ADOBE® ILLUSTRATOR® 7.0

An Introduction to Digital Illustration

PRENTICE HALL
Upper Saddle River, NJ 07458

Library of Congress Cataloging-in-Publication Data

Behoriam, Ellenn.
  Adobe Illustrator 7.0: an introduction to digital illustration.
    p.   cm. -- (Against the clock)
  ISBN 0-13-080166-6
  1. Computer graphics. 2. Adobe Illustrator (Computer file)
I. Title. II. Series.
T385.B453 1998
006.6' 869 -- dc21
                                                98-10913
                                                CIP

Acquisitions Editor: *Elizabeth Sugg*
Developmental Editor: *Judy Casillo*
Supervising Manager: *Mary Carnis*
Production Editor: *Denise Brown*
Director of Manufacturing & Production: *Bruce Johnson*
Manufacturing Buyer: *Ed O'Dougherty*
Editorial Assistant: *Leanne Nieglos*

Formatting/page make-up: *Against The Clock, Inc.*
Printer/Binder: *Banta/Harrisonburg*
Cover Design: *Joe Sengotta*
Icon Design: *James Braun*
Creative Director: *Marianne Frasco*
Marketing Manager: *Danny Hoyt*

©1998 by Prentice Hall, Inc.
Simon & Schuster/A Viacom Company
Upper Saddle River, New Jersey 07458

The fonts utilized in this training course are the property of Against The Clock, Inc., and are supplied to the legitimate buyers of the Against The Clock training materials solely for use with the exercises and projects provided in the body of the materials. They may not be used for any other purpose, and under no circumstances can they be transferred to another individual, nor copied, nor distributed by any means whatsoever.

A portion of the images supplied in this book are Copyright © PhotoDisc, Inc., 201 Fourth Ave. Seattle, WA 98121. These images are the sole property of PhotoDisc and are used by Against The Clock with the permission of the owners. They may not be distributed, copied, transferred, or reproduced by any means whatsoever other than for the completion of the exercises and projects contained in this Against The Clock training material.

Against The Clock and the Against The Clock logo are trademarks of Against The Clock, Inc., registered in the United States and elsewhere. References to, and instructional materials provided for, any particular application program, operating system, hardware platform or other commercially available product or products does not represent an endorsement of such product or products by Against The Clock, Inc. or Prentice Hall, Inc.

Adobe, Acrobat, Adobe Illustrator, PageMaker, Photoshop, Adobe Type Manager, and PostScript are trademarks of Adobe Systems Incorporated. Macromedia FreeHand is a registered trademark of Macromedia. QuarkXPress is a registered trademark of Quark, Inc. TrapWise and PressWise are registered trademarks of Luminous Corporation. Microsoft, MS-DOS, Windows, and Windows NT are either registered trademarks or trademarks of Microsoft Corporation.

Other products and company names mentioned herein may be the trademarks of their respective owners.

Printed in the United States of America

10 9 8 7 6 5 4 3 2 1

ISBN 0-13-080166-6

Prentice Hall International (UK) Limited, London
Prentice Hall of Australia Pty. Limited, Sydney
Prentice Hall Canada Inc., Toronto
Prentice Hall Hispanoamericana, S.A., Mexico
Prentice Hall of India Private Limited, New Delhi
Prentice Hall of Japan, Inc., Tokyo
Simon & Schuster Asia Pte. Ltd., Singapore
Editora Prentice Hall do Brasil, Ltda., Rio de Janeiro

Contents

PROJECTS

GLOSSARY

INDEX

PURPOSE

The Against The Clock series has been developed specifically for those involved in the field of graphic arts.

Welcome to the world of electronic design and prepress. Many of our readers are already involved in the industry — in advertising and design companies, in prepress and imaging firms, and in the world of commercial printing and reproduction. Others are just now preparing themselves for a career somewhere in the profession.

This series of courses will provide you with the skills necessary to work in this fast-paced, exciting, and rapidly expanding business. Many people feel that they can simply purchase a computer, the appropriate software, a laser printer, and a ream of paper, and begin designing and producing high-quality printed materials. While this might suffice for a barbecue announcement or a flyer advertising a local hair salon, the real world of four-color printing and professional communications requires a far more serious commitment.

THE SERIES

The applications presented in the Against The Clock series stand out as the programs of choice in professional graphic arts environments.

We've used a modular design for the Against The Clock series, allowing you to mix and match the drawing, imaging, and page layout applications that exactly suit your specific needs.

Titles available in the Against The Clock series include:

Macintosh: Basic Operations
Windows: Basic Operations
Adobe Illustrator: An Introduction to Digital Illustration
Adobe Illustrator: Advanced Digital Illustration
Freehand: An Introduction to Digital Illustration
Freehand: Advanced Digital Illustration
Adobe PageMaker: An Introduction to Electronic Mechanicals
Adobe PageMaker: Advanced Electronic Mechanicals
QuarkXPress: An Introduction to Electronic Mechanicals
QuarkXPress: Advanced Electronic Mechanicals
Adobe Photoshop: An Introduction to Digital Images
Adobe Photoshop: Advanced Digital Images
File Preparation: The Responsible Electronic Page
Preflight: An Introduction to File Analysis and Repair
TrapWise: Trapping
PressWise: Imposition

We've designed our courses to be "cross-platform." While many sites use Macintosh computers, there is an increasing number of graphic arts service providers using Intel-based systems running Windows (or WindowsNT). The books in this series are applicable to either of these systems.

All of the applications that we cover in the Against The Clock series are similar in operation and appearance whether you're working on a Macintosh or a Windows system. When a particular function does differ from machine to machine, we present both.

ICONS AND VISUALS

Pencil icon indicates a comment from an experienced operator. Whenever you see the pencil icon, you'll find corresponding sidebar text that augments or builds upon the subject being discussed at the time.

Bomb icon indicates a potential problem or difficulty. For instance, a certain technique might lead to pages that prove difficult to output. In other cases, there might be something that a program cannot easily accomplish, so we might present a workaround.

Pointing Finger indicates a hands-on activity — whether a short exercise or a complete project. This will be the icon you'll see the most throughout the course.

Key icon is used to point out that there is a keyboard equivalent to a menu or dialog-box option. Key commands are often faster than using the mouse to select a menu option. Experienced operators often mix the use of keyboard equivalents and menu/dialog box selections to arrive at their optimum speed.

If you are a Windows user, be sure to refer to the corresponding text or images whenever you see this **Windows** icon. Although there isn't a great deal of difference between using these applications on a Macintosh and using them on a Windows-based PC, there are certain instances where there's enough of a difference for us to comment.

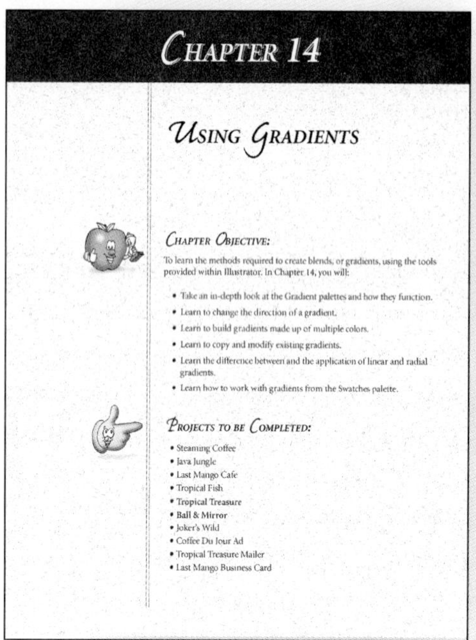

CHAPTER OPENINGS *provide the reader with specific objectives.*

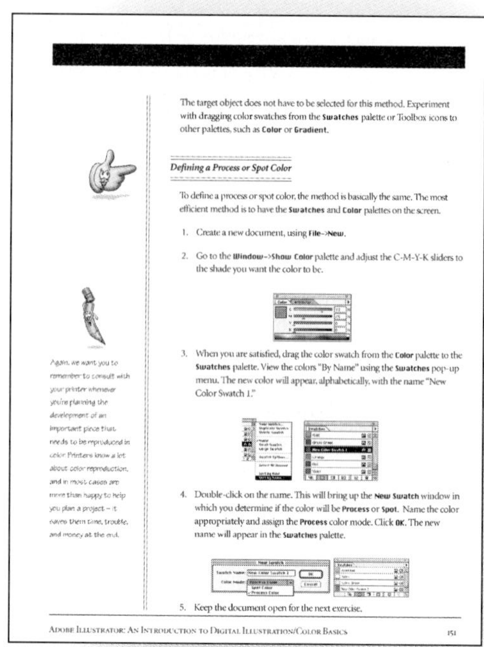

SIDEBARS and HANDS-ON ACTIVITIES *supplement concepts presented in the material.*

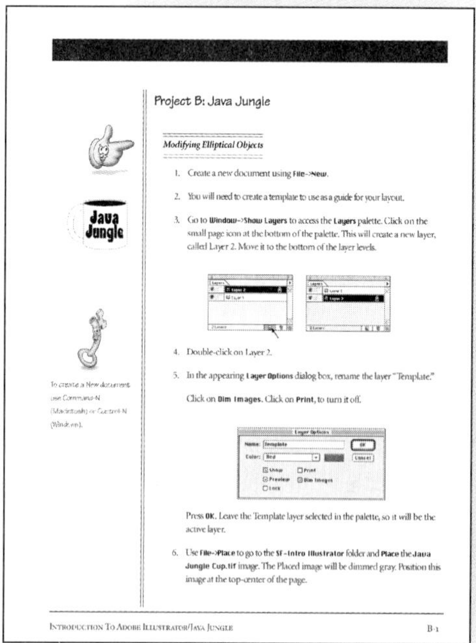

SUPPLEMENTAL PROJECTS *offer practice opportunities in addition to the exercises.*

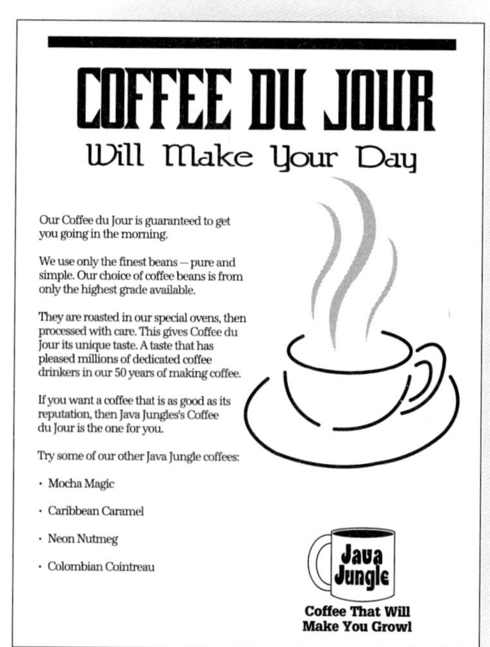

PROJECT ASSIGNMENTS *will result in finished artwork — with an emphasis on proper file construction methods.*

The Against The Clock course materials have been constructed with two primary building blocks: exercises and projects. Projects always result in a finished piece of work — built from the ground up, with you creating all the elements within the scope of the specific job.

This course, *Adobe Illustrator: Introduction to Digital Illustration*, makes use of several projects that you will work on during your learning sessions. You will find the projects that you will complete by the end of the course displayed on the inside front cover of the book. Here's a brief overview of each.

PROJECT A: STEAMING COFFEE

The *Steaming Coffee* project makes use of simple closed paths to create the actual steam puffs. The cup is constructed using the pen tool, setting paths to no-fill and ensuring that the end caps are properly configured to simulate the end of a pen stroke. Illustrator's default end cap is a sharp, square edge – not suitable for most drawings of this type.

PROJECT B: JAVA JUNGLE

Selecting and drawing objects that you, as a beginning illustrator, see around you every day can prove to be a very effective teaching tool. To build the *Java Jungle* coffee cup, you will cut an ellipse to create symmetrical shapes for the lower portion of the opening and the bottom of the cup. You'll also be required to place type on the object. You might try the cup with several different typefaces as the logo.

PROJECT C: LAST MANGO CAFE

The *Last Mango Cafe* logo combines type and linework to create a balanced, fun visual. The creation of the umbrella makes use of reflecting, editing, and modifying paths to create symmetrical shapes.

PROJECT D: TROPICAL FISH

Tropical Fish is built out of several primitive elements, including ellipses, freehand shapes, and random objects used for stylized shadings in the sand. To properly construct the artwork, you should use the Layers function – a critically important tool in the experienced artist's repertoire. The Pathfinder command set is also used to merge the shapes that make up the arms of the coral. Pathfinders are also very important time savers – far superior to manually connecting, merging, cutting, and altering shapes.

PROJECT E: TROPICAL TREASURE

Designing a logo that speaks elegantly of a company isn't easy. Here, you will create a retailer's logo block called *Tropical Treasure* using type, an illustration of the little treasure chest in the copy line, bordering rules, and a "deck" ("*Gifts from the Sea*"). This is a type-intensive project, with shadow techniques derived from using layers of overlapping type.

PROJECT F: BALL & MIRROR

The *Ball & Mirror* image uses the Pencil tool extensively for a hand-drawn look. The frame and the reflection are created using a linear gradient while the ball uses a radial gradient.

PROJECT G: JOKER'S WILD

A playing card is an excellent example of an illustration that takes advantage of Illustrator's powerful tool set. Throughout the project, you will create accurately spaced and mirrored elements. The stars around the Joker figure are repeated elements around an invisible circle created by the use of Repeat Transformation. This complex (and fun) drawing makes extensive use of templates, controlled cloning, layers, and guides.

PROJECT H: COFFEE DU JOUR

Utilizing Adobe Illustrator as a page-layout tool, the *Coffee Du Jour* ad uses elements from previous projects as the components of a display advertisement. We create the headline, the deck, and then import text from a file that is supplied with this course. As a page-layout tool, Illustrator offers sophisticated type controls as well as drawing tools all in one package.

PROJECT I: TROPICAL TREASURE MAILER

Another page-layout advertisement, the *Tropical Treasure Mailer* incorporates layers, imported copy files, and logos and visuals created in previous projects. This job emphasizes proper file construction for efficient output.

PROJECT J: LAST MANGO BUSINESS CARD

The *Last Mango Business Card* project requires careful attention to detail and the use of precision alignment. Business cards are often typeset in multiples based upon your printer's requirements. This project also makes use of visuals created in previous projects.

FOR THE STUDENT

On the CD-ROM you will find a complete set of Against The Clock (ATC) fonts, as well as a collection of data files used to construct the various exercises and projects.

The ATC fonts are solely for use while you are working with the Against The Clock materials. These fonts will be used throughout both the exercises and projects and are provided in both Macintosh and Windows format.

A variety of student files has been included. These files, necessary to complete both the exercises and projects, are also provided in both Macintosh and Windows formats.

FOR THE INSTRUCTOR

The Instructor Kit consists of an Instructor's manual and an Instructor's CD-ROM. It includes various testing and presentation materials in addition to the files that come standard with the student books.

- **Overhead Presentation Materials** are provided and follow along with the course. These presentations are prepared using Microsoft PowerPoint and are provided in both "native" PowerPoint format as well as Acrobat Portable Document Format (PDF).

- **Extra Projects** are provided along with the data files required for completion. These projects may be used to extend the course, or may be used to test the student.

- **Finished artwork (in Illustrator format)** for all projects that the students complete is supplied on the CD-ROM.

- **A Test Bank of Questions** is included on the instructor CD-ROM. These questions may be modified, reorganized, and administered throughout the delivery of the course.

- Halfway through the course is a **Review** of material covered to that point, with a **Final Review** at the end.

I would like to give special thanks to the writers, illustrators, editors, and others who have worked long and hard to complete the Against The Clock series. Foremost among them are Dean Bagley, Gavin Nagatomo, Julie LeMonte, Jim Wheaton, Tyler Robinson, and John Siebel, whom I thank for their long nights, early mornings, and their seemingly endless patience.

Thanks to the dedicated teaching professionals whose comments and expertise contributed to the success of these products, including Renée Prim of Central Piedmont Community College, Ron Bertolina of The Graphic Arts Technical Foundation, Dr. Mitchell Henke of Bemidji State University, and Rainer Fleschner of Moraine Park Technical College.

A big thanks to Judy Casillo, Developmental Editor, for her guidance, patience, and attention to detail.

A special thanks to my husband for his unswerving support and for living in a publishing studio and warehouse during the three years it took to develop the entire ATC series.

Thanks to my original partner and friend Steve Tripp, for his faith and patience in the early days. Thanks, too, to Jung Mills, who was with me each and every day.

Thanks to my "Fishin' Buddies" EW Spencer and Jeannie Pugh. And special thanks to my dogs, Spike (who left for the big rawhide factory in the sky before the project was completed), Boda, and Chase.

Ellenn Behoriam, December 1997

AGAINST THE CLOCK

Against The Clock (ATC) was founded in 1990 as a part of Lanman Systems Group, one of the nation's leading systems integration and training firms. The company specialized in developing custom training materials for such clients as *L.L Bean, The New England Journal of Medicine, Smithsonian,* the *National Education Association, Air & Space Magazine, Publishers Clearing House,* The *National Wildlife Society, Home Shopping Network,* and many others. The integration firm was among the most highly respected in the graphic arts industry.

To a great degree, the success of Systems Group can be attributed to the thousands of pages of course materials developed at the company's demanding client sites. Throughout the rapid growth of Systems Group, founder and General Manager Ellenn Behoriam developed the expertise necessary to manage technical experts, content providers, writers, editors, illustrators, designers, layout artists, proofreaders, and the rest of the chain of professionals required to develop structured and highly effective training materials.

Following the sale of the Lanman Companies to World Color, one of the nation's largest commercial printers, Ellenn embarked on a three-year project to fully redevelop a library of training materials engineered specifically for the professional graphic artist. The result of this effort is the ATC training library.

Ellenn lives in Tampa, Florida with her husband and her dogs, Boda and Chase.

ABOUT THE AUTHORS

Every one of the Against The Clock course books was developed by a group of people working as part of a design and production team. In all cases, however, there was a primary author who assumed the bulk of the responsibility for developing the exercises, writing the copy, and organizing the illustrations and other visuals.

In the case of *Adobe Illustrator: An Introduction to Digital Illustration,* that author was **Dean Bagley**. Dean is an experienced marketing and advertising expert. One of Dean's most effective skills is the development of hands-on activities, which, as you'll see, is the foundation of the ATC series.

Dean is a professional cartoonist, well-known for his imaginative and entertaining "Baggy Gator" series of comic characters. Dean lives in Winter Haven, Florida with his cat Nuci.

Platform

The Against The Clock series is specifically designed to apply to both Macintosh and Windows systems — the courses will work for you no matter what environment you find yourself in. There are some slight differences in the two, but when you're working in an actual application, these differences are limited to certain types of functions and actions.

Naming Conventions

In the old days of MS-DOS systems, file names on the PC were limited to something referred to as "8.3," which meant that you were limited in the number of characters you could use to an eight-character name (the "8") and a three-character suffix (the "3"). Text files, for example, might be called *myfile.txt*, while a document file from a word processor might be called *myfile.doc* (for document). On today's Windows-based systems, these limitations have been somewhat overcome. Although you can use longer file names, suffixes still exist. Whether or not you see them is another story.

When your system is first configured, the Views are normally set to a default that hides these extensions. This means that you might have a dozen different files named *myfile*, all of which may have been generated by different applications and be completely different types of files.

On a Windows system, you can change this view by clicking on *My Computer* (the icon is on your desktop) with the right button, and choosing View ->Options. From this dialog box you may choose whether or not to display these older, MS-DOS file extensions. In some cases, it's easier to know what you're looking at if they're visible. This is a personal choice.

To ensure that the supplied student files are fully compatible with both operating systems, we've named all the files using the three-character suffix — even those on the Macintosh.

Key Commands

Key commands are fairly consistent between the Macintosh and the Windows versions of Adobe Illustrator. The major difference lies in the names of special function keys. The Macintosh has a key marked with an Apple and an icon that looks like a clover leaf. This is called the Command key. Whenever you see this icon, you will need to hold this key down. The Command key is a *modifier* key; that is, it doesn't do anything by itself, but changes the function of a key pressed while it's being held down. A good example is holding Command while pressing the "S" key: this Saves your work. The same thing applies to the "P" key; hold down Command and press it to Print your work.

On Windows-based systems, the Control key is almost always the equivalent of the Command key on the Macintosh. (This is sometimes confusing to new users, since the Macintosh also has a Control-key, although, on the Macintosh, it's hardly ever used in popular applications).

Another special function key on the Macintosh is the Option key. It's also a modifier key, and you'll need to hold it down along with whatever other key is required for a specific function. The equivalent modifier key on a Windows system is called the ALT key (for alternative). Besides these two nomenclature issues, there isn't really a lot of difference between using a Windows system and a Macintosh system (particularly when you're within a particular application).

The CD-ROM and Initial Setup Considerations

Before you begin using your Against The Clock course book, you will have to set up your system so that you have access to the various files and tools you'll need to complete your lessons.

Student Files

This course comes complete with a collection of student files. These files are an integral part of the learning experience, as they're used throughout the course to help you construct increasingly complex elements. Having these building blocks available to you throughout your practice and study sessions will ensure that you will be able to experience the exercises and complete the project assignments smoothly and with a minimum of time spent looking for the various components required.

In building the Student Files folders, we've created sets of data for both Macintosh and Windows users. Locate the appropriate version of the "SF-Intro Illustrator" folder for your platform of choice and simply drag the icon onto your hard disk drive. If you have limited disk space, you may want to copy only the files for one or two lessons at a time.

Creating a Project Folder

We strongly recommend that you work from your hard disk. However, in some cases you might not have enough room on your system for all of the files that we've supplied. If this is the case, you can work directly from the CD-ROM.

Throughout the exercises and projects, you'll be required to save your work. Since the CD-ROM is "read-only," you cannot write information to it. Create a Project Folder on your hard disk and use it to store your work-in-progress. Create your project folder using Command-N (Macintosh) or Control-N (Windows) while you're looking at your desktop. This will create the folder at the highest level of your system, where it will be easy to find.

Fonts

Whatever platform you're working on — Macintosh or Windows — you will have to install the ATC font library to ensure that your lessons and exercises will work as they're described in the course book. These fonts are provided on the student CD-ROM. There is a version for Windows and one for Macintosh.

Instructions for installing fonts are provided in the documentation that came with your computer. If you're using a font utility such as Suitcase or Font Juggler, then be sure to refer to the instructions that came with the font management application for installing your ATC fonts onto your system.

Preferences

We recommend that you throw away your Preferences file before you begin the lessons in this course. The "Illustrator Prefs" file may be found inside your System folder.

Prerequisites

This book assumes that you have a basic understanding of how to use your system. Whether you're working on a Macintosh or a Windows workstation, the skill sets are basically the same.

You should know how to use your mouse to point and click, and how to drag items around the screen. You should know how to resize a window, and how to arrange windows on your desktop to maximize the space you have available. You should know how to access pull-down menus and how check boxes and radio buttons work. Lastly, you should know how to create, open, and save files.

If you're familiar with these fundamental skills, then you know all that's necessary to utilize the Against The Clock courseware library.

Notes:

CHAPTER 2

THE ILLUSTRATOR WORKING DOCUMENT

CHAPTER OBJECTIVE:

To introduce the student to the Illustrator Working Environment. Teaching the Illustrator Toolbox, Toolbox Pop up Menus, the location and function of the program's menus, and the philosophy behind Illustrator palettes. In this section, you will:

- Gain a basic understanding of the Toolbox, including the names of the tools and a description of their basic functions.

- Explore and use the alternative pop-up tools — often hidden under a standard tool's icon.

- See how menus operate and how they affect objects and conditions.

- Work with Palettes, one of Illustrator's basic components.

The Illustrator Working Environment

While very elegant and natural, Adobe Illustrator is a challenging program to master. In your efforts to learn the program, it's best to start with the basics, and for a program like Illustrator, that means learning some of the fundamental tools, menus, and palettes that the program offers. Each is a method of communicating with the software. The better you understand how to make the program do what you want, the quicker you'll be on your way to proficient digital illustration. It's sort of like learning to cook; first you have to know what a pot and pan is, and then you have to learn how to mix ingredients and apply the right amount of heat. In this chapter, we're going to learn about the pots and pans in Illustrator's kitchen.

The Toolbox

The Toolbox is a floating palette that contains a selection of tools that allow you to draw lines and shapes, paint them, size them, rotate them, and otherwise modify components of your drawings.

For people who are using this course to learn the differences between Illustrator 7.0 and earlier versions, the Toolbox is one of the most important places to start. There are considerable differences in the Toolbox of this and prior versions.

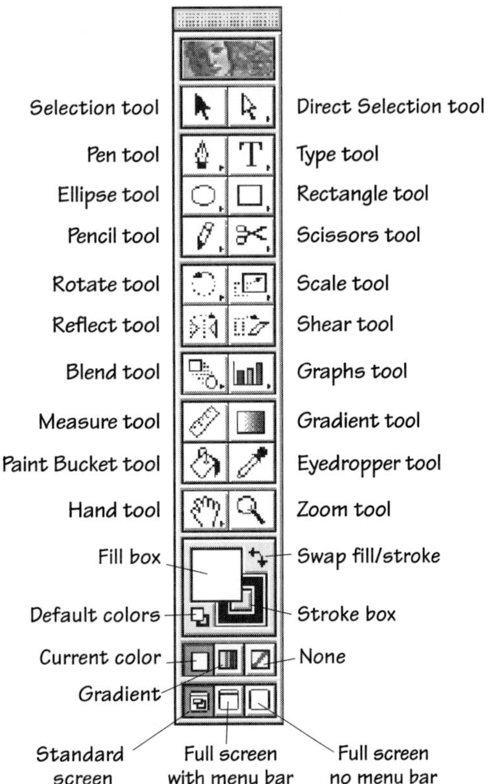

Toolbox Summary

For people who are using this course to learn the differences between Illustrator 7.0 and earlier versions, the Toolbox is one of the most important places to start. There are considerable differences in the Toolbox of this and prior versions. Many drawings are complex, and require the use of many of the tools available to you. Here are the tools you will see in the document window.

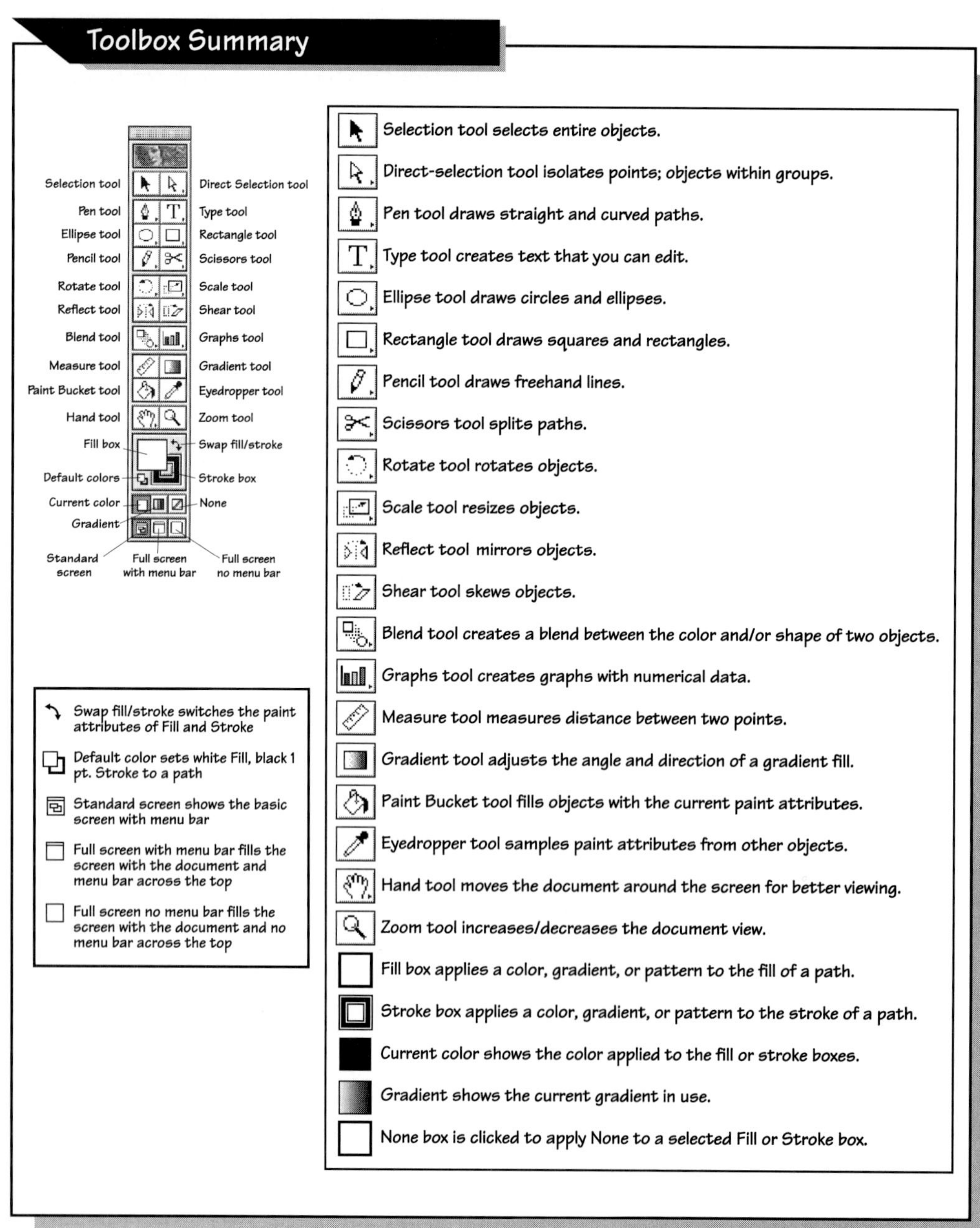

Toolbox Pop up Menus

Many of the tools that you first see when you look at the Illustrator Toolbox have more than one method of operation; in other words, there are options available for most tools. Here's an extended view of those "hidden" tools and a brief comment about what they can be used for.

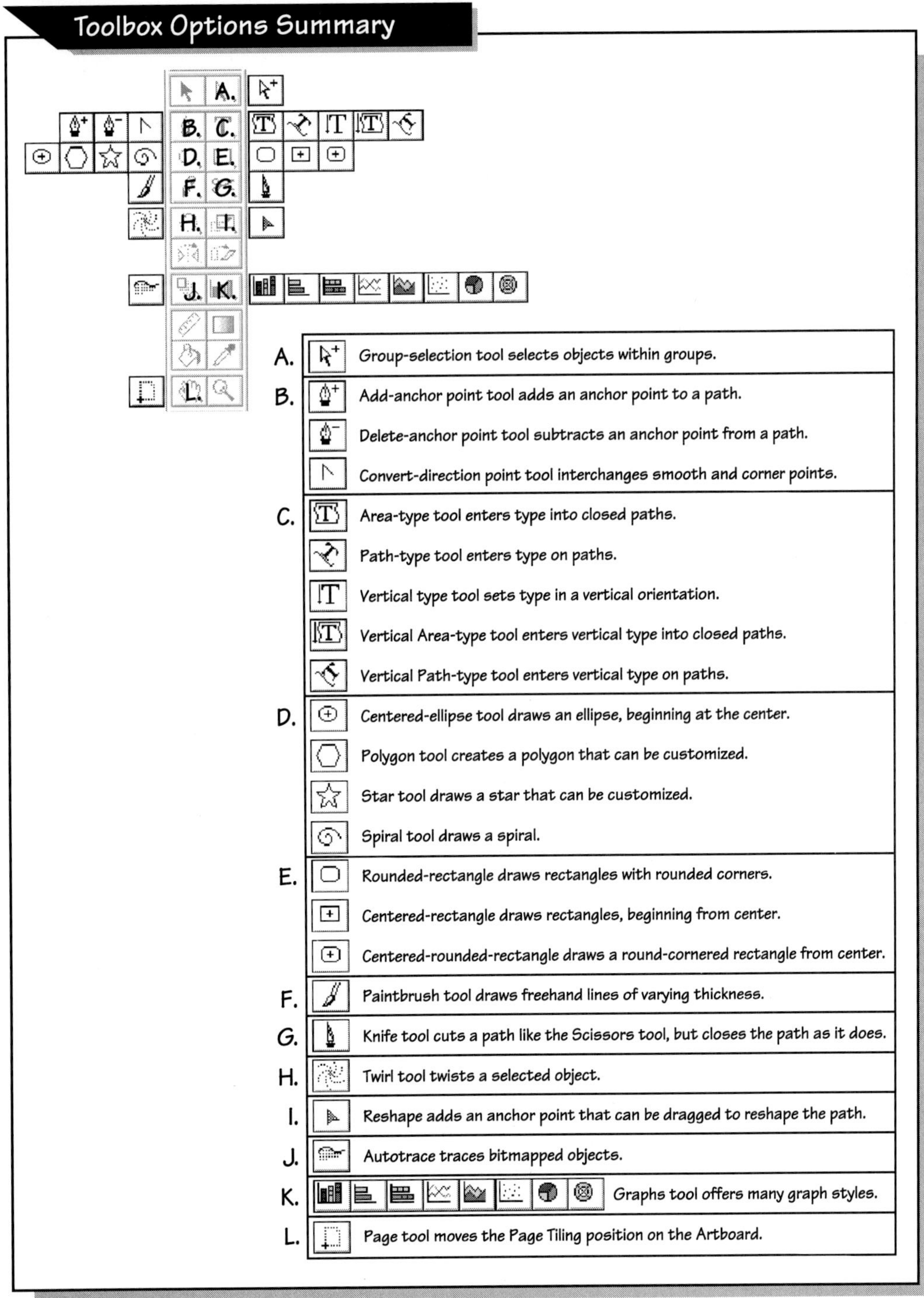

Toolbox Options Summary

A. Group-selection tool selects objects within groups.

B. Add-anchor point tool adds an anchor point to a path.
   Delete-anchor point tool subtracts an anchor point from a path.
   Convert-direction point tool interchanges smooth and corner points.

C. Area-type tool enters type into closed paths.
   Path-type tool enters type on paths.
   Vertical type tool sets type in a vertical orientation.
   Vertical Area-type tool enters vertical type into closed paths.
   Vertical Path-type tool enters vertical type on paths.

D. Centered-ellipse tool draws an ellipse, beginning at the center.
   Polygon tool creates a polygon that can be customized.
   Star tool draws a star that can be customized.
   Spiral tool draws a spiral.

E. Rounded-rectangle draws rectangles with rounded corners.
   Centered-rectangle draws rectangles, beginning from center.
   Centered-rounded-rectangle draws a round-cornered rectangle from center.

F. Paintbrush tool draws freehand lines of varying thickness.

G. Knife tool cuts a path like the Scissors tool, but closes the path as it does.

H. Twirl tool twists a selected object.

I. Reshape adds an anchor point that can be dragged to reshape the path.

J. Autotrace traces bitmapped objects.

K. Graphs tool offers many graph styles.

L. Page tool moves the Page Tiling position on the Artboard.

The Menus

Both Macintosh and Windows-based systems rely on what are called "context-sensitive" menus; that is, menus that are specific to the program that you're working in. Illustrator naturally has its own menu selections, and you will explore some of the more important ones.

The Illustrator menus offer features for modifying, editing, or arranging your artwork. Many menus have sub-menus marked with a triangle that, when clicked on, will show the further choices and options.

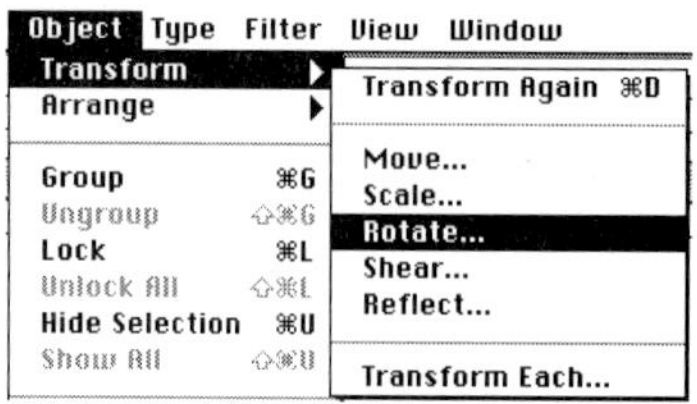

The Palettes

The Toolbox is one palette, but certainly not the only one. We are going to discuss how Illustrator's extensive palettes work; what sort of tools they provide, and how to arrange them using "docking," a method that lets you combine related palettes in one window, to take the best advantage of your particular screen's "real estate."

The palettes, most of which are found in the **Window** menu, have some consistent buttons and sub-menus that are very handy. The small dog-eared page icon is the shortcut to creating a new item. The trashcan icon next to it is the shortcut for deleting a palette item.

The upper-right triangle is the pop-up menu for more options for the palette.

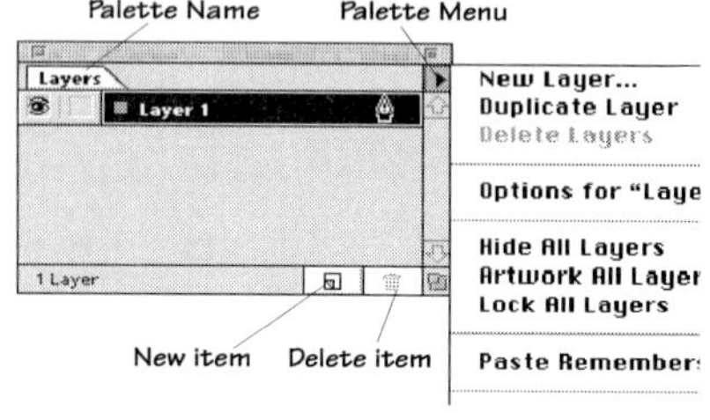

The folder headings that hold the names of certain functions can be clicked on to access the functions, or can be dragged away from the palette to be separate. Plus, folder headings can be dragged to other palettes, and combined or "docked." This is a very convenient way to have more palettes available, without having to go to the **Window** menu to access them individually.

Docking palettes is another way to reduce the clutter on your monitor.

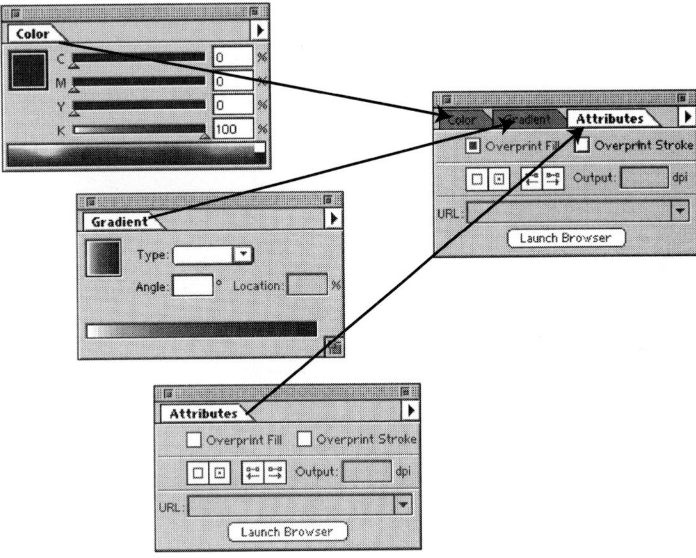

Notes:

CHAPTER 3

INITIAL SETUP

CHAPTER OBJECTIVE:

To explain how to create a new document, open a document, and save Illustrator and Illustrator EPS documents. To introduce the concept of preferences — changeable settings that can be used to control some of the program's basic features. In Chapter 3, you will:

- Learn how to create a new document.

- Learn the various components of a document "window" and how to work with them.

- Work with Document setup to control basic page size, orientation, margins, and other attributes of your documents.

- Learn to customize General Preferences to improve your productivity.

- Learn how to zoom in and out of your drawing to aid development of an illustration.

- Learn to save documents in formats that ensure they'll be compatible with other applications, such as page layout or painting programs.

Initial Setup

Before you can start using Adobe Illustrator, you should know how to do some basic tasks — things like creating a new document, how to control the size and shape of the page you're working on, and other ways to control the working "environment" of Illustrator. What we're learning is how to set up your drawing table. Another way of looking at what you're going to learn in this chapter is to think about the moment you first sit down to create a work of art, and you ask yourself the question: "Where do I start?"

Creating a New Document

As we launch the Illustrator application, it initializes itself with fonts and plug-in filter information. It will automatically open up a blank, untitled document.

New documents are created by using the **File** menu and selecting **New**. The new document window offers the following features:

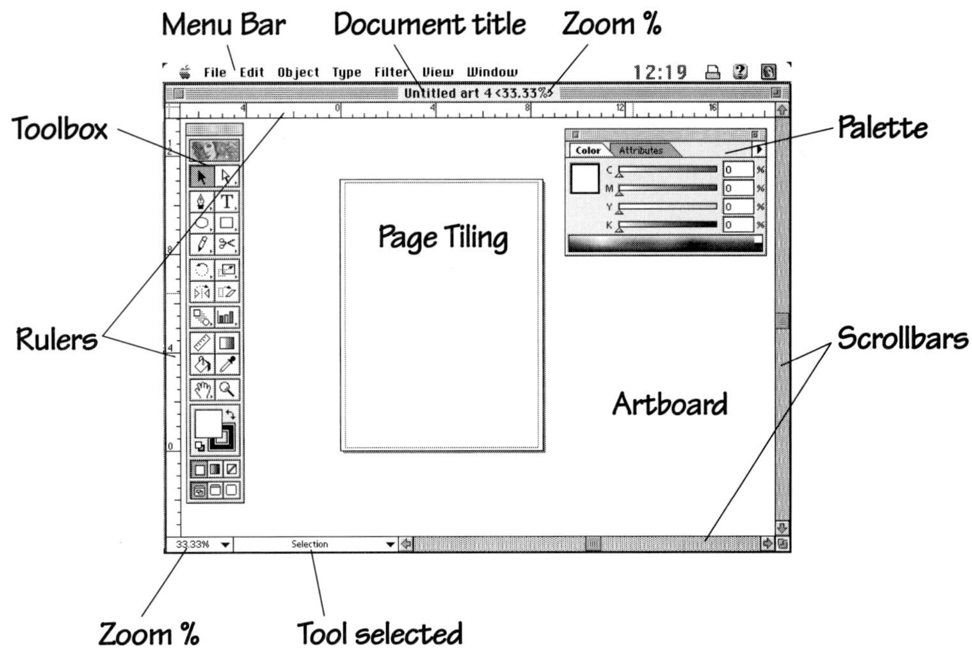

- The Illustrator Toolbox.

- The Menu Bar across the top of the screen that gives you access to many of Illustrator's functions. Additional floating palettes provide access to other functions.

- A new letter-size page to draw on, called the *Page Tiling*.

- Rulers that are very handy for measuring objects, setting up layouts, and creating guides.

- Illustrator's printable area is represented by the Page Tiling. Only objects within the Tiling area (enclosed by the dotted lines) will appear when the page is printed. Any objects outside of these lines will not print on the paper size selected in **Document Setup->Page Setup.**

- The surrounding Artboard area that holds unused art and type. These elements won't print as long as they do not overlay the page in any way. However, any anchor points, objects, paths, or text on the Artboard will be included in the saved EPS file, which greatly affects the *bounding box* dimensions, file size, and RIP time, when placed into a page layout document.

- Scroll bars that allow you to move around to see art more clearly.

- The Document name along with its current magnification. Illustrator allows multiple documents to be open at one time, so having the document name displayed is important. This way, you'll know which document is active.

- Zoom Percentage that shows the relative magnification of the document that is being viewed, where 100% is full size.

If you've worked with other applications, then the basic way the windows work and look should be quite familiar.

ADOBE ILLUSTRATOR: AN INTRODUCTION TO DIGITAL ILLUSTRATION/INITIAL SETUP

1. Create a **New** document from the **File** menu.

2. Click-hold on any of the menus in the Menu Bar to see their contents.

3. Click the mouse on the various tools in the Toolbox.

4. Click on the Rectangle tool in the Toolbox. Observe how the name of the tool appears at the bottom of the screen.

5. Select the Zoom tool and click it on the page. Hold the Option key (Macintosh) or Alt key (Windows) and click the Zoom tool on the page. Use the scroll bars to move the window around.

6. **Close** the file without saving.

Setting Up Your Document

Dialog boxes are regions of the screen where you're expected to provide parameters relative to a specific object or document. This dialog box controls things like page size and orientation.

The **Document Setup** (Macintosh) or **Print Setup** (Windows) dialog box, located under the **File** menu, offers control over the way the document looks.

Flatness is a term that refers to the complexity of a drawing – at a very fundamental, mathematical level. The higher the number, the more coarse the artwork – but often in a manner not visible to the naked eye. The resolution factor that this dialog asks for sets that flatness level. You can potentially reduce the quality of your artwork if you set this figure too low.

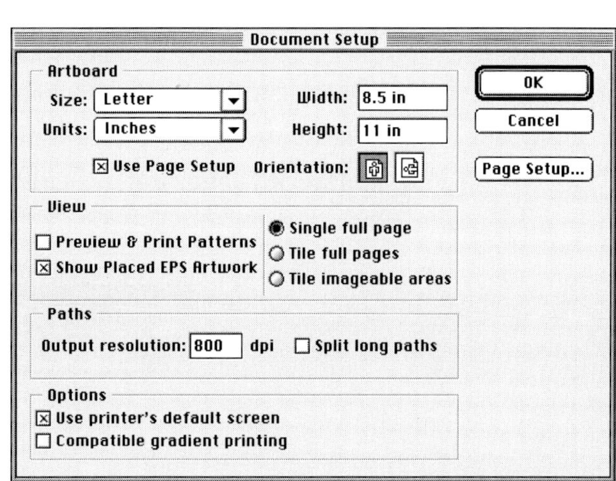

- **Artboard** — This section lets you select the page size and page orientation (portrait or landscape) of the Artboard. New documents default to the letter size in portrait orientation, but you can customize page dimensions in the Width/Height data boxes. If you check the **Use Page** (Macintosh) or **Print** (Windows) **Setup** box, the Artboard will accept the settings in the **Page Setup** dialog box. Otherwise, **Size** and **Orientation** options selected in the **Artboard** section will be used as you customize.

- **View** — You won't need to select **Preview & Print Patterns** at this time, so make sure it is deselected. You should click the **Show Placed EPS Artwork** box, so any placed EPS images will be visible.

  Use **Tile imageable areas** only when your artwork is too large for the chosen page size. It allows you to work on more than one Illustrator page at a time. **Tile Full Pages** is rarely used. The most common choice is **Single full page**.

- **Paths** — **Output resolution** determines the flatness of the printed paths. Printer resolution/output resolution = Flatness. Flatness controls the number of device pixels that create curved paths.

Preferences

Preferences are just that; the way you prefer to work. Examples of Preferences in Illustrator are whether objects are measured in inches, picas, or millimeters. There are plenty of other examples that we will discuss later.

The selection **File->Preferences** offers further selections that allow you to adjust Illustrator's operations. When you select **Preferences**, several choices appear, but **General** is most important for now.

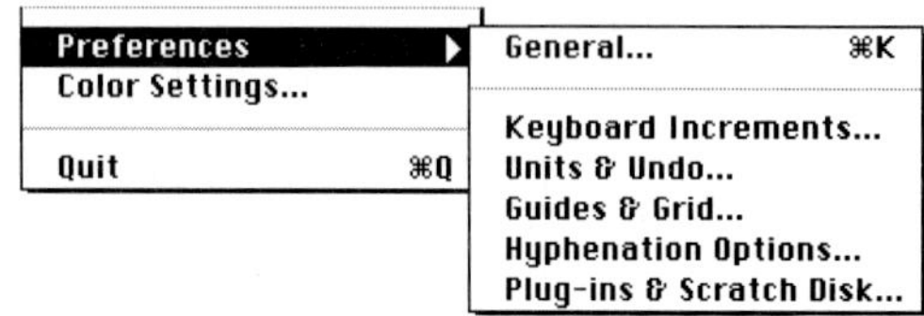

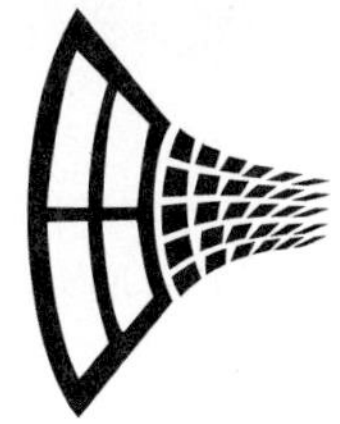

AI 6.0 Tool Shortcuts is
for Macintosh only.
Adobe Illustrator did not
come out with a 6.0
version for the PC.

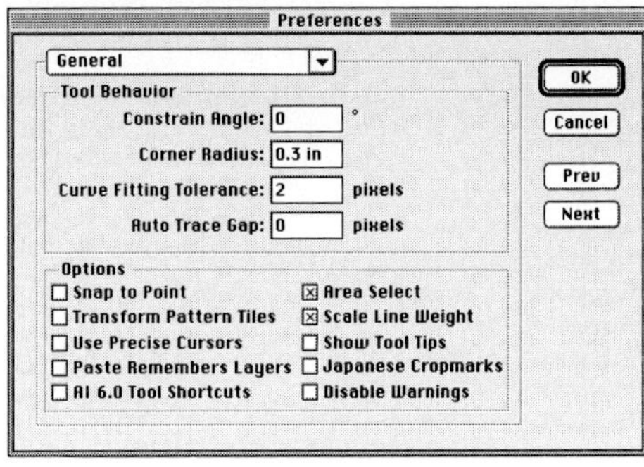

Macintosh

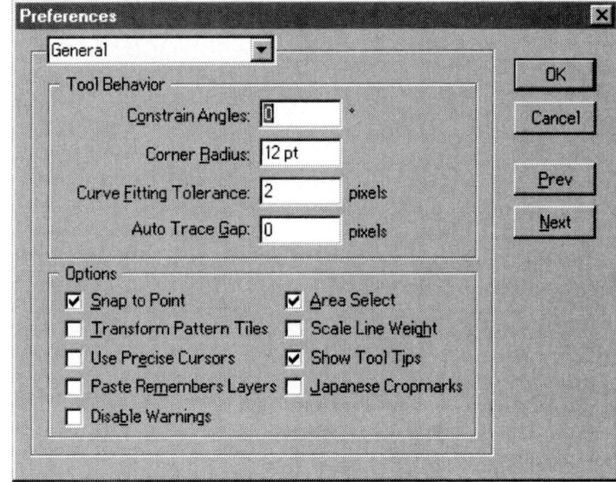

Windows

- **Snap to Point** should not be clicked for now. It interferes when using the Pen tool, by snapping to other close points.

- **Transform Pattern Tiles** should only be clicked with the use of Tiles.

- **Use Precise Cursors** changes the shape of the cursor to a cross-hair for more precision when clicking certain areas.

- **Paste Remembers Layers** is helpful when Cutting/Pasting objects to/ from different layers. See the chapter on Layers for more detail.

- **AI 6.0 Tool Shortcuts** retains some of the keyboard shortcuts from the previous version of the Illustrator application.

- **Area Select** makes it possible to click on a painted object in **Preview** mode and select it. This does not work in **Artwork** mode.

- **Scale Line Weight** automatically adjusts line weights in proportion to the selected scaling factor. This should be clicked.

- **Show Tool Tips** turns on balloon tips that explain a tool's functions.

- **Japanese Crop Marks** sets crop marks pertaining to Japanese measurement standards.

- **Disable Warnings** turns off certain warnings that might affect your work. Keep this unclicked to have the helpful warnings.

Saving Illustrator Documents

In the **File** menu, you will see two saving options:

- **Save** — If you are in an untitled new document, to use **Save** defaults over to **Save As** so you can determine the format of the file. Once a document is saved as a file, choosing **Save** in the future will save the file without giving you dialog boxes to make format decisions.

- **Save As** —The options available in **Save As** include formats compatible with many other applications and even other hardware platforms. **Save As** is necessary when you want to save a document as another name or a different file format. Once **Save As** is selected from the **File** menu, this dialog box appears. Click-hold in the **Format** selection box with the mouse to show these options:

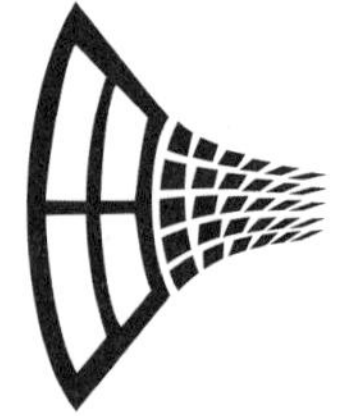

1-bit/8-bit Macintosh options are not available on the PC version of Illustrator.

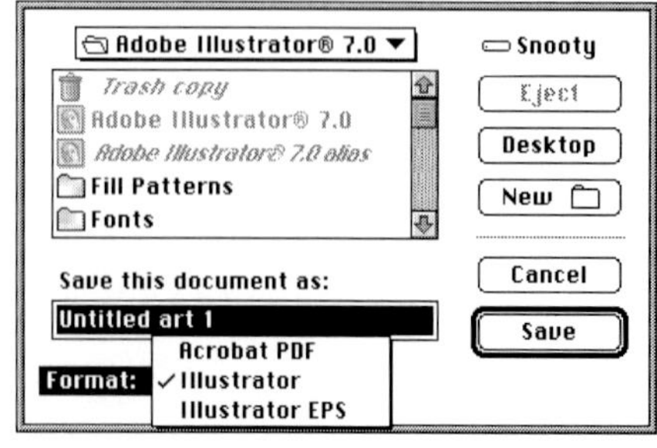

Macintosh

You can spend a lot of time looking for exactly the right folder into which to save your work. You might consider saving everything at the desktop level, then dragging them to their proper place when you're done working.

The Illustrator icons are marked to show their format.

An EPS shows that it is Encapsulated PostScript. AI means that it is a standard Illustrator document.

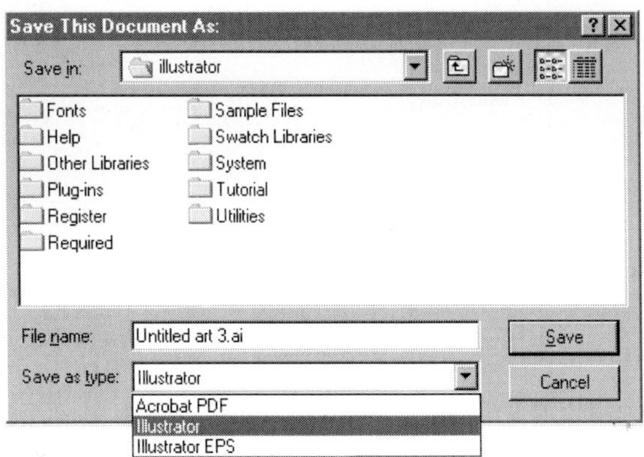

Windows

If your intention is to output your artwork from within Illustrator, you should save in the Illustrator 7.0 format. This will keep the file size small while enabling the full complement of features.

If the document is going to be used as a *placed graphic* in another application such as PageMaker or QuarkXPress, it should be saved as **Illustrator EPS**.

Saving As Illustrator EPS (Encapsulated PostScript)

Since the drawings that you'll be developing with Illustrator will often be used as part of larger projects (like a logo being used in an advertisement or on a stationery package), you will need to learn how to save your work in other formats. One of the most important formats is Encapsulated PostScript (EPS).

When you **Save As->Illustrator EPS**, this window appears.

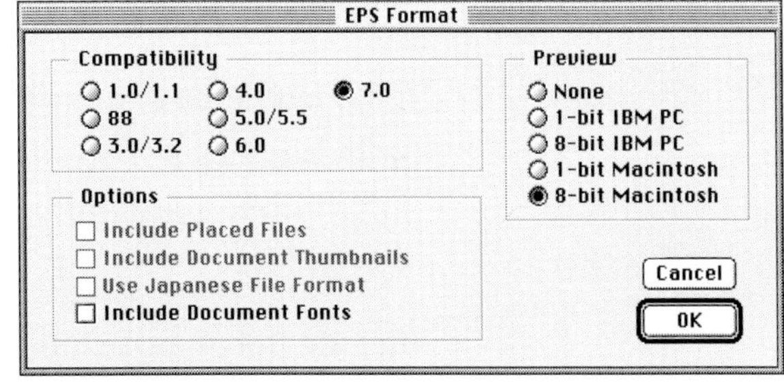

Macintosh

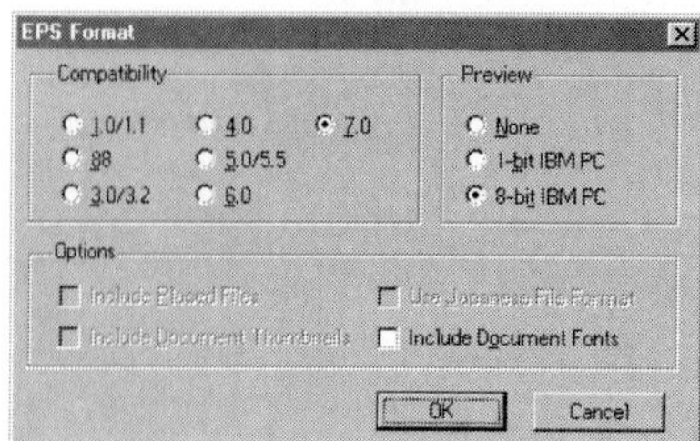

Windows

Compatibility refers to past/present Illustrator versions that the document can be saved in. Later Illustrator versions can open earlier versions of Illustrator documents, but not vice versa. This is known as Backward Compatibility. For example, Illustrator 7.0 can open an Illustrator 3.0 file, but a 3.0 cannot open a 7.0 document.

Preview is the low-resolution screen representation of the image that you see when the EPS is placed into a page-layout application.

None will give no preview. If placed in a layout, all you will see is a rectangular gray box.

1-bit IBM PC is a very coarse black/white screen preview. This choice is for saving to IBM format.

8-bit IBM PC displays color on a color monitor, or up to 256 shades of gray.

1-bit Macintosh is also a coarse, line art screen preview. It would be the best preview for a black/white monitor. Any color will be translated to a very coarse image representation.

8-bit Macintosh is the ideal preview choice. It was called Color Macintosh in past Illustrator versions. It will display color on a color monitor, or up to 256 shades of gray.

Options

Include Placed Files will include any graphics (photographic images or illustrations) placed in the file. This option is available only when the document has a placed image in it.

Include Document Thumbnails refers to a thumbnail image of the artwork that will appear in the **Open** file window. The thumbnail shows a preview of the illustration.

When saving files, it's a good idea to use descriptive names, and not something like Picture1 or Drawing1. That way, if you have to collect a number of components for a project, you'll have some idea of what to look for.

ADOBE ILLUSTRATOR: AN INTRODUCTION TO DIGITAL ILLUSTRATION/INITIAL SETUP

Use Japanese File Format — Saves the EPS image as a Japanese language file.

Include Document Fonts — Saves the image with those fonts used in the document. **Caution:** consult your printer or service provider as to their needs for the document fonts.

Saving the Document as an Illustrator EPS File

EPS is a very important file format. By saving a file as an EPS, you can almost assure yourself that the illustrations will work when placed in other applications, such as page layout software, or in manufacturing, imposition, and trapping software.

1. Create a **File->New** document and draw a simple oval using the Ellipse tool.

2. Go to the **File** menu and choose **Save As**. Save your document in the Student Folder.

3. Name the file "Test File.EPS."

4. In the **Format** choices window, select **Illustrator EPS**. For the Macintosh, click on the **Desktop** button and press **OK** to save it there. For the PC, go to **File->Save In->Desktop** to save the file.

5. In the next window, click on:

   • **Compatibility** — 7.0

   • **Preview** — 8-bit Macintosh or 8-bit IBM PC

   • **Options** — click nothing for now

6. Click **OK**.

7. Go to the **Desktop.** The file icon should have the letters EPS in it, so you will know what kind of file it is.

   You have saved a document as an **Illustrator EPS** that can be placed into page layout applications such as PageMaker and QuarkXPress.

8. **Close** this file. Then, go to the Student Folder and delete the file, so it will not be accidentally opened later.

The keyboard shortcut to opening a document is Command-O (Macintosh) or Control-O (Windows).

You can use the Command-Arrow (Macintosh) or Control-Arrow keys to move through folders. Up arrows move you up through the folder hierarchy, and down arrows (or the Enter key) takes you down into a folder.

Opening Illustrator Files

Throughout this course you will be instructed to open prepared Illustrator documents. The **Open...** option is found in the **File** menu.

When **Open...** is selected, the **Open** dialog box appears.

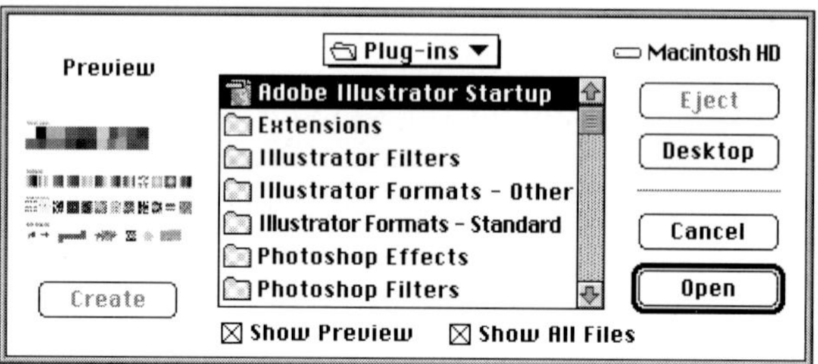

Macintosh

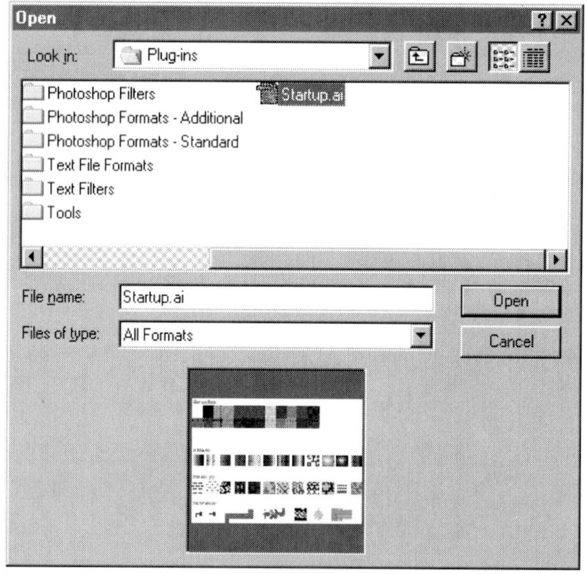

Windows

- **Show All Files** (Macintosh) will show every file in the folder. If not clicked, it will show only the files that Illustrator can open.

ADOBE ILLUSTRATOR: AN INTRODUCTION TO DIGITAL ILLUSTRATION/INITIAL SETUP

- **Show Preview** (Macintosh) will allow the Illustrator EPS image to be shown under the word **Preview**. This is only if the **Include Document Thumbnails** (Macintosh) was selected when the file was saved.

There is not an option for this in the Windows version of Illustrator.

- **Preview**. The space under Preview will be blank, unless the file selected has been saved with a thumbnail.

Notes:

CHAPTER 4

GRIDS & GUIDES

CHAPTER OBJECTIVE:

To learn how to use non-printing guides, and the built-in grid provided by the Illustrator environment. To learn how to create several types of guides; how to move them and manage them within a document, and how to delete them when they're no longer needed. In Chapter 4, you will:

- Learn the importance of grids and guides, and how they will help you develop more accurate drawings.
- Learn how to access the built-in grid, and how to modify its size and appearance.
- Learn how to create, lock, unlock, and accurately position guides.
- Convert regular objects into non-printing guides.
- Learn to reposition the rulers to simplify the process of measuring distances.
- Learn how to hide guides temporarily while you're working.

Grids & Guides

Since so many drawings require measuring objects and placing them in proper position — relative to themselves as well as relative to the page — it's very important that you learn how to use the various measurement tools available to you in the Illustrator environment.

We actually cover measurements in several places here in *Introduction to Adobe Illustrator*. In this chapter we start out showing you how to properly position your rulers, and later on, in another chapter, we provide some exercises that will build on the basic knowledge from this chapter. Here we're going to learn about rulers, and about using a scanned object as a guide in developing accurate drawings.

Grids

Are you familiar with the blue-line grid sheets that can be bought at the art store? The non-photographic blue lines are not photographically reproducible, so they are are excellent for creating artwork.

In the same way that blue-line grids are used for measurements, dimensions, and creating exact artwork, Illustrator, when **View->Show Grid** is selected, turns the complete background of the document into a blue-line grid.

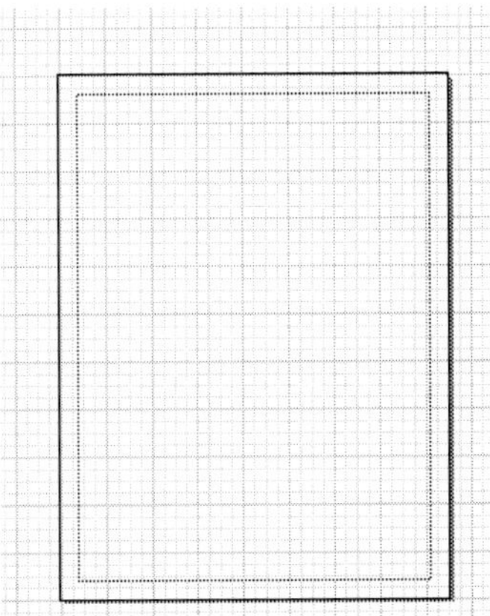

The Artboard and Page Tiling may be viewed as seen above. The grid, like guides, is non-reproducible.

In order to **Show Rulers**, press Command-R (Macintosh) or Control-R (Windows) on the keyboard.

Remember, always get rid of all the guides in your drawing before sending the final version out to the service bureau or output site. Save a working version for yourself, with the guides intact.

Controlling the Grid

The Grid feature is available from the **View** menu. **Show/Hide Grid** is one option, **Snap to Grid** is another. The same way objects snap to rulers and points, items will snap to the grid.

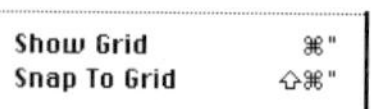

Where else do you obtain control over the grid feature? In the **File->Preferences->Guides & Grids.**

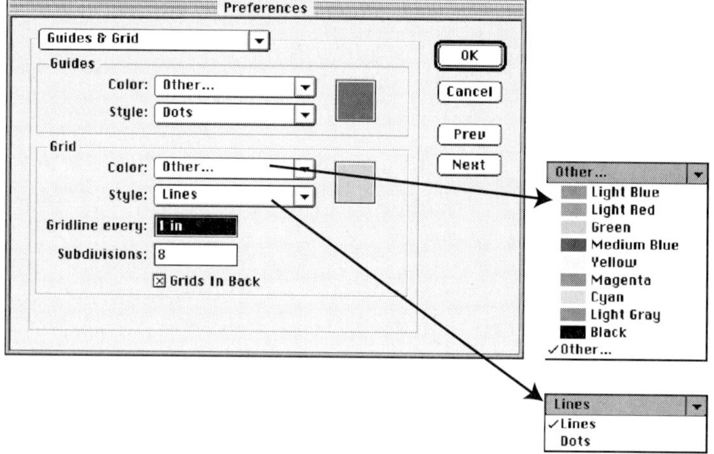

You may customize:

- **Color** — The color of the grid lines.

- **Style** — The grid can be lines or dots. You decide.

- **Gridline Every** — The thicker line can be set for whatever distance you desire. One inch is the default standard, but can be changed.

- **Subdivisions** — are the small, inner grids within each grid square. You can specify how many you want to appear.

Guides

Non-printing **Guides** are very useful (and sometimes essential) in keeping measurements and alignments consistent in designs and layout work.

Guides look like dotted lines. They're visible and can be moved or locked; however, they don't print.

. . . .

Guides are created in two ways:

As you become more proficient with Illustrator, you'll find yourself creating and deleting guides several times while developing complex illustrations. When you don't need them, get rid of them. Don't work in cluttered environments if you can help it.

- Dragging from the rulers in the document window. With the Selection tool, simply click the ruler area and drag the mouse to pull a guide into the drawing area.

- Selecting a path (or paths) and choosing **View->Make Guides** converts the path to a guide.

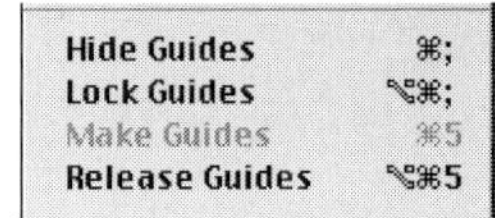

Hide Guides allows you to view the page without guides showing.

Lock Guides makes guides unselectable.

Make Guides creates a guide from the path you have selected.

Release Guides reverts guides back to paths.

Guides are very handy and may be used to maintain heights and widths, keep objects aligned on a level plane, or position objects you want to match with others in your design. You can also make objects snap to guides by selecting **Snap to Point** in the **General Preferences**.

Setting Ruler Zero Points

Illustrator, like many programs, provides simple rulers that can be used to measure an object's position on the page. The point from which objects are measured is called the Zero Point. It starts out in the corner of the page, but can be moved to make measuring things easier.

Measurement is a high priority for using guides, and it's important that you have control over your measuring system. Controlling where the ruler Zero Point is located is essential.

The ruler Zero Point control is located in the upper left corner, visible only when you have rulers turned on. To adjust the Zero Point location, drag from this corner onto the page and the zeros of the ruler will follow accordingly. The default Zero Point is the upper left corner of the Page Tile.

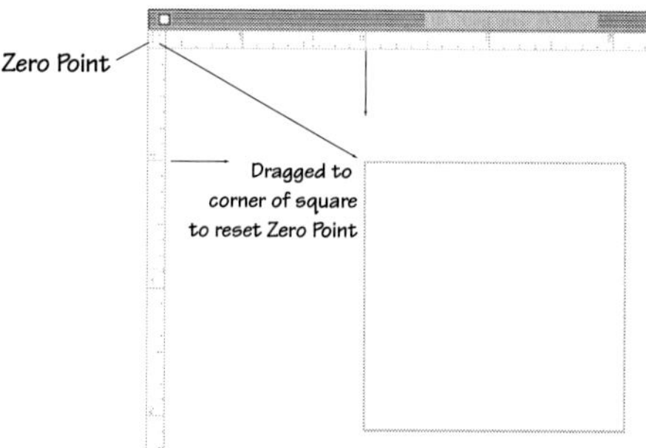

Creating a Two-Inch Square with Guides

1. Create a **New** document. Go to **File->Preferences->Units & Undo** to set the **General** units to **Inches**.

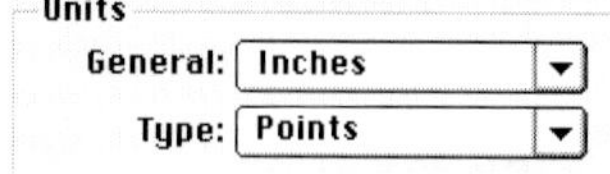

2. Press Command-R (Macintosh) or Control-R (Windows) to show the **Rulers**.

3. From the Zero Point box, drag the crosshair to the upper left corner of the Page Tiling. This will reset the ruler Zero Point.

4. Drag a guide from the vertical ruler. Position it on the zero in the horizontal ruler. Drag a guide from the horizontal ruler. Position it on the zero mark of the vertical ruler.

5. Drag a guide from the horizontal ruler. Position it on the 2" mark of the vertical ruler. Drag a guide from the vertical ruler to the 2" mark of the horizontal ruler.

6. A 2" square has been created using the guides. Dragging guides is a fast, simple way to build the layout of a job.

7. **Close** the file without saving.

Making Guides from Paths

You can easily drag from the rulers onto the page in order to create horizontal and vertical guides — lines that won't print out in the final artwork, but are used only to place elements accurately. You aren't limited to straight guides, though; you can create non-printing guides from any shape.

The second way to create a guide is to convert a path to a guide. This is the most flexible technique for creating guides because they can be made from a simple, single segment or a complex design. This method is very convenient for using paths that cannot be used as templates, but need to be traced or used for position.

Keep the guides **Locked**. If objects are marqueed, unlocked guides will be selected. If the paths are moved, the guides will be moved as well.

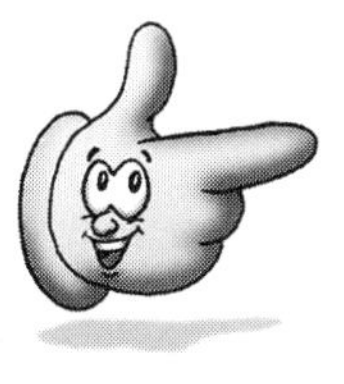

Experimenting with Guides

1. From **SF-Intro Illustrator**, **File->Open** the document **Primitive Objects.AI**.

2. Go to **View->Artwork** mode. In the **View** menu, toggle **Lock Guides** so that it has no check mark next to it. This means the guides are not locked.

Hide Guides	⌘;
Lock Guides	⌥⌘;
Make Guides	⌘5

3. Click on the circle at the top of the page with the Selection tool.

4. Go to **View->Make Guides** to turn the circle (a.) into a guide (b.).

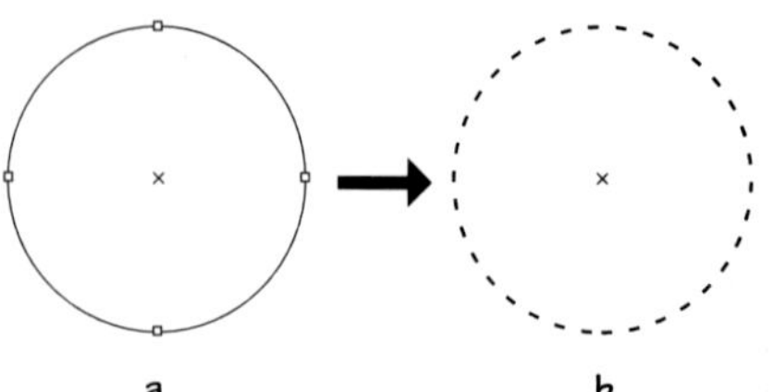

5. Click on the new guide to select it. Go to **View->Release Guides.** Observe how the circular guide reverts back to being an object.

6. With the released guide still selected, press Command-5 (Macintosh) or Control-5 (Windows). This is a shortcut to turning objects into guides.

7. Go to **View->Lock Guides.** Now try to select the guide. Locked guides cannot be selected. Keep guides locked for safety measures.

8. **Close** the file without saving.

VIEWING MODES

CHAPTER OBJECTIVE:

To learn the various methods of viewing and working within a drawing window. In Chapter 5, you will:

- Understand the difference between Artwork and Preview modes

- Learn how to use Artwork mode to make difficult selections.

- Learn how to isolate and view selected portions of a drawing.

- Save custom views of your drawings.

Viewing Modes

When you're developing a piece of artwork, you'll find yourself continually needing to change the portion of the drawing that's visible on your monitor. Sometimes you need to get really close in order to work on a detail; other times you need to see the whole page, so that you can position elements across the entire drawing surface. To accomplish this, you need to understand how to zoom in and out of an illustration, focusing on specific areas where you need to work. You'll also learn how to save specific views so that you can return to them whenever you need to.

Using Preview and Artwork Modes

There are two ways to look at a drawing: preview and artwork. **Preview** mode shows what the illustration will look like when it's printed; **Artwork** mode shows the elements as raw components.

Illustrator was first developed to take advantage of the PostScript page description language while implementing a clear and easy-to-use interface that would appeal to professional graphic artists. These drawing elements are vectors or paths that can be Stroked and Filled (painted) with colors.

In the early versions of Illustrator, the process of drawing and painting was to draw the shape first and Paint it in **Artwork** mode, then to view the colors in **Preview** mode.

Now Illustrator permits work in the **Preview** mode. The **Artwork** mode still removes all the painting effects and allows you to see the paths without Fill or Stroke as anchor points connected by segments. Here is an object seen in **Artwork** mode:

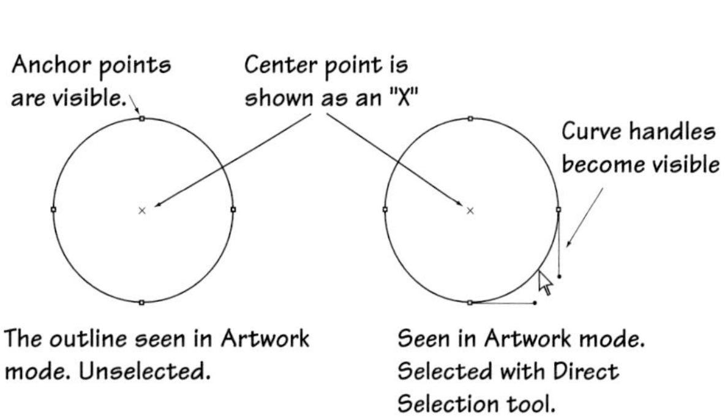

If you're working on a very complex document, or a slow workstation, you can turn off preview — it does make the program run a lot faster. You can always choose to preview just the selected object. This selection preview also works well when you've changed your preferences to not display high-resolution images such as scans.

The keyboard shortcut to toggle back and forth from **Preview** to **Artwork** mode is Command-Y (Macintosh) or Control-Y (Windows).

The **Preview** mode allows you to see the object, after being painted, as it really looks with colors, etc. Below is the same outline as above, seen in **Preview**.

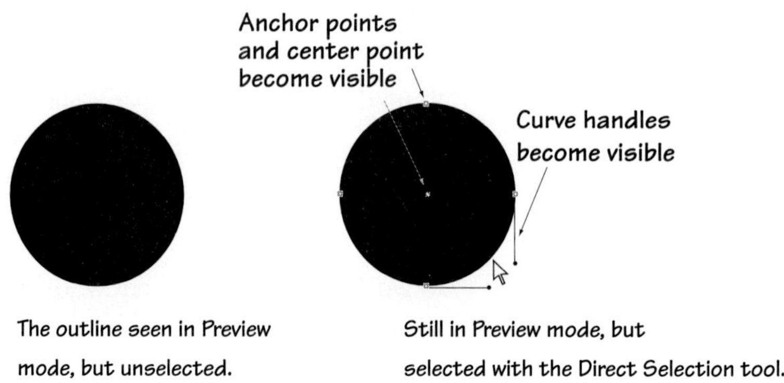

The outline seen in Preview mode, but unselected.

Still in Preview mode, but selected with the Direct Selection tool.

There are times when it is desirable to draw and Paint in the **Preview** mode. Sometimes is it necessary to go to the **Artwork** mode to see the shapes being worked on more clearly.

The **Preview** mode toggles to **Artwork** mode when selected. Both options are available from the **View** menu.

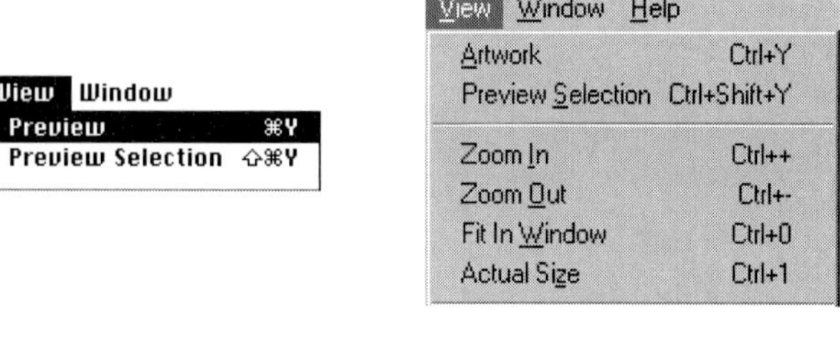

Macintosh

Windows

Preview Selection

When a drawing is very complex, you may want to work in **Artwork** mode (to maximize the speed at which you can work), but will need to preview a single component or group of components.

A view that is sometimes useful is **Preview Selection**. It will preview only the objects that are selected. Other unselected objects remain in **Artwork** mode. This saves time when you wish to view a portion of the art and don't want to wait as the whole design previews in color.

Here is an example of how **Preview Selection** works. The three objects are seen first in **Preview** mode. You can tell which object is in front of another by the way they look. In **Artwork** mode, it's impossible to tell which object is in front.

Preview Selection allows you to see only the selected object in **Preview** mode, but only gives some indication of front/back positioning if two or more objects are selected.

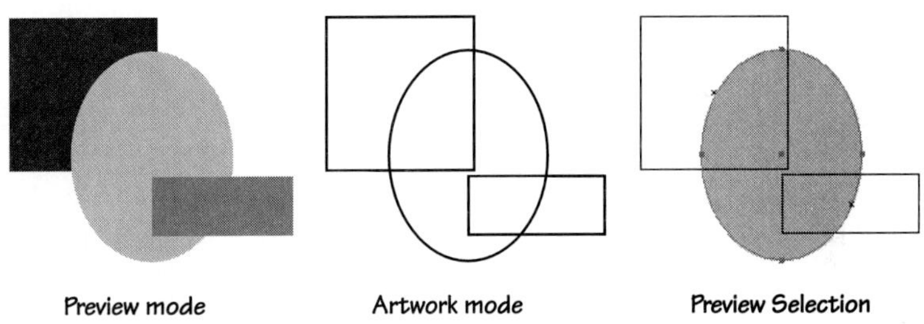

Views Maximize Drawing Efficiency

There are times when the various painted objects of a design either overlap, obscure, or cause problems that a change in viewing mode can fix. Here are some guidelines to how **View->Preview/Artwork** modes affect the appearance and working aspects of your design.

Preview mode is best when you are merely drawing circles, ovals, and squares, or when arranging the objects to fit your design.

Preview mode is not good for drawing paths with the Pen tool unless you are experienced with Illustrator. When you click the path, it will **Preview** as you draw. If **Fill** is on while you are drawing a line, you might be surprised by the preview as you click.

Artwork mode is best when drawing with the Pen tool. You will see exactly what shape you are drawing. You can then go to **Preview** to see it painted.

Personal choice will dictate whether you will tend to create in **Preview** or **Artwork** modes. You may find that intricate or complex drawings with many overlapping elements can best be edited in **Artwork** mode. Coloring and finalizing a drawing will almost always be easier in the **Preview** mode.

Just like anything else, whether you like to work in preview or artwork mode is a matter of preference, and we know excellent operators that argue the relative benefits of one over another. We prefer **Preview mode** and big, bad workstations.

Whenever you have to move scroll bars, or use the grabber hand too often, it's time to consider saving several custom views. We know mapmakers who use Illustrator and often have dozens of custom views in a single document.

Custom Views

Custom views are a feature of Illustrator that allows you to save specific areas of the page as named views. If, while you're developing a drawing, you find yourself constantly zooming into the same general region of the illustration, then you should consider building custom views for that page.

Saving a few mouse clicks by creating such custom views might not seem like a time-saver, but if any feature can save mouse clicks, rest assured that they'll build up over time, making you a more productive operator.

Located at the bottom of the **View** menu are two options, **New View** and **Edit Views**:

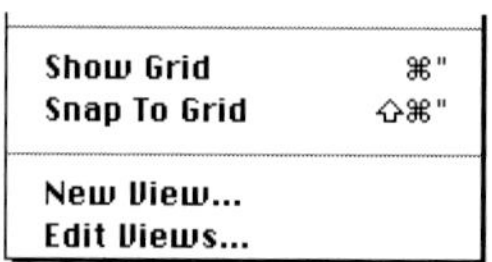

The sequence in creating a custom view is to use the Zoom tool to get the image on the screen at the size you want it.

The **New View** option is then chosen from the **View** menu. The **New View** window appears. It is then possible to type in the name of this particular view in order to access it later. Once new views are created, their names appear at the very bottom of the **View** menu for selection.

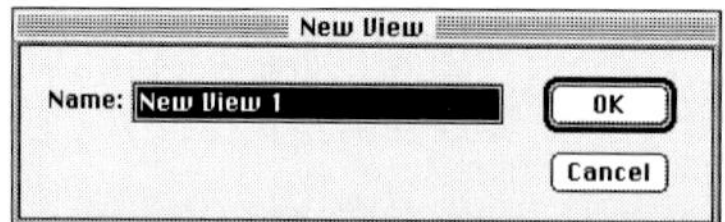
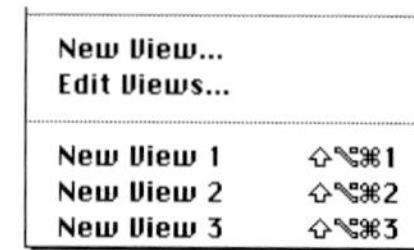

The other option, along with **New View**, is **Edit Views**. This is rather misleading. You cannot actually edit the view itself, you can only either rename a view or delete the view from the list.

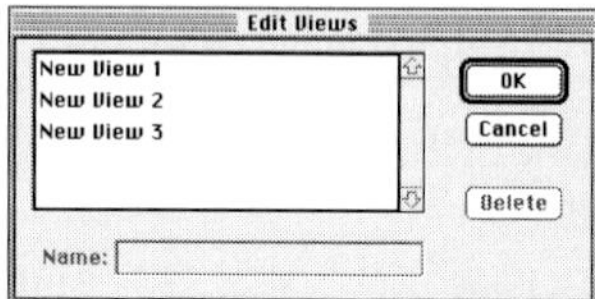

1. Use **File->Open** to go to the **SF-Intro Illustrator** folder and open the **Primitive Objects.AI** document.

2. With the Zoom tool, enlarge 400% on the black outline square.

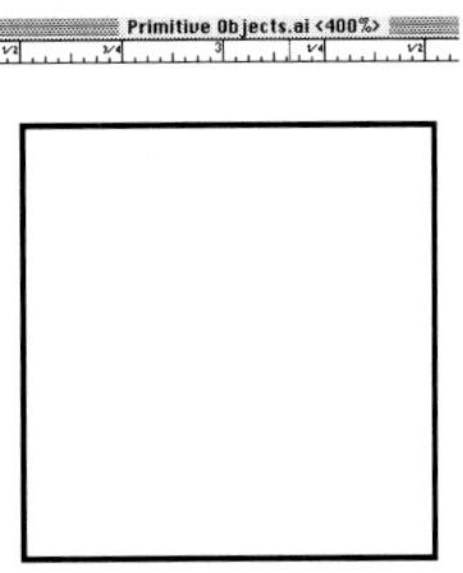

3. Go to **View->New View**. Name the view "Close-up 400%." Click **OK**. Go to **View->Fit In Window**; then to **View->Artwork** mode.

4. In the **View** menu, go to the bottom and select **Close-up 400%**. Observe how the screen jumps to this previously made view.

5. **Close** the file without saving.

Notes:

CHAPTER 6

ORGANIZING YOUR ART WITH LAYERS

CHAPTER OBJECTIVE:

To learn the use, behavior, and functionality of the Layers commands. To learn to manage layers within your document, and to learn when and how they can be utilized to best advantage. In Chapter 6, you will:

- Learn how layers are organized and how to manage them.

- Learn to create and modify layers within an existing drawing.

- Learn to assign objects to specific layers, and how to move objects from one layer to another.

- Learn to lock, hide, and delete layers to reduce complexity and to aid in the development of complex artwork.

Organizing Your Art with Layers

In this section, we're going to explore the many different things that can be accomplished with the use of layers.

A good visual analogy for layers can be had by thinking about the plans for a new house. There would be a lot of drawings involved; electrical components would be on one drawing, plumbing on another. Yet more "layers" might be required for things like walls and windows, doors and openings, foundation and cement work, even the pool area might be on its own set of plans. That's the best way to think about layers. Imagine if you could put all of these components on their own separate pieces of paper — and could turn them on or off, lock or hide them, or move them around in relationship to each other. Different layers could even be colored differently to help them stand out.

The Layer Concept

The layer concept is quite easy to understand. It is best compared to color separations where various elements appear on different color plates. In the same way, the elements you assign to the layers are separated from the other elements in the design.

In this example, the coffee steam, the cup/saucer, and the border are put on three different layers. Here's how they look.

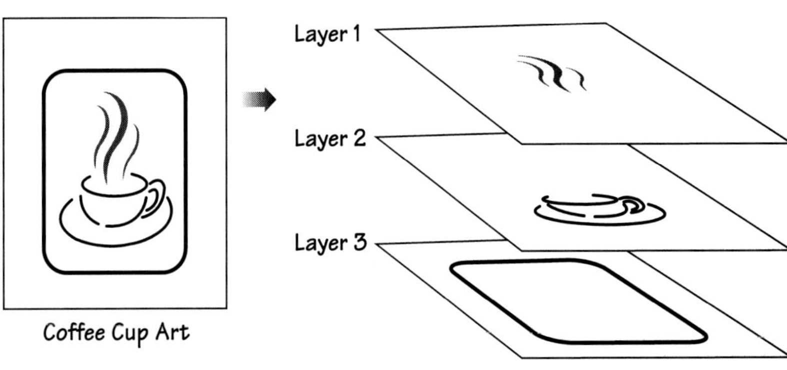

Certain types of drawings, like architectural drawings, technical drawings, and maybe some types of ads and designs can be easier to develop — and easier to modify — if you develop them with layers.

Organizing the Elements

The first question asked when considering layers is "What goes where?" The design may have a multitude of paths, objects, groups, placed images, etc.

The first step is to break down the design to its basic elements. How you view the elements of a design depends perhaps on your own style, or how the design will be output. You can be very conservative, or you can overdo it.

In this example, conservatively speaking, the Coffee Du Jour ad contains only two basic design elements: the type (headline, body copy, logo tag-line), and the graphics (border at top, coffee cup art, logo at bottom). You could put all text on one layer and the graphics on another.

But, to carry the breakdown further, the border at the top could have its own layer, the headline and its sub-head could be on one layer, the coffee cup art on another layer, and the Java Jungle logo with its tag line at the bottom could be on its own layer. In essence, break the design down to its various elements and assign each to its own layer.

The Layers .

The control you can obtain with layers depends on how well the **Layers** palette and the **Layer Options** dialog box are understood and used.

The **Layers** palette is accessed from **Window->Show Layers**. This is the main palette you will use to create layers, assign elements to layers, and **Lock** and **Hide** the layers.

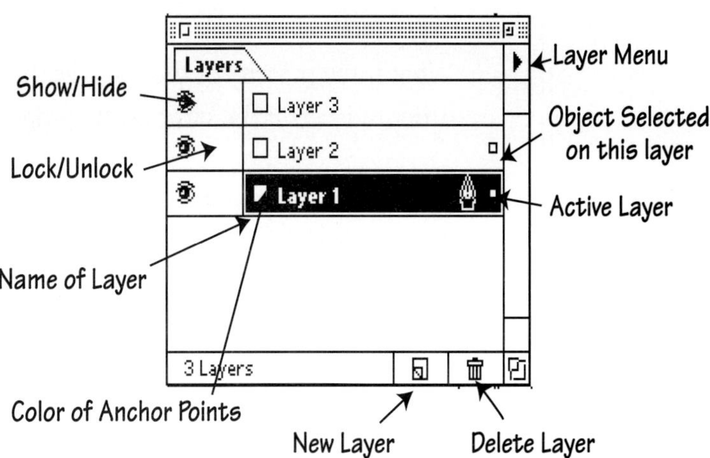

Basic Rules for Layers

Layers work in a logical manner, one on top of another. You can shuffle them, lock them, hide them, or delete them at any time.

The procedures for using layers must be observed, or you are going to end up with problems that will take some time to find and fix.

- If a layer is selected, and new items are created or placed, they will default to be assigned this layer.

- Layers can be relocated up and down the list in the **Layers** palette.

- Objects can be reassigned to other layers by dragging the colored dot. You cannot simply click on layers to reassign art objects to the layers.

- The layer color is the color of the Edges of selected paths and objects.

- If a layer is locked, and accidentally remains the selected layer, all tools or cursors will be the crossed-out pencil icon. You must select another unlocked layer to work on.

- Be careful when deleting layers. If a message says there are objects on the layer that will delete them, go back and reassign them, if needed.

- Layers, when selected to be the active layer, turn black and show a pen tip icon.

The Order of Layer Levels

What is the priority of the levels as they appear in the **Layers** palette? The order of layers is the same as the order in the list from top to bottom.

Example: in this palette window, Layer 3 is in front of all others. Next is Layer 2, then Layer 4. The bottom-most layer is Layer 1.

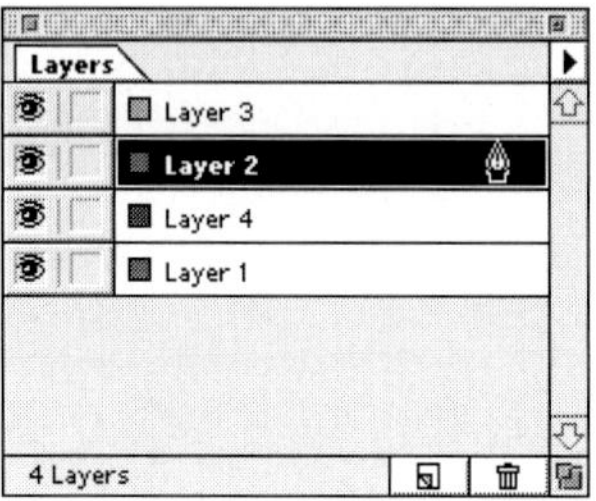

Changing Layer Levels

There will be many times when a layer needs to be moved to another level. The layer is dragged up or down to the new level desired. When you click-hold on the layer, a clenched fist appears to show you are grabbing the item.

You then drag the clenched fist and layer to its new location. In this example, Layer 4, at the top of the list, needs to be relocated to be at the bottom. Keep in mind that even Locked layers can be moved.

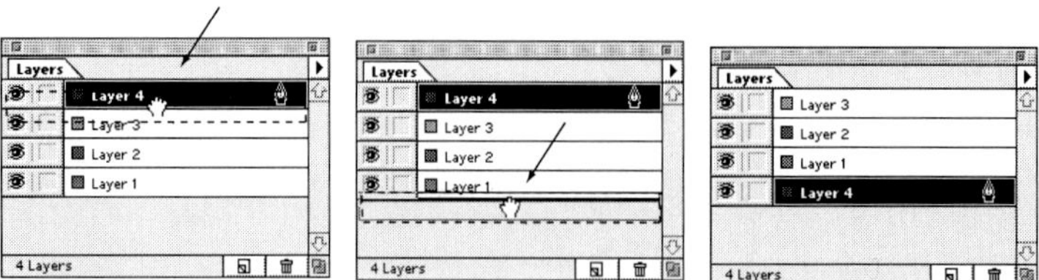

Layers with dots show that the objects on the layer are selected. Even though a single layer is selected as the active layer, the other dots will show when their corresponding objects are selected.

Appearances sometimes deceive. In this example, the square is selected and the Layer 2 is highlighted as the active layer. Is the square assigned to Layer 2? No. When the square was selected, the small colored dot appeared on Layer 1. That is the square's assigned layer.

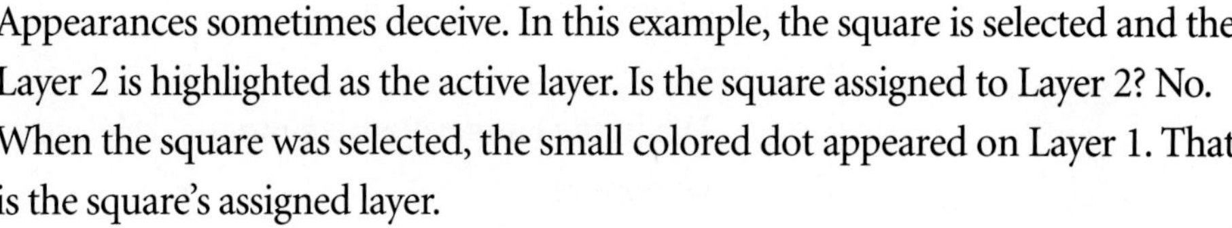

Reassigning Objects to Other Layers

There will be times when objects need to be reassigned to another layer. When an object is selected, a small colored dot appears to designate the layer it is assigned to. The black square in this example is assigned to Layer 1 because its colored dot shows there when selected. To reassign the square to Layer 2, the colored dot is dragged down to Layer 2.

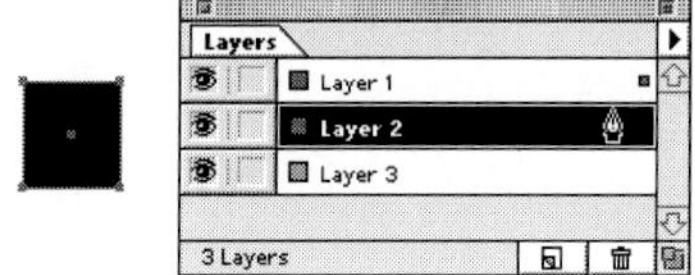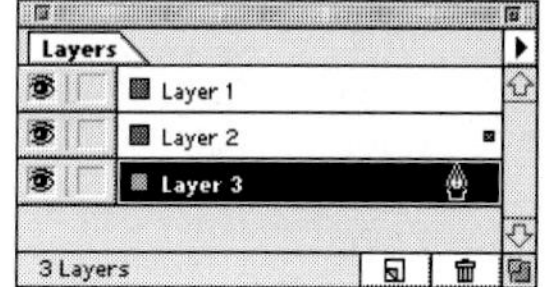

How do you assign many objects, residing on various layers, all to one layer? You **Edit-Select All**. The selected objects will show their colored dots on each assigned layer. You simply drag the colored dots to the desired layer. Any layer without a dot can then be deleted without a warning message.

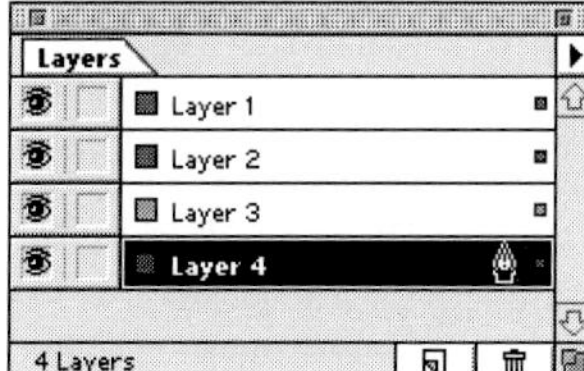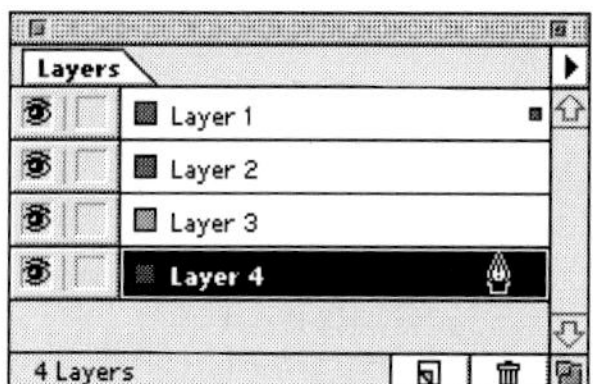

The shortcut for accessing the **Layer Options** dialog box is to double-click the layer in the palette.

Paste Remembers Layers
keeps track of objects and
their assigned layers, even
when Cut or Pasted.

If **Paste Remembers
Layers** is On, the object,
regardless of where it is
pasted, will retain its layer.

If **Paste Remembers
Layers** is Off, the object,
though assigned to a
certain layer, will lose this
connection if it is pasted
behind another object on a
different layer. It will be
assigned to the layer of
the object it was pasted
behind.

Layer Options for a
particular layer can be
accessed at any other
time by double-clicking the
layer.

The Layers Palette Menu

When the **Layers Palette Menu** is selected from the **Layers** palette, several options are given.

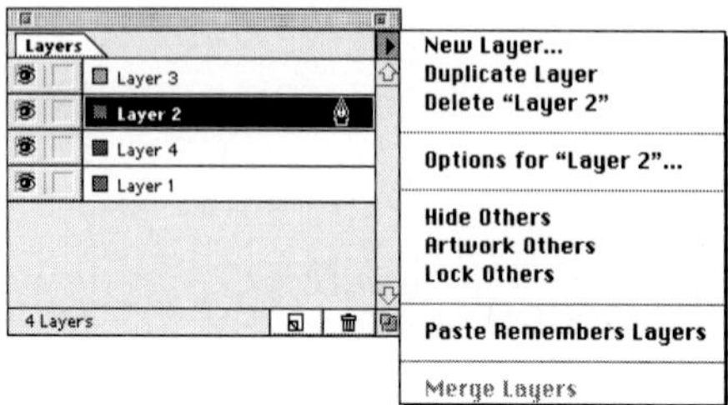

- **New Layer** allows you to create a new layer.

- **Duplicate Layer** makes a copy of the selected layer.

- **Delete** is used to eliminate specific layers.

- **Layer Options** offers many choices.

- **Hide Others** will **Hide** all layers except the one selected.

- **Artwork Others** sends all layers, except the one selected, into the **Artwork** View mode. This is similar to **Preview Selection.**

- **Unlock All** will unlock all layers that are **Locked.**

- **Paste Remembers Layers** controls how elements that are **Cut** and **Pasted** will retain their layer levels. Without this turned on, elements pasted behind another layer will default to that layer.

- **Merge Layers** eliminates all layers but one, and assigns all objects to this layer.

Layer Options

The **Layer Options** dialog box appears when you create a new layer through the **Layers Palette Menu.**

- **Show** refers to Hide/Show. If you click this Off, the objects on the layer will Hide.

- **Preview** refers to **View->Preview/Artwork** modes. If you click this Off, the objects on the layer will appear only in **Artwork** mode.

- **Lock** will lock and unlock the objects on the layer.

- **Print** will allow the objects to print or not print, when output.

- **Dim Images** refers only to Placed images. This option is used mostly for dimming graphics to be used as templates.

The options it offers can give you absolute control over the elements residing on that layer.

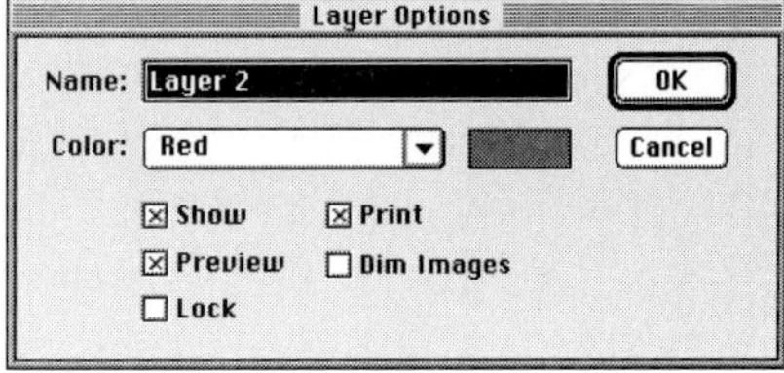

You might consider looking around in magazines, books, and other publications for artwork that may have been developed on a computer. It's getting harder to tell these days. Once, computer-developed artwork stuck out like a sore thumb.

Trying to reproduce artwork and illustrations you find laying around is a great way to develop your own skills. Just remember that published artwork is protected by copyright laws. Using it for practice is, we're sure, just fine with any professional artist.

1. Open **Tubing Turtle.AI** from the **SF-Intro Illustrator** folder.

2. Go to **Window->Show Layers**. The **Layers** palette will appear.

3. Click on the New Layer icon. The new layer will appear at the top of the layer list.

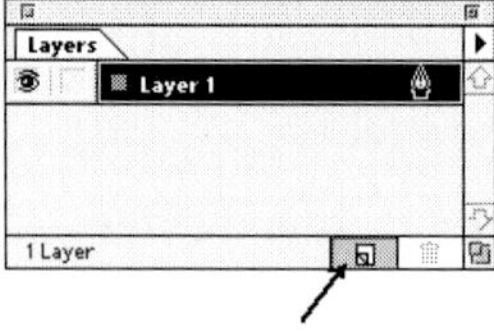
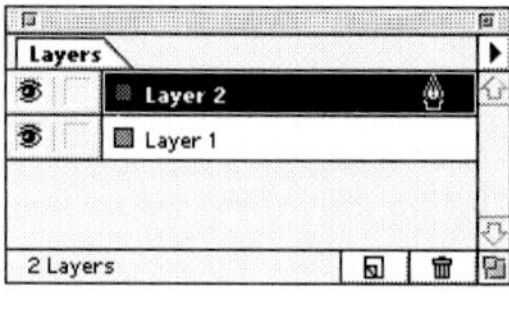

4. Create two more new layers this way.

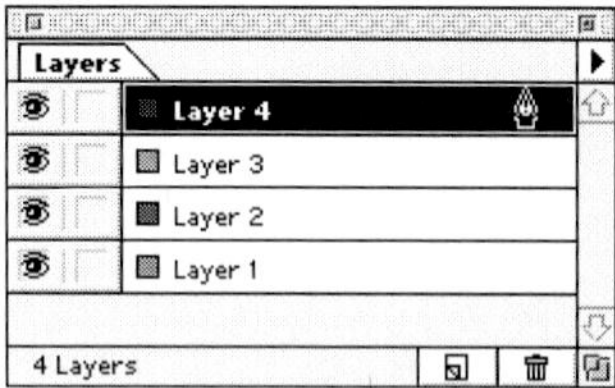

5. All the objects are on Layer 1. Leave the turtle assigned to Layer 1. Click on the "Life's A Beach" headline. Pull its square icon to Layer 2.

6. Click on the body text block. Pull its colored dot to Layer 3.

7. Click on the rounded-corner border. Pull its colored dot to Layer 4.

8. The objects have all been assigned to their own layers.

9. Double-click on Layer 1. In the **Layer Options** dialog box, rename the layer "Turtle Layer." Click **Ok.**

Keep working with layers until you're comfortable. Remember, some artists find them indispensable, and others hardly touch the palette.

Rename the other layers in the same way. You will appropriately rename the layers as follows:

> Layer 2 becomes "Headline Layer"

> Layer 3 becomes "Text Layer"

> Layer 4 becomes "Border Layer"

10. The order of the layers needs to be rearranged.

11. Click-hold on Turtle Layer. The cursor will become a clenched hand. Drag Turtle Layer up to the top of the list.

12. Click-hold on Border Layer and move it to be the second in the order.

13. Click-hold on Text Layer and move it to be the third in the order.

14. Click-hold on Headline Layer and move it to be the fourth in the order.

15. The **Layers** palette should look like this.

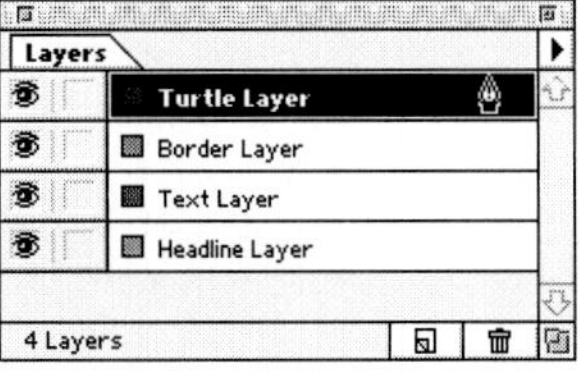

16. Experiment with **Show/Hide** in the **Layers** palette. Click on the Eye icon to the left of the layers and observe the effects on the objects and the **Layers** palette.

    Hold the Option key (Macintosh) or Alt key (Windows) and click on the Eye icon of the Turtle Layer. Observe how this affects the other objects.

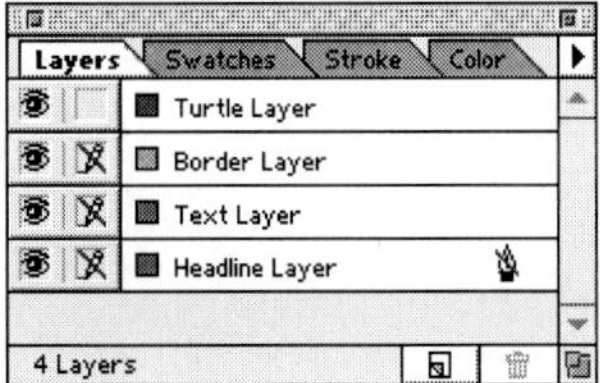

Again, hold the Option key (Macintosh) or Alt key (Windows) and click on the same Eye icon.

17. Experiment with **Lock**ing in the **Layers** palette.
Click on the **Lock/Unlock** square to the left of the layers and observe the effects on the objects and the **Layers** palette.

Hold the Option key (Macintosh) or Alt key (Windows) and click the **Lock/Unlock** square. Observe how this affects the other objects.

Again, hold the Option key (Macintosh) or Alt key (Windows) and click the **Lock/Unlock** square.

18. Press Command-S (Macintosh) or Control-S (Windows) to **Save** the file.

19. **Close** the document.

CHAPTER 7

TEMPLATES

CHAPTER OBJECTIVE:

To learn how to create and manage the use of templates as a tracing aid. To learn how to use a scanned pencil sketch to develop artwork. In Chapter 7, you will:

- Use Layers and Layer options to turn a scanned or imported graphic into a template.

- Learn how, in certain instances, it's better to start with a rough sketch and then convert it into an Illustrator Template.

- Learn to draw a design using a template as a tracing guide.

- Use the Autotrace tool on a template to automatically trace an imported image.

As we've said earlier, it's a good idea to develop drawings in a logical manner – and that usually means doing a rough pencil sketch before you start clicking and dragging. These sketches can become the templates we describe in this section.

When using bitmapped images (TIFF, PICT, JPEG, etc.) it is mandatory that you stay in Preview mode to see your template. Artwork mode will not show the image.

Templates

Many artists find it easier to start a drawing with a rough sketch and refine it using tools such as Adobe Illustrator. Start with a rough scanned image as a basis of your drawings. Some of the most professional, well-seasoned illustrators routinely rely on their manual drawing skills to *begin* their designs.

We've already told you that the book is built on exercises and projects. Exercises are scattered throughout the course and often result in the creation of small components, shapes, and objects. Projects are self-contained, and result in the creation of finished elements that are often combined to create completed jobs. In keeping with this popular and effective method of developing designs, we've built all of the Projects on sketches — scanned and supplied on the CD that were included with this course material.

When you import a template, Illustrator automatically creates a Layer — the scanned image can be dimmed so as not to interfere with your drawing efforts.

The Making of a Template

You can Place the image you want for a template into Illustrator. This can be a scan of a rough sketch or a graphic created from a computer application. The image format can be Raster (bitmapped) or Vector paths (EPS). If the image you use is of Raster format, you will always need to be in **View->Preview** to see this image. Artwork mode will show only its bounding box.

Prior to placing the image, the **Layers** palette (**Window->Show Layers**) is used to create a new layer by clicking the New Item icon at the bottom of the palette. This will create a new layer called Layer 2 which will be located at the top of the layers list.

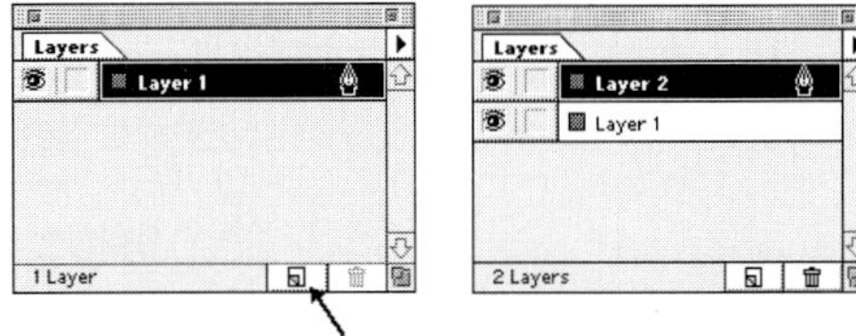

Layer 2 is double-clicked to bring up the **Layer Options** dialog box. In this box, the layer is renamed "Template" for identification purposes. Also, **Dim Images** is selected to dim the image to a gray. **Print** should be clicked off, so as not to print the template image. **OK** is then clicked.

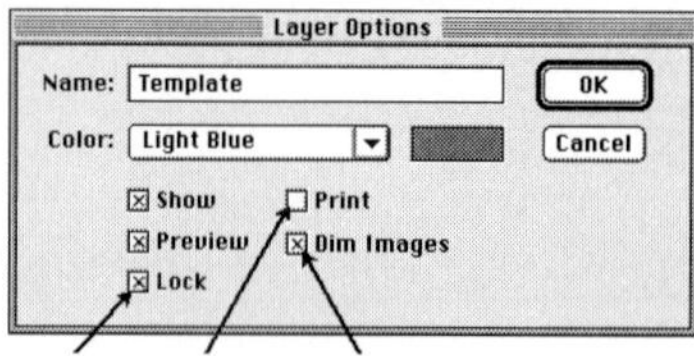

In the **Layers** palette, the Template layer is moved down to the level under Layer 1.

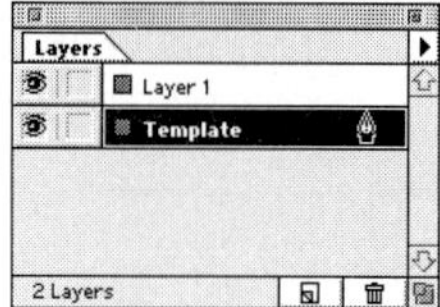

With the Template layer clicked on to be the active layer, the desired template image is **File->Placed** into the document. It is automatically assigned to the active Template layer. The image will appear as a dimmed, gray image.

The placed image is still selectable and should be moved on the page to act as a template. Once the image is in position, it should be **Locked** in the **Layers** palette to avoid accidental moving or deleting. This is done by clicking the **Lock** button on the Template layer. When clicked, a crossed-out pencil icon appears to show that no work can be done on that layer because it is locked. Afterwards, you should always click on Layer 1 to continue drawing.

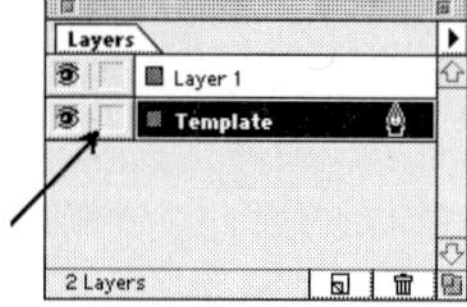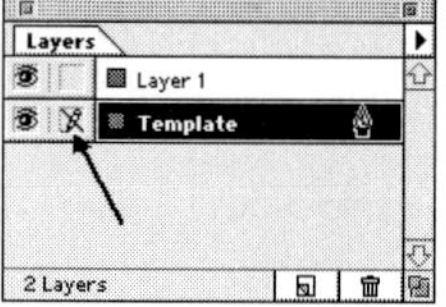

The document page will then have a template that you can trace using either the Pen or Pencil tool.

Creating a Template with Layers

1. Use **File->New** to create a new document. Go to **View->Preview** mode.

2. Go to **Window->Show Layers**. In the **Layers** palette, select the pop-up menu and select **New Layer** to create a new layer.

3. In the appearing **Layer Options** dialog box, change the name of the layer to "Template." Click on **Dim Images**. Click the **Print** option off. Click **OK**.

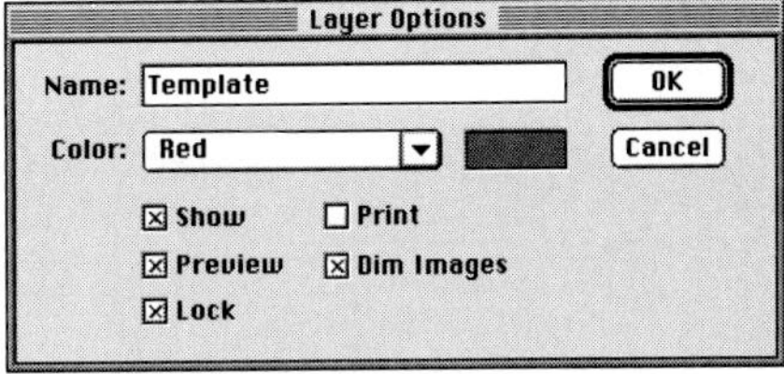

4. Move the new Template layer to be under Layer 1. Keep the Template layer clicked to be the active layer.

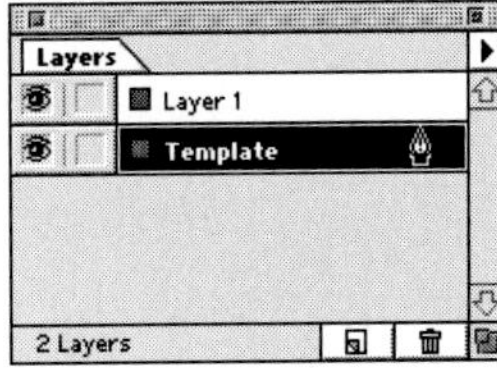

5. Use **File->Place** to go to **SF-Intro Illustrator** and place the graphic **Flower.TIF**. The image will automatically be assigned to the Template layer you created.

Here's an excellent use of Layers that we didn't really cover in the last section.

6. Position the placed image to the top-center of the page.

Click the Lock button on the Template layer.

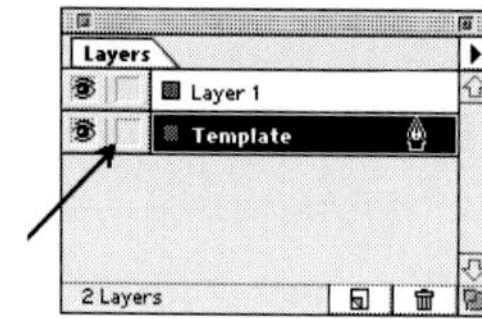 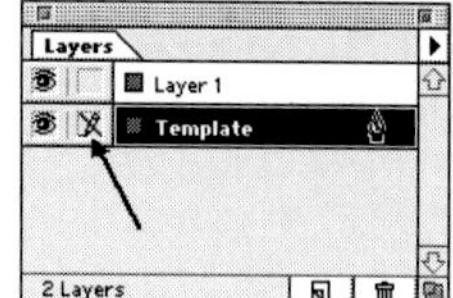

7. Click on Layer 1 to make it the active layer.

8. **Close** the file without saving.

Tracing a Template by Hand

1. Create a new document with **File->New**. Use the Layers technique to dim a **Placed** image to be a template. Go to the **SF-Intro Illustrator** folder, and place the file **Manual Trace.TIF**, turning it into a template.

2. Select the Pen tool. Click on the top-left corner and, moving to the right, click on all corners of the template, in sequence. Finish by clicking the Pen tool on the first anchor point clicked. This will complete a closed path.

Adobe Illustrator: An Introduction to Digital Illustration/Templates

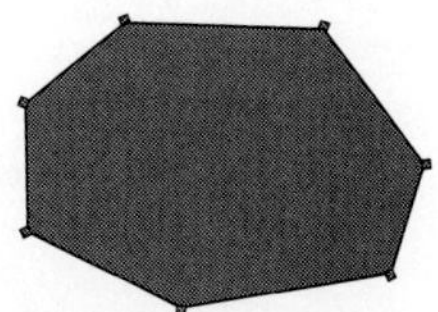

3. Click on this new path with the Selection tool. Go to the Toolbox. Near the bottom, you will see a small icon with the larger **Fill** and **Stroke** icons.

This small icon is the default setting of **Fill** = White, **Stroke** = 1 pt. Black. Click on this icon to paint your path.

4. With the Selection tool, click on the Artboard to deselect the artwork. Go to **View->Preview** mode. The tracing should look like this.

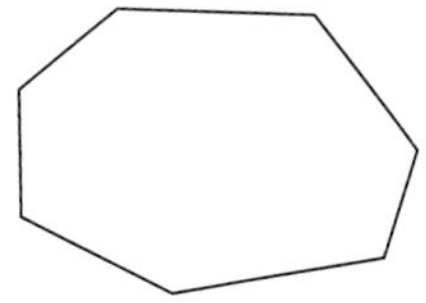

5. **Close** the document without saving.

Autotracing a Template Image

When you click-hold the mouse on the Blend drawing tool icon, the Autotrace tool pops up. This tool will trace Raster (bitmapped) and Vector EPS images **Placed** in the document.

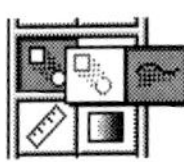

When you choose the Autotrace tool, the cursor becomes a crosshair. This crosshair is moved to the edge of the image you wish to trace, and clicked. The exterior edge of the image will be traced. In areas where the bitmapped image does not touch, the tracer will cease the flow and continue on to the next available touching bitmap.

Autotrace will work on template images, even if they are on a Locked layer.

Autotracing can definitely save you some time, but don't rely on it as a standard practice. Using the regular pen and shape tools results in better, cleaner artwork.

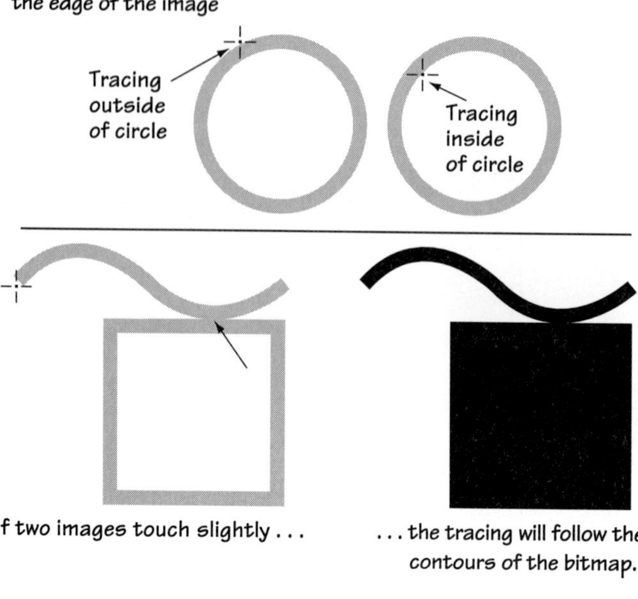

Placed Vector EPS images (Illustrator EPS) are not a good example to use. The Preview of an EPS image is so coarse, it lacks continuity. Also, it is a very rough representation of the image and Autotrace will give an even rougher tracing.

Our suggestion is to use Autotrace only in dire moments when the speed of Autotrace is needed for a deadline. We feel the seasoned Illustrator artist chooses the drawing tools needed to achieve the end result.

If you must use Autotrace, it is best used on TIFF images.

Using Autotrace

1. Use **File->Place** to go to the **SF-Intro Illustrator** folder. Place the graphic **Flower.TIF**.

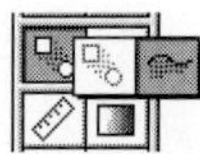

You can always use Autotrace as a starting point, and then push, pull, and tweak the anchor points until the shape is as refined and cleaned as it needs to be.

2. Click-hold on the Blend tool to access the Autotrace tool.

3. Click the crosshair cursor on the outside edge of the image. It will automatically trace the exterior of the image. The result will be an outlined path that can be painted. In **View->Artwork** mode, it will look like this.

4. With the Autotraced path selected, click on the default paint icon for **Fill** and **Stroke**. The flower will look like this.

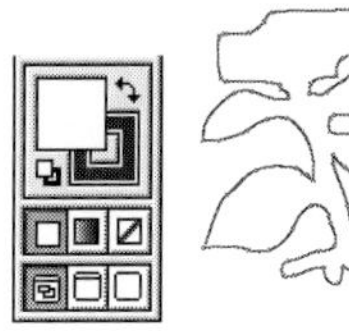

5. **Close** the file without saving.

 **Notes:**

ADOBE ILLUSTRATOR: AN INTRODUCTION TO DIGITAL ILLUSTRATION/TEMPLATES

CHAPTER 8

DRAWING PRIMITIVE SHAPES

CHAPTER OBJECTIVE:

To learn how to create the most basic shapes within the Illustrator environment. To learn the functions of the Ellipse and Rectangle tools. To learn to create other shapes. In Chapter 8, you will:

- Draw shapes manually, and by entering specific sizes into a dialog box.

- Use the Rectangle and Ellipse tools to create components of a more complex drawing.

- Learn to modify the actions of certain tools by using them in conjunction with the keyboard.

- Experiment with tools that create custom shapes, such as starbursts, spirals, and polygons.

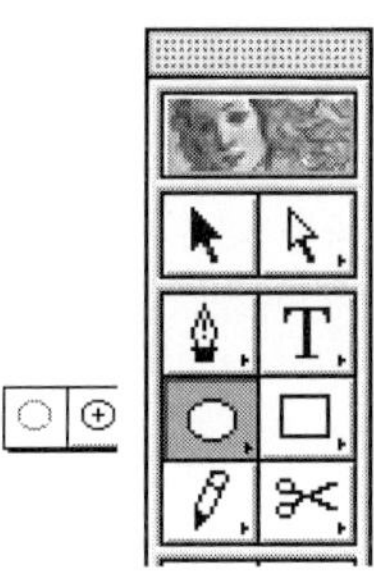

Drawing Primitive Shapes

Almost all drawings — whether very simple or highly complex — make use of basic shapes like squares, rectangles, circles, and ovals. This section will introduce you to the tools Illustrator provides for the creation of such simple elements. We'll discuss several different ways of creating them; visually, and mathematically. Both methods come in handy as you're developing your designs.

Later on, as you learn more about paths and shapes, you'll find that the circles and squares, drawn with the tools we're learning in this chapter, are actually groups of paths — and can be drawn in several ways.

The Ellipse Tool

The Ellipse tool may be used to create perfect circles, or, if you want, eggs, ovals, squished circles, and any remotely circular shape. When using this tool without the Shift key, ellipses of any shape and size can be drawn. If the Shift key is held down while drawing, this tool creates circles.

Click the Ellipse tool crosshair on the page to access its dialog box. You can set the exact dimensions of the ellipse you wish to draw. The dialog box also remembers the dimensions of the last ellipse drawn.

Drawing from the Center Point

The Ellipse tool draws starting from the upper left corner of its bounding box. This is acceptable in most cases, but if you want the center point to be an important aspect of where the ellipse or circle is drawn, then you have an option of drawing starting from the center. This can be done in two ways:

- Hold down the Option key(Macintosh) or the Alt key (Windows) when drawing the object.

- Click-hold on the Ellipse tool icon in the Toolbox. The extensions will appear. Choose the icon with a center point.

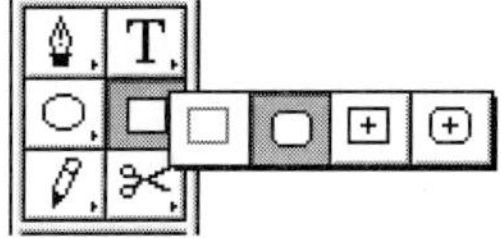

Whenever you're working on a hands-on activity, try to visualize what it is you're learning — as opposed to simply following the steps. There's always a reason we've used an exercise.

Using the Ellipse tool

1. Create a **File->New** document. Go to **View->Artwork** mode. Click on the Ellipse tool in the Toolbox.

2. Experiment with drawing an ellipse by moving the mouse around to see how the ellipse changes shape as you drag.

3. Hold down the Option key (Macintosh) or Alt key (Windows) while drawing another ellipse. This will start the ellipse from its center point.

4. Hold down the Shift key and draw a circle.

5. Hold down both the Shift and Option (Macintosh) or Alt (Windows) keys to draw a circle from its center point. With the circle selected, notice the four anchor points and the center point.

6. Delete the ellipses. Leave the document open for the next exercise.

Creating a Rounded Header

1. In the same document, draw a circle. Stay in **View->Artwork** mode.

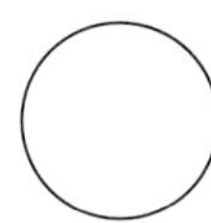

2. Select the circle with the Selection tool and drag it to the right, holding the Option (Macintosh) or Alt (Windows) and Shift keys. This will duplicate it.

3. Click on the facing side anchor points with the Direct Selection tool to select them and press the Delete key.

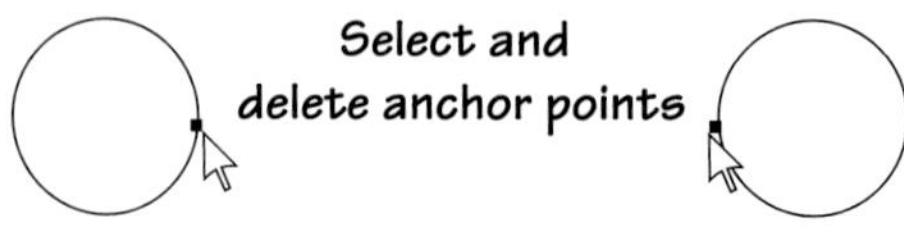

Drawing from the Center Point can be done two ways:

• Hold down the Option key (Macintosh) or Alt key (Windows) when drawing the object.

• Click-hold the Ellipse tool icon in the Toolbox. From the extensions, select the tool with plus symbol.

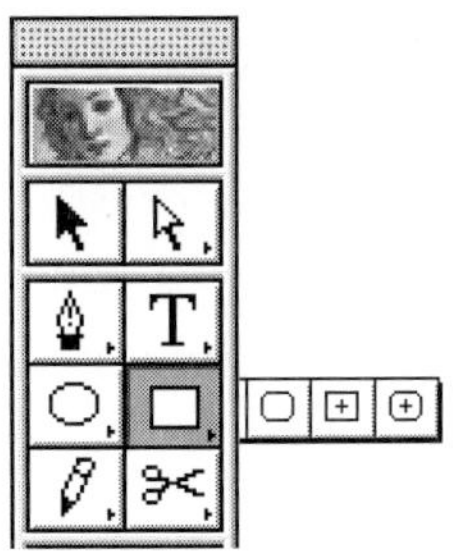

4. With the Direct Selection tool, drag a marquee to select the two top endpoints, then go to **Object->Path->Join.** Do the same to the bottom anchor points.

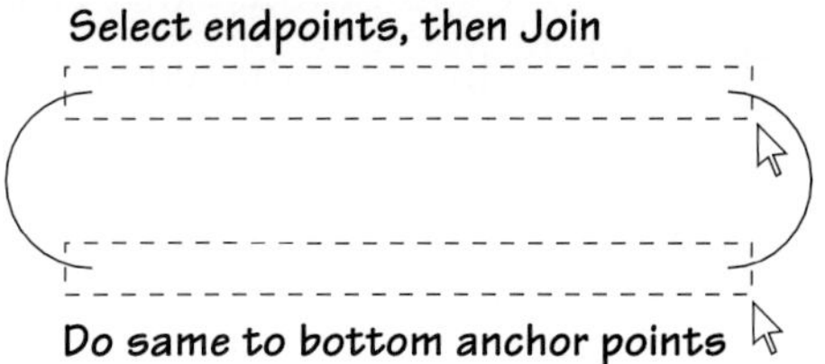

5. Click on this path with the Selection tool and go to the Toolbox. Click the Default paint icon to paint it: **Fill** = White, **Stroke** = 1 pt. Black. Go to **View->Preview** mode.

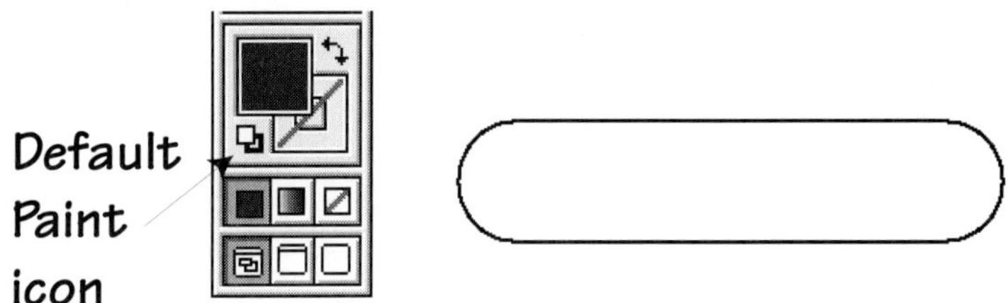

6. **Close** the file without saving.

The Rectangle Tool

The Rectangle tool will draw rectangles or squares. When using this tool without the Shift key, rectangles of any shape and size can be drawn. If the Shift key is held down while drawing, this tool creates a square.

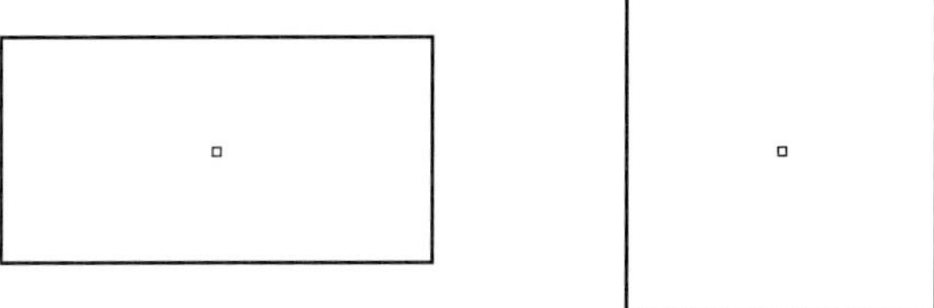

The center point is helpful in showing the center of the object so that proper alignment is attained when lining up with other objects.

The Command (Macintosh), Control (Windows), Option (Macintosh), Alt (Windows) keys, as well as Shift (both) have the same effect on the Rectangle tool and the Ellipse tool for their drawing operations.

The Ellipse and Rectangle tools draw complete closed paths with Center Points. The Center Point looks like an **X** in Artwork mode. It looks like a small square when seen in Preview mode. In the menu **Window->Show Attributes**, the **Show Center Point** will toggle between letting the center point be on/off.

Drawing from the Center Point

The Rectangle tool draws starting from the upper left corner. This can be acceptable in most cases, but if you want the center point to be an important aspect from where the rectangle or square is drawn, you can draw the object starting from the center by holding down the Option key (Macintosh) or Alt key (Windows).

Rounding the Corners

All rectangles can have rounded corners. This can be done using a variety of methods. The roundness of the corner is determined by the **Corner Radius**.

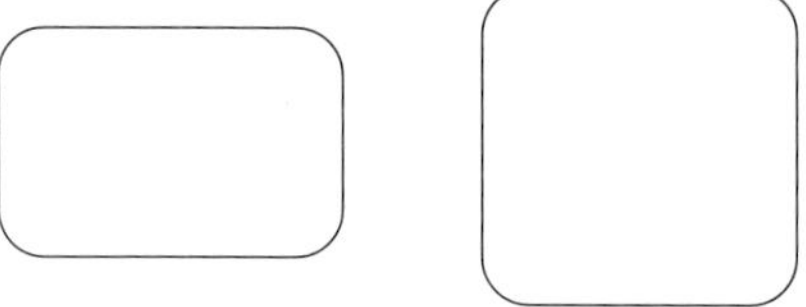

When you select any of the rectangle tools and click its cursor on the page, the **Rectangle** dialog box appears. It is here that you control the **Corner Radius** when drawing the object from the dialog box.

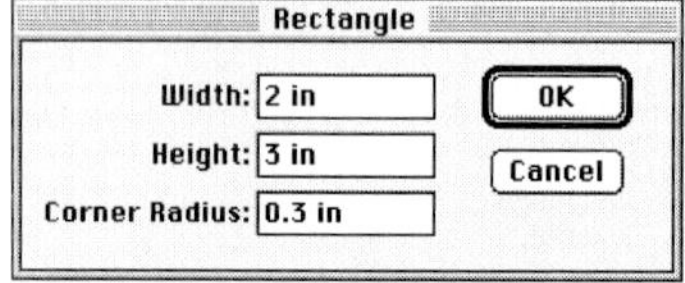

Corner Radius is based, as the name implies, on the radius of a circle. If you divide a circle in quarters, you actually have four corners. The curvature of the corners is determined by the actual radius of the circle, when whole.

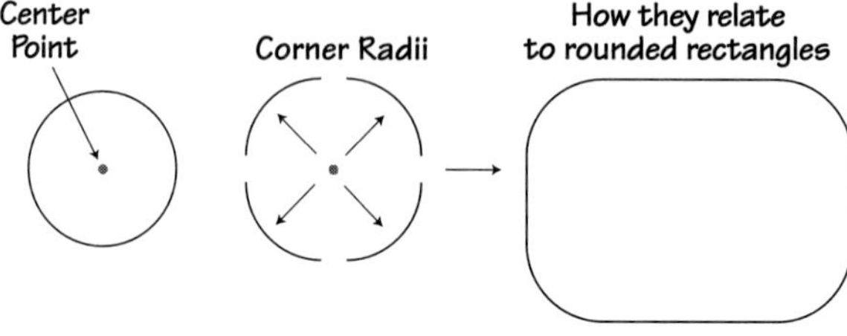

There are several methods to draw or apply rounded corners.

 ADOBE ILLUSTRATOR: AN INTRODUCTION TO DIGITAL ILLUSTRATION/PRIMITIVE SHAPES

- **Manually** — Select the Rounded Corners tool and manually draw the object by dragging the crosshair on the page.

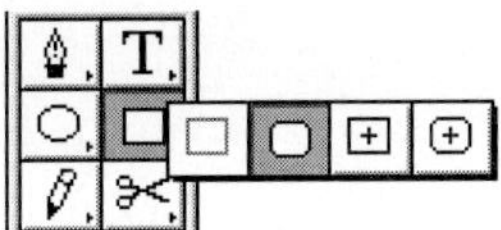

- **Dialog box** — Click on one of the Rectangle tools in the Toolbox. Click the tool's cursor on the page. In the next window, **Corner Radius** allows you to specify the corner's curvature. When you click **OK**, a rectangle of the dimensions you set will appear on the page.

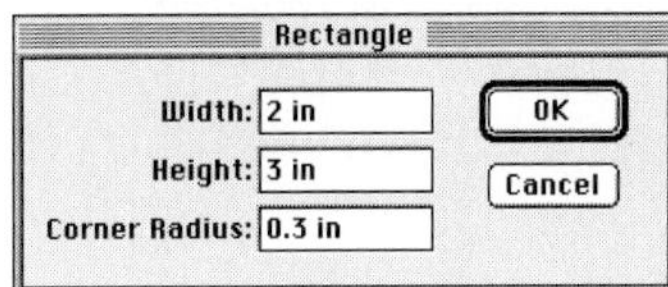

- The Rounded Corners tool can be used manually without going through the dialog box. You select the tool in the Toolbox, then drag the cursor on the page to draw the rectangle. How do you set the **Corner Radius** before drawing? In the **File->Preferences->General** window. There is a **Corner Radius** option in which to type the radius that the Rounded Corner tool will create when you draw manually.

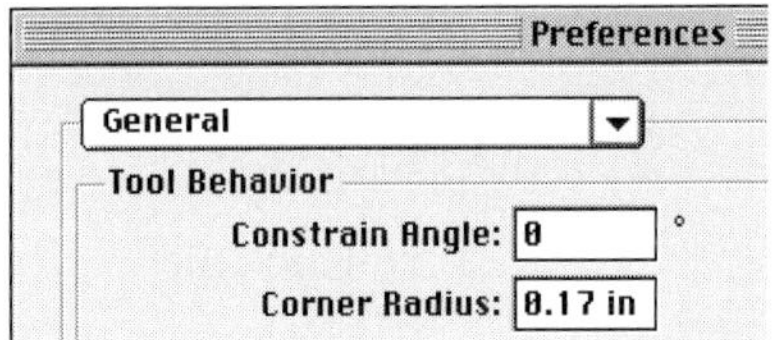

- Square-cornered objects can be selected. Then, from the **Filter** menu, the **Stylize->Round Corners** is accessed. In the dialog box that appears, an entered **Radius** number gives the rectangle rounded corners.

Practicing with the Rectangle Tool

1. Create a **New** document.

2. Click on the Rectangle tool in the Toolbox. Experiment with drawing a rectangle by moving the mouse around on the page.

3. Hold down the Option (Macintosh) or Alt (Windows) key to start the rectangle from its center point. Add holding the Shift key to constrain the object to a square.

4. Hold down the Option (Macintosh) or Alt (Windows) and Shift keys to draw a square that begins from the center point.

5. When finished, leave the file open for the next exercise.

Creating Rounded Corner Objects

1. Click on the Rounded Corner tool in the Toolbox. Experiment with drawing rectangles with round corners.

2. Click on the Rectangle tool. Hold the Option (Macintosh) or Alt (Windows) key and click on the page. In the dialog box, type: **Width** = 2, **Height** = 3, **Corner Radius** = 0.25 in. Click **OK**. Observe the results. **Undo** this to perform another operation.

3. Go to **File->Preferences->General**. Type 0.30 into the **Corner Radius** box. Click **OK**.

4. Select the Rounded Corner tool and draw a square. It will have the corner radius you specified in **Preferences** in Step 3.

5. Select the Rectangle tool with square edges. Draw a square or rectangle. Click on the object to select it.

6. Go to the **Filter->Stylize** (first "Stylize" in the Filter menu). Select **Round Corners**. In the next window, type 0.5 in the **Radius** box. Click **OK**. Observe the object's corners.

7. **Close** the file without saving it.

ADOBE ILLUSTRATOR: AN INTRODUCTION TO DIGITAL ILLUSTRATION/PRIMITIVE SHAPES

Other Tools

Besides circles and squares, Illustrator provides tools to draw other shapes, including stars, polygons, swirls, and spirals. In the Toolbox you will find assorted tools that either perform different effects on paths, or create shapes on their own. Some of these tools have dialog boxes, accessed by clicking the crosshair on the page, in which you can make your own settings.

Twirl

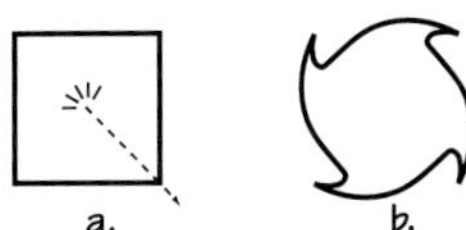

Twirl has no dialog box. To use Twirl requires that you first select the object you wish to twirl. Then, using the Twirl tool, drag on the object. Text can be Twirled, but must first be turned into outlines with **Type->Create Outlines**.

Spiral

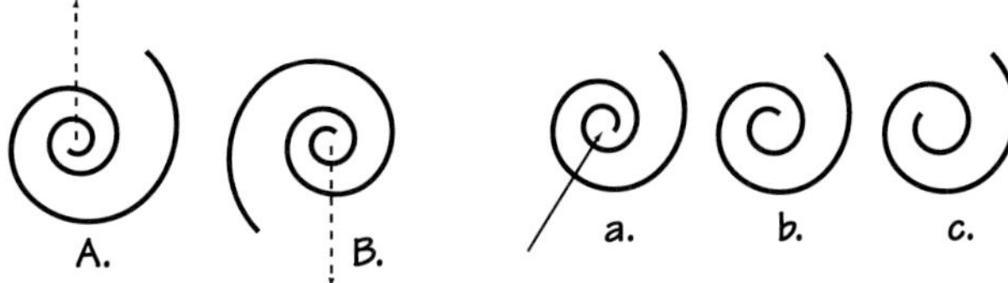

Spiral is a tool that is used by dragging on the page. The direction of the drag determines where the opening of the spiral occurs. Dragging upward (sample A.) points the opening toward the top. Dragging downward (sample B.) points the opening toward the bottom.

While dragging the crosshair, simultaneously press the Up Arrow of the keyboard to add anchor points from the center. Pressing the Down Arrow will delete anchor points from the center (samples a., b., c.). Spiral has a dialog box that custom settings can be made in.

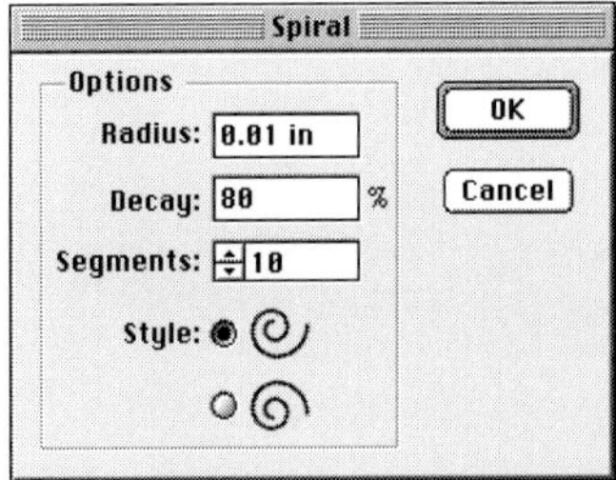

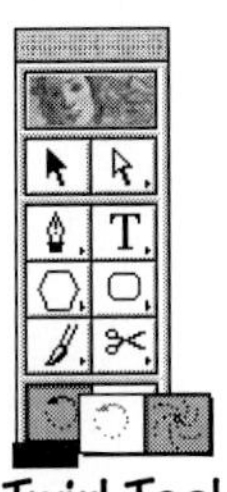

Twirl Tool

Spiral Tool

Later, when you learn about text, and how to turn type into artwork, remember the Twirl tool — you can produce some nifty designs when combined with type elements.

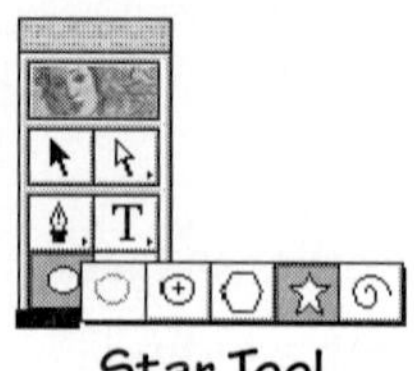

Star Tool

We were excited when we first saw the Star tool. We drew about a million of them, and colored them everything under the rainbow. We haven't used it since.

Star is a tool that draws a star when you drag the tool on the page. There are several keyboard options available while dragging that change the attributes of the star.

- If dragged without pressing a key, the star will have slightly bloated stems and five points.

- Hold the Option (Macintosh) or Alt (Windows) key while dragging and stems will straighten out.

- When you begin dragging the star defaults to a number of points. The Up Arrow key will add points while dragging. The Down Arrow key will reduce the number of points, allowing you to construct a star with as little as three points.

- Star has a dialog box in which you can make custom settings.

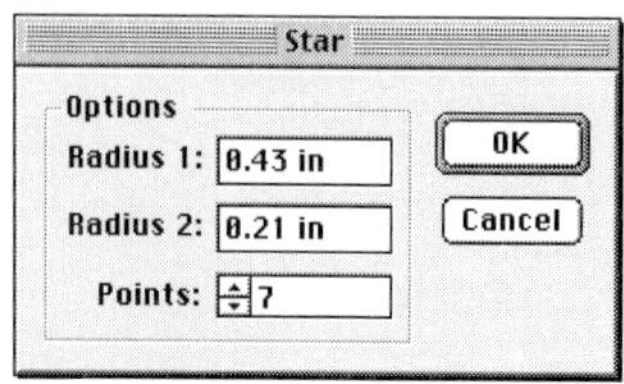

Adobe Illustrator: An Introduction to Digital Illustration/Primitive Shapes

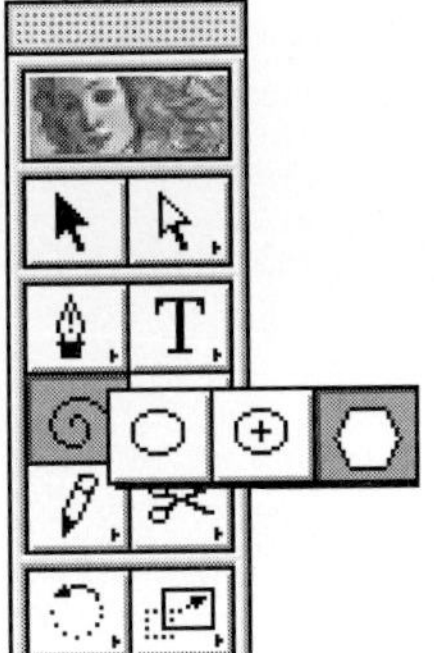

Polygon

The Polygon tool draws a multi-sided closed object. Holding the Shift key while dragging constrains it perpendicular. The Up Arrow key adds sides; the Down Arrow deletes sides.

Polygon has a dialog box to make custom settings.

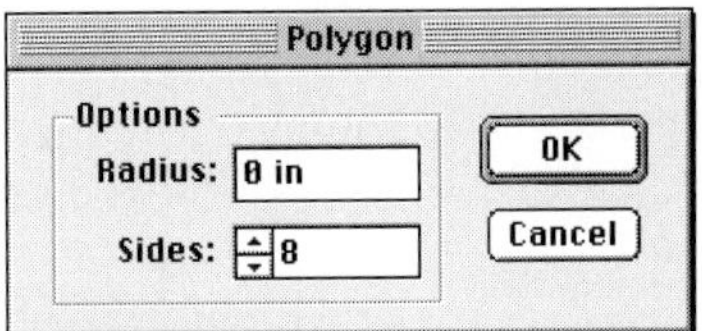

Experimenting with Geometric Tools

1. Create a **File->New** document.

2. Go to **View->Artwork** mode. With the Rectangle tool, draw a square and leave it selected.

3. With the Twirl tool, drag from the center of the square, toward the lower right corner. Observe the results. Delete the square.

4. With the Rectangle tool, draw a very thin rectangle.

With the Twirl tool, drag from the center of the rectangle at a 45° angle toward the upper left. Observe the results. Delete the result.

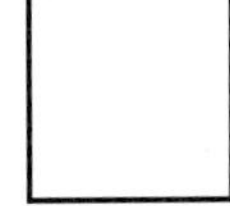

As with the Star and Spiral tools, you can use the arrow keys to increase the number of sides as you're drawing the object. Very cool for drawing honeycombs, by the way, or game boards.

5. Select the Spiral tool. Drag the mouse downward.

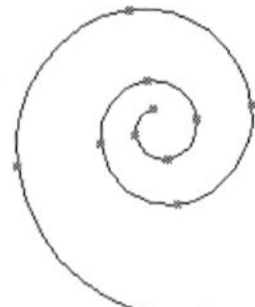

Hold the mouse button down, press the Up Arrow three times. Press the Down Arrow three times. Observe the results. Delete the spiral.

6. Click again on the Spiral tool in the Toolbox. Click the crosshair on the page to bring up the dialog box. Make these settings and click **OK**.

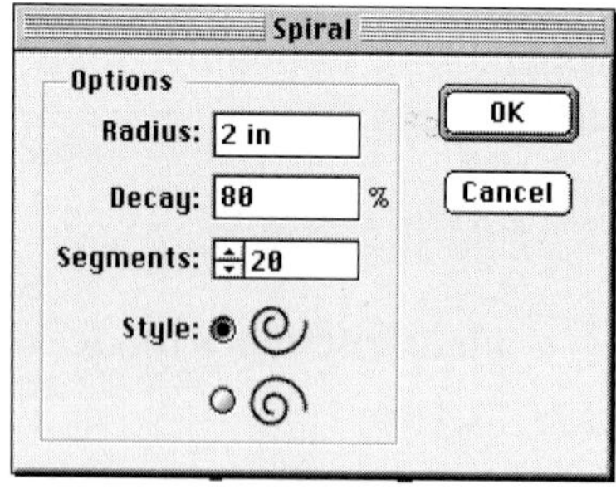

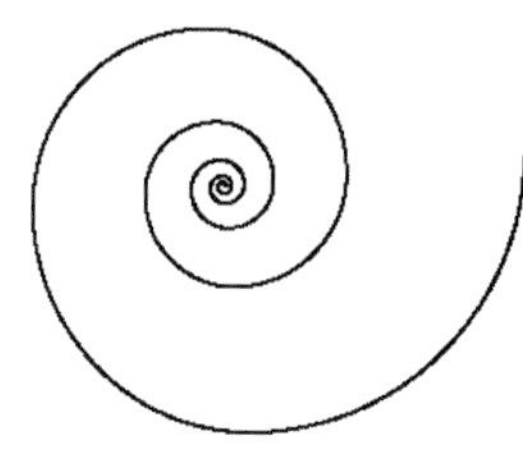

7. Select the Star tool. Drag the tool to create a star.

While holding the mouse down, press the Option key (Macintosh) or Alt key (Windows). Add the Shift key at the same time, and observe the results. Delete the star.

The Spiral tool can produce some great effects. You have to experiment with colored strokes and fills, and try putting them over backgrounds as repeating patterns.

8. Click again on the Star tool in the Toolbox. Click its crosshair on the page to bring up the **Star** dialog box. Make these settings and click **OK**.

9. Select the Polygon tool. Drag the tool to create a polygon.

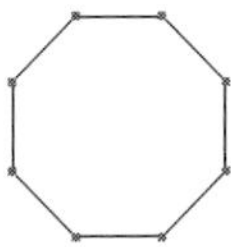

While holding down the mouse, press the Up Arrow key several times. Press the Down Arrow several times. Observe how the number of sides of the polygon increases/decreases.

10. Click again on the Polygon tool in the Toolbox. Click the tool's crosshair on the page to bring up the dialog box. Make these settings and click **OK**.

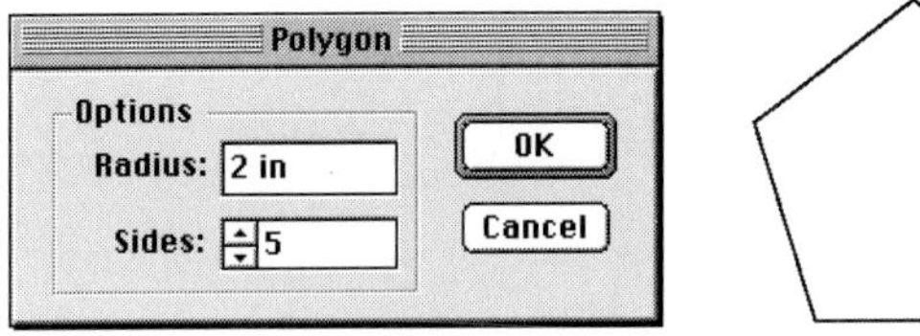

11. **Close** the file without saving.

Notes:

CHAPTER 9

CREATING PATHS

CHAPTER OBJECTIVE:

To learn the basic use of the Pen Tool, Illustrator's most important function. To learn the difference between anchor points and segments. To learn the use of the Pencil and Paintbrush tools. In Chapter 9, you will:

- Learn to use the Pen Tool to draw straight lines.

- Learn how to draw basic curves — the foundation of almost every illustration you will ever develop.

- Learn about open and closed paths.

- Work with the Direct-Selection tool to modify existing elements.

- Learn two optional methods of creating paths — the Pencil and Paintbrush tools.

Creating Paths

Drawing shapes and controlling their appearance is at the heart of all illustration. This chapter — the longest and most demanding in the entire course — will provide the foundation for the skills you'll need to be a successful artist who's able to use Illustrator in the demanding real-world environment of the graphic arts. Study this chapter, work with its hands-on exercises, and master the creation of paths, and you're more than halfway there.

The Pen Tool

The Pen is Illustrator's most useful and important tool. You'll use it more than any other tool (with the exception, perhaps, of the Type tool). While you're first learning the tool, you might find it strange, but as time goes on and you become increasingly familiar with how it works to create shapes, it will become quite natural to use.

The Pen tool creates by clicking the tool on the page. Each time it is clicked, it sets an anchor point. Anchor points and the segments that connect anchor points comprise paths.

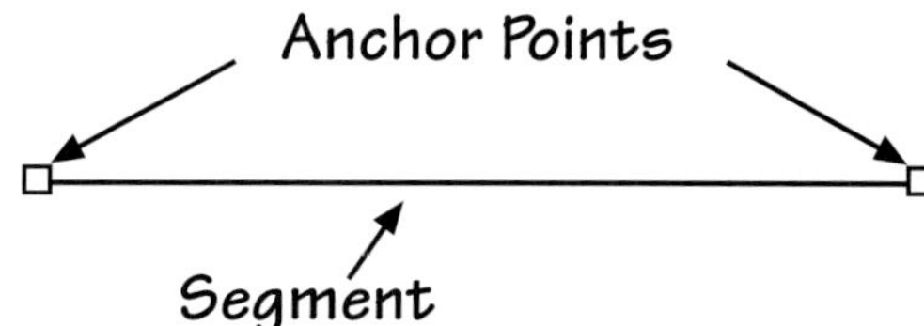

Using the Pen tool is simple: you click it, move the tool cursor to another position, then click again. Holding the Shift key while clicking constrains the segments to 90° and 45° increments.

Straight and curved segments are the only two types of segments that construct paths.

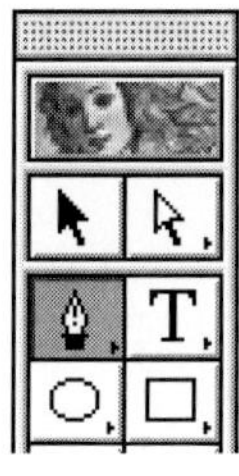

Drawing and modifying paths is the heart and soul of Illustrator. If you can draw paths, and learn to understand how they work, the rest is a cake walk.

Every time you click the pen tool, a point is created. This is called an Anchor Point. As you continue to click away, the points are connected with lines called segments. A line, a seg-ment, and a stroke are all the same thing.

Clicking the Pen tool once to create a single anchor, then deselecting, leaves a "Stray Point," which is one of the major troublemakers of unexpected results you get in your file size, when saved as an Illustrator EPS. Stray Points, if any are present, should be located and removed. The Object->Path->Cleanup feature does this for stray objects.

Drawing Straight Lines

Click in one place, and click in another, and a line appears. Illustrator is a very sophisticated drawing program that offers some simple features. Once you grasp the concept of how to draw and paint, you'll be creating designs ready for output.

Think of drawing with the Pen tool as a game of connect-the-dots. First, you click your first Anchor Point (dot). You then select the next Anchor Point location and click again. When the second point is made, Illustrator connects the points with a Segment. This is called a Path.

Anchor Points & Segments

This section will explore the difference between lines and anchor points. When you're talking to people or reading about Illustrator, you will hear several different terms for the line between the points. They're called lines, paths, and segments — depending on whom you're talking to. Sometimes people use all three terms. They all mean basically the same thing.

The Pen tool can be used to click-move-click a shape. A beginning point is made by clicking once to start the process; this positions an *anchor point.* The mouse is moved forward, then clicked again to continue the drawing; this creates a second anchor point and a *segment* connecting it to the first anchor point. To click on and drag an anchor point creates a curved segment, which we will discuss later in the chapter.

Two anchor points connected by a segment is the minimum path that can be defined. After having clicked several times, the Pen tool has extended the uninterrupted path. Ending the clicking process can be done by either clicking on the beginning point to complete a *closed path*, or selecting the Selection tool and clicking in an open area away from the path to deselect it.

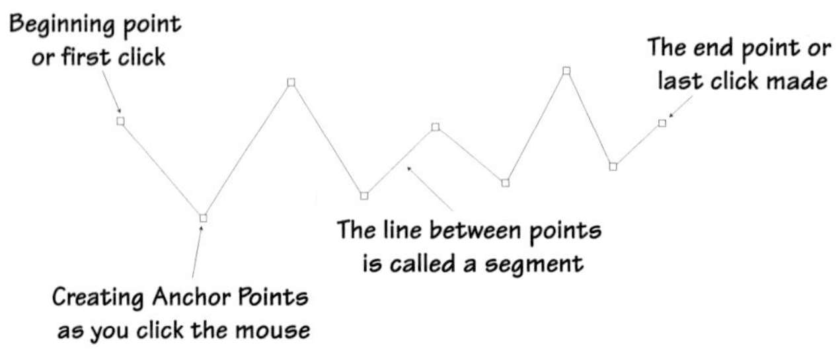

 Adobe Illustrator: An Introduction to Digital Illustration/Creating Paths

Open and Closed Paths

A path (which is really a collection of points and lines) can either return to its starting point (in which case it's closed), or just have two ends hanging out somewhere (in which case it's open).

- Open paths — The beginning and endpoints of open paths do not meet. A minimum of two anchor points connected by a segment, is an open path.

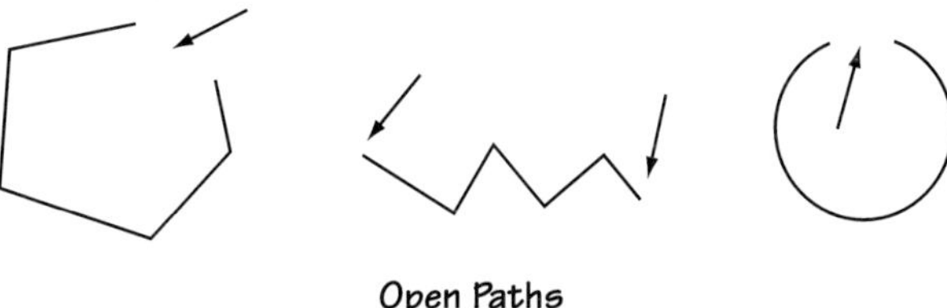

Open Paths

- Closed paths — The endpoints of closed paths meet to become one.

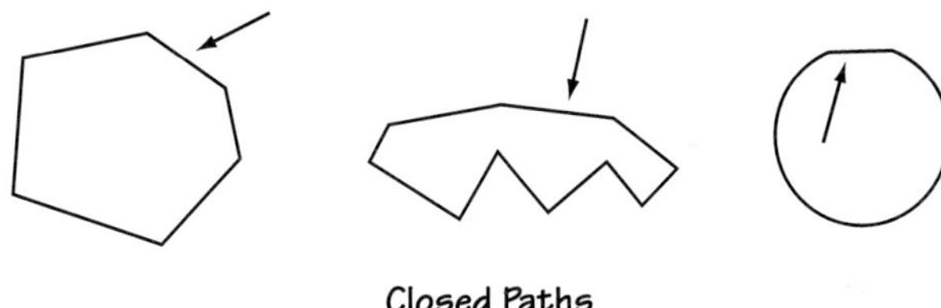

Closed Paths

Handy Pen Tool Symbols

When drawing paths, the Pen tool has small symbols in the bottom right. This changes when the tool touches anchor points.

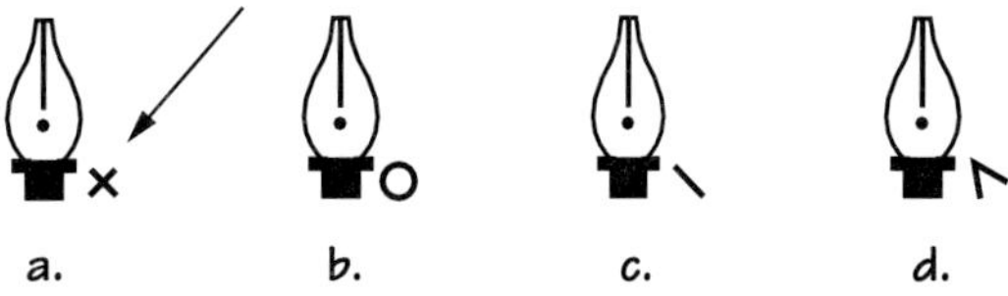

It is an "X" when you are about to start a new path (a.). It becomes a circle (b.) when it touches the beginning point of the path you are drawing. This signifies that the path will be complete, or a "Closed Path." The slash "\" (c.) appears when the Pen tool touches an endpoint of a path. The angled "V" (d.) appears when the Pen tool clicks an endpoint of a path.

Drawing Basic Paths with the Pen Tool

1. With **File->Open,** go to **SF-Intro Illustrator** and open the **Primitive Objects.AI** document. Go to **View->Artwork** mode.

2. Click on the zig-zag object with the Selection tool. You will see its anchor points. Select the Pen tool from the Toolbox and click the tool on the last anchor point of the object. This will reinstate the continuity of the drawing process.

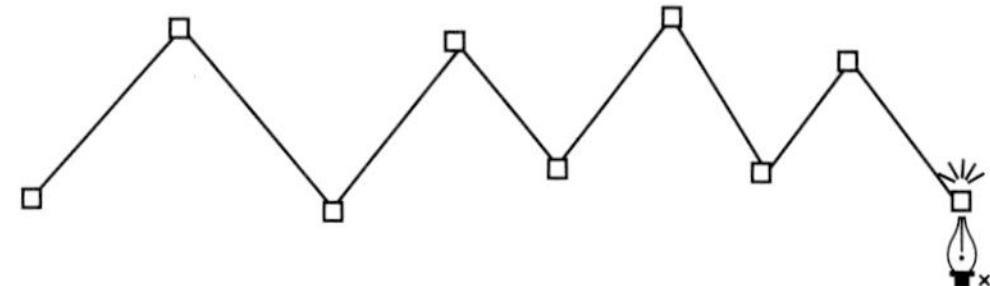

3. Begin clicking on the page so as to imitate the zig-zag pattern in progress. Add two extra anchor points. Click on the Selection tool and click the Artboard to deselect.

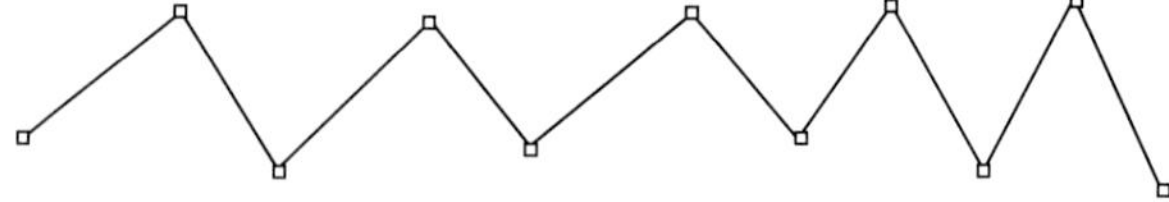

4. Go to **View->Preview** and observe how the anchor points disappear, showing the path as it will look when printed.

5. **Close** the file without saving.

Holding the Shift Key to Constrain as You Click

1. Use **File->New** to create a new file. Go to **View->Artwork**. Click on the Pen tool in the Toolbox.

2. Click once on the page to create the beginning point (a.). Move the Pen tool to the right and, pressing the Shift key to constrain, click again (b.).

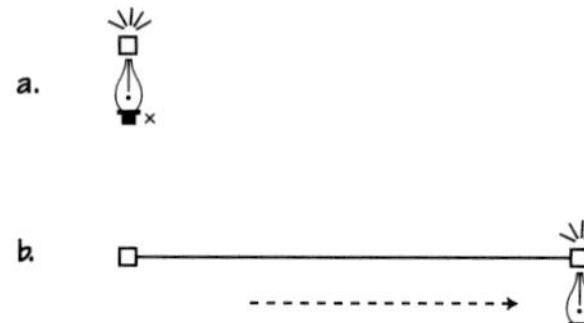

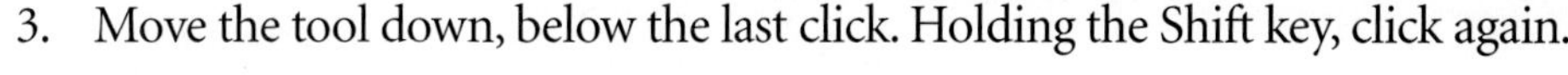

3. Move the tool down, below the last click. Holding the Shift key, click again.

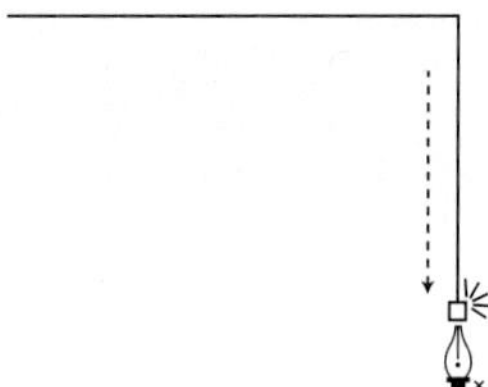

4. Move the tool to the left of the last click, so that the tool is under the beginning point. Pressing the Shift key, click again.

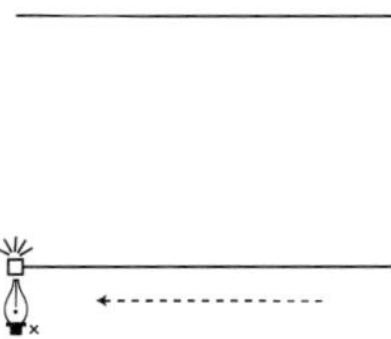

Drawing straight lines is quite simple. Soon you'll move on to learning how to draw curves.

5. Click on the Selection tool in the Toolbox to deselect and end the progress of this path. You will pick it back up in the next exercise.

6. Keep the file open.

There are times that path continuity is interrupted. It is quite simple to pick up where you left off. Merely click the Pen tool on the last anchor point of the path and continue clicking.

Continuing Paths That Have Been Interrupted

1. In the open document, continue in **Artwork** mode.

2. Select the Direct Selection tool in the Toolbox. Click on the path you began last exercise. You will see the anchor points.

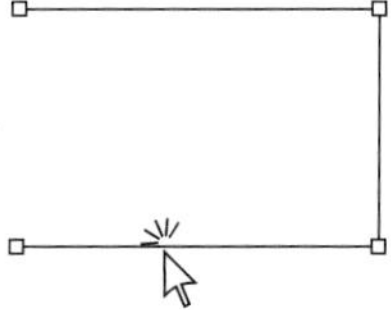

If the Shift key is pressed while you are clicking anchor points, the drawing will be constrained to 45° increments.

You should always use this when drawing segments that you want to be level and aligned.

3. Access the Pen tool. Click the tool once on the last point you created on the path. This will reinstate the path's continuity.

4. Move the tool up to the first anchor created and click it.

5. You have regained the continuity, and gone on to close the path. Delete this path.

6. Keep the file open for the next exercise.

Creating Multiple Simple Paths

1. In the open document, go to **View->Artwork** mode.

2. Select the Pen tool in the Toolbox. The task is to draw many independent segments that crisscross each other. Click the tool once to set the beginning point. Move down and right about an inch and click again.

3. Hold the Command (Macintosh) or Control (Windows) key so the cursor turns into the Selection tool.

4. Click the Selection tool once on the page to deselect the path. Release the Command (Macintosh) or Control (Windows) key. The tool will go back to being the Pen tool. Continue to make many segments this way (click beginning point — click end point — deselect). Draw the segments so they cross over one another.

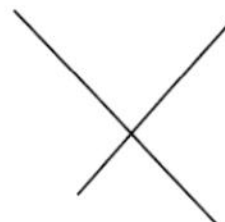

5. Continue to click - click - deselect so that you have created an interesting collage of segments that crisscross each other.

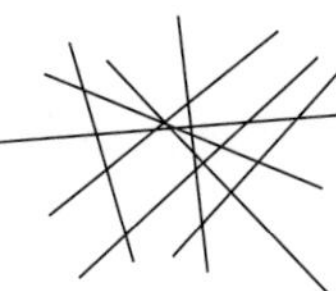

6. Press Command-A (Macintosh) or Ctrl-A (Windows) to **Select All** segments, then press Delete. Keep the file open for the next exercise.

Connecting Anchor Points

1. In the open document, go to **View->Artwork** mode.

2. Click on the Pen tool in the Toolbox. Click the tool on the page. Move the tool upwards (holding the Shift key) and click again.

3. Click on the path with the Selection tool. Hold the Option (Macintosh) or Alt (Windows) key and drag this segment to the right (holding the Shift key after the drag has started) to duplicate it. Release all keys.

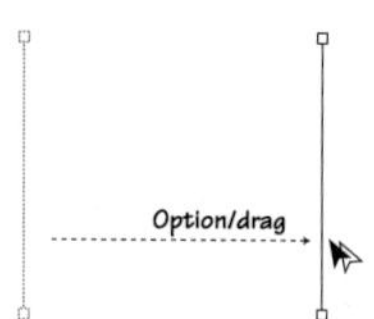

Click the Selection tool in the Toolbox to deselect the segment.

4. Select the Pen tool, click on the top anchor point of the original segment. Hold the Shift key and click on the top anchor point of the duplicate segment. Click the Selection tool in the Toolbox to deselect the segment.

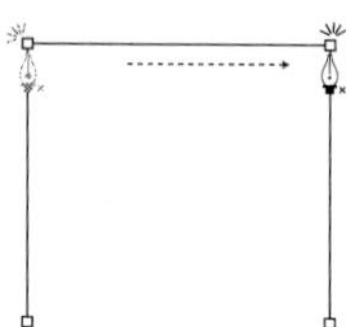

5. Select the Pen tool, click on the bottom anchor point of the duplicate segment. Hold the Shift key and click on the bottom anchor point of the original segment drawn. Click the Selection tool to deselect. You have used the Pen tool to connect anchor points into a closed path.

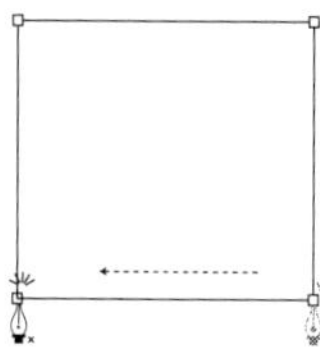

6. **Close** the document without saving.

Drawing Curves

We've already discussed how to create straight-line segments using the Pen tool: click a point, move the mouse, and click a second point. To draw a curve, you simply drag the mouse after you click.

Click in one place, click in another, and a line appears between the two. Hold down the mouse button and pull, though, and the line starts to bend. Use the Pen tool to draw curves. Each curve segment has control handles that allow you to control or fine-tune curve shapes.

Getting the square perfectly right is a trick. When you're drawing an object like this, rough it in first, then move the points around until you've got it just right.

Simple and Compound Curves

1. Create a **New** document.

2. Click with the Pen tool to establish an anchor point. Then, without releasing the mouse button, drag the cursor about an inch straight up, in the direction you want the curve to be drawn. Hold down the Shift key as you drag, to constrain the line to vertical. Notice that as you drag, control handles, connected to the anchor point, are formed in both directions.

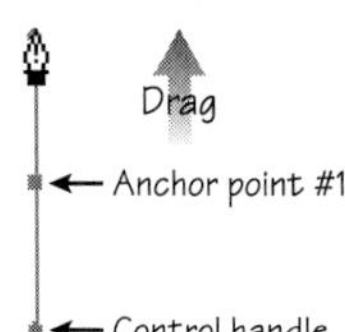

3. Release the mouse button, move it a short distance right, and click-drag again. This time, drag straight down about an inch.

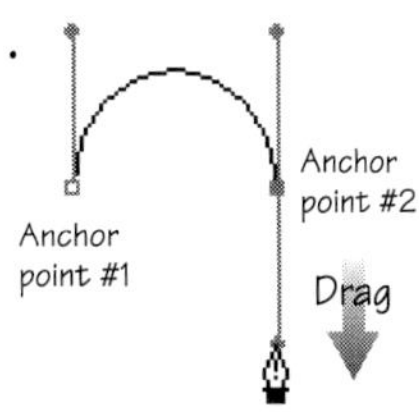

From this second anchor point, the end of the curve is formed. This point has its own control handle. You have now created a simple, curved path.

4. Finally, release the mouse button. Again, move the mouse to the right, about the same distance as the first move.

Then, click to create a third anchor point and drag straight up about an inch to create a second curved segment.

This is a compound curve, with the second anchor point as the center point.

After curves have been set on an anchor, such as a Smooth or Corner point, the only tool that can modify or transform the anchor point is the Convert Direction Point tool.

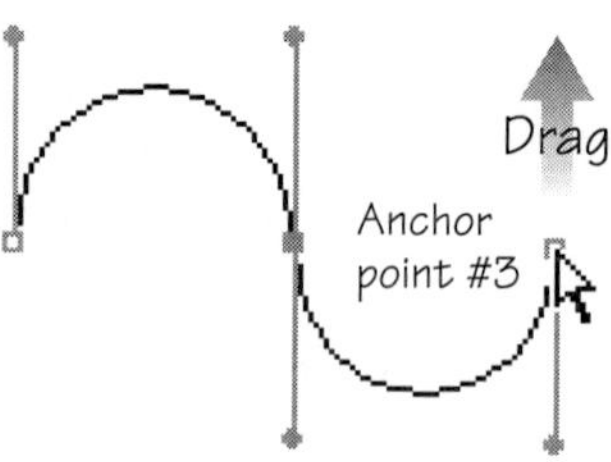

5. **Close** the document without saving.

The Many Shapes of a Curve

As the illustrations below show, the position of a control handle controls the general shape of a curve. The distance of the control handle from the anchor point controls the depth of a curve.

Curves don't always feel natural when you first learn them. This graphic will help.

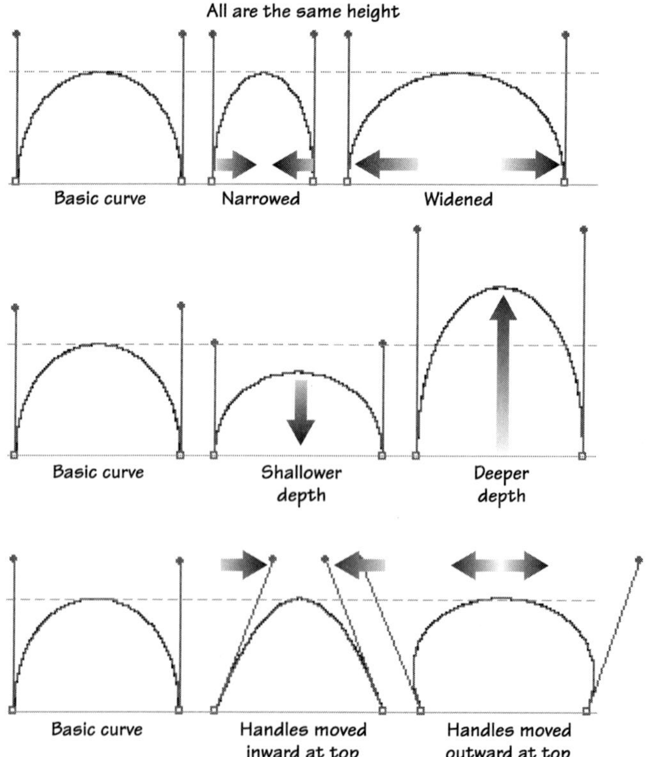

Expect to work with curves for a while before you feel completely comfortable with them.

The Smooth Point

The Smooth Point is called "smooth" because curves passing through it are smooth, continuous lines. Smooth Points ensure that the curves are connected by smooth segments.

The Smooth Point is identified by the two control handles that protrude from it in opposite directions. Use the Smooth Point to create free-flowing, elegant curves. The Smooth Point curve pivots on the anchor point between two adjacent segments. When you change the position of the control handle for one segment, the adjacent segment's curve is modified as well.

Creating a Smooth Point

1. Create a **New** document. With the Pen tool, click to create the first point of Segment A. Create the second point, which is the Smooth Point, by dragging the mouse (a.).

2. Click again to the side to complete the Smooth Point (comprised of "segment before—Smooth Point—segment after") with Segment B (b.).

3. With the Direct Selection tool, click on the Smooth Point — two handles appear (c.). Change the position of the control handle to modify the shape. Notice that when one segment changes, the other segment also changes.

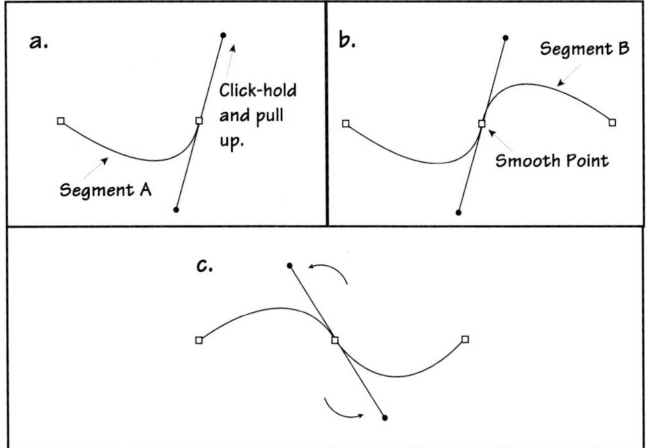

Remember, clicking and pulling is how you develop curves. The more you pull, the bigger the curve.

4. **Close** the file without saving.

Corners on curves are important in any drawing. Recognize a corner from its pointy shape.

The Corner Point

A Corner Point has handles that come out of the point in two different directions. There are three places to have a Corner Point: between two straight segments, at the end of a straight line segment, and between consecutive curves linked together.

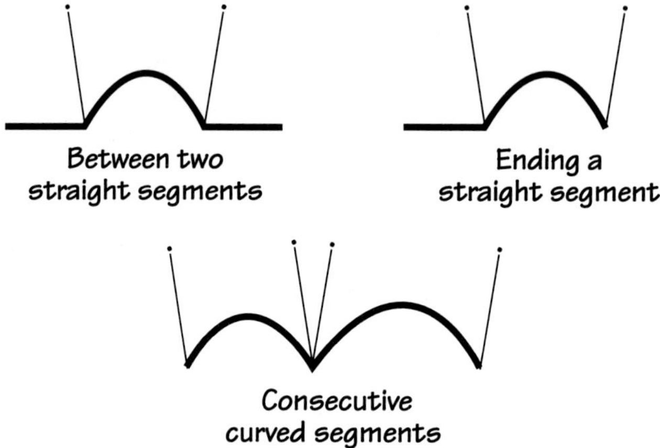

The Corner Point can have two control handles that work independently of one another; each controls a curve segment ending at the Corner Point.

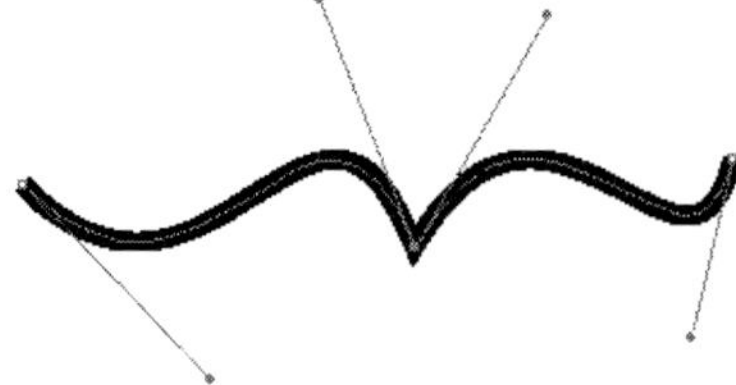

Corner Points are versatile because you can modify a curve segment without affecting other segments. Also, if you need to put a Smooth Point where there is a Corner Point, use the Convert Anchor Point tool to convert the point. If you click/drag with the tool on the point, new control handles will appear.

1. Create a **New** document.

2. Using the Pen tool, click and drag slightly to the right and up (a.).

3. Move the mouse to the right, and drag upwards (b.).

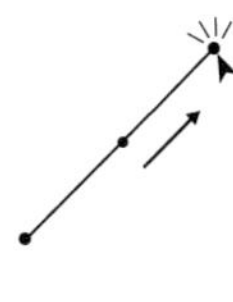
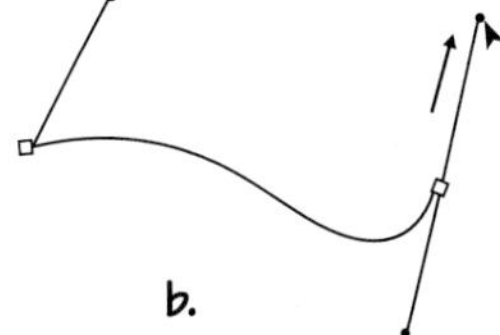

a.   b.

4. Release the mouse button. Hold the Option (Macintosh) or Alt (Windows) key and drag on this same point. Drag the second control handle in a different direction (c.).

5. Move the mouse to the right, then drag upwards (d.).

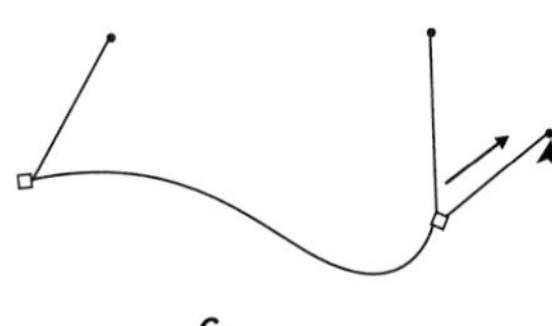
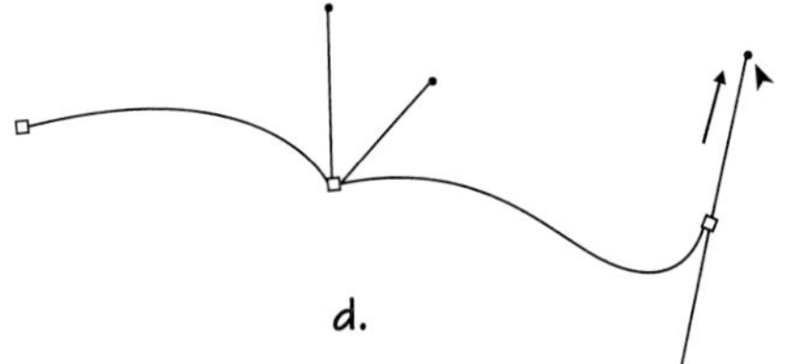

c.   d.

6. With the Direct Selection tool, click on the first segment. Adjust the curve to look like this (e.). Do the same with the second segment (f.).

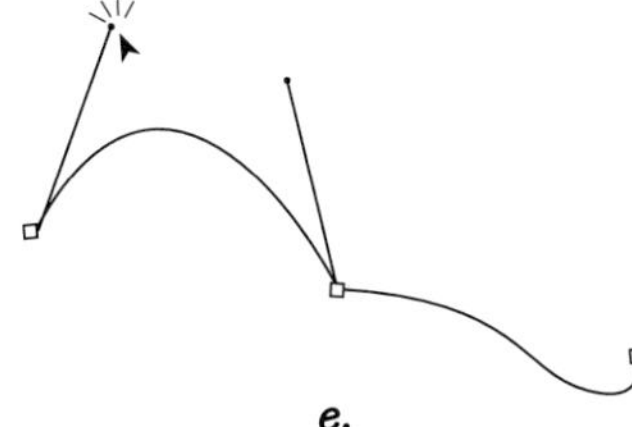
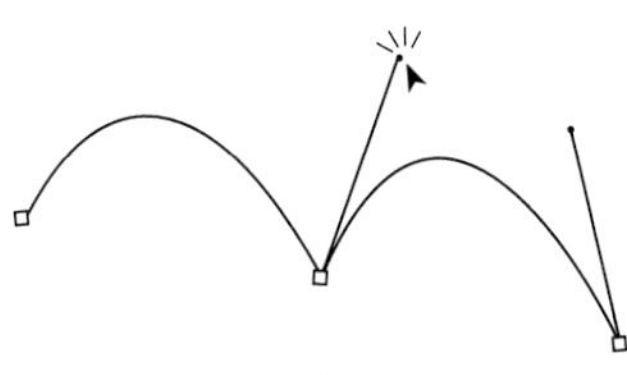

e.   f.

7. **Close** the file without saving.

Don't be afraid to experiment. If you make a curve that you want to get rid of, just hit the Delete key. The first time you hit it, the last point you made will be deleted. The next time you hit it, the whole shape will go away. Use Command-Z on the Macintosh or Control-Z on the PC to undo it if you accidentally blow away one of your shapes.

Combining Straight Lines with Curves

Many shapes require a combination of corners and curves, smooth round shapes, and pointy or jagged corners. Using the Pen, you can easily create combinations that exactly meet your needs.

Creating a Closed Path with Straight Lines and Curves

1. Create a **New** document.

2. With the Pen tool, single-click to establish a beginning point. Move the mouse to the right and up, then single-click again(a.).

3. Drag on the 2nd anchor point, and pull out a control handle. Release the mouse button. Move the mouse to the right and down, then single-click to establish a 3rd point (b.).

4. Move the mouse to the left and down. Single-click again to create the 4th point(c.).

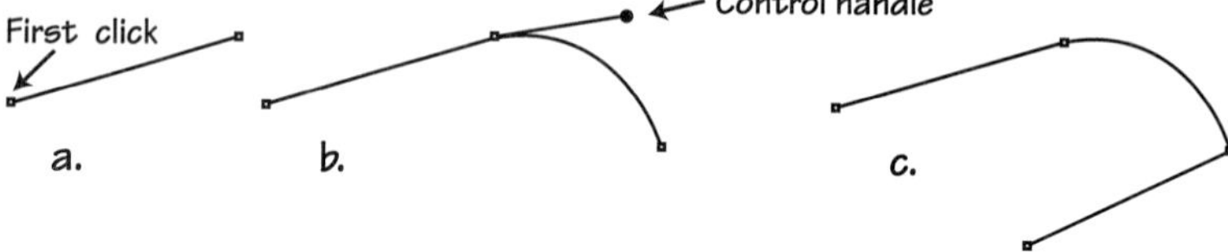

5. Drag on the 4th point, and pull out a control handle (d.). Release the mouse button. Single-click on the 1st point you created. This makes the path a Closed Path (e.).

6. Select the **Swatches** palette.
Paint the path: **Fill** = Black, **Stroke** = None (f.).

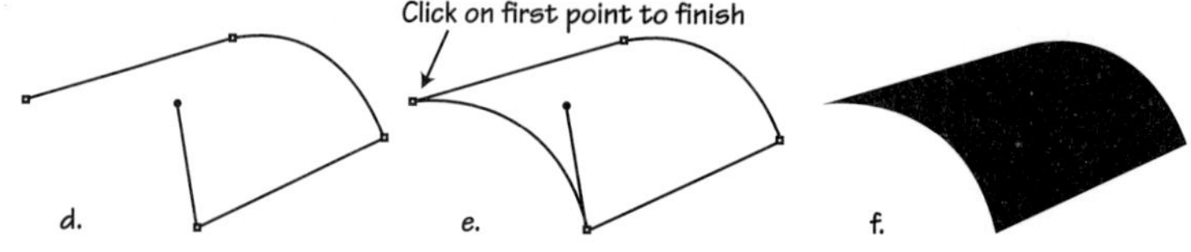

7. **Close** the file without saving.

As you learn how objects are filled with color, the concept of using shapes to develop your drawings will begin to make sense to you.

The Pencil tool is tough for some people to use. Many artists opt for a tablet, which lets you use a physical pen as the pencil tool.

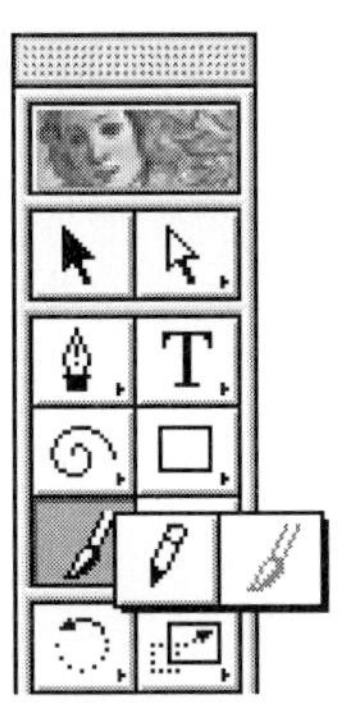

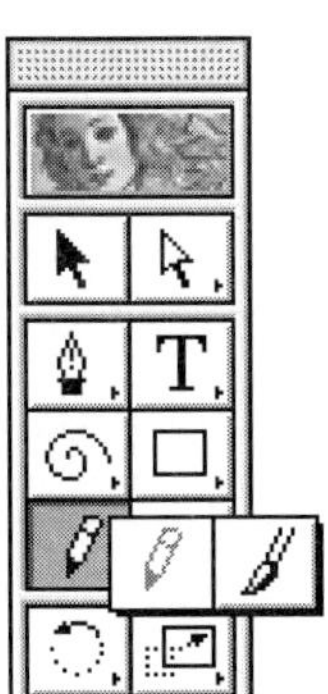

The Pencil and Paintbrush Tools

There are two other ways to create paths — with the Pencil tool (which is a "freehand" drawing tool); and the Paintbrush, another "freehand" tool that can provide interesting effects like calligraphy and custom brushes.

Shown here in **Artwork** mode, you can see the paths that each creates. The Pencil tool creates a single, open path. The Paintbrush tool creates a closed path.

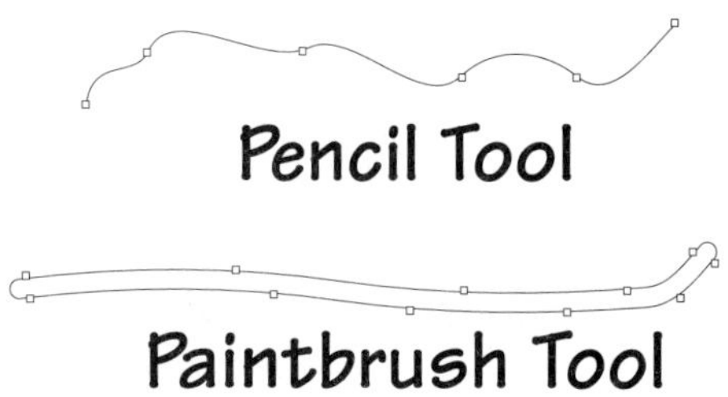

The Pencil Tool

The Pencil tool imitates the single line created with a pencil on paper. It draws a continuous "hand-drawn" effect.

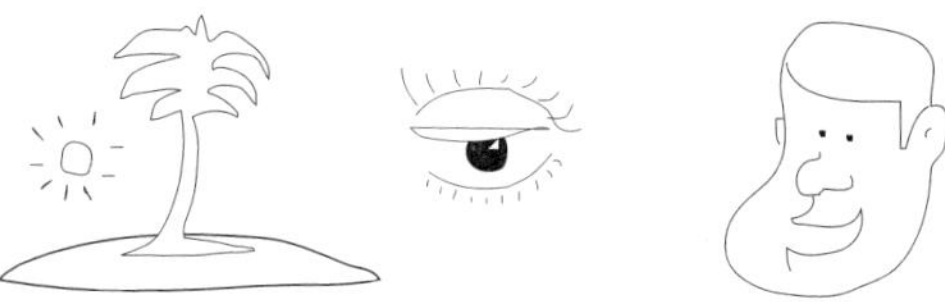

The Paintbrush Tool

The Paintbrush tool works much the same way as the Pencil tool, except that its width is adjustable. The Pencil tool draws a single, open path. The Paintbrush tool's path is a closed path.

The **Paintbrush Options** window can be accessed by double-clicking on the Paintbrush tool icon in the Toolbox. It is here that the width of the pen stroke can be set as well as the endcaps. Also, you can perform calligraphy script by clicking in the **Calligraphic** box.

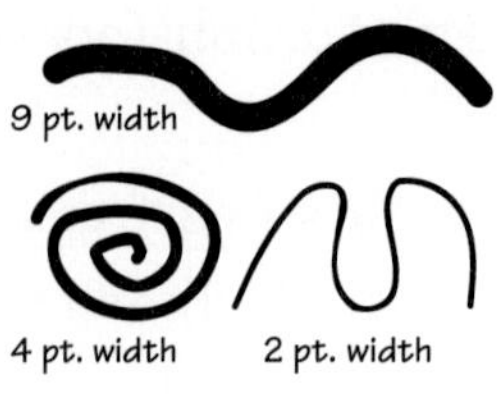

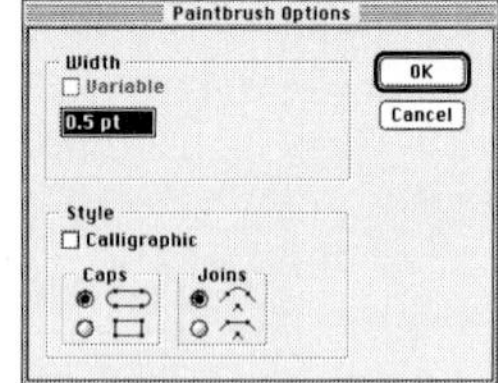

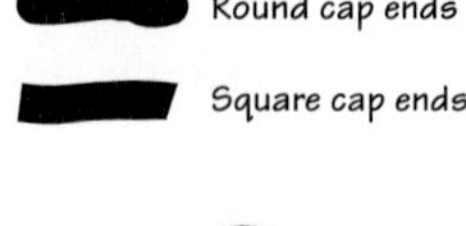

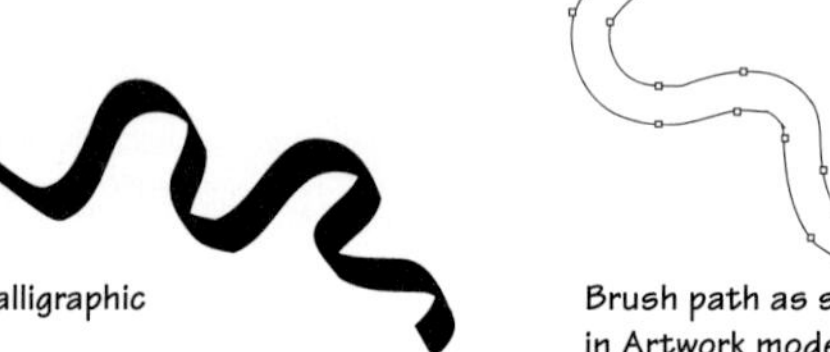

Using the Pencil & Paintbrush Tools

1. Go to the **SF-Intro Illustrator** folder and **Open** the document **Primitive Objects.AI.**

2. Go to **View->Artwork** mode. Click on the Pencil tool in the Toolbox.

3. Experiment with the tool by drawing various shapes and long lines. Draw short line strokes, such as the eyelashes and sun rays on the previous page.

4. Double-click on the Paintbrush tool to access the Paintbrush window.

5. Set the **Width** for 9 pt. and the **Caps** for rounded ends.

6. Drag the tool around on the page and experiment with using the tool. Go back and set different widths of the stroke.

7. Double-click on the Paintbrush tool icon to access the **Paintbrush Options** window again. Click on the **Calligraphic** style. Leave the angle at 120°, but for the **Width**, type in 24. Now drag the tool on the page and write your name in the calligraphy style. Experiment with different widths.

Fat, hollow lines are excellent for drawing roads and maps.

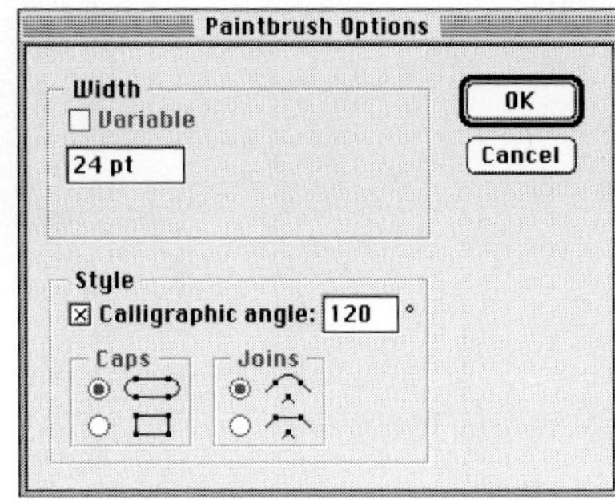

8. **Close** the file without saving.

Notes:

REVIEW #1

CHAPTERS 1 THROUGH 9:

In Chapters 1 through 9, we studied the basic drawing environment that Adobe Illustrator provides to the graphic artist, designer, or illustrator. Through a study of the materials that were presented in these chapters, and the completion of the hands-on activities, you should, by this point, be familiar with:

✓ The Toolbox, which contains most of Illustrator's important tools. You should understand that many of the tools contained in the Toolbox provide alternative tools with modified functionality.

✓ Menus and how they work. While you may not — at this point in your development — have them all memorized, you should have gone through them all and looked at the many options available to you. You should also understand how Illustrator's palettes operate, how they can be combined (or "docked"), and how to arrange them on screen.

✓ The importance of grids and guides. You should know how to create and control non-printing grids and guides; how to lock them, unlock them, delete them, and reposition them to suit your design. Rulers and measurement systems should also be a familiar concept.

✓ Know how to use both artwork and preview mode, and how to use magnification, zooming, and custom views.

✓ Layers and how they're used to build complex designs. You should be comfortable with creating, arranging, managing, locking, hiding, and deleting layers.

✓ How to use layers and imported images as templates, allowing you to trace rough sketches as a first step in developing a digital illustration. You should also understand the use of the Autotrace tool.

✓ How the Pen tool is used to draw simple paths. You should also know the difference between an "open" and a "closed" path. You should know how to draw a path with either the Pencil tool or the Paintbrush tool.

✓ How to use the Direct Selection tool to select and move an individual portion of a path.

✓ How to draw circles, ellipses, squares, and rectangles with the primitive tools. You should be able to draw them manually or through the use of a dialog box in which you can enter exact measurements for the object(s).

✓ How to draw more complex shapes using the custom shape tools such as Polygons, Stars, and Spirals. You should also understand how using certain keyboard combinations can affect the actions of certain tools.

CHAPTER 10

MODIFYING PATHS

CHAPTER OBJECTIVE:

To learn to modify paths in order to refine and develop complex drawings.
To learn about filters that affect lines and paths. In Chapter 10, you will:

- Work with editing tools to modify the position and characteristics of an object's paths.

- Learn more about the Direct Selection tool and the role it plays in modifying existing elements.

- Learn various ways to connect and reposition anchor points.

- Learn how to slice objects into separate elements.

- Learn more about filters (called *Vector* filters) that affect anchor points, segments, and objects.

PROJECTS TO BE COMPLETED:

- **Steaming Coffee**
- Java Jungle
- Last Mango Cafe
- Tropical Fish
- Tropical Treasure
- Ball & Mirror
- Joker's Wild
- Coffee Du Jour Ad
- Tropical Treasure Mailer
- Last Mango Business Card

Modifying Paths

Drawings don't just happen; they develop over a period of time. The professional artist is constantly tweaking and fine-tuning their drawings until they're totally satisfied with the results.

This often results in a design going through several phases — a rough, often referred to as a thumbnail, a second pass where the idea is executed and turned into a comprehensive, and a final stage where everything comes together to meet the designer's criteria for the final artwork.

Even small shapes are like that — developed as they're visualized and required. This section will discuss how to edit and change segments and anchor points so that your objects and shapes are as perfect as they need to be.

Anchor Points and Segments

When you learned how to create circles and squares with the Ellipses and Rectangle tools, we mentioned that all these shapes (as well as the stars, polygons, swirls, and spirals) were actually automatic versions of shapes you can draw yourself.

The paths that represent squares and circles may be modified on a point-by-point basis. Knowing how to select anchor points and segments is critical to working with paths.

The very minimal path that can be created is two anchor points connected by a line segment, whether the segment be straight or a curve.

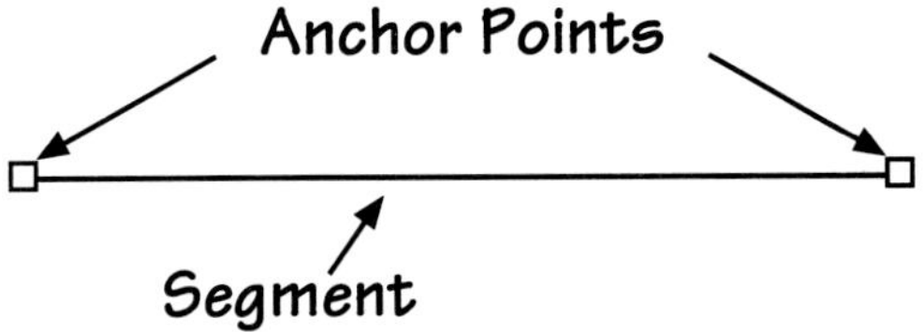

Anchor points and segments are the building blocks of objects. Knowing how to create, edit, and modify points and segments is the foundation of the more sophisticated art pieces produced with Illustrator.

In a traditional environment, the development of a drawing follows a certain process: thumbnail sketch, rough-in, comprehensive, then finished (inked, colored, etc.). You should try to work the same way in Illustrator.

The Selection tool will automatically select all anchor points in an object or group of objects. The Direct Selection tool will select individual anchor points and segments.

Here are the basics:

- When a path is clicked with the Selection tool, all anchor points are solid. The whole path is selected (a.).

- When the same path has a segment clicked with the Direct Selection tool, all anchor points appear, but are hollow (unselected). Only the segment clicked is actually selected and can be moved or deleted (b.).

- When a single anchor point is clicked with the Direct Selection tool, it becomes solid, indicating it is selected. Only the selected point can be modified. The other anchor points are unselected (c.).

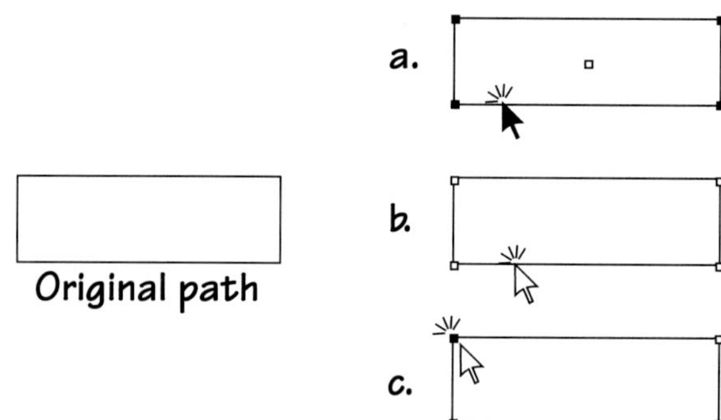

In the real world, you'll find yourself using the direct selection tool (the hollow arrow) more often than the regular (solid) selection tool.

Selecting Single Anchor Points

Selecting a single anchor point is necessary when modifying an object. Selecting one anchor point can be done in two ways:

- Marquee the point by dragging the Direct Selection tool to create a small, dashed selection box around it. (a.).

- Click on the single point with the Direct Selection tool, making it movable as shown (b.).

The keyboard shortcut for Join is Command-J (Macintosh) or Control-J (Windows).

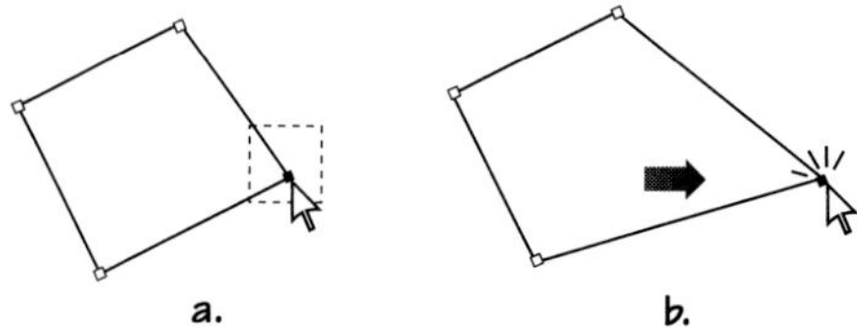

Isolating Segments for Repositioning

With the Direct Selection tool, click on a segment to select and reposition it.

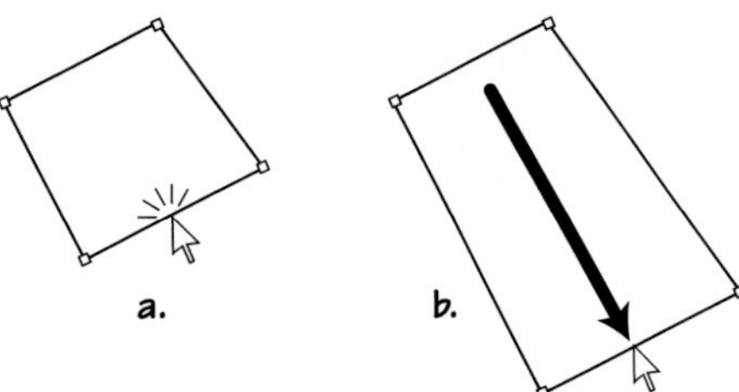

Deleting Single Segments of an Object

Single-click on a segment with the Direct Selection tool and press Delete to erase that segment. **Caution:** after deleting the segment, all remaining anchor points become selected — you will erase the entire object if you press Delete again.

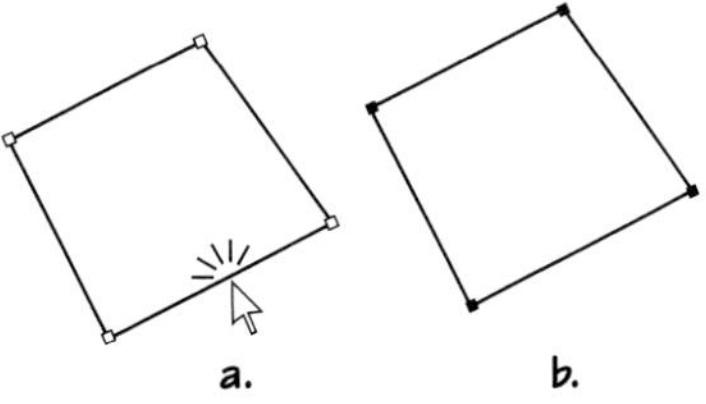

Duplicating Paths and Objects

The easiest way to duplicate a path is to click on it with the Selection tool, and hold down the Option (Macintosh) or Alt (Windows) key as you drag the object.

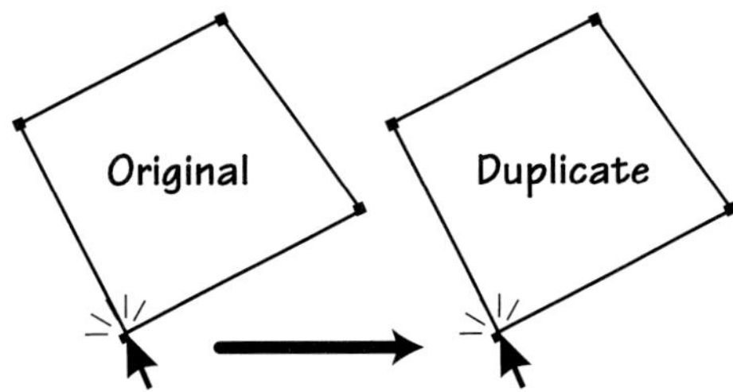

Note that this illustration shows the use of the Selection tool to select the entire path. Selecting the entire object with the Direct Selection tool while holding the Option (Macintosh) or Alt (Windows) key will do the same thing.

The Path Editing Tools

Occasionally, you'll need to make more drastic changes to a path than simply moving a point around. The Scissors, Add-Anchor Point, and Delete-Anchor Point tools can perform these alterations to a path without disturbing other points or control handles.

    a.   The Scissors tool, as its name implies, cuts paths either at the anchor points or within a segment.

    b.   The Add-Anchor Point tool will add an anchor point anywhere on a segment. It will not place an anchor point on top of another point. The new anchor point can be used to reshape the path.

    c.   The Delete-Anchor Point tool will remove an anchor point from a path, when the point is clicked on. Other points on the path remain undisturbed, but the removal of the point may cause the path to change shape.

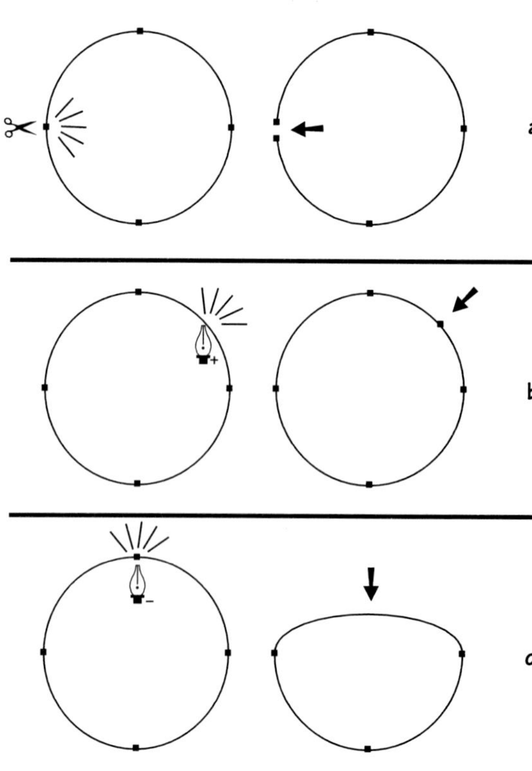

At the place where the Scissors tool makes its cut of the path, there will appear to be only one anchor point.

Don't be misled. There are actually two anchor points present, one positioned on top of the other.

Deselect, then, using the Direct Selection tool, you can move them apart to see the points.

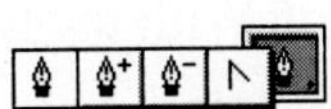

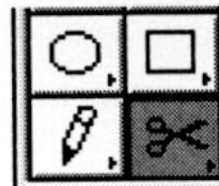

✂ **Scissors**

Add

Delete

Joining and averaging points is another one of the really important concepts you'll need to understand. Sometimes, the only way to get a shape right is to average and join anchor points. It's far better than trying to click in just the absolutely perfect place.

Connecting Anchor Points

Often, separate anchor points need to be connected to other points to complete a Closed Path. This is not as simple as it sounds, because there are many ways to select and connect two points.

The Join command is used to create a segment between two selected anchor points. The Join command should not be confused with the Group command which is used to bind whole paths and other objects together. Get to know these techniques and when to use them:

- Using a marquee to select two anchor points, **Join** to connect them

- Using the Direct Selection tool on anchor points to select, **Join** to connect

- Using the Pen tool to bridge the continuity between two anchor points

- Using the Pencil tool to both select/connect

Selecting and Connecting Anchor Points

1. Open **Select & Connect.AI**, located in the **SF-Intro Illustrator** folder.

2. Using the Direct Selection tool, marquee the first two anchor points to select them. Selected points become solid filled. Unselected points are hollow. Once selected, go to the **Object->Path** menu and choose **Join**.

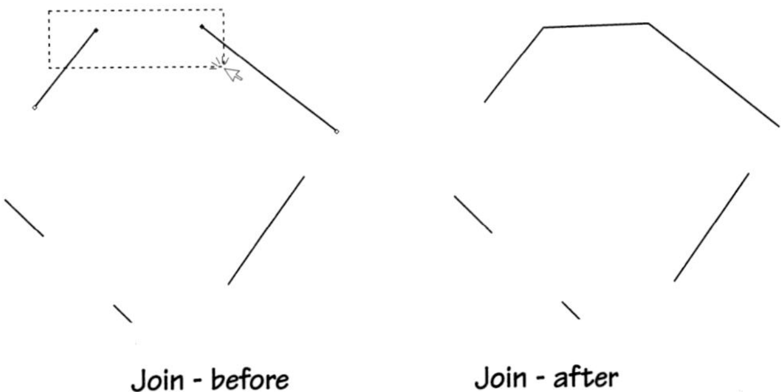

---

3. Select the next two points by clicking on the first with the Direct Selection tool. Hold the Shift key when clicking on the second point. With the two points selected, go to the **Object->Path** menu and choose **Join.**

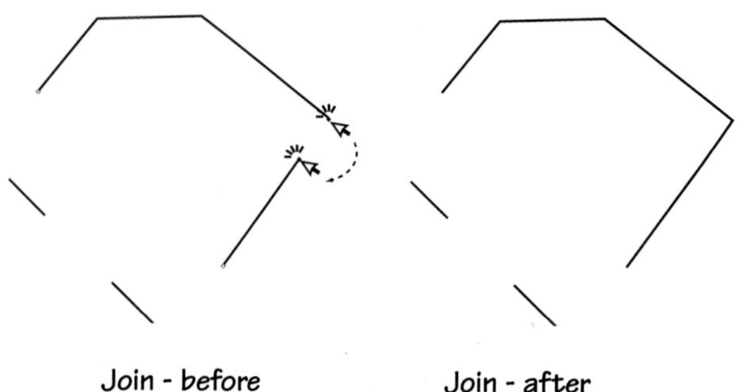

4. Access the Pen tool, click on the endpoint of the path, then click on the next single endpoint. This will connect the two.

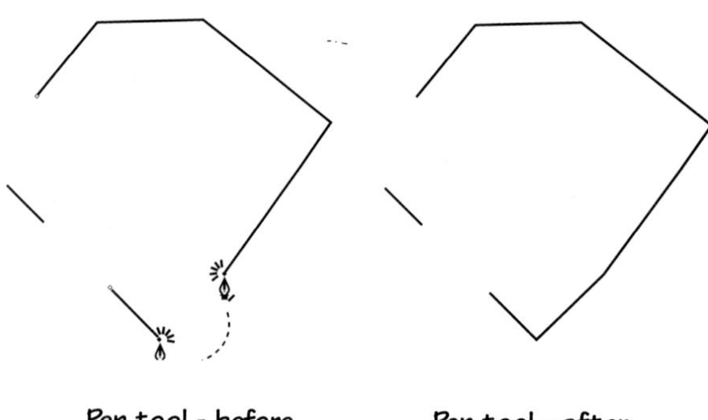

5. Using the Pencil tool, click on the next endpoint of the path and draw a connecting path that touches the next single endpoint.

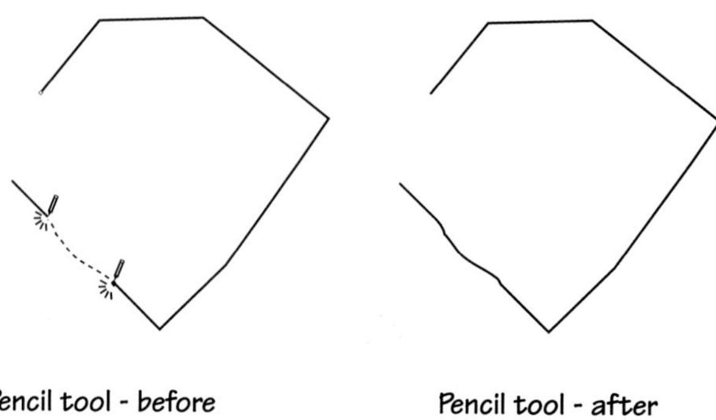

6. **Close** the document without saving.

If you're using the pencil tool to draw a shape, let's say a circle or square, you will know when you've completed the shape, because a small circle will appear over the first point when you put the pencil over it. This indicates that you're about to close the path.

If you just click once, and then select another tool or command, you can end up with anchor points that aren't connected to anything – they're just hanging out there. Later, you'll learn how to clean these up.

1. Create a **New** document. With the Pen tool, draw several unconnected paths.

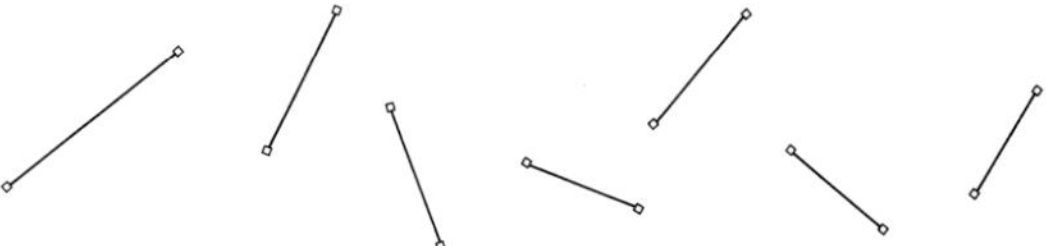

2. Use the techniques learned in this section to connect all the anchor points.

   The final open path should look similar to this.

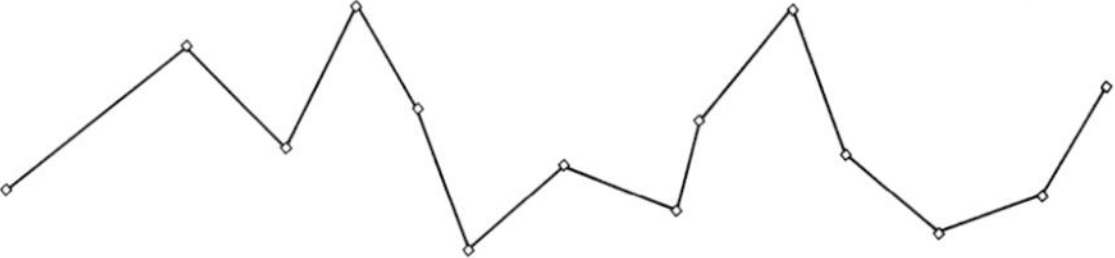

3. Now, use the Delete-Anchor Point tool to click on various anchor points to modify this new path. Use your own judgment when doing this. Remember, **Undo** is quite handy for doing something to see what the effect will be, then going back to the previous state.

4. Use the Scissors tool to cut the path in different places. The Scissors tool can cut on a segment or on an anchor point. When the cut is made, be sure to use the Direct Selection tool to move the anchor points where the cut was made, to see the separation.

5. Use the Add-Anchor Point tool to add anchor points to the various line segments.

6. Experiment with these tools to alter this path into a new, and considerably different looking path. It will give you practice in using the tools.

7. **Close** without saving.

The Slice command is just like using a cookie cutter to make those great holiday sugary, sticky dough lumps like Ma used to bake. Mmmmm.

The Slice Tool

Slicing allows you to use one shape to cut out another. The Slice command is another way to create a shape with a tool rather than going through a tedious manual effort to accomplish the same thing. You could create a guide, use the Scissors tool to make the cuts, and take an object apart, but why bother when you can just slice it?

The **Slice** feature works just like a cookie cutter. The cutting object is placed on top of the target object. Only the cutting object should be selected; then, **Object->Path->Slice** is accessed. The target object will have the cutting shape modified into its path.

In this example, the star was placed over the square (a.). The star was selected, and **Object->Path->Slice** was accessed. The star took on the color of the square (b.). We moved the star (c.) to show the cut that was made into the square. Note how the star was cut off at the edge of the square (b., c.).

a.   b.   c.

Using Slice on a Closed Path

1. Go to the **SF-Intro Illustrator** folder, and **Open** the document **Primitive Objects.AI**. Set the view to **View->Preview** mode.

2. In the document, scroll to the painted circle and square.

a.   b.   c.

When you cut something apart, each object has its own stroke and fill – taken from the original object.

3. With the Selection tool, move the circle so that it overlaps the lower left corner of the square. Keep the circle selected.

4. Go to **Object->Path->Slice**. Don't be alarmed when the circle takes on the same color as the square, and seemingly disappears. Deselect the objects.

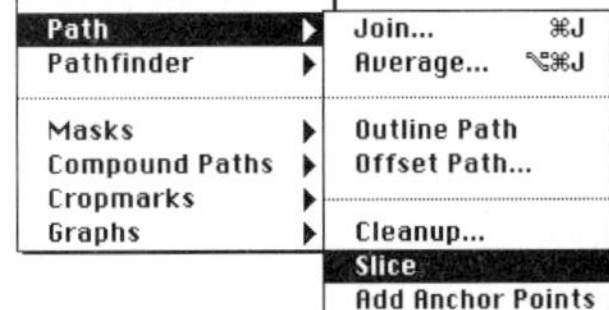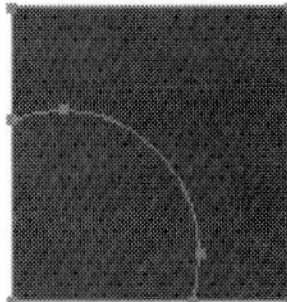

5. With the Selection tool, click on the circle and move it away from the square to see what the effects were to both objects. Observe how the operation cut off the circle, as well, using the square's path.

6. **Close** the file without saving.

Filters

Many drawing and image editing programs offer filters, and Adobe Illustrator is no exception. Several special-effect filters come with the program, and others can be purchased from third parties. Here we will focus on how some of the more common filters function and how they can be used to modify existing artwork.

Filters are preprogrammed operations that may be used to accomplish in seconds what it would take considerable time to do by hand.

Here is a sampling of some of the many filters found in the **Filter** menu.

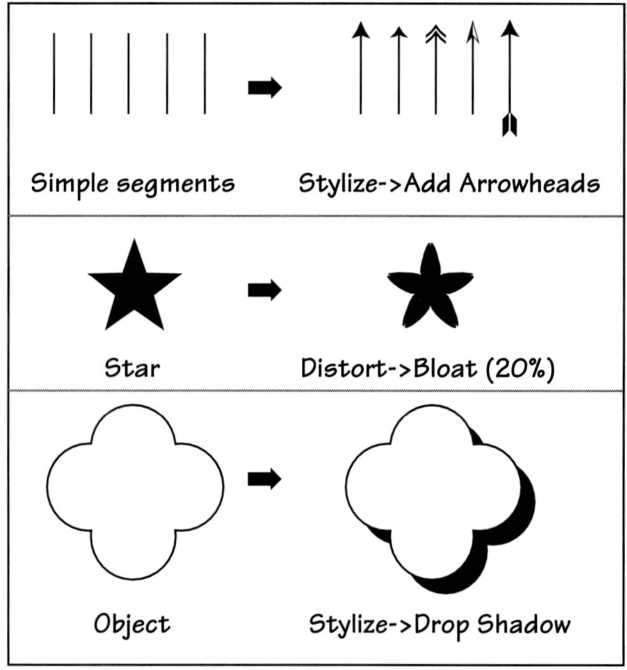

Using Filters on Objects

1. Create a **New** document. Go to **View->Artwork** mode.

2. With the Pen tool, draw (holding the Shift key) a single path segment.

3. Select this path, then go to **Filter->Distort->Zig Zag.**

     Adobe Illustrator: An Introduction to Digital Illustration/Modifying Paths

Many of the filters allow you to develop ideas quickly. You can accomplish anything a filter can by using the regular tools, but drawing a bloated object like a star can take much longer than simply using a filter.

4. Experiment with the settings. Make sure **Preview** is clicked in the **Zig Zag** dialog box, so you can see the effects as you set them.

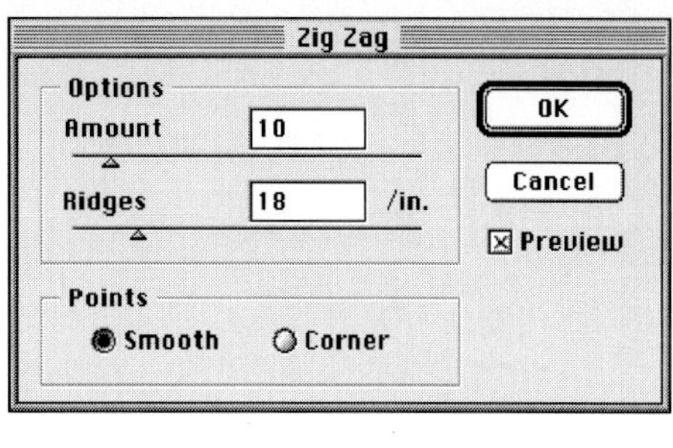

5. Select the Star tool in the Toolbox, then click the crosshair on the page. Set the dialog box to create a 5-pointed star shape, then click **OK**. Click on the star to select it.

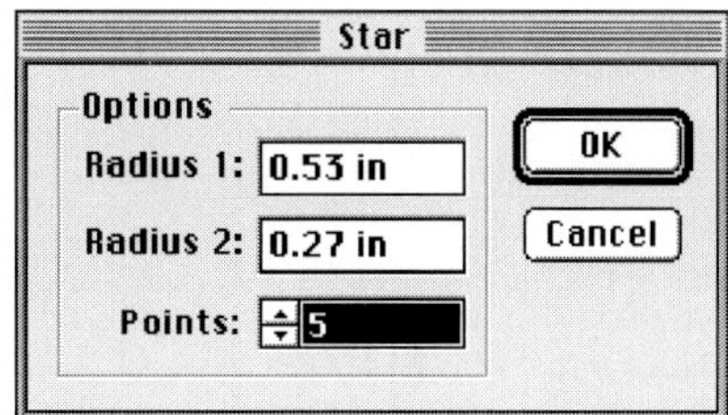

6. Go to **Filter->Distort->Punk & Bloat**. Make sure **Preview** is clicked so you can see the results as you experiment with the slider from Punk to Bloat.

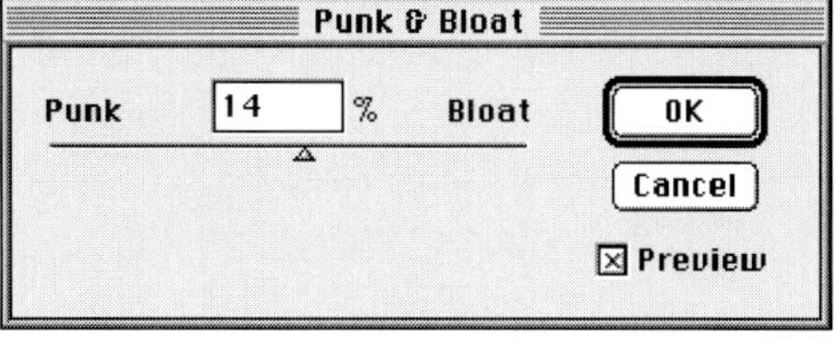

7. Observe how the corner points of the star are distorted.

8. **Close** the document without saving.

Project A: Steaming Coffee

Notes:

CREATING & EDITING TYPE

CHAPTER OBJECTIVE:

To learn the use of Illustrator's extensive typographic features. To learn how to place type on the page, both as an individual element and within a container. In Chapter 11, you will:

- Learn to enter type onto the page.
- Learn to use the Character palette to control the attributes of type.
- Convert type into outlines that can be modified the same way as any element on the page.
- Learn how to put copy into linked boxes, and to facilitate the placement and positioning of text within any design.
- Wrap text around standard or irregular objects.

PROJECTS TO BE COMPLETED:

- Steaming Coffee
- **Java Jungle**
- Last Mango Cafe
- Tropical Fish
- Tropical Treasure
- Ball & Mirror
- Joker's Wild
- Coffee Du Jour Ad
- Tropical Treasure Mailer
- Last Mango Business Card

Creating and Editing Type

Typography and typographic elements are among the most important design elements you have to work with. Type, whether long blocks of body text, or tastefully applied font characters within a company's logo, adds character, and communicates the core message of many designs. In every typeface there are dozens of individual illustrations.

Illustrator's type controls are sophisticated enough for the most demanding designer — whether you're concerned about the space between characters, the space between lines, or even the shapes of individual characters you want to modify and use as a component in a larger piece. In this chapter we're going to cover many of the features of Illustrator that offer this high level of control and creative license.

Text blocks can be created in two ways:

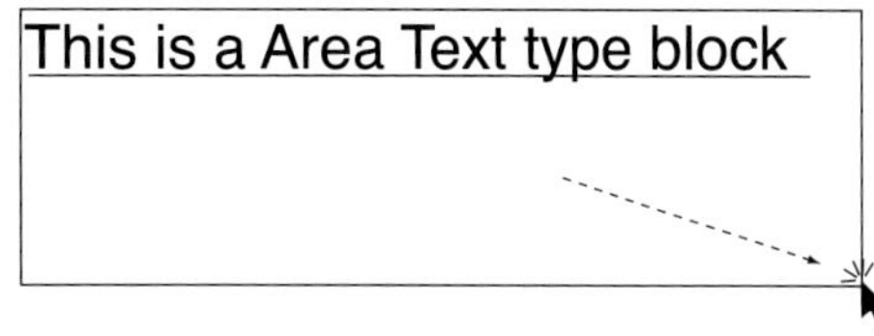

- Point Text — is created simply by clicking the Type tool "I-beam" cursor in the drawing area and typing. This will create a text block that has no right margin. Text will continue to the right as long as you type, or until you press Return (Macintosh) or Enter (Windows).

  Point text is mostly used for headlines, short sentences, or phrases that do not require a text wrapping right margin.

  Isolated text can be highlighted with the I-beam. The entire text object can be selected by clicking on or marqueeing the object with the Selection tool.

- Area Text — is a text container (text block) created by dragging the Type tool cursor and drawing a box. Text is selected by highlighting the type with the text cursor, or by clicking on the text block with the Selection

Selecting a text block (or several blocks with the Shift key), the Selection tool will allow you to perform physical changes to the box itself, such as move, duplicate, or transform it.

Also, when a text block is selected with the Selection tool, you can apply all the font attributes found in the Font and Type menus.

In **Preferences->Keyboard Increments**, make sure **Type Area Select** is clicked.

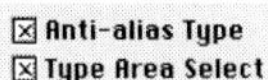

This allows text blocks to be selected by clicking on the text characters.

tool. After selecting the type, you can apply attributes from the Type menu or the Type **Character** palette. It's convenient to use the Selection tool method of selecting if you want to apply changes to several text blocks simultaneously.

Area text containers must be used with a large amount of text requiring a right margin to force text wrap.

Selecting text

Text, regardless of its container, can be selected in only two ways. You may choose to highlight it with the Type tool, or click on the text block with the Selection tool.

Use of the Type tool is preferred to isolate letters or words and apply text attributes to them.

The Selection tool comes in handy when you need to select an entire block of text quickly. Also, if you have several text containers that need the same attribute changes, they all can be Shift-selected. This allows you to make the change one time for all selected containers. Shift selecting involves selecting the first container and with the shift key depressed the remaining containers can be selected.

Another very popular species, this warm-growing orchid is found in the old-world tropics: places like Vietnam, Thailand, New Guinea, and Australia. It is often grown in slatted wooden baskets, which closely mimic its natural habit of growing in the "crotches" of

Highlighting the text using the Type tool allows you to select specific words or sections of text.

Another very popular species, this warm-growing orchid is found in the old-world tropics: places like Vietnam, Thailand, New Guinea, and Australia. It is often grown in slatted wooden baskets, which closely mimic its natural habit of growing in the "crotches" of

The Selection tool selects all text in the text block.

Resizing an Area Text Block

If you have an Area text block, and you want to widen the margins and lengthen the depth, use the Direct Selection tool. When you click on the Area text block with this tool, you'll see the anchor points and segments. Drag a segment, holding Shift to constrain, and adjust.

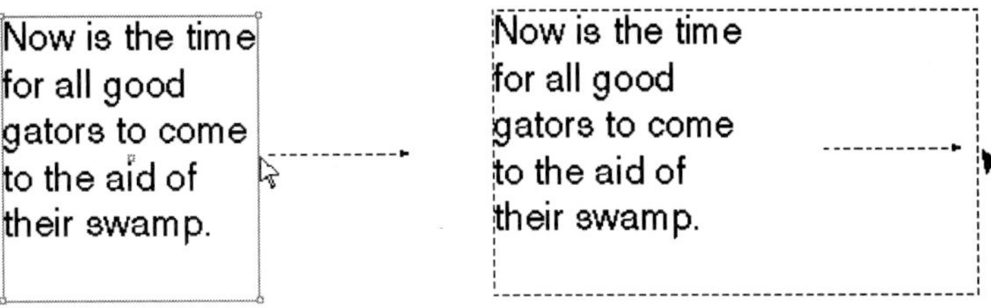

Typographic Basics

Typography is a broad area that fills libraries with volumes on the subject, and requires years of study for those who want to master the profession. For the purposes of type's use in Illustrator, we will show you the basics. The entire palette can be displayed (as shown) using the submenu **Show Options**.

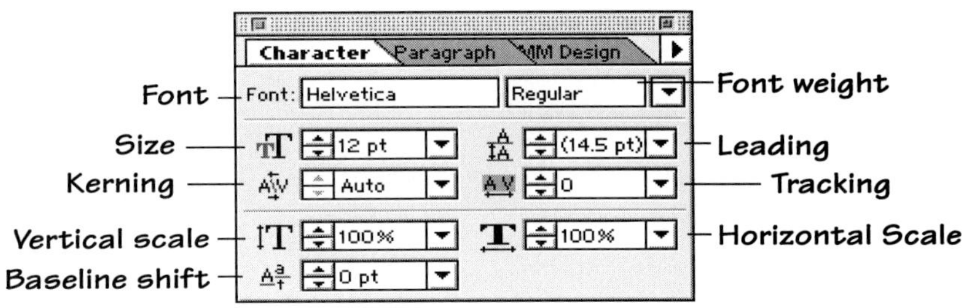

Font

The font is the physical appearance of the letters. Typeface is another term used to speak of the look of the alphabet. A full alphabet of letters is called a "font." Here is a sampling of various typefaces. The Font weight refers to Bold, etc.

Avant Garde   Cheltenham   **Cooper Black**

Helvetica   Souvenir   **STENCIL**   Tekton   Times

There are thousands of typefaces, but they actually fit into three catagories:

- Serif refers to the small extensions from the letter's stems.

- Sans is French for "without." Sans Serif means "without serifs."

- Decorative is a hybrid style of physical features that can't actually be classified as "serif" or "sans serif."

Size

The size of the letters is measured vertically in Points. There are 72 points in one inch. The vertical measurement extends from the baseline to the top of the ascender.

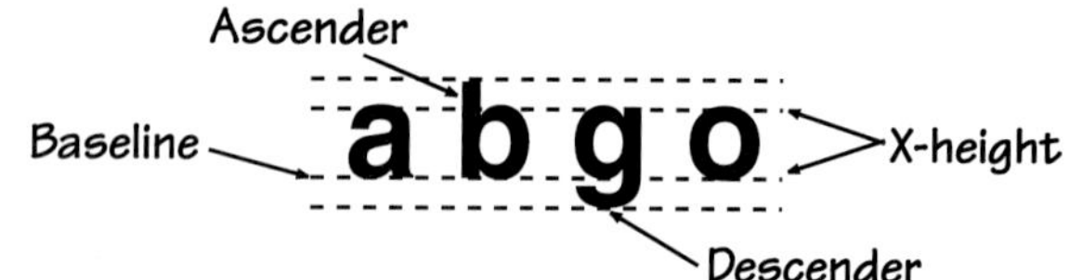

Special typographic rulers are available in art stores to measure type for what is called "type fitting," or adjusting type to fit a specific available area.

The text you are reading, such as this sentence, is 12 pt. type.

Leading

Leading is the spacing between two or more lines of type. The line can be a single letter, word, or sentence. Leading is measured from the baselines of two lines.

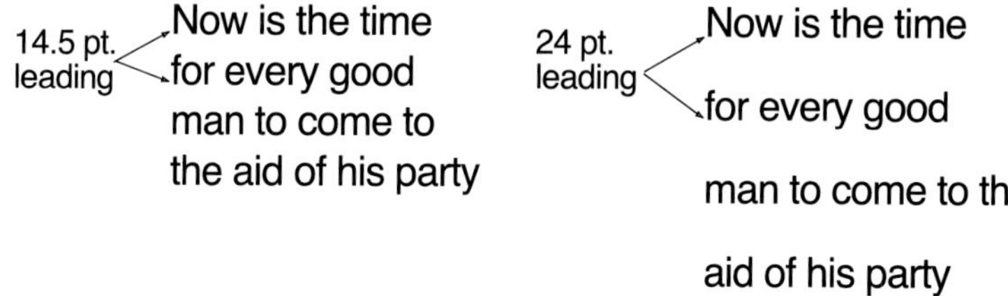

Tracking

Tracking is the spacing between letters. There are several descriptive words often used to describe tracking: loose, normal, or tight. In Illustrator, the tracking is measured in numeric increments. Zero (0) could be called "normal."

A setting of -20 could be called "tight." You adjust the increments to your own liking in the **Type Character** palette. Any type or text blocks selected can be modified in this palette.

The basis for measuring Tracking is in the increments of the Em space.

The Tracking Menu

(0)	This tracking is set for 0.
-100	This tracking is set for -25.
-75	
-50	This tracking is set for -50
-25	
-10	This tracking is set for 15.
-5	
✓ 0	This tracking is set for 25.
5	
10	This tracking is set for 50.
25	
50	
75	
100	
200	

The keyboard shortcut to adjust tracking of selected text is to hold the Option (Macintosh) or Alt (Windows) key and press either the Left or Right arrow keys. The Left arrow will reduce the distance, making the spacing tighter. The Right arrow will add spacing between the letters, making them less tight.

Kerning

Kerning is adjusting the spacing between two letters. The text cursor is placed between the two letters, then the Tracking keyboard shortcuts are applied as you observe the results.

The term for the two letters is called "Kerning Pairs." This is because certain letters do not fit together, unless kerned.

Kerning, or controlling the amount of space between specific characters, contributes greatly to the readability and "look" of copy – particularly headlines.

Letter's left/right dimensions butt up to each other.

This looks bad, and makes reading difficult.

Kerning makes the letters fit better.

Kerning can be done on two types of text.

- On a "kerning pair" of two letters

- On all selected text

For selected text, the type is highlighted with the text cursor (I-beam). Then, when the keyboard tracking shortcuts are applied, all the selected text will respond.

Scaling Type

Scaling refers to changing the actual width of the character itself — either condensing or expanding its shape.

Horizontal Scale

Adjusting the horizontal width of letters is called Horizontal Scale. This is measured in percentages.

This text is set for 50% Horizontal Scale.

This text is set for 150% Horizontal Scale.

Vertical scale

Adjusting the vertical height of letters is called Vertical Scale. This is measured in percentages.

This text is set to 75% Vertical Scale.

This text is set to 200% Vertical Scale

Baseline shift

The imaginary line that letters sit on is called the Baseline. To move the baseline of letters up or down is called Baseline Shift. This feature is extremely valuable when creating logos that have certain letters that rise above or go below the Baseline. In the **Type Character** palette, Baseline Shift is offered to alter its vertical location. If you want to alter the Baseline of characters by two point increments, then use the keyboard shortcut. You can also alter Baseline Shift by highlighting the characters you wish to change and pressing Option-Shift-Up Arrow to move up or Option-Shift-Down Arrow to move down.

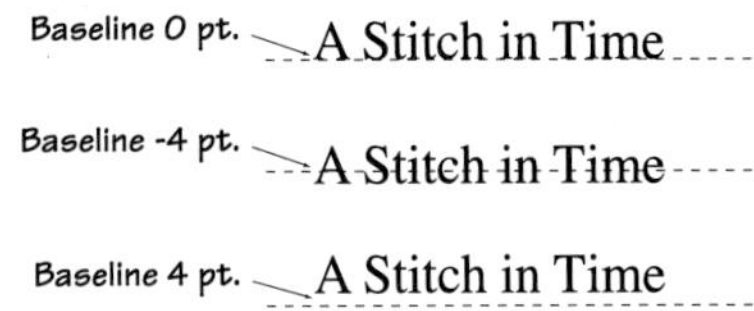

Creating and Manipulating Type

1. Create a **New** document. Select **View->Preview** mode.

2. Select the Type tool and click the tool on the page to create a text block.

3. Type your name for the first line, your address on the second line, your City, State, and Zip code on the third. Make a return after each line.

   > User's Name
   > 12234 Silicon Valley Rd.
   > Anywhere, USA 33615

4. With the Type tool cursor, highlight all this text. Press Command-T (Macintosh) Ctrl-T (Windows) for the Type **Character** palette. Use this palette to make all your changes.

5. To the right of the Font weight is a pop-up menu to select fonts and their weights. Apply the following: **Font**=Times, **Size** =14 pt. , **Leading** =24 pt., **Tracking** =-20, **Horizontal scale** =125%, **Vertical scale** =110%, **Kerning** = Auto, **Baseline shift** =0. Now press Return (Macintosh) or Enter (Windows).

Be careful of using techniques like vertical and horizontal scaling, which we just covered. It sometimes looks artificial, and has a computer-generated feel.

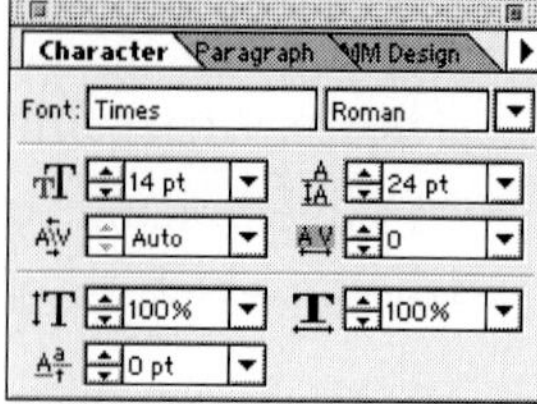

The Paragraph formatting capabilities of Illustrator makes it a perfect choice for doing single-page layouts. It provides a tremendous amount of control over type elements.

6. Highlight your name and change the Font weight to Bold. Change the Tracking of your name to 200.

7. Highlight the first letter of your first name. Change the Size to 20 pt. Hold the Shift key and the Option (Macintosh) Alt (Windows) key, and press the Down arrow key two times to change the Baseline shift.

8. Highlight the First letter of your last name, and repeat all the changes you made in Step 7.

9. Click the text cursor between the first and second letters of your first name. Hold the Option (Macintosh) or Alt (Windows) key and press the Left arrow key three times.

10. Do the Step 9 kerning to the first and second letters of your last name.

11. **Close** the document without saving.

Paragraph

In the **Paragraph** dialog box, you can further adjust the formatting of type. From alignment and indentations to word and letter spacing, you can adjust settings to make type look the way you want.

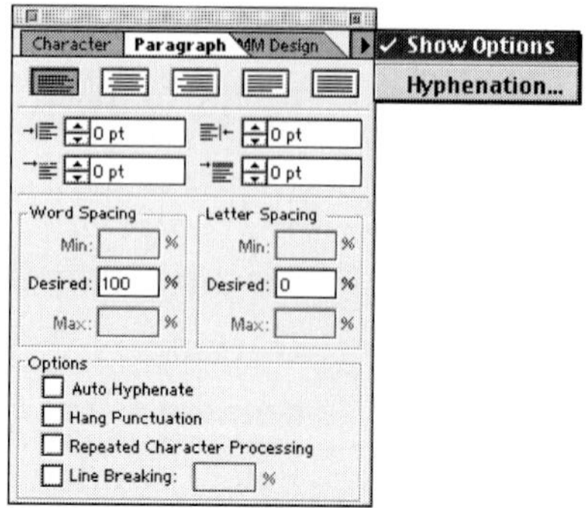

Some of the Paragraph controls are for more advanced typographic typefitting. We will only address the Alignment (top)section of the dialog box for now.

Learning key commands for paragraph alignment will save you lots of time. On the Mac, they're Command-C (Center), Command –L (Left), Command-R (Right), and Command-J (Justified). If you're a Windows user, just substitute the Control key for the Command key.

Alignment

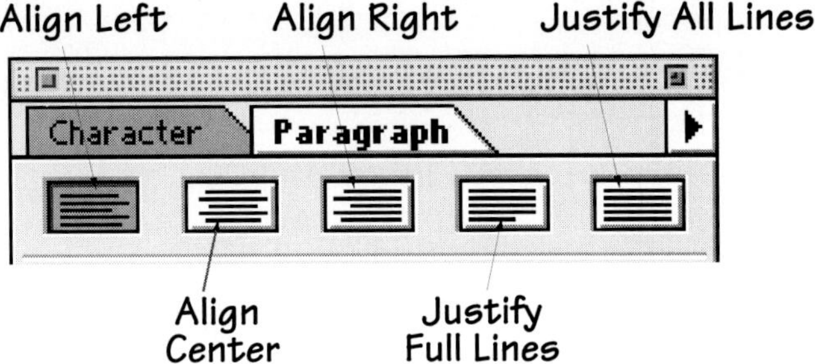

Text needs alignment for either readability or aesthetic purposes. There are nicknames that the typographers use for alignment.

Align Left is called either "Flush Left" or "Ragged Right" by typographers, because the left margin is even, or flush, and the right margin is ragged, or uneven.

You should study some magazines and books, as well as advertising, to see how alignment varies from media to media. The two aspects of alignment to keep in mind are readability and the aesthetic visual appeal.

Formatting Text

1. Go to **SF-Intro Illustrator** and **Open** the document **Format Text.AI.**

2. With the Selection tool, click on the text container. Press Command-T (Macintosh) or Ctrl-T (Windows) to access the Type **Character** palette.

3. Make the **Font** = Times, **Font weight** = Roman, **Size** = 14 pt., **Leading** = 21. Press Return (Macintosh) or Enter (Windows) to apply.

4. With the Type tool, highlight "Latin Nonsense, by, Oedipus Wrecks." Make the **Font** = Times, **Font weight** = Roman, **Size** = 18 pt., **Leading** = 24 pt. Press Return (Macintosh) or Enter (Windows) to apply .

5. Press Command-M (Macintosh) or Ctrl-M (Windows) to access the **Paragraph** palette. Click on the Align Center box.

6. Highlight only the body text. Click on Force Justify, then Justify. Observe how the spacing between words is affected.

7. Click on Align Left, then on Align Right. Observed the difference. Finally, click on Align Center.

8. Highlight only the title "Latin Nonsense." Make the **Font weight** = Bold, **Size** = 24 pt.

9. **Close** the file without saving.

Text Effects

Working with text as a designer goes far beyond merely typesetting. The use of type in logos, artistic headlines, and decorating a page tests the designer's imagination.

Working with Text Outlines

If you want to do creative things to text, such as making a distinctive headline, you may first want to convert the text to an outline, or path. Outlined text no longer contains some of the characteristics of type on the page. Hinting, one of the features of high-quality PostScript and TrueType fonts, will no longer be supported if the type is converted to outlines.

You may notice that the type turned to outlines will look somewhat rougher on your screen and heavier on some low-resolution devices. The final high-resolution output from Illustrator will be unchanged, however.

Outlined type can also be used to create an Illustrator file that can be opened and printed without needing the fonts used in the file. It can be very useful, for example, in creating ads that will be incorporated in a page layout package as an EPS file.

You can **Fill** and **Stroke** standard text, but it doesn't offer anchor points for stretching, distorting, and curving the outline of the letters in creative ways. Before you can do this, text must be converted to an outline path.

There are times when an illustration placed in another program (like a page layout application) simply won't print. You might try converting the text elements to outlines, and replacing the image. Always save a version with the actual type elements intact, in case you need to change a word or two.

 ADOBE ILLUSTRATOR: AN INTRODUCTION TO DIGITAL ILLUSTRATION/CREATING AND EDITING TYPE

Creating a Design with Type Outlines

1. Create a **New** document. Click the Type tool on the page to begin typing.

2. Type "TROPICAL TREASURE." Highlight it with the cursor. Make these settings: **Font** = ATC Tequila, **Size** = 72 pt., **Tracking** = -40.

3. Click on the Selection tool in the Toolbox. The text object will be automatically selected (a.). In the **Type** menu, choose **Create Outlines.**

4. Go to **View->Artwork** mode. The text letters will become outlines (b.). Select all the outlines and **Object->Group** them.

a. **TROPICAL TREASURE**

b. TROPICAL TREASURE

5. Select the headline group and choose **Edit->Copy.** Go to **Edit->Paste in Back**, to paste a duplicate behind the original group. When pasted, the duplicate will be the selected object.

6. Press the Right Arrow key 2 times; the Down Arrow key 2 times .

TROPICAL TREASURE

7. Paint the duplicate: **Fill** = Black, **Stroke** = None.
   Paint the original group: **Fill** = White, **Stroke** = Black 0.5 pt.

8. The design should look like this in **Preview** mode.

TROPICAL TREASURE

9. **Select All,** then Delete the outlines. Keep the file open.

Shadow type, hollow type, and other special effects have their place, but shouldn't be overused just because they're easy to apply.

1. Continue in the open document. Click on the page with the Type tool and type these words, on separate lines:

    Logo
    Type

2. Access the Type **Character** palette.

3. Highlight the text and make these settings: **Font** = ATC Cozumel, **Size** = 72 pt., **Leading** =60, **Tracking** = 0, **Horizontal scale** = 100%. Press Return (Macintosh) or Enter (Windows) to apply. Select the text block with the Selection tool. In **Artwork** mode, go to **Type->Create Outlines**.

 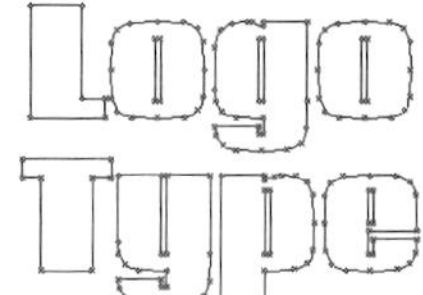

4. Turn your rulers on. Drag a horizontal guide down to the bottom of the letter "g" in "Logo." Drag another guide to the bottom of the "p" in "Type."

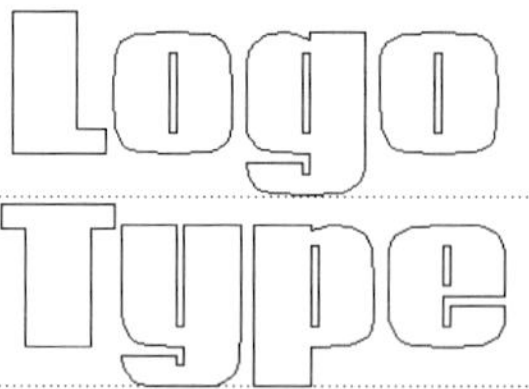

5. Zoom in on the "L." With the Direct Selection tool, marquee the lower anchor points of the "L" to select. Drag the points, holding the Shift key, so that the bottom segment touches the guide.

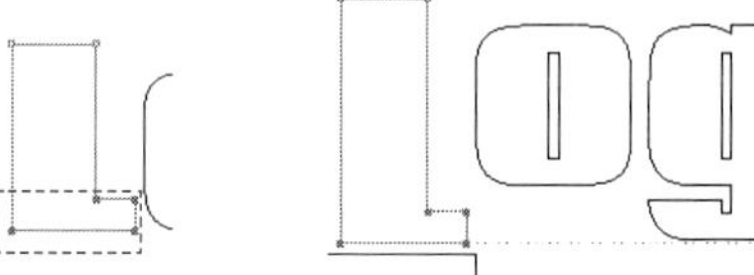

Look around in popular literature and advertising for logos that are made up of type elements — there are plenty to find. Many of them were done in Adobe Illustrator.

When you reshape a font for a logo, make sure you don't destroy the balance of the character by distorting it too much.

6. With the Selection tool, select the "ogo" letters and move them closer to the "L."

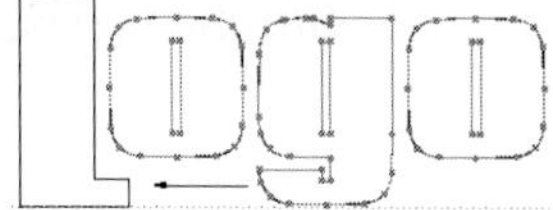

7. With the Direct Selection tool, marquee the bottom anchors of the "T." Drag them down, holding the Shift key, so the bottom segment touches the guide.

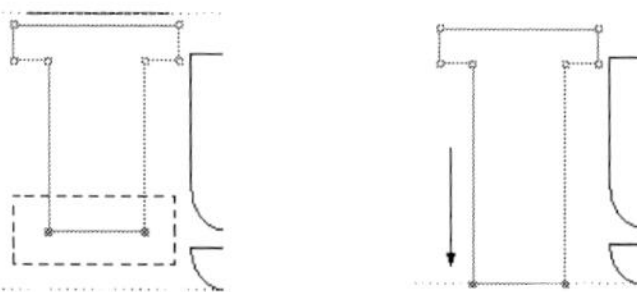

8. With the Direct Selection tool, highlight the top anchor points of the "T." Drag the points upward, holding the Shift key, so the top of the "T" touches the bottom of the "L."

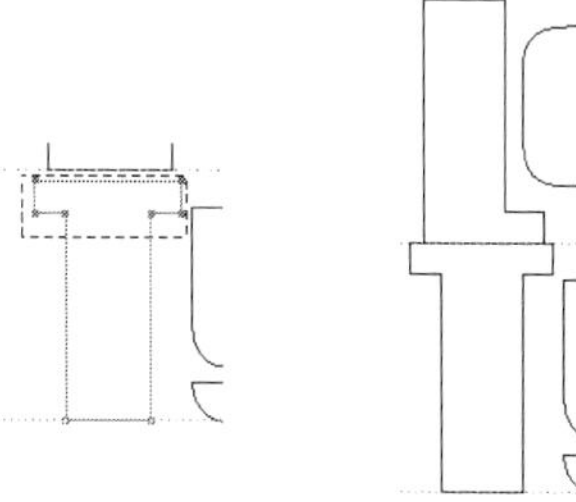

9. Select the "ype" outlines with the Selection tool, and move them closer to the "T."

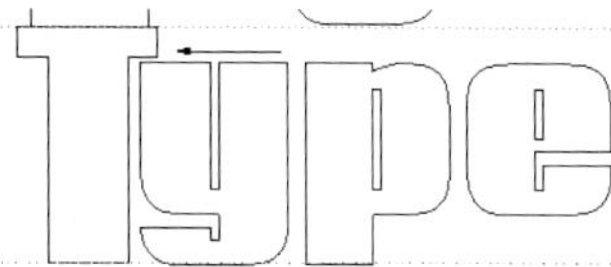

10. With the Direct Selection tool, highlight the bottom anchor points of the "o" in "Logo." Drag the points, holding the Shift key, so the bottom touches the guide.

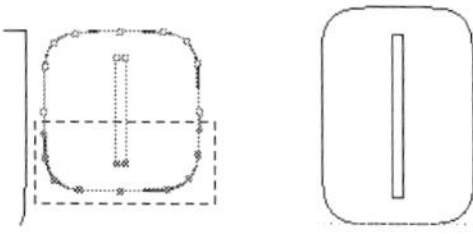

Once type has been converted into outlines, it's just like any other shape, and responds to the arrow tools, fills, strokes, and other attribute tools in the same way.

11. With the Direct Selection tool, do not marquee, but simply click on the top segment of the "y" in "Type." This will select the segment and its anchor points. Drag upward, holding the Shift key, so that the segment is level with the descender of the "g."

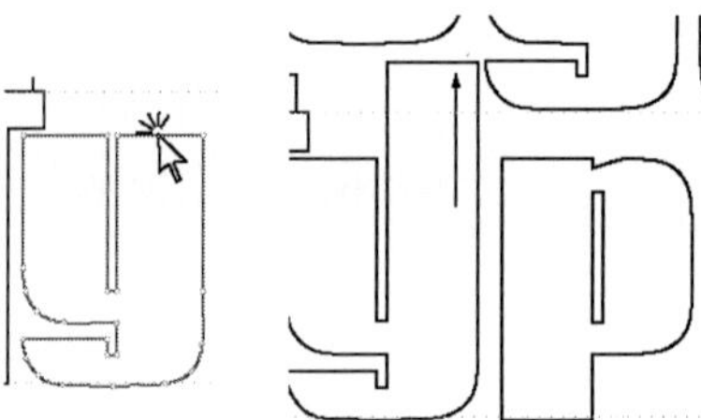

12. The logo design is finished. You have edited and modified type in such a way that would be impossible if the letters were to stay in text format.

It should look similar to this:

13. **Close** the file without saving.

Creating Text on a Curving Path

1. Create a **New** document. With the Pen tool, draw a curving path. Click-hold on the Type tool in the Toolbox to access the Path Type tool from the Toolbox.

If you delete the path, you delete the type that follows it. You might consider turning path-based type into outlines before you print it. Again, always save a version with the actual type intact, to facilitate edits and corrections.

2. Lay the crossbar of the text cursor on top of the path and click once. Type the words "Typing text on a path."

3. With the Selection tool, click on the path. You will see the I-beam text cursor. Drag the I-beam to the left with the Selection tool. Enlarge the Point size of the type so that it fits the path from left to right.

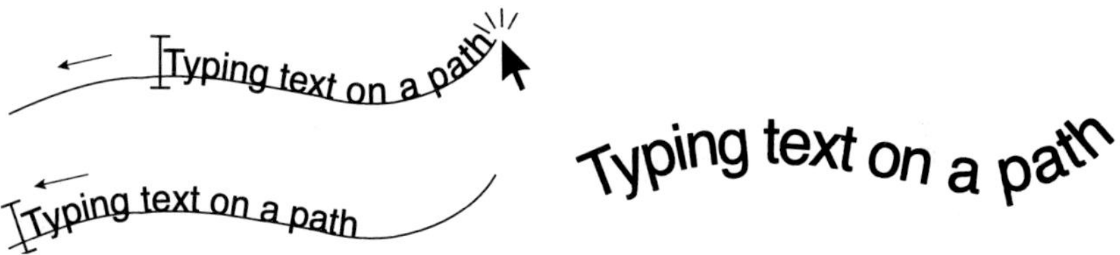

4. With the Direct Selection tool, alter the curves of the path to see how the type moves with the path as you change it.

5. **Close** the file without saving.

Project B: Java Jungle

Notes:

CHAPTER 12

PAINTING OBJECTS

CHAPTER OBJECTIVE:

To learn how to apply colors to objects in your drawings. To learn how to apply fills and strokes, and how to control the colors of each individually. In Chapter 12, you will:

- Learn the difference between a stroke and a fill.
- Learn how fills affect open and closed paths.
- Learn to use the Swatches palette to change the colors of strokes and fills on objects or type.
- Learn to use the Paint Bucket and Eyedropper tools to fill and select colors.
- Learn to import or export colors from one drawing to another.

PROJECTS TO BE COMPLETED:

- Steaming Coffee
- Java Jungle
- **Last Mango Cafe**
- Tropical Fish
- Tropical Treasure
- Ball & Mirror
- Joker's Wild
- Coffee Du Jour Ad
- Tropical Treasure Mailer
- Last Mango Business Card

Painting Objects

Painting refers to an object's fundamental attributes: the color that fills a shape and the rule, or stroke, that surrounds it. All objects have a fill and stroke attribute – even if both are set to none and the shape is invisible. It's only a matter of changing the two values and the shape appears.

A wide variety of painting tools is available within Adobe Illustrator. In this section we're going to explore the use of these tools, and how they can be used to color and fill various objects and shapes within your illustrations. Drawing with color dramatically expands the options available to the artist, and effective use of color is a critical skill.

Think of your drawing in Illustrator as a page from a coloring book. Each path you create can be assigned a fill attribute and a stroke attribute. The fill is what color, and or pattern, the object will be. Stroke is the thickness and color of the path itself. An object can have none, either, or both fill and/or stroke attributes applied to it.

Painting any path is based on two styles: **Fill** and/or **Stroke**.

- **Stroke** — To **Stroke** is to paint the path. This is usually measured in Points, abbreviated as "pt." This rectangle was Stroked 6 pt. with no Fill.

- **Fill** — To **Fill** is to paint the interior of an open or closed path with color, tint, gradient, or pattern choices from the **Swatches palette.** This rectangle was **Filled,** but given no **Stroke.**

- Both **Fill** and **Stroke.** Any path can have both a **Fill** and **Stroke** applied together. This rectangle was painted as: **Fill** = 30% Black. **Stroke** = 6 pt. Black.

Stroking and Filling a Path

A path can be filled and stroked. The stroke defines the outside edge of any path, and can have a color and width. This section discusses the methods whereby you can assign color and width attributes to an object or path.

Closed paths can be painted with either a Stroke, a Fill, or both. Stroke and Fill selections are made in the Toolbox, using the Fill and Stroke icons.

The Stroke

The **Stroke** is the painted thickness of the path. Its weight (i.e., thickness or width) is measured in points.

This Open Path has been painted with **Fill** = None and **Stroke** = 3 pt. Black

The Fill

Applying an attribute to a path's interior is known as a **Fill** because you are "filling" the object. The **Swatches** palette offers different **Fill** attributes: colors, gradients, and patterns.

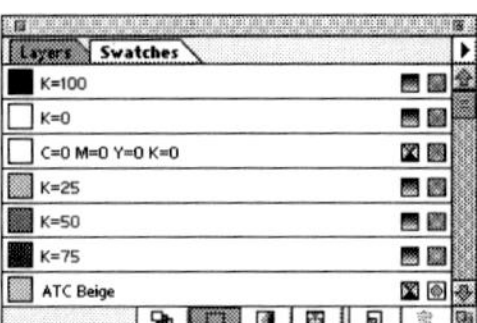

The Fill box in the Toolbox has to be selected to apply the Fill.

Stroke and Fill Together

The appearance of painted paths depends on how you **Fill** and **Stroke** them. Here is the same path shown painted in three different ways.

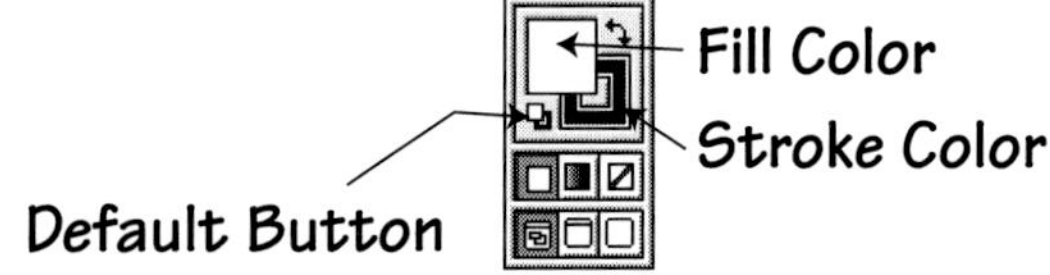

 Adobe Illustrator: An Introduction to Digital Illustration/Painting Objects

---

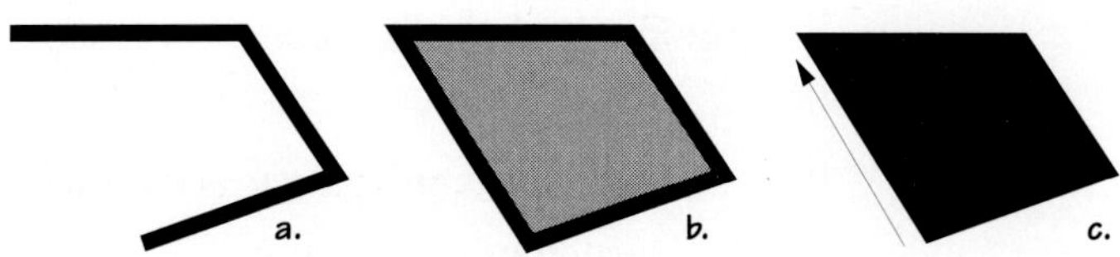

a. **Fill** = None, **Stroke** = 8 pt. Black

b. **Fill** = 30% Black screen tint, **Stroke** = 8 pt. Black. Notice how the rule is not completely connected, yet the **Fill** bridges the open gap.

c. **Fill** = Black, **Stroke** = None

Various Painting Methods

There are many methods available to paint your paths and objects. Here are the most common. With the object to be painted selected:

- Touch the swatch in the **Swatches** palette.

- Drag the swatch from **Swatches** palette to touch the **Fill** or **Stroke** boxes in the Toolbox.

- Drag the swatch from **Swatches** palette to touch the target object.

- Drag the **Fill** /**Stroke** box from the Toolbox to touch the object. The object does not have to be selected.

- Use the Paint Bucket tool to touch the object.

- The Eyedropper tool turns into the Paint Bucket tool when you hold the Option (Macintosh) or Alt (Windows) key.

Caution: Open paths, when Filled, connect from the Endpoint to the Beginning Point. In Preview mode, this can sometimes create questionable effects, as you may not recognize whether it is an open or closed path.

The Swatches Palette

The **Swatches** palette is the main window to access colors and styles. The icon swatch next to each name can be dragged to paint your objects.

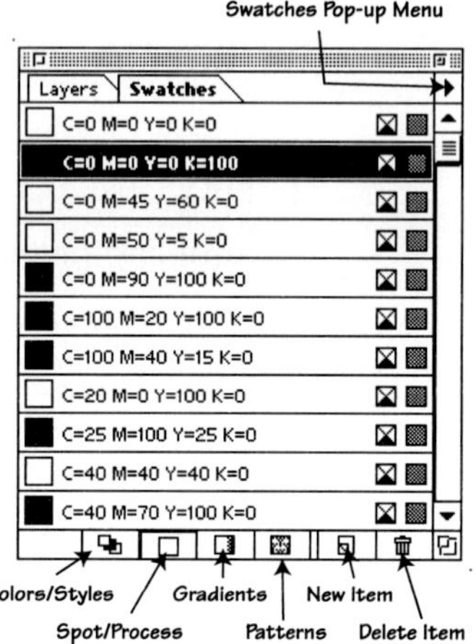

Almost all jobs that are reproduced in color rely on a process known as four-color printing. The four inks used are Cyan, Magenta, Yellow, and Black. Take a magnifying glass and look at a color photo in a magazine and you'll see the technique at work.

- **K 0%** — Paints the object White. Though White may seem transparent, it will be opaque and hide any objects behind it.

- **K 100%** — Paints the object 100% Black. The selected color tint can be adjusted using the sliders in the **Color** palette.

- **Process Colors** — Objects will be colored using standard four-color process (CMYK) printing ink colors. The mix is controlled by moving the four sliders in the **Color** palette.

- **Spot Colors** — Paints the object with a Spot or custom color. These colors can be built from Pantone, TruMatch, or other color systems. They can also be made within the working document.

- **Patterns** — Fills objects with **Pattern** tiles.

- **Gradients** — Gradients are created in the **Gradients** palette (under the **Window** menu) using selected colors for the starting and ending points, as well as intermediate colors.

You will find yourself changing strokes and fills often during the development of a drawing. You can save time by having common elements, such as a 1 point stroke with no fill, lying around on the outside of the page. That way, you can click on them and automatically set the fill and stroke to match that object.

Painting the Stroke Only

1. Create a **New** document. Working in **View->Artwork** mode, draw a basic open path by clicking seven times with the Pen tool. Select the path with the Selection tool.

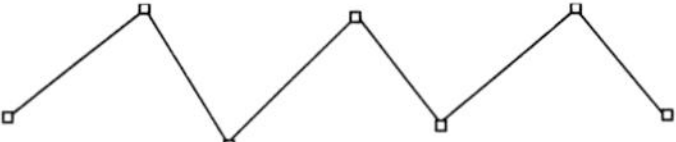

2. Go to **Window->Show Swatches**.

3. In the Toolbox, click on the Fill box. Then, click on the None box. This tells Fill to be None.

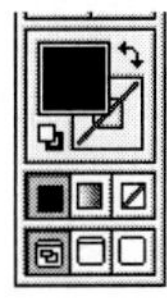 

4. Click on the Stroke box in the Toolbox.

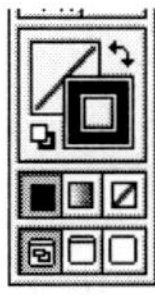

5. From the **Swatches** palette, viewed by "name," drag the **K=100%** swatch to touch the Stroke box in the Toolbox.

6. Go to **Window->Show Stroke**. In the **Weight** box, type **4**.

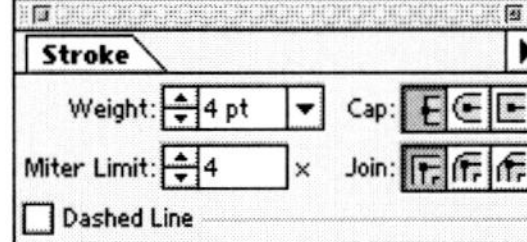

7. In **View->Preview** mode, the resulting path should look like this.

8. Keep this file open and continue.

Filling and Stroking

1. Continue in the same document. Go to **View->Artwork** mode.

2. With the Rectangle tool, draw a square. Keep it selected.

3. Go to **Window->Show Swatches** to access the **Swatches** palette.

4. In the Toolbox, click on the Fill box.

5. From the **Swatches** palette, drag the C=0, M=50, Y=5, K=0 swatch to touch the **Fill** box in the Toolbox. This tells Fill to be of that color.

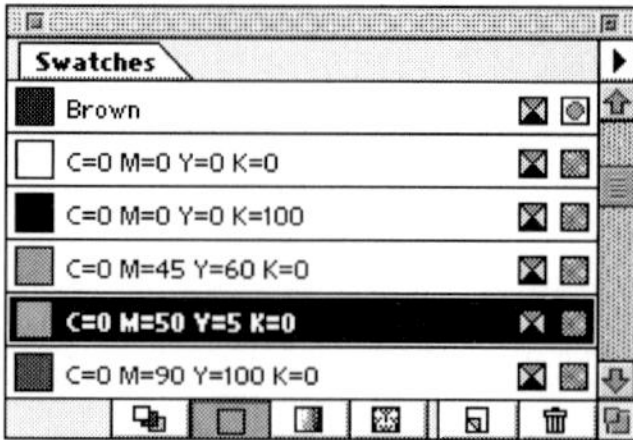

6. Click on the Stroke box in the Toolbox. Drag the C=0, M=0, Y=0, K=100 color from the **Swatches** palette so the Stroke will be 100% Black.

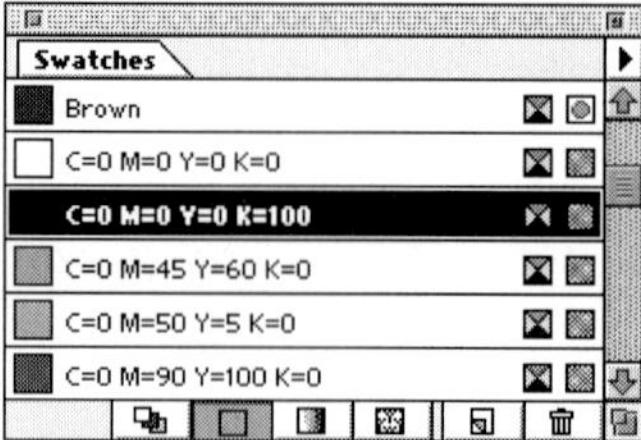

7. Go to **Window->Show Stroke**. In the **Stroke** palette, type 5 for the Weight. Press Return (Macintosh) or Enter (Windows) to apply.

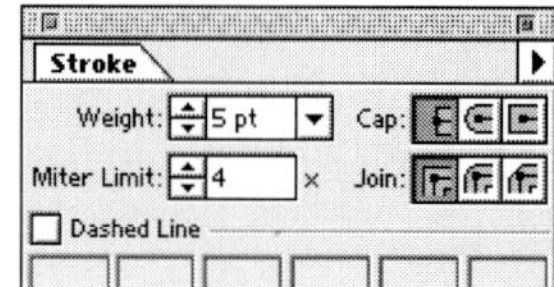

You can drag a color from the palette onto a shape and automatically fill it with that color. You can also drag a color onto the Stroke and Fill swatches in the bottom of the toolbar and accomplish the same thing (if an object's selected when you do it).

8. The closed path has been Filled and Stroked. In **View->Preview** mode, the square should look like this.

9. **Close** the file without saving.

The Paint Bucket and Eyedropper Tools

The Paint Bucket allows you to fill shapes with a color; the Eyedropper tool lets you grab a color from an object — even if that object is in another drawing. If a color is already applied to an object, you may "sample" that color by clicking that object with the Eyedropper tool. This sampled color can then be applied to other objects with the Paint Bucket tool. These two tools can reduce the time it takes to paint objects.

Using the Paint Bucket and Eyedropper Tools

1. Create a **New** document.

2. Create a series of objects to color and paint them all the same. Once done, change one of the object's colors. Select the Eyedropper tool from the Toolbox. Click on the object that is painted in the style you wish to obtain. This will load the Fill/Stroke boxes with the sampled styles.

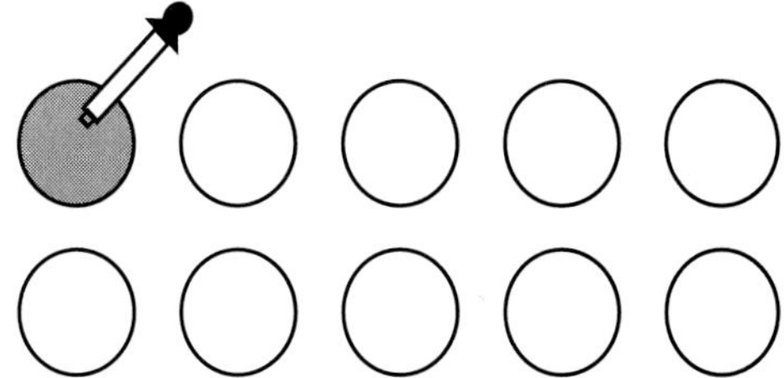

You can toggle back and forth from the Paint Bucket to the Eyedropper tools by holding the Option (Macintosh) or Alt (Windows) key while using the tools.

The part of the Paint Bucket that actually paints an object is the tip of the "spilling paint."

Dragging a color swatch does the same thing as using the Paint Bucket.

3. Next, select the Paint Bucket tool. Click on an object you want to paint. You don't have to select the object itself. The object clicked with the Paint Bucket tool will be painted with the color style sampled with the Eyedropper.

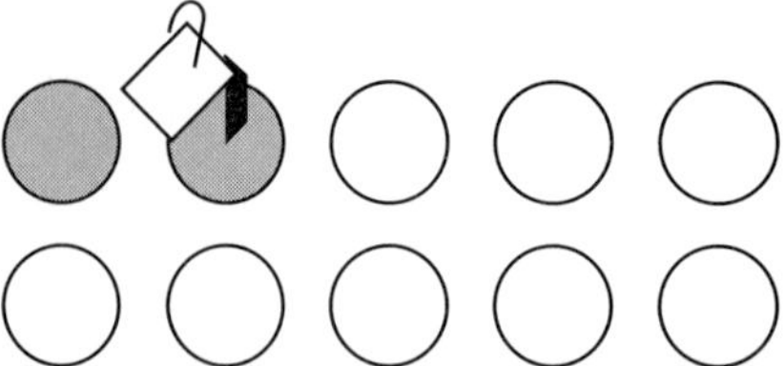

4. Continue clicking on the rest of the objects until they are all painted the new color style.

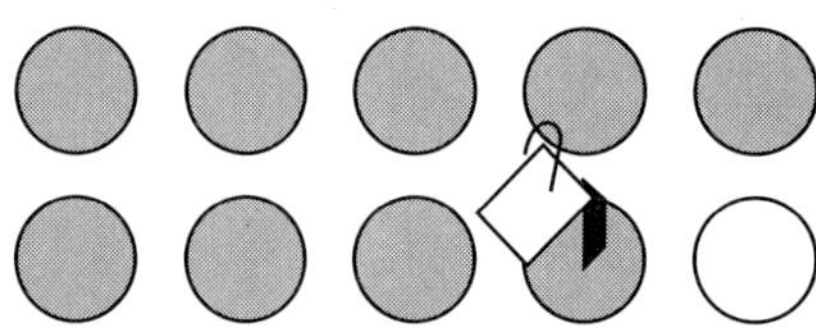

5. **Close** the file without saving.

Importing Colors, Styles

Gradients, Process Colors, Custom Colors, Patterns, etc. — all are features that can be quite time consuming to redefine manually in each document you create. You can import paint styles from other Illustrator documents or libraries, such as Pantone.

By selecting **Window->Swatch Libraries**, you can choose **Other Library.**

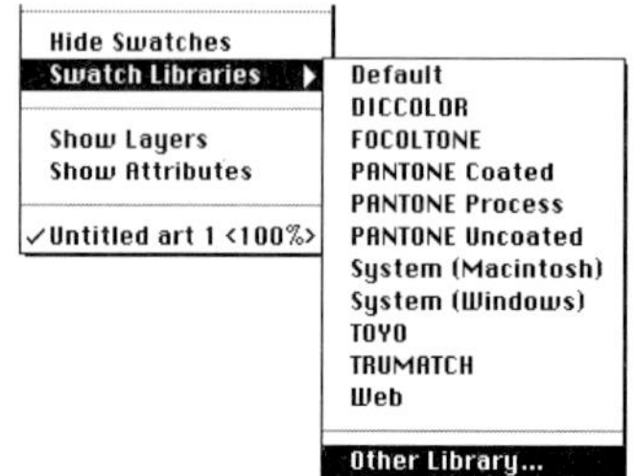

In the dialog box that appears, you can choose the document from which you wish to import the styles into your current **Swatches** palette.

Importing Styles

1. Create a **New** document. Go to **Window->Show Swatches.**

2. Go to **Window->Swatch Libraries.**

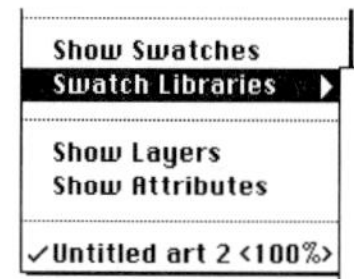

3. From the **Swatch Libraries** menu, select **Other Library.**

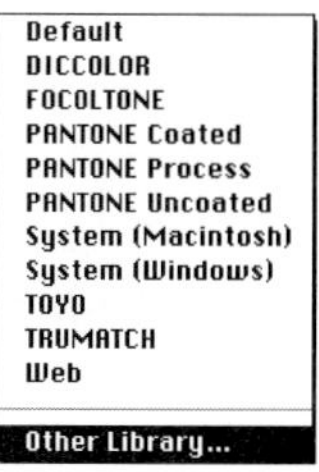

Talk with your printer about what color library you should use when developing your artwork. In most cases, they're going to recommend one of the Pantone™ libraries.

4. In the following dialog box, locate the file **ATC Custom Colors.AI** in the **SF-Intro Illustrator** folder. Click **Open.**

5. Observe how Illustrator creates a separate color swatch library that you can choose colors from.

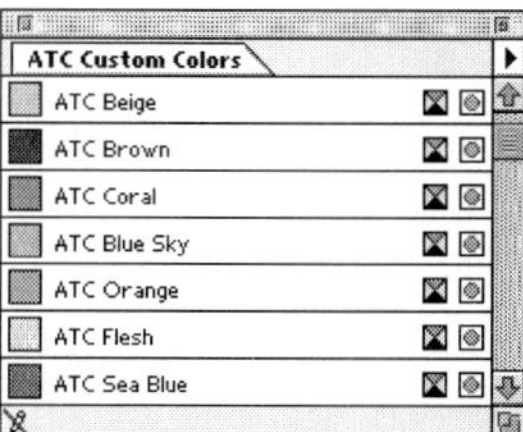

6. Scroll through the colors of this palette to see the new colors and names.

7. **Close** the file without saving.

1. Create a **New** document.

2. With the Type tool, click on the page (click and release).

3. Type in the single letter "W." Click the Type tool icon in the Toolbox. This will deselect the letter. The cursor will still be the Type cursor.

4. Click again on the page and type the letter "O."

    You should have two text blocks: "W" and "O."

5. With the Selection tool, marquee a rectangle that will select both blocks.

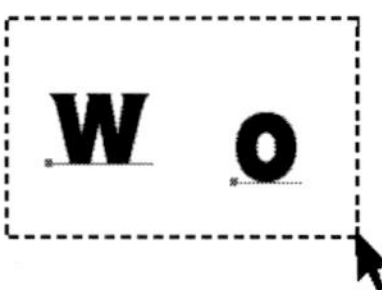

6. With the text blocks selected, apply these settings to the text: Font = **ATC Plantation**, Size = **36 pt**.

7. Select only the "O" and change its size to 60 pt. in the **Type** menu.

8. Move the "O" closer to the "W" so that it fits, almost touching the "W."

9. With the Selection tool, click on the baseline of the "W" to select it. Press Command-C (Macintosh) or Ctrl-C (Windows) to copy the "W."

    Press Command-F (Macintosh) or Ctrl-F (Windows) to **Paste in Front** the duplicate in the exact position where the original is.

10. With the Selection tool, move the duplicate "W" (holding the Shift key as you do to maintain the horizontal level) over to the right, nudged up to the "O."

Some people have great color sense, and others are horrible, dressing with socks that don't match. We're of the latter breed.

11. Use the Selection tool to click on the bottom of the "O" (which is the baseline) to select it.

12. Show the **Swatches** palette (**Window->Show Swatches**), if it is not currently on the Artboard. Use the pop-up menu to **Sort by Name** the colors. They will arrange themselves alphabetically.

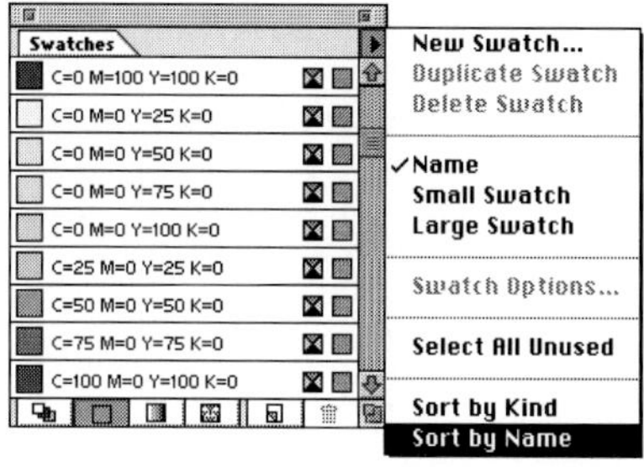

13. With "O" still selected, and with the **Swatches** palette open, make sure the Fill icon of the Toolbox is clicked on and selected. Drag the swatch of the color ATC Red to touch the Fill icon.

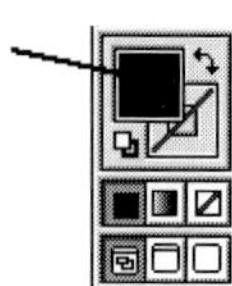

14. The "O" will be painted red, and will stand out against the black "Ws."

15. You have created and painted a simple logo. **Close** the file without saving.

Project C: Last Mango Cafe

Notes:

CHAPTER 13

COLOR BASICS

CHAPTER OBJECTIVE:

To learn the basics of color output, and how colors relate to each other and affect each other within a drawing. In Chapter 13, you will:

- Read a basic discussion of color output and theory.
- Learn the difference between a process color and a spot color.
- Learn to define and modify existing colors.
- Learn to work with industry-standard color definitions and libraries, such as those provided by Pantone™ and included with Illustrator.

PROJECTS TO BE COMPLETED:

- Steaming Coffee
- Java Jungle
- Last Mango Cafe
- Tropical Fish
- Tropical Treasure
- Ball & Mirror
- Joker's Wild
- Coffee Du Jour Ad
- Tropical Treasure Mailer
- Last Mango Business Card

Color Basics

Adobe Illustrator is a very colorful program, and provides a wide range of methods for using colors in your designs. Not only does the program come with a complete selection of popular color definitions, but it allows you to create custom colors through a simple-to-use interface. We will explore these methods and as we move forward to the following chapters, provide extensive hands-on exercises where you'll get to apply them.

There are several different color models that can be used to define colors for use in Illustrator. The color model you select will affect how the color looks on your monitor and will also control the color in the final output.

Color Output

Output and reproduction of your illustration may be accomplished via a multitude of channels. Possibly with commercial print manufacturing, via a *web page* on the Internet, as a CD-ROM graphic, or as a component of a multimedia presentation.

There are two types of color "models"; spot, which refers to solid ink colors, and process colors — the use of four primary inks (cyan, magenta, yellow, and black).

- **Spot Color (Custom Colors)** — the color is defined by the custom color ink used on the press. Spot color printing can also employ *tints* of the spot color to extend the apparent range of color being printed. One type, Pantone inks, are formulated to match the widely used *Pantone Matching System (PMS)*.

- **Process Color** — also known as 4-color (4/c), in which a range or *gamut* of colors is printed according to the specific combination of halftone tints of cyan, magenta, yellow, and black inks (CMYK). These halftone dots are arranged in a specific *rosette* pattern with each ink having a unique halftone *screen angle*. Errors in specification or placement of these halftones can result in a repeating pattern called a *moiré*.

Any color can be rendered as either a process or a spot color for output purposes; however, the accuracy of the color reproduction may not be satisfactory when some spot colors are converted to process inks. That is because process color printing cannot duplicate all of the colors that can be printed with spot colors, especially the highly saturated, the fluorescent, and the metallic colors. Converting these from custom to process will result in a *color shift*. Check with your printer for guidance.

Color Definitions

Illustrator makes extensive use of color palettes, including "swatch" books which can be used to drag and drop color chips directly onto an object — a very quick and easy way to define the color of a shape.

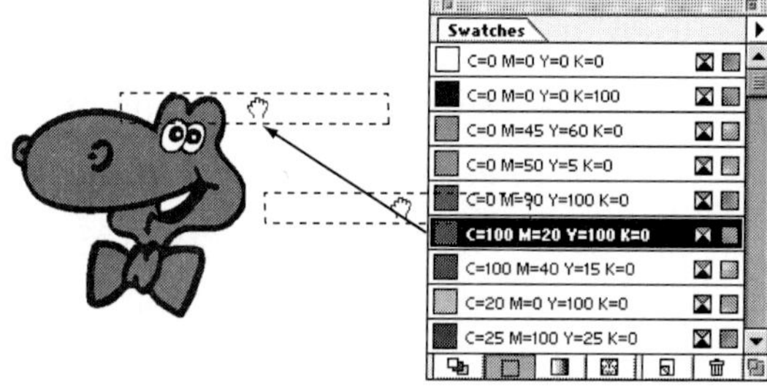

If desired, a new color can also be stored in the **Swatches** palette by dragging the Fill box from the Toolbox to the palette.

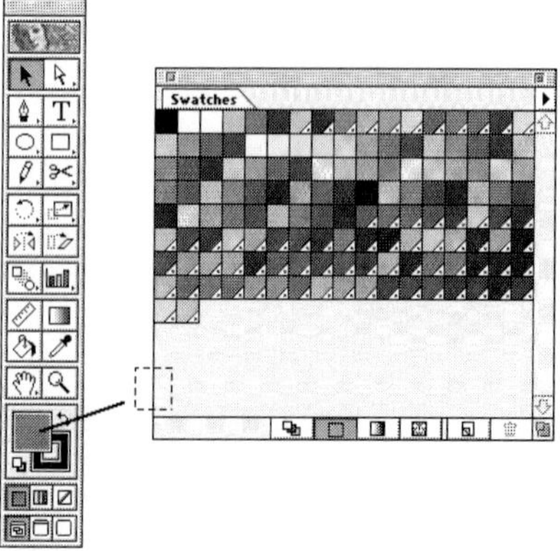

The drag and drop method is a quite common way to move colors, store colors, and apply a color to an object. It is now easy to paint an object, just by dragging the color from either the Toolbox Fill/Stroke boxes, or from the **Swatches** palette, and touching the target object.

The target object does not have to be selected for this method. Experiment with dragging color swatches from the **Swatches** palette or Toolbox icons to other palettes, such as **Color** or **Gradient**.

Defining a Process or Spot Color

To define a process or spot color, the method is basically the same. The most efficient method is to have the **Swatches** and **Color** palettes on the screen.

1. Create a new document, using **File->New**.

2. Go to the **Window->Show Color** palette and adjust the C-M-Y-K sliders to the shade you want the color to be.

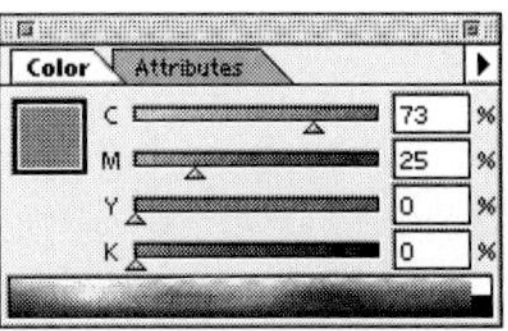

3. When you are satisfied, drag the color swatch from the **Color** palette to the **Swatches** palette. View the colors "By Name" using the **Swatches** pop-up menu. The new color will appear, alphabetically, with the name "New Color Swatch 1."

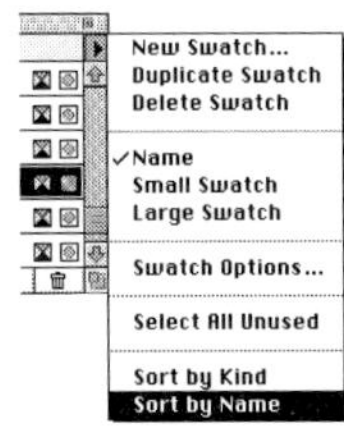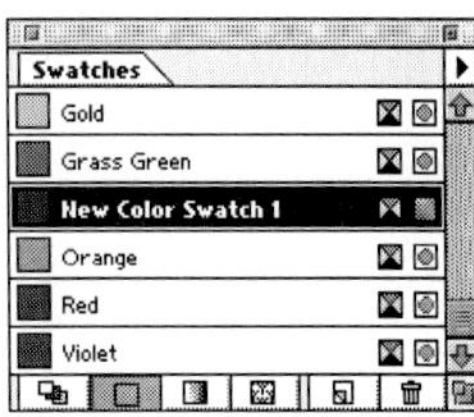

4. Double-click on the name. This will bring up the **New Swatch** window in which you determine if the color will be **Process** or **Spot**. Name the color appropriately and assign the **Process** color mode. Click **OK**. The new name will appear in the **Swatches** palette.

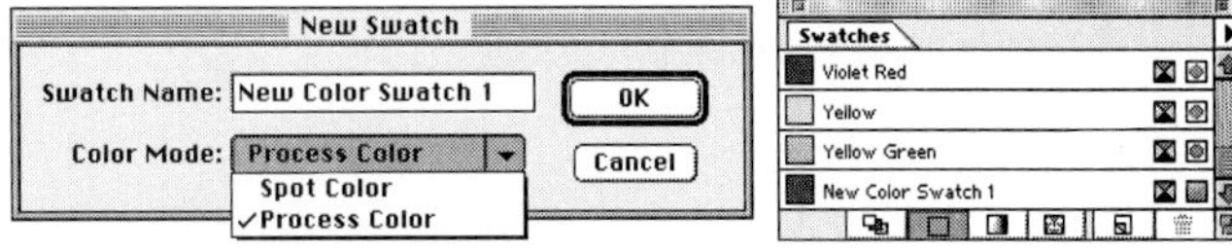

5. Keep the document open for the next exercise.

Adding PMS Colors

1. Continue in the open document.

2. Go to **Window->Swatch Libraries.** Select **PANTONE Coated.**

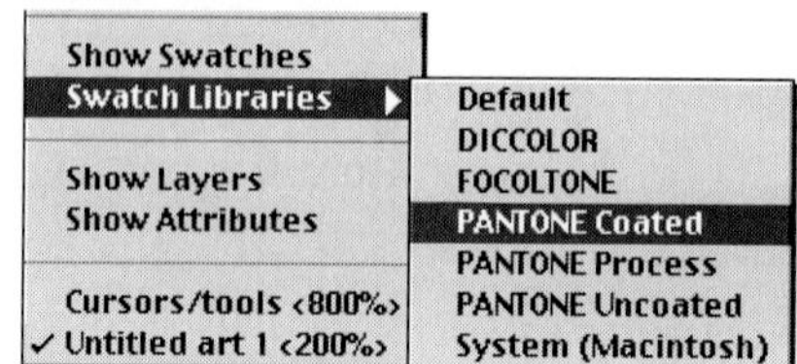

3. This library will appear in its own palette.

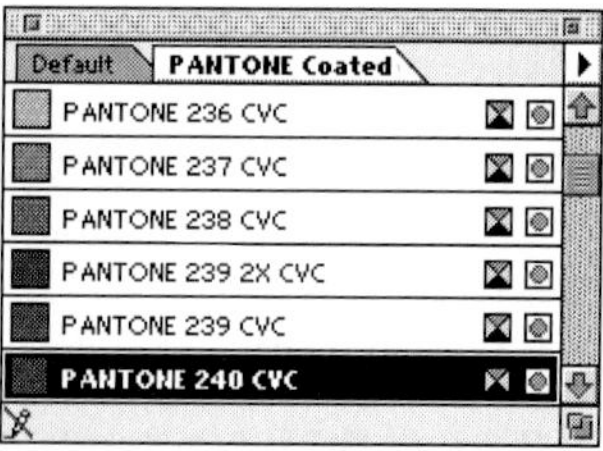

4. Scroll to **Pantone 357 CVC** in the color list. Drag it from the list to the **Swatches** palette. This color will now be easier to access, rather than constantly referring back to the Pantone library.

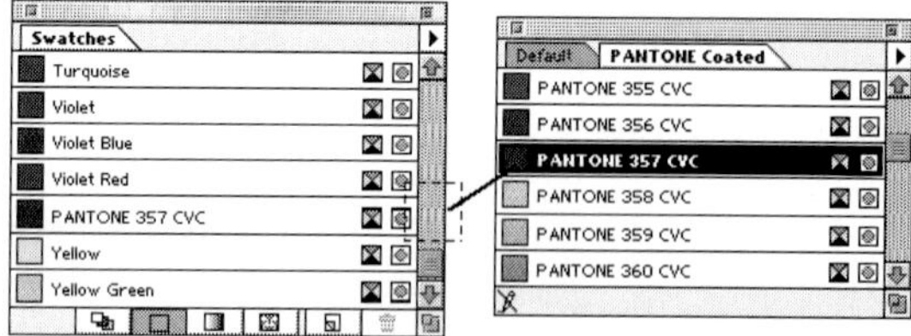

5. Keep the file open for the next exercise.

PMS colors are sometimes solid inks. Not all colors can be matched with four-color process. Solid inks are known as Spot colors. Some jobs have the four primary colors and a fifth ink added to achieve these difficult shades.

Adobe Illustrator: An Introduction to Digital Illustration/Color Basics

The Color Palette

The **Color** palette creates and adjusts both Process and Spot colors. The color swatch is for dragging colors to and from the palette. It also shows you how the color will appear.

- Process (CMYK) is for building or modifying process colors. You use the color sliders to adjust the percentages of CMYK to achieve the desired color. Or, you can type the known percentage in the boxes next to the sliders. The color sampler is a spectrum of color tones that you can click on to shop around for the color you want.

- Spot Color appears when you select a spot color from the Swatches palette. You cannot adjust the CMYK colors that build a spot color here. You can only adjust the tint or percentage of the color. Either move the slider or type in a desired percentage. The color sampler allows you to click on the tonal area that you like, which will automatically move the slider appropriately.

You can name a color anything that suits you — as long as it's created with proper amounts of the four primary colors, or is designated as a spot (additional) color and output properly.

Process (CMYK)

Spot Color

1. With the same document open, go to the **Window** menu and access the **Color** and **Swatches** palettes. In the **Swatches** palette, click on the process color C=0, M=40, Y=15, K=0. Notice how this color instantly appears in the **Color** palette.

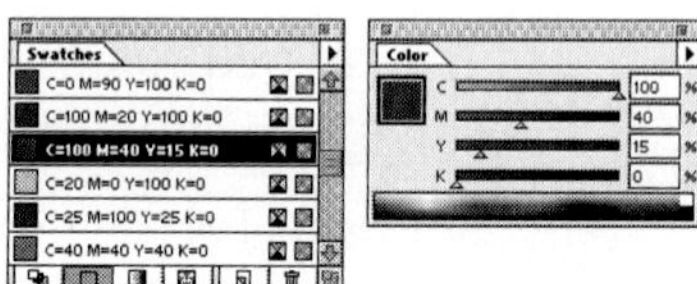

2. In the **Color** palette, click on the color sampler to experiment with how the color swatch changes as you do. Now, move the sliders to change the CMYK percentages to achieve a desired color.

   When satisfied with the color, drag the color swatch from the **Color** palette back to the **Swatches** palette. You will see a new color item appear, named "New Color Swatch 1."

3. Double-click on the new color in the **Swatches** palette. You will see the **Swatch Options** dialog box.

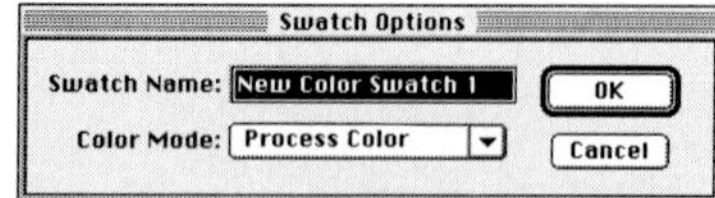

4. Name the color "New Process Color 1" and click **OK**. Observe how the color takes on the new name in the **Swatches** palette. In the **Swatches** palette, scroll to the colors that are named. These are Spot colors. Drag the color Red from the **Swatches** palette to the **Color** palette.

5. Observe how the **Color** palette changes to allow for tints of a Spot color.

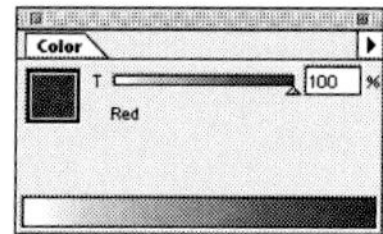

You can use tints or shades of a single color and make a piece look as if way more than that one color was used. Judicious use of tints (also called screens) is an important skill. In particular, be on the lookout for marketing materials that only use two colors — usually black and one other PMS color. They often make smart use of screens.

6. Move the slider to observe how the color swatch changes tint, and the percentage box changes its numbers. Click on the color sampler to see how these changes occur automatically. Finally, set the tint for 50%.

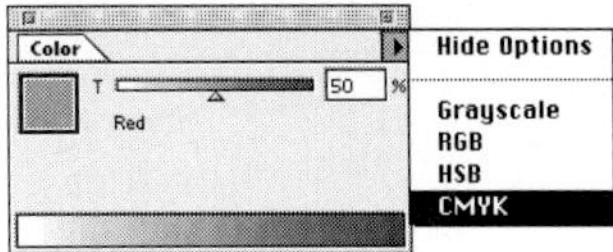

7. Imagine that you like the color you have set, but final output dictates that the color be Process. How do you do it? Simple. Click on the Options pop-up menu and select CMYK. The tint will remain as you set it, but the new Process palette will reflect the appropriate percentages.

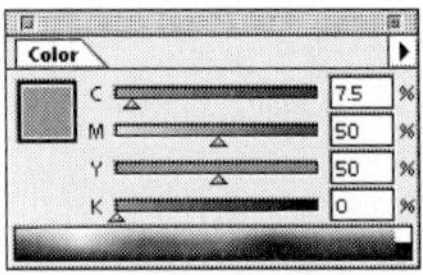

8. Go to **Edit->Undo** to undo this conversion. You will be back at the Spot Color palette. Drag its color swatch to the **Swatches** palette. You will notice that it didn't replace the original Red color. You will see two Red colors. This is because the second Red you made is a tint of the original. As long as you keep modifying the tints, you can have as many Red items in the palette as you want.

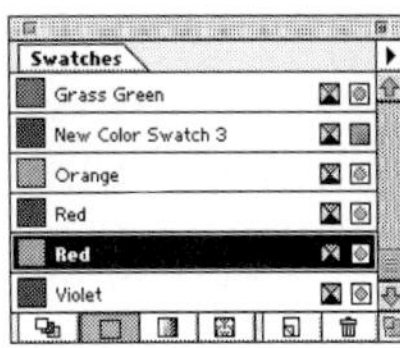

If you make many tints of a color, the name will appear many times. You should rename the tints, to avoid confusion.

9. In the **Swatches** palette, double-click on the new 50% Red tint you made. Rename the color "Red 50%."

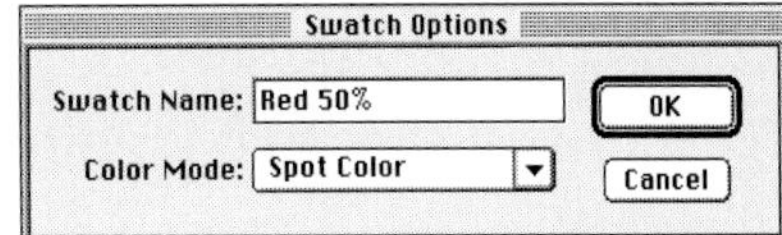

10. You want the tint to remain with its original name alphabetically. That's why the new name was not "50% Red." It would not have been listed with the original Red. Here is how the Red 50% color will appear in the list.

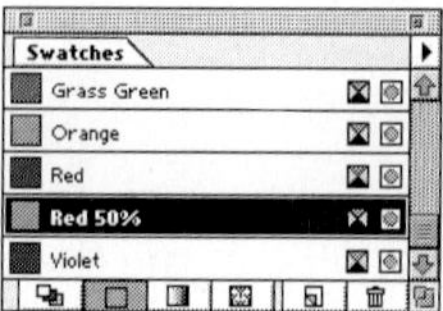

To keep any custom Process or Spot colors you make, so that they will be available whenever you use Illustrator, and without accessing libraries, you need to save the colors in the **Adobe Illustrator Startup** document.

11. With the Rectangle tool, draw a small square. In the Toolbox, click on the **Fill** box. From the **Swatches** palette, drag the Red 50% color swatch so that it touches the rectangle to paint it.

12. Use the Selection tool to select the rectangle. **Edit->Copy** it to Clipboard.

13. Use **File->Open** to go to the folder where the Illustrator 7.0 application is located. Inside this folder, you will find the folder Plug-ins, where the **Adobe Illustrator Startup** (Macintosh) or **Startup.AI** (Windows) file is located. **Open** this file.

14. In the Adobe Illustrator Startup document, **Paste** the rectangle. Now, **Save** the document and **Close** it. You will be back in your working document. **Close** it without saving.

15. Go to **File->Quit**. Once the application quits, launch Illustrator again.

16. Create a **File->New** document and go to the Swatches palette. Scroll to the Red color. You will also see your Red 50% tint.

17. Experiment with the **Color** and **Swatches** palettes to create and adjust Process and Spot colors.

18. **Close** the file without saving.

Project D: Tropical Fish

U SING G RADIENTS

C HAPTER O BJECTIVE:

To learn the methods required to create blends, or gradients, using the tools provided within Illustrator. In Chapter 14, you will:

- Take an in-depth look at the Gradient palettes and how they function.
- Learn to change the direction of a gradient.
- Learn to build gradients made up of multiple colors.
- Learn to copy and modify existing gradients.
- Learn the difference between and the application of linear and radial gradients.
- Learn how to work with gradients from the Swatches palette.

P ROJECTS TO BE C OMPLETED:

- Steaming Coffee
- Java Jungle
- Last Mango Cafe
- Tropical Fish
- **Tropical Treasure**
- **Ball & Mirror**
- Joker's Wild
- Coffee Du Jour Ad
- Tropical Treasure Mailer
- Last Mango Business Card

Using Gradients

Subtle variations in shades is a critical component in complex drawings. Shading and gradients can be used for a wide variety of effects; from realistic drawings, to subtle backgrounds, to color shifts, to special effects in type elements.

Illustrator provides specialized tools to create gradients, and you should be aware that their overuse can result in overly complex drawings that might even prove difficult to print. We mention this because it's very tempting to use gradients — since they're so easy and dramatic. Be judicious in their use.

Gradients that come standard with Illustrator are located in the **Swatches** palette (**Window->Show Swatches**). The third icon at the bottom of the palette is the Gradient icon. Click this to see small images of what the gradients look like, as well as the name (when viewed by name).

To paint your object, you drag the Gradient swatch either to the Fill icon of the Toolbox, or directly to touch the object itself.

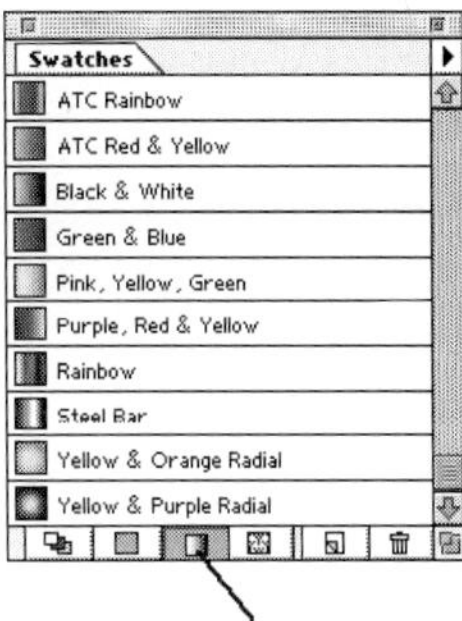

The upper-right, pop-up menu offers a variety of options to create new or delete gradients, plus choices on how they will be viewed and sorted in the **Swatches** palette.

If your intention is to reproduce your artwork with process color printing, convert all custom and spot colors to process using **Filter->Colors->Convert** to the CMYK option. This will enable all of your colors to be printed using a four-color process.

Creating Custom Gradients

Even the best selection of pre-defined blends won't meet all your needs. Here we will learn about linear and radial gradients, and how to add them to the swatch palettes.

Select **Show Gradient** from the **Window** menu to create or adjust a gradient. This window appears. When you build a gradient, you can drag the **Gradient** swatch over to the Fill icon of the Toolbox (or to the object itself) and Fill it with your new gradient.

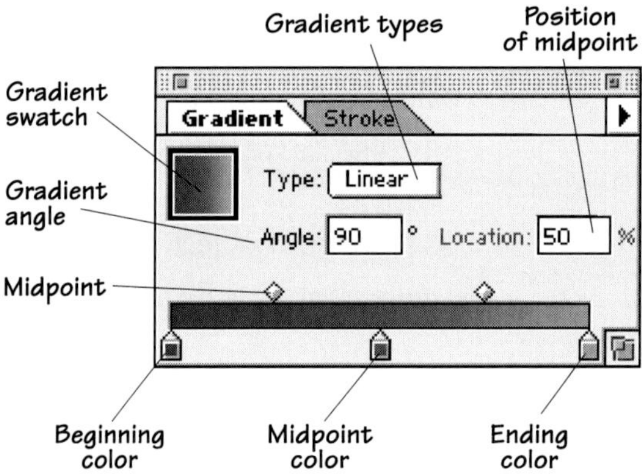

Among the many options listed to fill a path, is the **Gradient** choice. Keep in mind, though, that gradients will work only when set on the Fill swatch in the Toolbox.

When the **Gradient** option is clicked in the **Swatches** palette, the names of available gradients will appear in a list to choose from. If any gradient name is clicked, the Fill swatch will change to look like the gradient, so you can see what you are getting. The **Angle** box allows you to change the angle of the gradient.

There are only two types of Gradients:
- Linear
- Radial

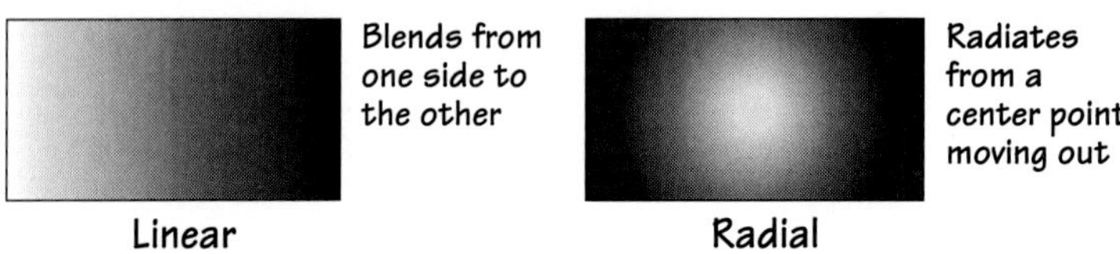

ADOBE ILLUSTRATOR: AN INTRODUCTION TO DIGITAL ILLUSTRATION/USING GRADIENTS

1. With the Ellipse tool, holding the Shift key, draw a circle.

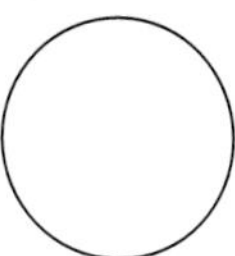

2. Draw curved paths to fit the circle, making it look like a ball. Select all the curved paths and **Object->Group** them.

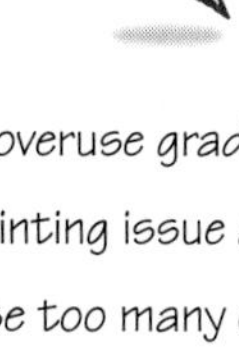

Don't overuse gradients. The printing issue aside, if you use too many of them, your artwork might look as if it was generated by computer — something you usually want to avoid.

3. Position the group of curves onto the circle to make it resemble a basketball. Paint the curves: **Fill** = None, **Stroke** = 1 pt. White.

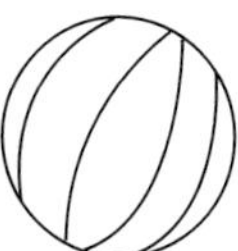

4. Click on the circle to select it.

5. Paint the circle: **Fill** = Yellow & Purple Radial gradient, **Stroke** = 2 pt. Black.

6. **Close** the file without saving.

Changing Angles and Directions of Gradients

Learning how to change the angle and direction of a blend is very important — especially when you're attempting to create shading effects. In the **Gradient** palette, the **Angle** box allows you (only on Linear gradients) to type an angle number to change the gradient's direction.

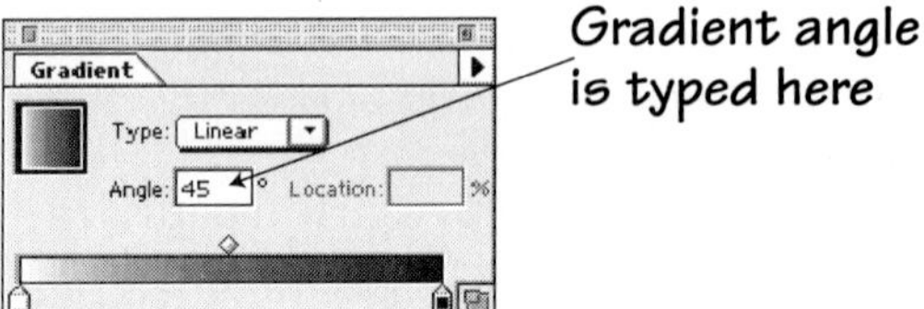

Another way to change the direction is to use the Gradient tool in the Toolbox. When an object Filled with a gradient is selected, this tool, when accessed, turns into a crosshair. It is clicked at the point where the gradient is to start, then dragged to the point where the gradient is to end.

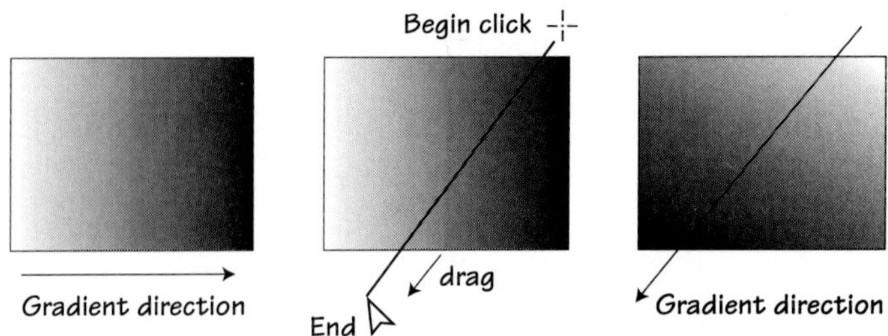

If several objects are painted individually with gradients, the tool will adjust them all from the beginning of the drag to the end.

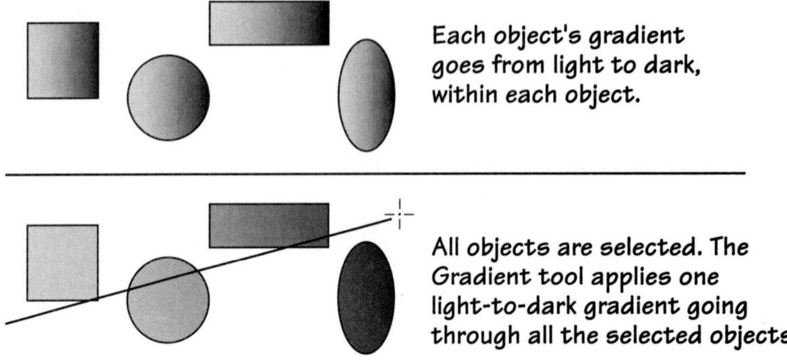

Using the Gradient Adjustment Tool

1. In **Preview** mode, draw several objects, such as squares, circles and ovals.

    Select all the objects with the Selection tool.

2. Access the **Swatches** palette.

3. **Fill** all the objects with the Black & White gradient.

4. Click on the Gradient tool in the Toolbox.

5. Select all the objects and experiment with this tool by positioning the crosshair cursor near the objects and dragging to another location on the other side of the objects.

6. Observe the effect this tool has on the selected objects and how all the gradients change to look as if one gradient were applied to them all.

7. **Close** the file without saving.

Making Gradients

Gradients are predefined "blends" that require some working knowledge of the Gradient dialog box, but are actually quite simple to make.

In earlier versions of Illustrator, Gradients were very complicated, required much knowledge of "steps" in between the colored objects, and were somewhat difficult to build.

With the Gradient window, it's possible to use many colors, but too many can complicate the final result, so keep the number of colors under five.

The **Gradient** selection is found under the **Window** menu.

If your design has many gradients in it, you might want to consider working in Artwork mode, to expedite the screen's painting. Gradients take several seconds to paint, and if you have many, it could be counter-productive waiting for the screen to view.

Creating a Simple Linear Gradient

1. Create a new document using **File->New**.

2. Access the **Gradient** palette, through **Window->Show Gradient**. Double-click on the swatch in the gradient window to see the color sliders.

3. Access the **Swatches** palette through **Window->Show Swatches**. Click on the Process color swatches icon. In the upper-right, pop-up menu, select **Name** to view the colors by name.

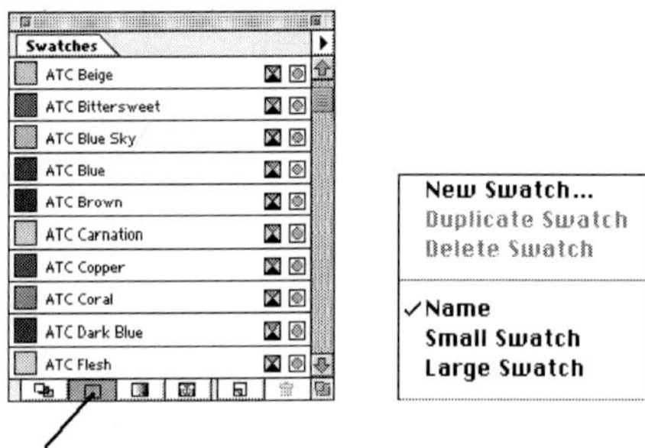

4. From the **Swatches** palette, drag the color **Blue** to the Beginning Color square.

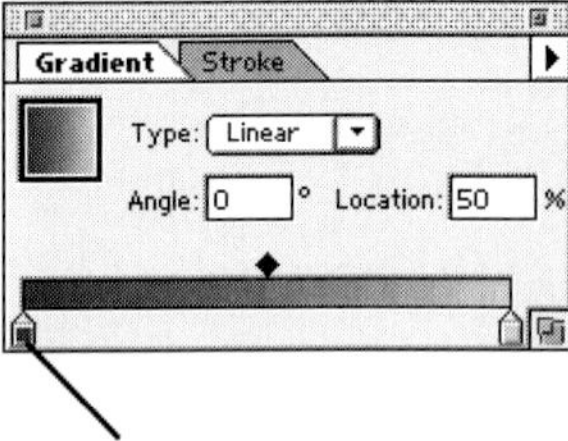

5. From the **Swatches** palette, drag the color **Yellow** to the Ending Color square. Leave the **Angle** at 0. Set the Midpoint **Location** percentage to 50%.

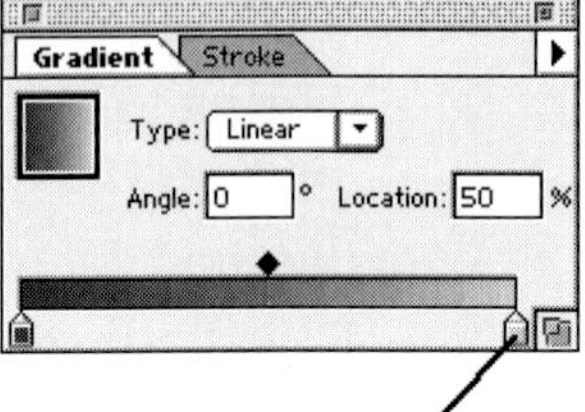

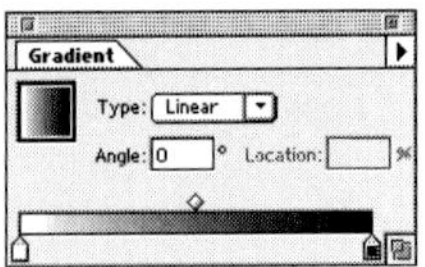

If you see no color sliders underneath the **Gradient** ramp, then double-click on the swatch in the gradient palette.

You should consider saving cool gradients. Just put them in a document, save it, and load that document if you need to use the blend in another drawing. Just copy the shape containing the gradient and paste it into your new illustration.

6. From the **Gradient** palette, drag the **Gradient Swatch** over to the **Swatches** palette. A new gradient will appear called **New Gradient Swatch**.

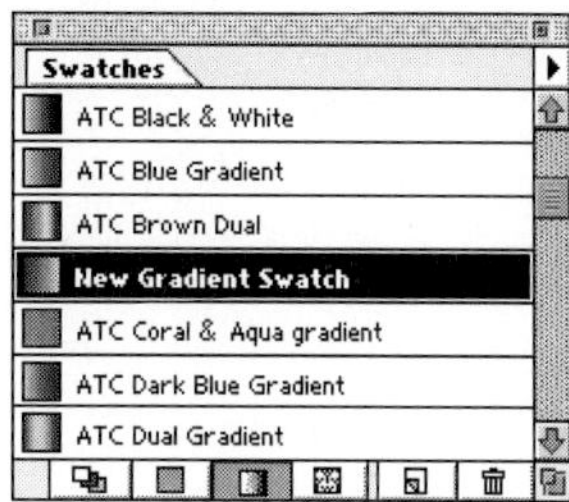

7. Double-click on the new name panel.

8. In the **Swatch Options** dialog box, change the name to "My Gradient." Click **OK**.

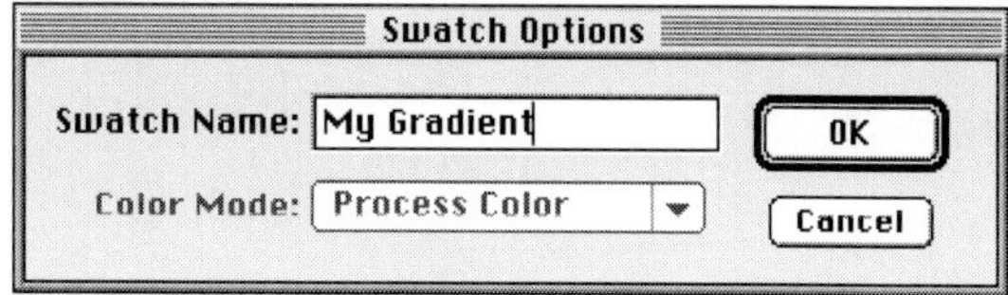

9. You have now created a custom gradient that is accessible to paint objects you draw.

10. **Close** the document without saving.

Project E: Tropical Treasure

Project F: Ball & Mirror

Notes:

TRANSFORMATION TOOLS

CHAPTER OBJECTIVE:

To learn the many functions available in Illustrator that will transform, or modify, an existing object. In Chapter 15, you will:

- Learn the four basic transformation tools: Rotation, Scaling, Reflecting, and Skewing.
- Learn how to apply them, and how they're affected by the so-called "point of origin."
- Learn to transform objects both visually and mathematically.
- Learn to transform objects sequentially to create many interesting and often-used effects.

PROJECTS TO BE COMPLETED:

- Steaming Coffee
- Java Jungle
- Last Mango Cafe
- Tropical Fish
- Tropical Treasure
- Ball & Mirror
- Joker's Wild
- Coffee Du Jour Ad
- Tropical Treasure Mailer
- Last Mango Business Card

Transformation Tools

Developing a drawing efficiently requires more than just being able to draw shapes — you have to know how to transform shapes for a variety of needs. This section covers Transformation methods — powerful tools that let you stretch, grow, shrink, rotate, and reflect the shapes you create with the geometric and Pen tools.

Transformational Basics

The transformation of objects can be done two ways:

- Manually

- Dialog Box

Manual Transforming

To manually transform a selected object means that you do the transformation by hand, pulling or moving the object to change its characteristics.

To do this requires that you click on the Transformational tool in the Toolbox, such as the Rotation tool, then move the cursor to the object and perform the necessary movements with the mouse.

Origin of Transformation

Any Transformation has to have a point of reference from which to perform its operation. Once a tool is selected, it requires an Origin of Transformation to be this point of reference.

When you click on the transformational tool in the Toolbox, the exact center of the selected object defaults as the immediate Origin of Transformation.

If you do not click another Origin of Transformation point, the operation will extend from the default point.

Beware of stray objects after transformations are made.

You can accidentally select objects you didn't wish to. Holding Shift to select is the main culprit here.

Using the dialog boxes of the transformational tools is the suggested method for transforming objects. Manually, if you drag a duplicate, and then do Transform Again several times, you might have also duplicated other objects that were selected. If they are out of view of the page, you won't catch your mistake.

Unattended objects can be off on the Artboard, in "no man's land." These objects, even though they are not on the page, will be included if you choose "Illustrator EPS" when saving. The file size, both physically and in kilobytes, will be astronomical.

If you choose to do manual transformations, do so with care.

Example:

As shown here, the square was selected and the Rotate tool clicked in the Toolbox (a.)

Then, the Origin of Transformation point was clicked for the rotation to axis around (b.).

The square was pulled on with the tool cursor (c.), which rotated it on the set Origin axis.

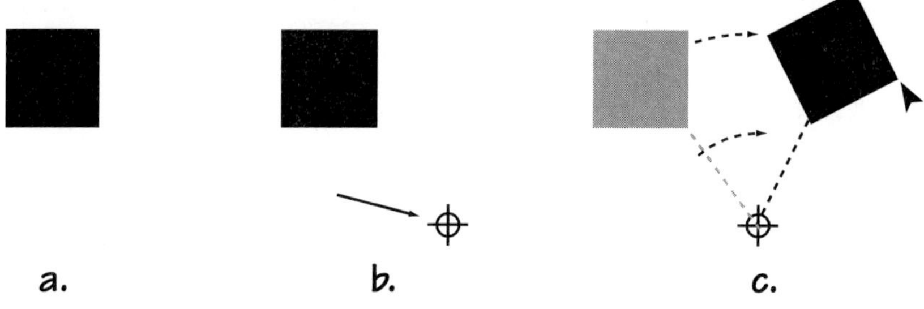

Unless you click an Origin point, the default Origin of Transformation is always the center of the selected object(s). If the default Origin point is acceptable, then you can simply select the transformation tool and drag on the object with the cursor. For quick transformations, such as scaling an object, the default Origin of Transformation works well.

As shown here, the oval was selected and the Rotate tool clicked in the Toolbox. The Origin of Transformation crosshair appeared in the default center of the object (a.). The crosshair cursor was clicked on the top of the oval to begin the manual rotation. The crosshair cursor turned into an arrow (▶) shape (b.). The oval was then dragged, which rotated it on the default center Origin point (c.).

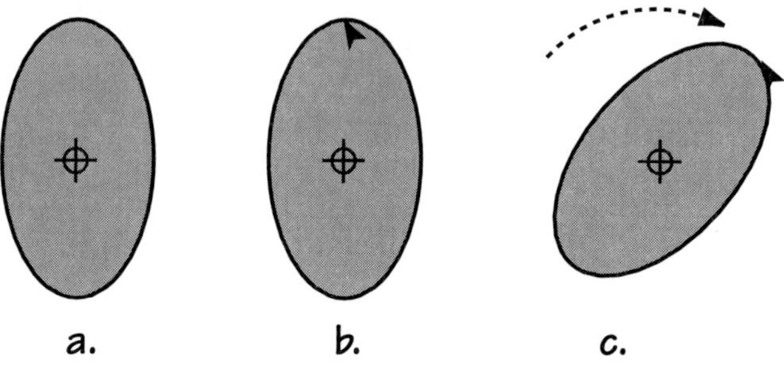

Selecting objects for transformation must be done with either the Selection tool or the Direct Selection tool.
You must hold the Option (Macintosh) or Alt (Windows) key when selecting with the Direct Selection tool, or you will only select a segment to be transformed.

The objects to be Reflected need to be selected, then the Reflect tool is selected. Holding the Option key (Macintosh) or Alt key (Windows) and clicking on the page brings up the Reflect dialog box. Here, you will choose a horizontal or vertical axis and decide if the objects will duplicate.

Dialog Box

If the Transformation tool is accessed, and the crosshair clicked on the page while holding the Option (Macintosh) or Alt (Windows) key, this will mark the Origin of Transformation to be used by the appearing dialog box. This is the preferred method of executing a transformation, given that you know the amount of transformation you wish to apply.

Each transformation dialog box has the settings for the tool that you can customize.

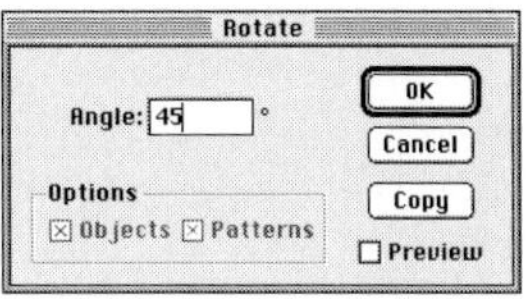
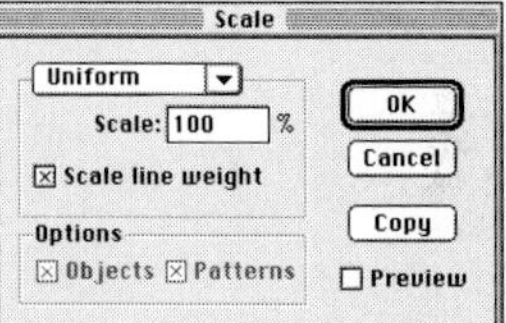
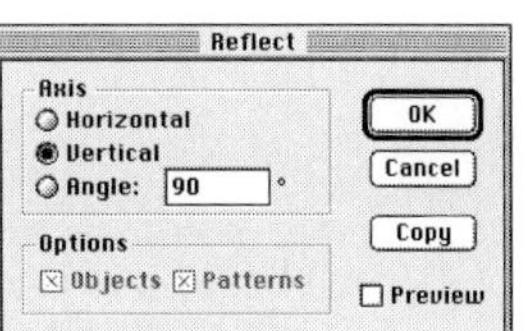
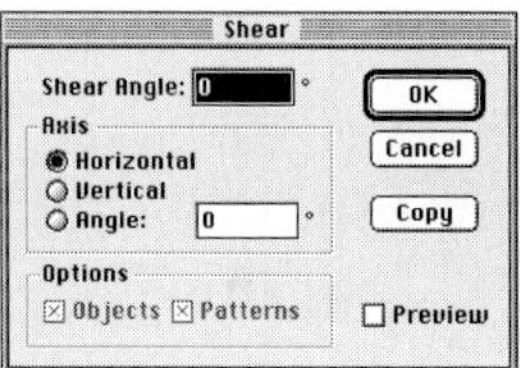

The dialog boxes can be accessed two ways.

- Double-clicking on the tool in the Toolbox

- Holding Option (Macintosh) or Alt (Windows) keys

If an object is selected, and then you double-click on the Transformational tool in the Toolbox, the tool's dialog box will appear. If you access the dialog box this way, be aware that you are restricted to the default Origin of Transformation, which is the center of the object.

If an object is selected, the tool selected in the Toolbox, and you click the crosshair on the page, while holding the Option (Macintosh) or Alt (Windows) key, you will access the dialog box. The advantage to this method is that where you click the crosshair on the page is where the Origin of Transformation will be set. Then, any settings you make in the dialog box will transform around or from this point.

Reflect

Reflecting is another word for mirroring – the technique whereby you can flip-flop an object (or a duplicate). Think of how many objects in life are shaped the same on each side and you'll get an idea of how important reflection is during the development of a design.

The Reflect tool, when clicked on the page while holding the Option (Macintosh) or Alt (Windows) key, mirrors the selected object across a Horizontal, Vertical or Angled axis when set in its dialog box. It will produce a mirrored duplicate by selecting **Copy** in the dialog box.

Holding down the Shift key as you reflect will ensure that the object reflects exactly across its own axis.

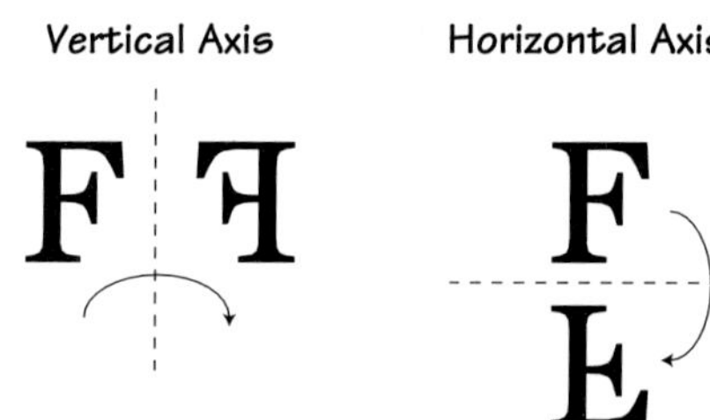

This tool is very useful in generating symmetrical components in artwork — any time you need to have one side of an illustration mirror the other.

Reflecting Objects

1. Create a **New** document using **File->New**.

2. With the Pen tool, hold the Shift key, and draw a simple 45° path. Select this object. Click on the Reflect tool in the Toolbox.

3. With the crosshair cursor, click near the base of object, holding the Option (Macintosh) or Alt (Windows) key as you do.

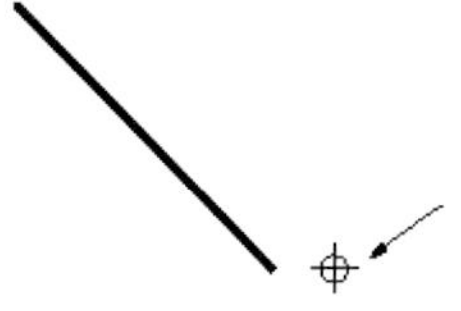

In the **Reflect** dialog box that appears, select **Vertical**, then click **OK**.

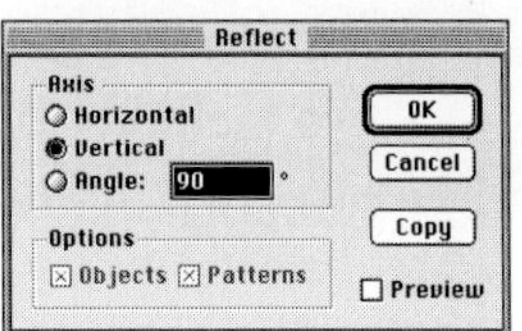

The object will flip-flop in the opposite vertical direction.

4. With the Reflect tool still selected, click near the base of the path again, holding the Option (Macintosh) or Alt (Windows) key as you do. Select **Horizontal** in the appearing dialog box. Click **OK**.

5. Double-click on the Reflect tool in the Toolbox. This will bring up the dialog box with the Origin point set for the default exact center of the path. Select **Vertical** and **Copy** in the dialog box. The duplicate will flip-flop exactly on the Origin point. You have created an "X."

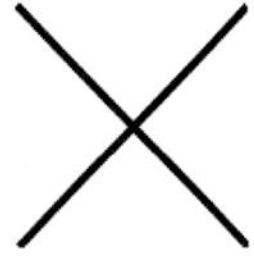

6. **Close** the document without saving.

One of the drawbacks to manually transforming an object is that you can't tell how much, in mathematical terms, that you transformed it. If you access the dialog box after doing a manual transformation, the settings in the box will reflect the action just performed.

Scale

To scale an object is to change its size, whether proportionally or not. There are two methods to scale objects. For both methods, the scaling can be **Uniform** (proportional) or **Non-Uniform**.

- Manually

- Dialog box

Manual Scaling

Think of the Origin of Transformation for the Scale tool as the vanishing point. The closer the tool cursor is moved toward the Origin of Transformation by the Scale tool, the smaller the object will become. Conversely, moving it away will make the object larger.

In this example, the flower was selected, the Scale tool clicked in the Toolbox, then the crosshair cursor clicked to set the Origin of Tranformation (A.). The cursor turned into a chevron point and was dragged at a 45° angle, holding Shift key to constrain, to scale the flower proportionally (B.) The flower was enlarged because the cursor was dragged away from the Origin point (C.).

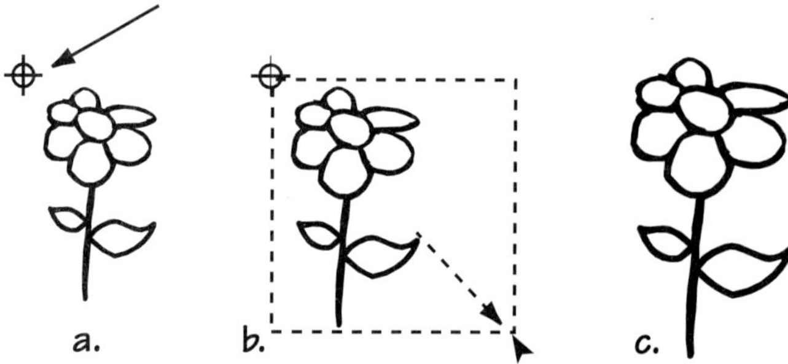

Scaling with the Dialog Box

For more precise, mathematical scalings, use the **Scale** dialog box. The dialog box is accessed by two ways:

- Double-clicking the Scaling tool icon in the Toolbox. When doing this, the Origin of Transformation defaults to the exact center of the selected object(s).

- Selecting the tool in the Toolbox, then clicking on the page while holding the Option (Macintosh) or Alt (Windows) key. When clicking on the page, you are setting your own Origin of Transformation.

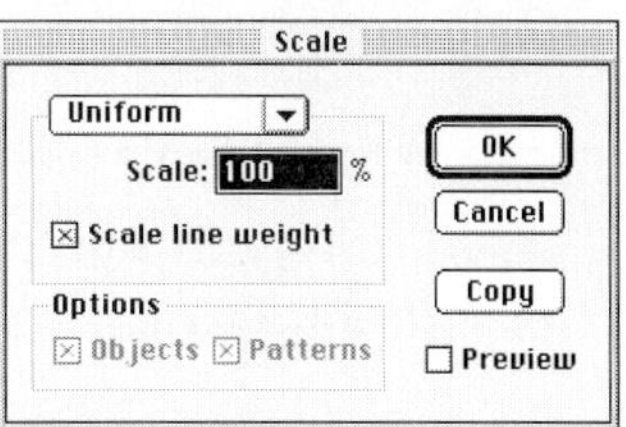

The **Uniform** pop-up menu also offers **Non-Uniform**.

In the dialog box, the percentage of the scaling is typed in. It is important to make sure that **Scale line weight** is selected to keep Stroke weights proportional. When you have set the percentage, you then click **OK**. If you want a scaled duplicate made, click **Copy**, instead.

Scaling Objects

1. Create a **New** document. With the Rectangle tool, draw a square.

2. Double-click on the Scale tool in the Toolbox. Notice that a crosshair automatically appears in the exact center of the square. The Scale dialog box will also appear. Set the scaling for **Uniform**, then type "50" in the percentage box. Click **OK**. Observe how the rectangle's reduction was concentric with the Origin point set by the crosshair.

3. Now, click the crosshair cursor next to the upper left corner of the rectangle, while holding the Option (Macintosh) or Alt (Windows) key.

You should be in the habit of holding down the shift key whenever you stretch something — unless you deliberately want to distort the object horizontally or vertically.

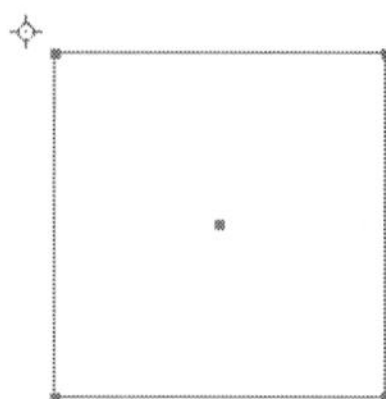

4. The Scale dialog box will appear. Set the scaling for **Non-Uniform**, and type in: **Horizontal** = 75, **Vertical** = 125. Click **Preview** and you will see the rectangle take on these dimentions. This is handy for seeing transformations before you click **OK**.

    Click **OK**.

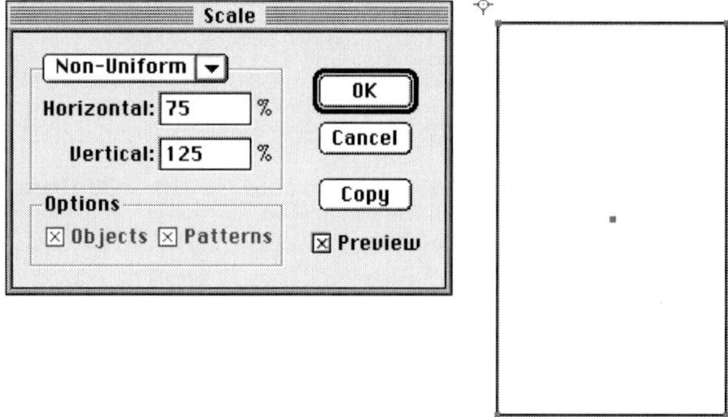

5. Click the crosshair next to the upper right corner of the rectangle (a.). Move the chevron cursor to the lower left corner (b.).

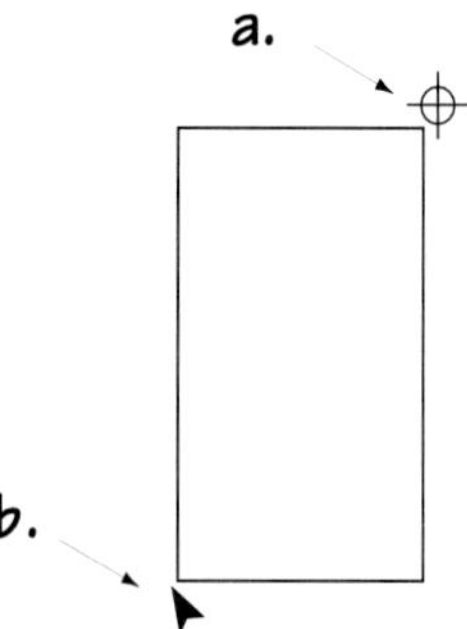

While manually rotating an object, you can duplicate the original by holding the Option (Macintosh) or Alt (Windows) key as you drag the rotation.

6. Without holding the Shift key, drag the mouse around to see how the object changes its dimensions, stemming from the Origin of Transformation set in the upper right corner.

ADOBE ILLUSTRATOR: AN INTRODUCTION TO DIGITAL ILLUSTRATION/TRANSFORMATION TOOLS

Now, hold the Shift key and observe how the scaling becomes constrained to 45° angles. This has to be used carefully when manually scaling for Uniform purposes. You have to keep control over this by visual observation while the object is scaling.

7. When you are satisfied with the manual scaling you have performed, release the mouse.

8. **Close** the document without saving.

Rotate

The Rotation of objects is sometimes one of the best shortcuts to creating other needed objects, such as rotating a square 45° to get a diamond shape.

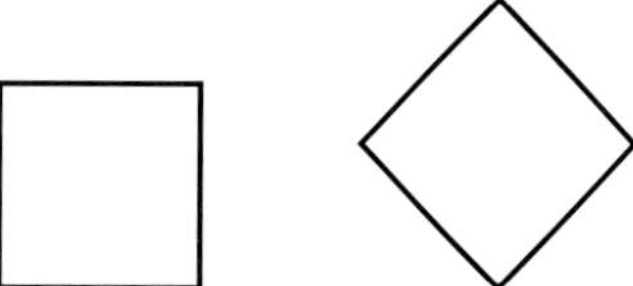

As with the other transformational tools, Rotate can be performed either manually or by dialog box.

Manually, you simply select the object, select the Rotate tool, then click-hold the crosshair on the object, and pull to rotate it around the default Origin point.

To access the dialog box, either double-click on the tool in the Toolbox, or click the crosshair on the page while holding Option (Macintosh) or Alt (Windows).

Positive numbers will rotate the object counterclockwise. Add the negative symbol (-) to create a negative number to achieve a clockwise rotation.

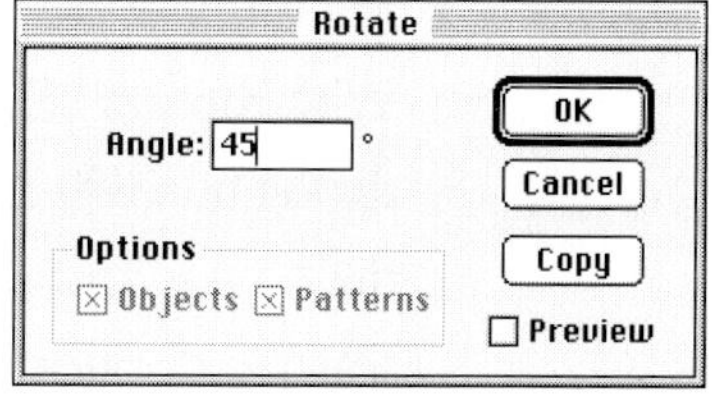

The Shift key plays a role in rotation as well. Hold it down while you're rotating, and you will constrain the rotation to 45-degree changes.

Using Rotate

1. Use **File->New** to create a new document.

2. With the Star tool, draw a star while holding the Shift key. Click on the Rotate tool in the Toolbox. The Origin of Transformation crosshair will appear in the center of the star.

3. With the crosshair cursor, click-hold on the top point of the star and pull to the right to rotate it. When you have rotated it slightly to the right, release the mouse.

Many shapes are constructed from identical objects rotated around a central point. Can you think of any shapes that are built this way?

4. **Edit->Undo** the transformation. With the star still selected, click the rotate crosshair at the lower right of the star to set an Origin point. Click the cursor on the top point of the star, and drag to rotate it. Observe as you drag how the star is rotating on the Origin point set in the lower right. When you are through rotating, release the mouse, then **Undo**.

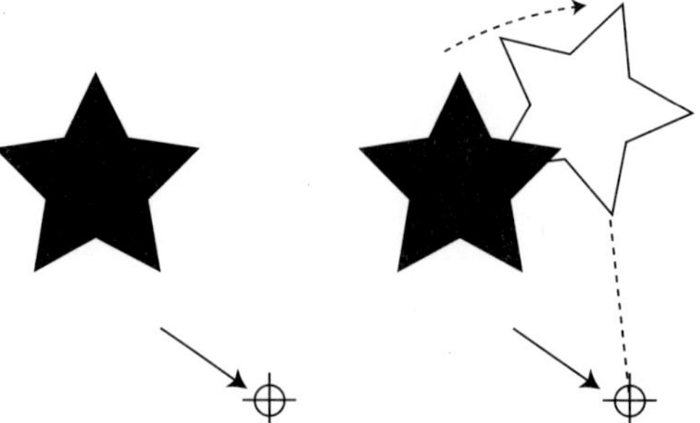

5. With the star selected, double-click on the Rotate tool in the Toolbox. The dialog box will appear. Type "45" for the angle. Click **Preview** in this dialog box and watch the selected star rotate. Press **Copy** in the dialog box watch a duplicate star appear, rotated 45˚.

6. **Undo** this rotation. Click on the Rotate tool in the Toolbox, then click the crosshair to the right of the star, holding the Option (Macintosh) or Alt (Windows) key as you click. Type 22.5 for the angle, then click **OK**.

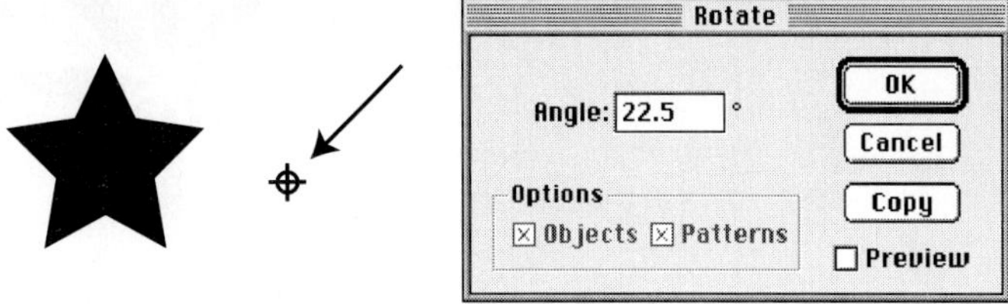

Observe how the star rotated the set angle, and around the Origin point you clicked.

7. **Close** the file without saving.

Transform Again

A designer's secret feature may be found in the **Object->Transform** menu. See **Transform Again**.

When you transform an object, **Transform Again** will repeat the transformation as many times as you press the keyboard shortcut of Command-D (Macintosh) or Control-D (Windows).

The creative aspect of this feature is limited only by the imagination.

• Rotating an oval will create a flower object.

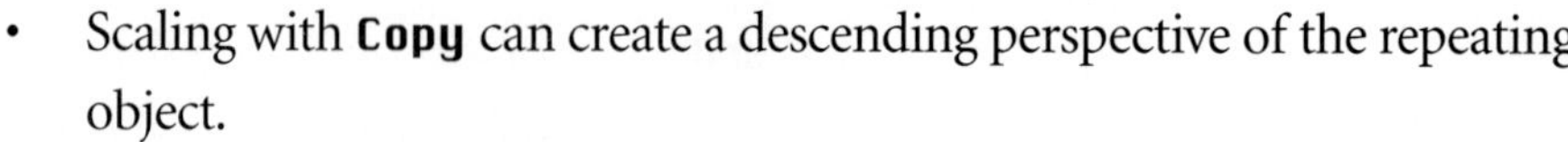

- Scaling with **Copy** can create a descending perspective of the repeating object.

- Reflecting is not a good tool for **Transform Again** because it merely goes back and forth.

- Shearing with **Copy** can create interesting designs.

Creating with Transform Again

1. Use **File->New** to create a new document.

2. With the Ellipse tool, draw an oval that is approximately 3/4-inch tall.

3. With the oval selected, click on the Rotate tool in the Toolbox; then, hold the Option (Macintosh) or Alt (Windows)key, and click just below the oval to set the Origin of Transformation. The **Rotate** dialog box will appear. Type 45 for the angle and press **Copy**.

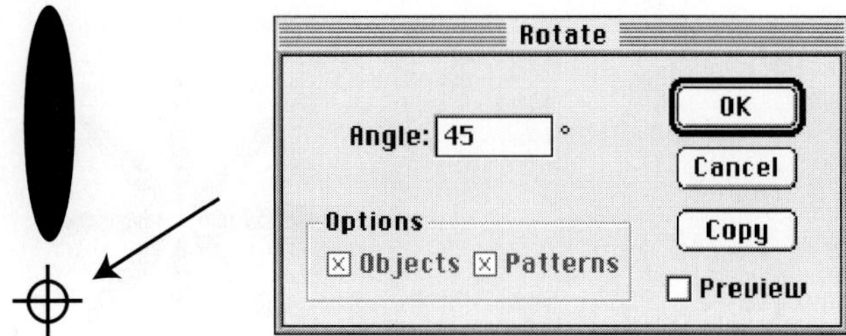

4. The oval will rotate 45° and duplicate.

5. Press Command-D (Macintosh) or Control-D (Windows) six times.

6. **Transform Again** has created a flower object.

7. **Close** the document without saving.

Shear

Shearing distorts an object, slanting it in one direction or another. It's a very important technique if you ever want to develop perspective drawings; that is, ones that contain a vanishing point. While it's not used as often as rotating, scaling, and reflecting, if you need it, it's good to know.

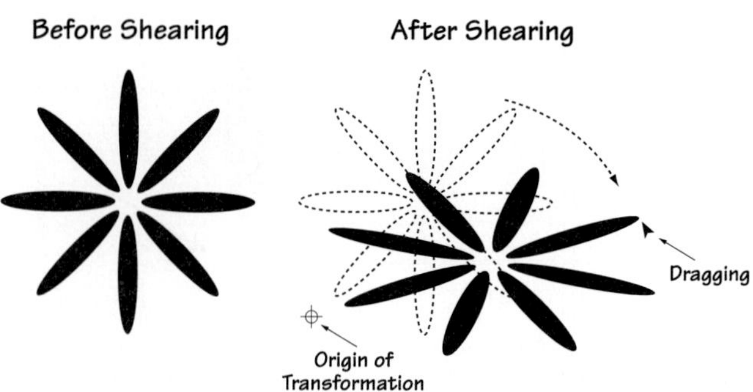

How Shearing Works

Like the other transformation tools, Shearing can be done either manually, or with the dialog box.

Manually, Shear works like the other transformational tools. For Shearing, it is of great importance where you click the Origin of Transformation, and where you drag the object to shear it. You might become quite frustrated trying to do a simple shear, and find the object skewing off into all directions.

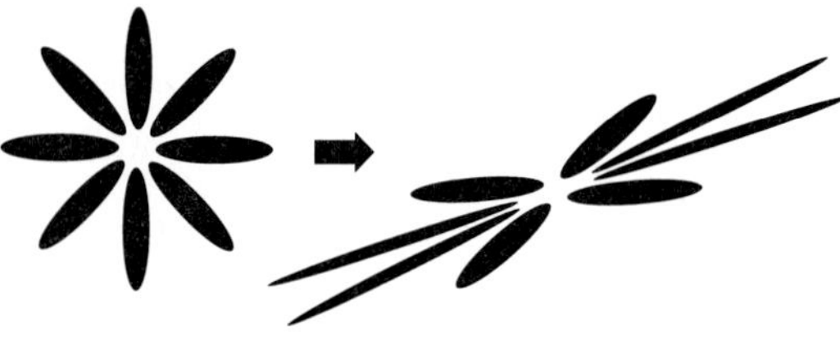

The worst location for the Origin of Transformation is in the default center of the object. If this is the Shearing axis, the erratic skewing is almost impossible to control. Be sure to set the Origin of Transformation yourself.

The best places to set the Origin point are the four corners of the Bounding Box around an object (A.) and to drag from the 90° sides of the Box (B.).

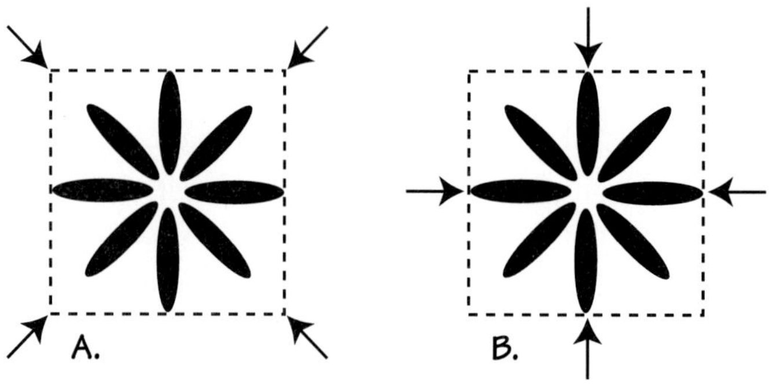

With the dialog box, the angle of the shear is typed into the designated box. It is very important to click the Shear tool crosshair where you want the Origin of Transformation, while holding the Option (Macintosh) or Alt (Windows) key. You can set the Origin point and have the dialog box for exact angles.

Shearing Text

What if you were creating a logo for a racecar company, and they wanted the letters of the name to slant in the extreme, showing speed? There is no transformation tool that accomplishes this, except Shear.

In the example below, the first text block (a.) was set as normal text. Then, with the block selected by the Selection tool, the Shear tool was clicked in the Toolbox. Using the Shear dialog box keeps the object constrained, so the angling maintains proper alignment.

In this example, the Origin of Transformation was clicked at the lower left base of the block, while holding the Option (Macintosh) or Alt (Windows) key. In the appearing dialog box, the **Angle** was set for 20% **Horizontal. OK** was then clicked (b.).

Shearing an Object

1. Open **Shearing Flower.AI** from the **SF-Intro Illustrator** folder and select the flower with the Selection tool.

2. Select the Shear tool in the Toolbox.

Shearing text can result in something that looks like italicized type, but isn't. Shearing is a good technique to simulate perspective.

3. Click the crosshair at the bottom left of the flower.

4. With the chevron cursor, pull to the right on the top part of the flower. Be careful not to pull too far. Shearing has bad "explosive" qualities when overdone.

   Observe how the Shearing affected the flower.

5. **Close** the document without saving.

Creating a Shadow with Shearing

1. Use **File->New** to create a new document.

2. Select the Type tool and click on the page. Type the word "REFLECTION." Highlight the word and, in the Type **Character** palette, set the **Font** = ATC Cozumel, **Size** = 48 pt. Press Return (Macintosh) or Enter (Windows).

REFLECTION

3. Click on the Selection tool in the Toolbox. The text will automatically be selected. Go to **View->Artwork** mode; then, go to **Type->Create Outlines**.

4. **Object->Group** all the type outlines.

5. Reflect the duplicate on a Horizontal axis in the Reflect dialog box, and click **Copy**.

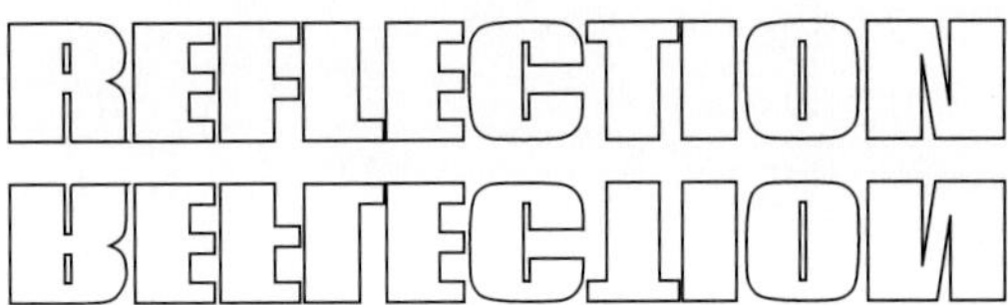

6. Select the Shear tool, and click the crosshair at the top left corner of the duplicate's "R." Drag the bottom right corner of the duplicate to Shear.

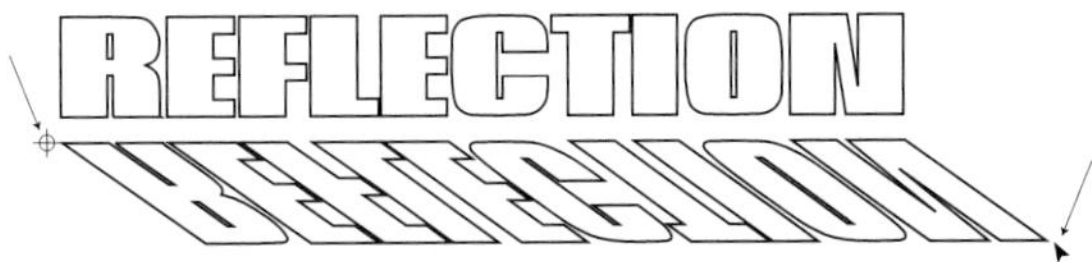

7. The idea is to shear the duplicate so as to create a shadow, as if the sun were in the far distance, shining on the original REFLECTION word.

8. When satisfied with the sheared duplicate, move it into place with the original to create the shadow effect. Paint the shadow: **Fill** = Black, White Gradient, **Stroke** = None.

9. **Close** the file without saving.

Project G: Joker's Wild

Notes:

 Adobe Illustrator: An Introduction to Digital Illustration/Transformation Tools

WORKING WITH PLACED IMAGES

CHAPTER OBJECTIVE:

To learn how to import scanned and other photographic images into the Illustrator working environment, and how to work with them once they're there. In Chapter 16, you will:

- Learn the differences between line art (also called *Vector* art) and scanned or photographic images (known as *Raster* artwork).
- Learn how to link images from one location into your drawing.
- Learn how to place various file formats into your Illustrator drawings.
- Learn to manage scanned or placed images within your drawings.
- Learn to save Illustrator documents that contain placed images.

PROJECTS TO BE COMPLETED:

- Steaming Coffee
- Java Jungle
- Last Mango Cafe
- Tropical Fish
- Tropical Treasure
- Ball & Mirror
- Joker's Wild
- **Coffee Du Jour Ad**
- Tropical Treasure Mailer
- Last Mango Business Card

Working with Placed Images

There is a lot to learn about working with scanned images. Color correction, proper scanning resolution, and a host of other technical issues all crop up when you're attempting to produce high-quality, four-color materials. While we cannot cover all of these issues here in an illustration course, it is important that you know how to incorporate scanned and photographic images into your illustrations. Whether an important, central visual, or simply a background, knowing how to get them onto the page is an important skill.

If you're going to be working on a lot of jobs that use color photographs, it's probably a good idea to study Adobe's Photoshop program — the industry standard method of manipulating digital images.

Graphic Formats

Placed images fall into two categories:

- Vector graphic (Illustrator EPS)

- Raster (Bitmapped)

A Vector graphic is created by outline paths, in programs such as Illustrator, and saved as an Encapsulated PostScript (EPS) file format. This EPS file can be placed into the Illustrator document.

Keep in mind that even though it was originally created by Illustrator, you cannot Place it and then work on it with any editing tools. Placed images can be modified with the transformational tools (Scale, Reflect, Rotate, Shear), and the images can be Masked, but you cannot access and edit its paths.

The Raster image is a bitmapped image, such as a photograph or art created in such programs as Adobe Photoshop.

Illustrator now has capabilities to **Export** a Vector graphic as a Raster image. Also, Illustrator has the Rasterize feature that will turn paths into a Raster image directly inside the Illustator document. For this to be a final Raster image, though, it must be **File->Exported.**

Placed Raster images can be transformed only with Scale, Rotate, Reflect and, Shear. They can also be Masked, and also be modified by the Rasterize feature in the Illustrator document.

Linking Placed Images

When Raster images are Placed in Illustrator, the Place dialog box automatically sets the Link button to be On. If the image is Vector EPS, the Link box will become gray to make it inaccessible. The Linking is so the Placed images can be kept track of in your documents. You can click it Off, if you don't want to deal with linkage.

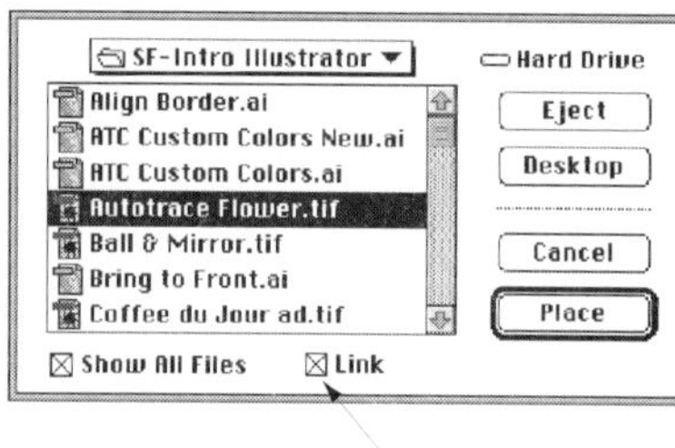
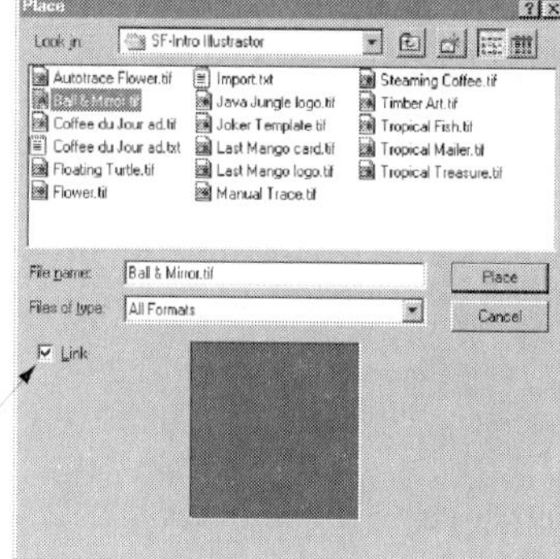

Macintosh   Windows

To see more information on the Linked images, you go **File->Document Info.** When you select it, you will see this window. The pop-up menu offers you a variety of information about the document, including **Linked Images.**

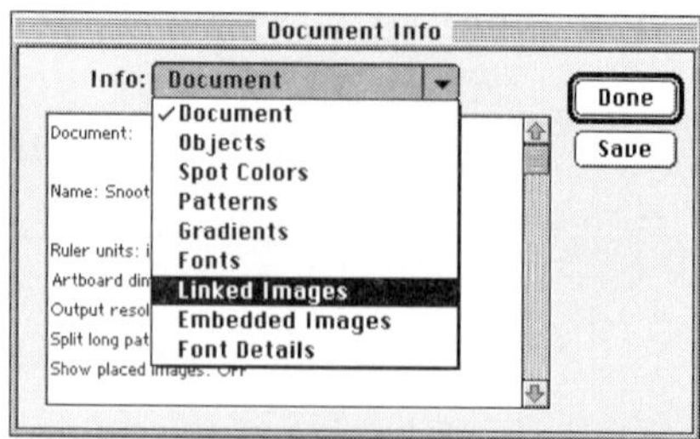

Identifying Placed Images

If you are Placing both Vector EPS and Raster images into the document, how do you tell them apart? When viewed in **Preview** mode, there is no way to distinguish between them. You have to go to **Artwork** view for the answer.

Raster Images

In **Artwork** mode, Raster images have a definite appearance. They definitely show nothing but the bounding box. To see a Raster image, you have to go to **Preview** mode.

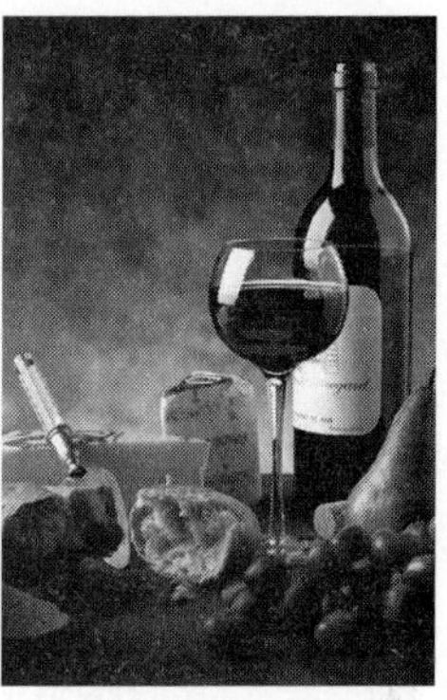

Artwork mode   Preview mode

Vector EPS Images

Vector EPS images can be seen in Artwork mode, but only if **Show Placed EPS Artwork** is clicked on in the **File->Document Setup** window

When viewed in **Artwork** mode, the Vector EPS image can be identified two ways. If **Show Placed EPS Artwork** is not clicked, all that will be seen is a bounding box with a criss-cross (a.).

If **Show placed EPS Artwork** is clicked on, a rough, 1-bit representation will be seen (b.).

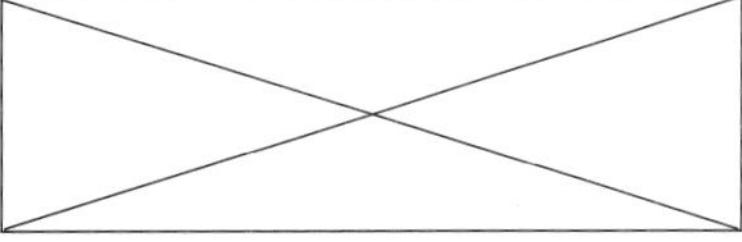

a.   b.

The most important aspect of a Placed EPS image is that the external file has to be intact for the Illustrator document to locate, when the document is reopened. Don't be misled by the **Include Placed Files** option in the EPS Format window. Including the EPS image in the file is merely to show the preview of the document when the Illustrator EPS file is placed into another program. If the **Include Placed Files** option is not clicked, the Illustrator EPS file can still be placed in other programs, but the image will appear as a gray box.

Photographic EPS Images

Photographs, and other bitmapped Raster images, can be saved as Encapsulated PostScript (EPS) format. When these are Placed in Illustrator, they look rough in **Artwork** mode, but look natural in **Preview** mode.

Artwork mode

Preview mode

Include Placed Files?

Don't be fooled by the **Include Placed Files** option when saving your document as an Illustrator EPS. The assumption most user's have is that once the image is Placed and Include Placed Files is clicked, there is no more need for the original that was placed. Some people trash it, store it, or put it in a different folder.

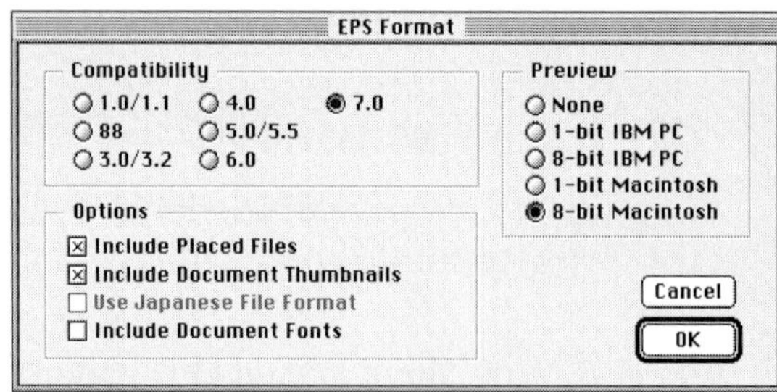

Doing the above is acceptable as long as you will never have to open the Illustrator document for modifications. If the Placed original EPS graphic has been moved from where Illustrator Placed it, you will get a warning message.

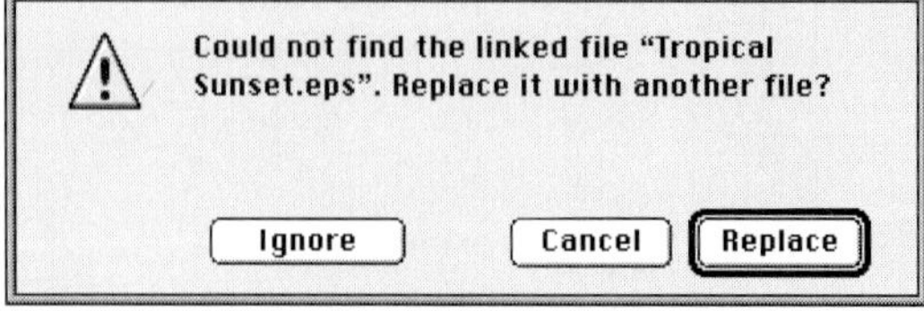

If you choose **Ignore**, the document will open, but an empty bounding box will be substituted for the missing graphic. Replace will allow you to re-link the document to the original file.

In the EPS Format window, if you do not choose **Include Placed Files**, you will get a different warning.

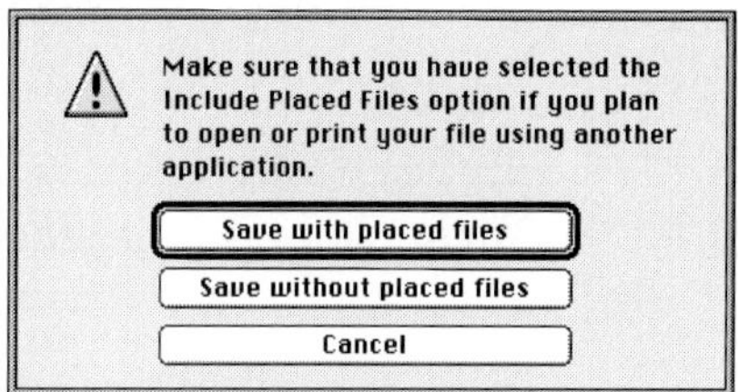

If Placed files are not saved with an Illustrator EPS, the preview image will not appear when the EPS is used in other applications such as PageMaker or Quark. You will see only a gray box.

What is the final verdict on including Placed files in your document?

> DO click on **Include Placed Files** in the **EPS Format** window.
> Better safe than sorry.

> DO NOT delete, move, or trash the original files once they are Placed and saved in the document.

The best strategy is to keep the Illustrator document and the original images in one folder. That way, if you do have to open the Illustrator document for modifications, it will instantly find the original image and not give you a warning.

Placing Several Images

If you are Placing several images in a document, then be sure to deselect the previously Placed image before going back to Place more.

If a former Placed image is selected and you try to Place another image, you will get an unexpected window.

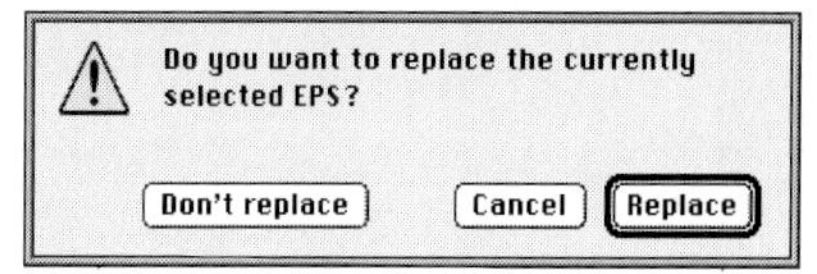

Don't replace will Place a new image in the document without affecting the previous image.

Replace will allow the image you are Placing to replace the selected image in the document.

The **Replace** option is a fast way to update images without having to **Close** the document, then reopen it for updating.

Placing Images into Illustrator

1. Go to **File->New** to create a new document. In **File->Document Setup**, click on **Show Placed EPS Artwork**.

2. Go to **View->Preview** mode. Use **File->Place** to go to the **SF-Intro Illustrator** folder and **Place** the TIFF graphic, **Tropical Sunset.TIF**.

3. Deselect the image and go back to **File->Place->SF-Intro Illustrator** and Place the image **Tropical Sunset.EPS**. Move this Raster EPS file to the right of the previous image, so they are side by side.

4. Go to **View->Artwork** mode and observe how the images change.

5. Deselect the images. Go to **View->Preview** mode.

Placing scanned images into Illustrator drawings adds an entirely new element to the drawing process. Some things just can't be drawn, no matter how good you are. Mixing scans and drawings can result in very powerful and professional artwork.

6. Use **File->Place->SF-Intro Illustrator** to **Place** the Vector EPS file, **Tropical Treasure Logo.EPS**.

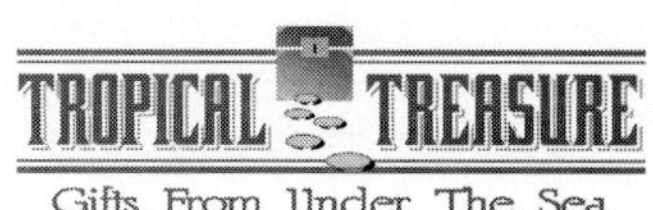

7. Go to **View->Artwork** mode to see how the image looks in that view. Go back to **View->Preview** mode.

8. Select the logo with the Selection tool. Double-click on the Rotate tool in the Toolbox. In the dialog box, type 45 for the angle. Click **OK**.

9. Double-click the Scale tool and type 50 for **Uniform** scale in the dialog box. Click **OK**. This is to show you how Placed images can be transformed.

10. Go to **File->Document Info**. In the appearing window, click on the pop-up menu to access the **Linked Images** option.

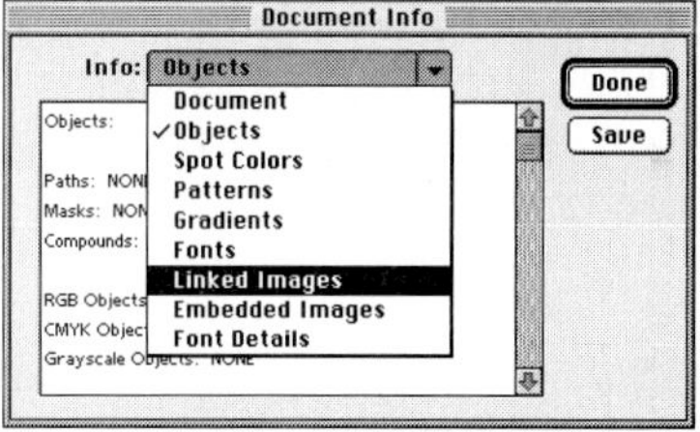

11. Observe how the images are listed. Scroll through the listing to read all the information about the images.

12. **Close** the file without saving.

Project H: Coffee Du Jour Ad

Notes:

 Adobe Illustrator: An Introduction to Digital Illustration/Working With Placed Images

MANIPULATING OBJECTS

CHAPTER OBJECTIVE:

To learn some of Illustrator's more advanced features to control, modify, and manipulate objects and to refine your drawings. In Chapter 17, you will:

- Learn how to lock, unlock, hide, and show objects within a drawing.
- Learn how to create groups of objects that act as if they were a single element.
- Learn how to modify individual elements within a grouped selection.
- Work with precision alignment tools that will allow you to align and distribute objects in a wide variety of ways.
- Learn how to use palettes to apply modification and transformation functions to a selected object.

PROJECTS TO BE COMPLETED:

- Steaming Coffee
- Java Jungle
- Last Mango Cafe
- Tropical Fish
- Tropical Treasure
- Ball & Mirror
- Joker's Wild
- Coffee Du Jour Ad
- **Tropical Treasure Mailer**
- **Last Mango Business Card**

Manipulating Objects

Drawings can get complicated, and as they develop, objects that are lying around the page can really get in the way sometimes. After objects are created and positioned on the page, they could be obscuring other objects that need modifications.

Locking

Objects can be locked and unlocked, and when locked, are impervious to any changes you might make on surrounding elements. You can lock certain elements, select everything else on the page, and change or transform them without affecting the locked items.

At times, clicking on a path is not easy because points and segments of another path may get in the way. The **Object->Lock** option freezes the offending path so it cannot be selected, even though it's still visible. Choose **Object->Unlock All**, to make all **Locked** paths accessible again.

Using Locking

1. Create a **New** document. With the Rectangle tool, draw three rectangles.

2. Click on the middle rectangle and **Object->Lock it.**

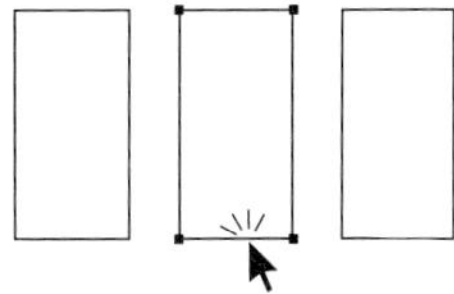

3. Marquee the rectangles with the **Selection** tool to select them.

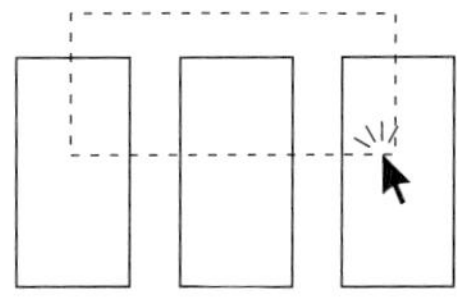

Although you can **Lock** several objects in sequence, one after another, to **Unlock** any single object in a group of Locked objects is impossible. The **Unlock All** option releases all Locked objects at once.

Although you can **Hide** several objects in se-quence, one after another, to **Show** any single object from a Hidden group is impossible. The **Show All** option releases all Hidden objects at once.

4. The locked path will not be selected. Go to **Object->Unlock All**. The rect-angle will again be accessible.

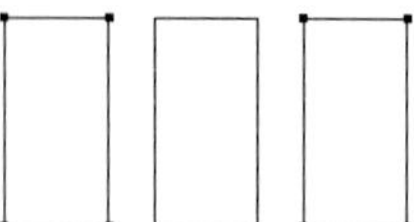

5. Keep this file open for the next exercise.

Hiding

By hiding things, they totally disappear from the page — out of the way and out of sight. They can easily be recalled though, with a click of the mouse. The **Object->Hide** option removes the selected object from view. It's still present and in position, but invisible.

With **Object->Show All**, all hidden objects become visible again. Also, if the document is **Closed** while objects are hidden, they will automatically show when the document is opened again.

Hiding an Object

1. In the same document, click on the middle rectangle to select it.

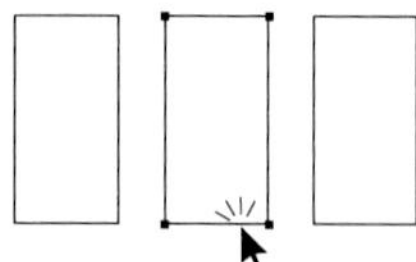

2. Go to **Object->Hide**.

3. The object will disappear from view, yet will still be present.

Objects can be grouped, then independent groups can be grouped with other groups. As many times as the Group command is used, that is how many times Ungroup will have to be used to go back to the beginning of the Grouping process.

Also, it is sequential. Whatever was the first Grouping in a series will be the last to be Ungrouped as you reverse the process.

4. Go to **Object->Show All**. The hidden rectangle will return to view and still be in position.

5. **Close** the file without saving.

Grouping

Complex components are often built of several different elements. Grouping lets you take a selection of objects and turn them into one component. Here we will learn how to group and ungroup objects, and how the Direct Selection (Hollow-Arrow) tool can change elements even within a group.

If you're spending too much time selecting many of the same paths to transform them together, then combine them with **Object->Group**. Once the objects are grouped, simply click on any member of the group with the Selection tool and you'll select them all. To release all the objects from the group, select **Object->Ungroup**. If you need to select only one object in a group, use the Direct Selection tool.

Using Group

1. Create a **New** document. Draw several objects such as these.

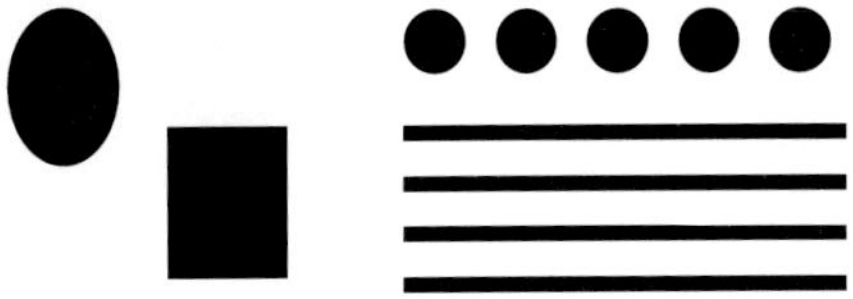

2. Marquee the objects with the Selection tool. Press Command-G (Macintosh) or Ctrl-G (Windows) to **Group** them.

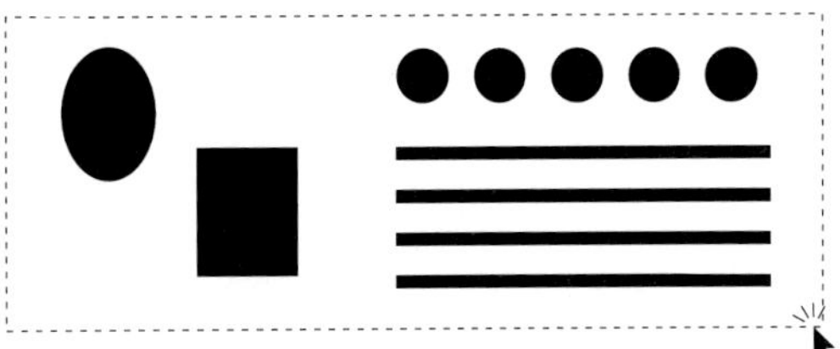

3. Click on one object in the group with the Selection tool. All objects will be selected. Remember, the Direct Selection tool allows selection of a single object.

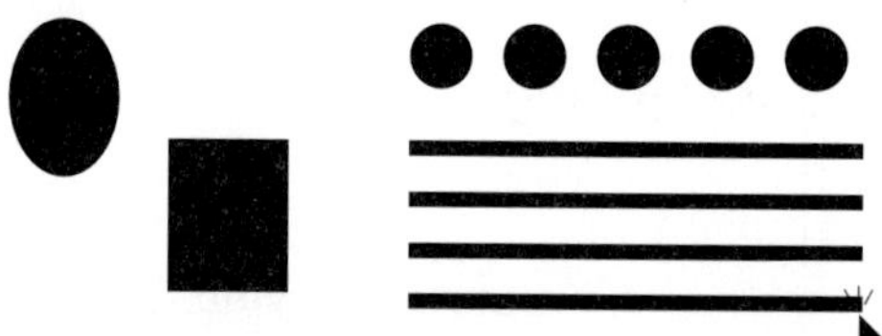

4. **Close** the document without saving.

Working With Front/Back

As you draw objects, they maintain the order in which you drew them. Draw a square, and draw a circle on top of it, and it covers the object behind it. Here we will learn how to control the stacking order of elements: which item is in front, which is in back, and how to move objects up one level at a time.

If a Filled object is on top of (in Front of) another object, it can ruin the effect you are trying to achieve. Here is an example:

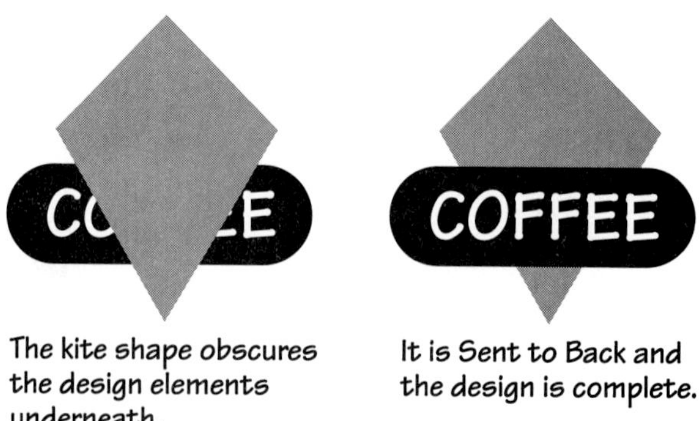

The kite shape obscures the design elements underneath.

It is Sent to Back and the design is complete.

The objects selected can be maneuvered to eliminate the interference by using **Bring To Front** or **Send To Back** found in the **Object->Arrange** menu.

Keep in mind that any new objects that are drawn are immediately in Front of everything else in the design, if they are all on the same layer.

1. Open **Bring to Front.AI** from the **SF-Intro Illustrator** folder. Observe the objects with **View->Preview.**

2. Go to **View->Artwork** so that you can see the path outlines.

3. Select the kite-shaped object, and **Object->Arrange->Send to Back.**

4. Select the Coffee text and **Object->Arrange->Bring to Front.**

5. Go to **View->Preview.** Observe the objects again.

6. **Close** the file without saving.

Arranging Objects

Sometimes you'll need to align the bottoms of objects; other times the tops. You might even find yourself needing to align the centers or sides of different elements.

Under the **Window** menu you will find several tools and palettes that can aid you in performing your drawing skills with greater speed and accuracy. Here are two of these options.

Aligning and Distributing Objects

Keep in mind that each alignment occurs immediately when selected and is cumulative. For example, aligning all the objects on their left edges, then on their top edges will pile them all up into a stack.

Designs with several objects that need to be moved so they line up in an orderly pattern are time-consuming to construct. This is because moving and measuring, combined with maintaining alignment, is a tedious process. It would be simpler to select the objects and say, "Line up to the left."

In a manner of speaking, this is actually what you can do to objects when using the **Show Align** option found under the **Window** menu. Both **Align Objects** and **Distribute Objects** are accessed under **Show Align.**

These many alignment options are quite handy and can save quite a bit of time. To use this function, simply select the objects that need alignment, go to the **Align** palette, and click on the appropriate button that aligns or distributes the objects.

The alignment of objects in a design is critical to the nature of the work. In final output, any discrepancies in spacing or alignment become too apparent.

The **Align** palette selections look like this:

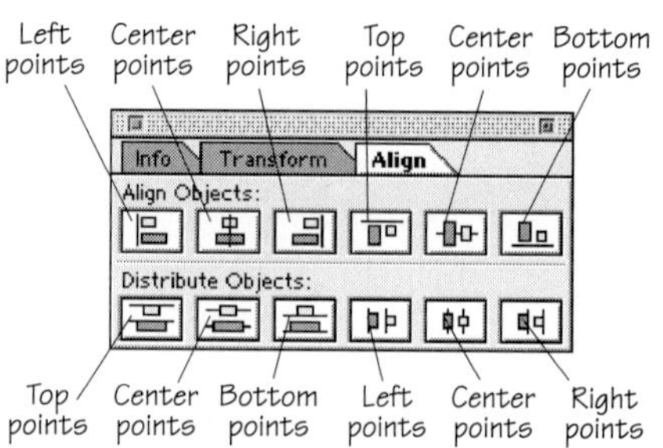

Here are descriptions of the **Align** and **Distribute** sections of the palette.

Aligning objects is much easier using the alignment tools than it is by eye. At the very least, you should use guides to make sure that something is lined up. Just looking at the screen isn't accurate enough.

Align Objects

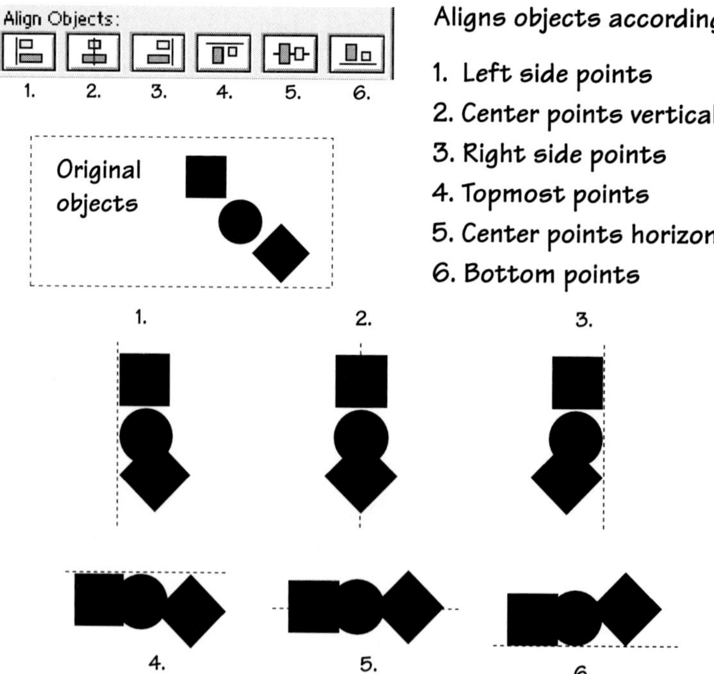

Aligns objects according to their:

1. **Left side points**
2. **Center points vertical**
3. **Right side points**
4. **Topmost points**
5. **Center points horizontal**
6. **Bottom points**

If you accidentally align a group of objects incorrectly (for example, they all wind up on top of each other), just undo the process and try again.

Distribute

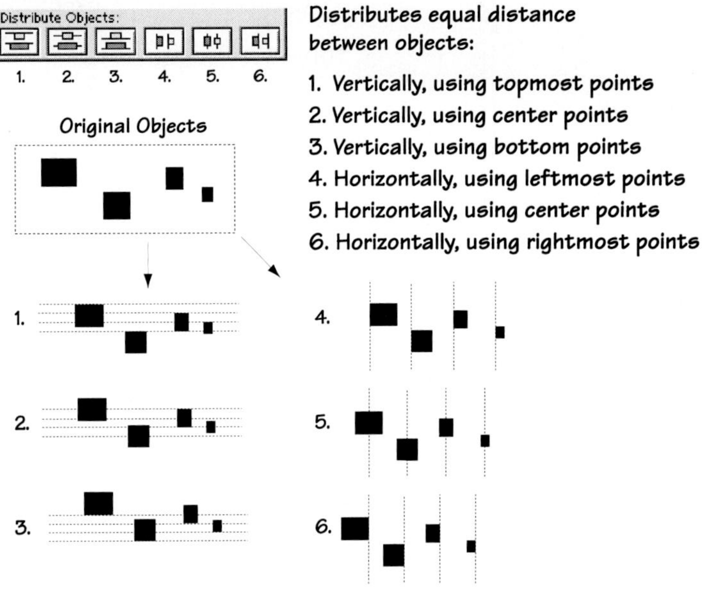

Aligning and Distributing Objects

1. Go to the **SF-Intro Illustrator** folder and **Open** the document **Primitive Objects.AI.** Scroll to the four geometric objects and select them all. Their center points are highlighted the purposes of this exercise.

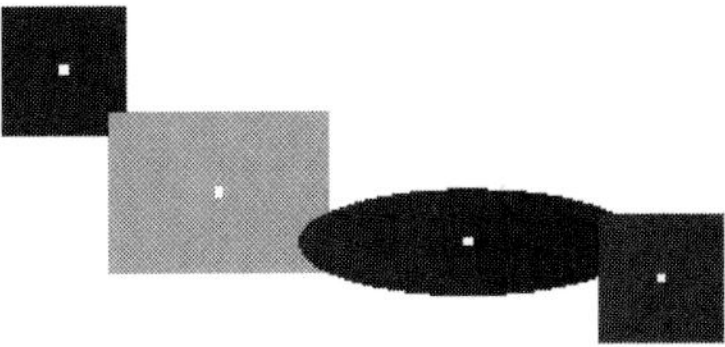

2. Go to **Window->Show Align.**

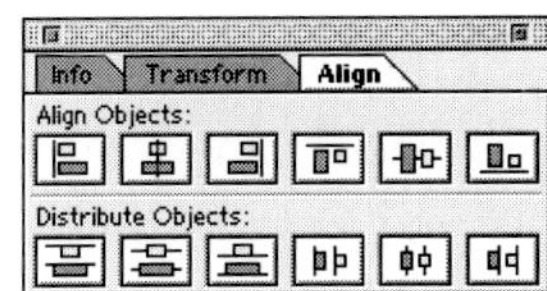

3. Experiment with the many options to get an idea of how the objects are aligned and distributed. Use **Undo** and **Redo** to go back and forth after an alignment is done. It will give a better visual understanding of how the objects were changed. This is important because the changes are sometimes very slight.

    In many cases you will not see much of a change. Drag guides to mark the edges and center points of the objects and you will see more clearly how they were arranged.

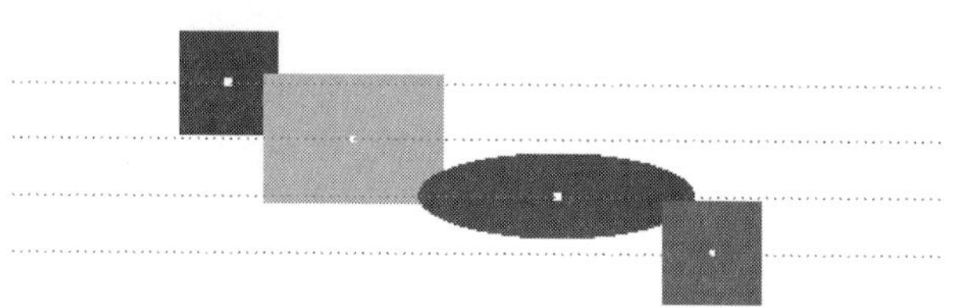

4. **Close** the file without saving.

Precision Alignment Techniques

Earlier in the course, we discussed how to use Illustrator's rulers — how to set them and how to move them onto the page. Let's build on this knowledge and focus on some very accurate methods for measuring and positioning items on the page.

There are times when two or more identical objects need to be positioned exactly on top of each other. However, what is seen on the screen is very seldom the exact alignment. How does one truly know that the alignment of the objects is exact and precise? There are several methods, but here are two quick ones.

- Manual alignment

- Paste In Front and Paste In Back

Some drawings — like technical or scientific illustrations — have to be very accurate. Fortunately, Illustrator provides you with the methods to accomplish the most demanding positioning and alignment techniques.

Manual Alignment

When aligning objects by hand, the cursor is the identifying piece. The cursor, when moving the object, is solid (a.). When the point you drag is perfectly in alignment with another anchor point, the cursor becomes hollow (b.). This works only when **Snap to point** is selected in **Preferences -> General.** Be sure this is clicked before using this technique.

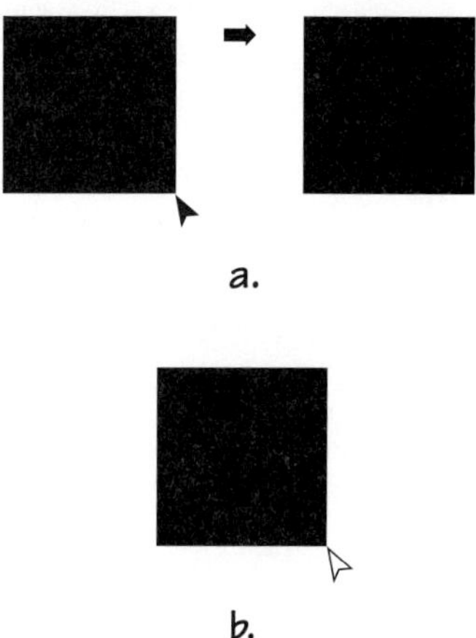

a.

b.

Paste in Front, Paste in Back

When an object needs a duplicate aligned in its same position, it is possible to **Copy** the original, then use either **Edit->Paste in Front** or **Edit->Paste in Back.** These two operations will paste the copied object exactly in alignment, either in front or in back of the original.

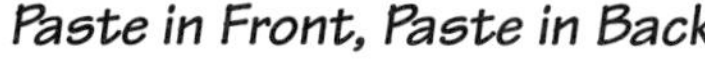

Using Alignment Techniques to Create a Design

1. In the **SF-Intro Illustrator** folder, **Open** the document **Align Border.AI.**

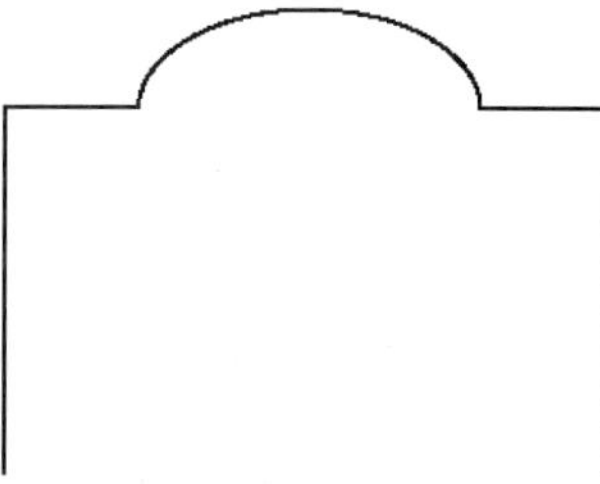

2. Go to **View->Artwork** mode. Select the object. Double-click on the Reflect tool in the Toolbox. In the dialog box, select **Horizontal** and press **Copy**.

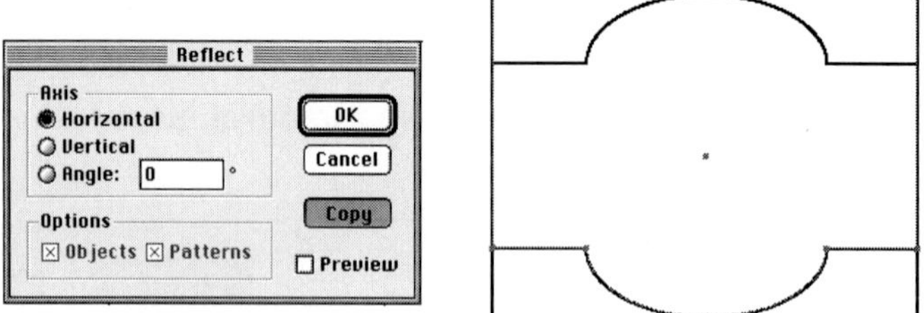

3. With the Selection tool, pull the duplicate downward until the ends meet in the middle, between the two paths.

4. Select the two right side anchor points with the Direct Selection tool, and **Join** them. Select the two left side anchor points and **Join** them. You now have one closed path.

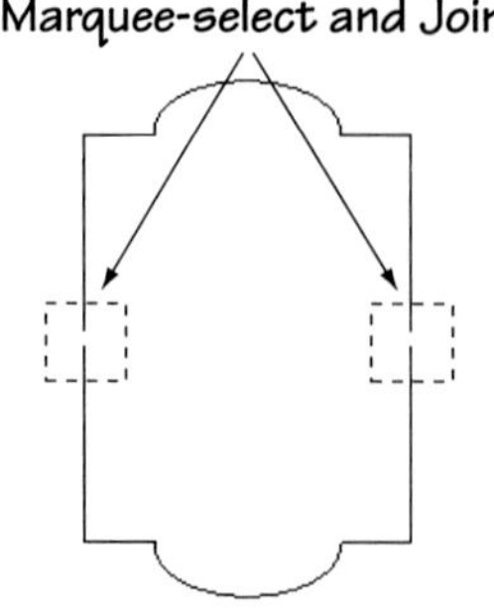

5. Paint the path: **Fill** = Black, **Stroke** = 12 pt. Black.

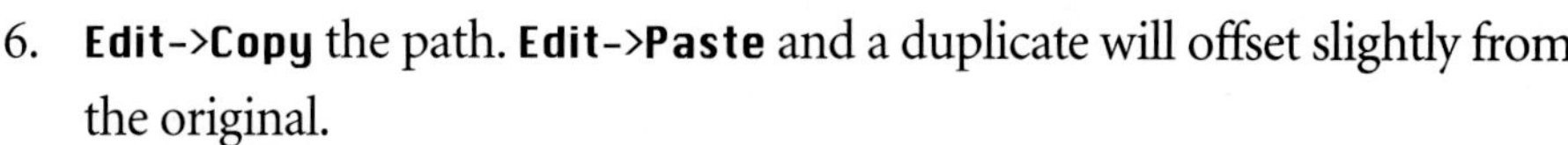

6. **Edit->Copy** the path. **Edit->Paste** and a duplicate will offset slightly from the original.

7. Go to **File->Preferences->General** and click on **Snap to Point**. This must be on for the following alignment procedure. Click **OK**.

   With the Zoom tool, zoom in on the upper left corner of the path. With the Selection tool, click-hold on the upper left anchor point and move it down slightly. After you move the object, the cursor will turn into a solid arrowhead shape (▶).

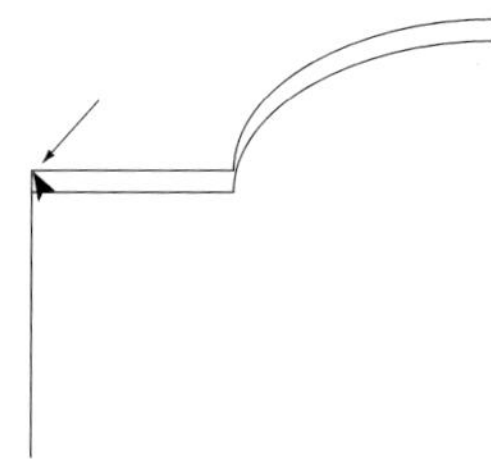

8. Hold the Shift key to constrain the moving object as you bring it down to match exactly on the original path. When the two have come into exact alignment, the cursor will become hollow (▷).

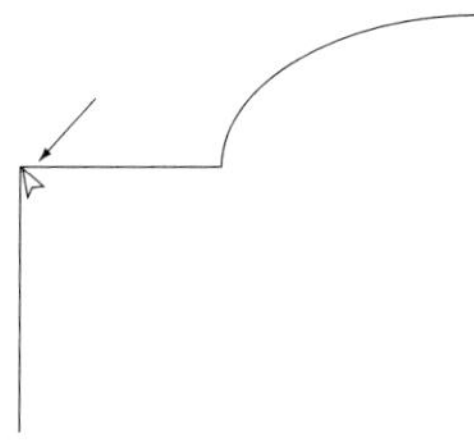

9. Even though you have aligned the two with this method, we will show you another way to achieve exact alignment. Delete the duplicate you just moved.

10. Select the original path. **Edit->Copy** the object, then **Edit->Paste in Front**. This will paste the duplicate exactly in front of the original, with perfect alignment. Keep it selected.

11. The dashed border is created in a very different way. The dashes are Stroked with a dashed line. Paint the selected duplicate: **Fill** = None, **Stroke** = 2 pt. Yellow.

    The unique way to create the dashed border is to make the **Stroke** a dash style with rounded caps. Apply these settings to the Yellow **Stroke**:

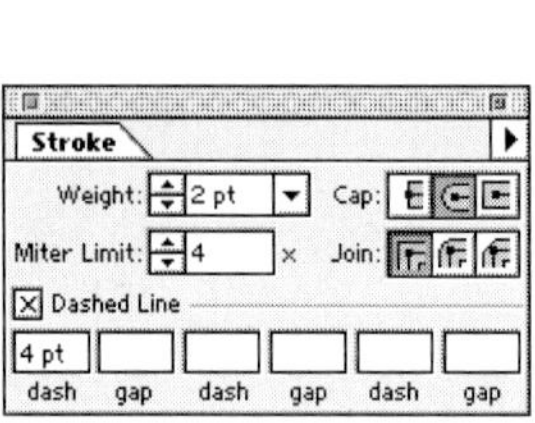

12. The background border is complete. Select the two objects and **Object ->Group** them. Go to **Object-Lock** to lock the group.

13. You will now create type on the design. Select the Type tool, then click the tool on the middle of the background border. Type the words:

    Now Appearing in the Banana Boat Lounge

    BAGGY GATOR and his Rock-a-billy Rats

    With the cursor in the text block, **Edit->Select All** the text. Press Command-Shift-C (Macintosh) or Control-C (Windows) to Align Center.

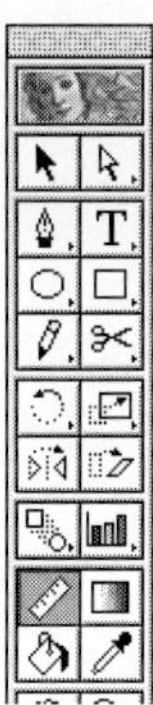

14. Highlight "Now Appearing in the Banana Boat Lounge." Access the **Type ->Character** palette and make these settings: **Font** = ATC Margarita Bold, **Size** = 32, **Leading** = 35.5. Press Return (Macintosh) or Enter (Windows) to apply the settings.

15. Highlight "BAGGY GATOR and his Rock-a-billy Rats." Apply these settings: **Font** = ATC Margarita Bold, **Size** = 40, **Leading**, 43.5, **Tracking** = -40. Press Return (Macintosh) or Enter (Windows) to apply the settings.

16. Highlight all the text and paint it: **Fill** = White, **Stroke** = None. The text block should be on the background border, but has not been aligned yet.

    Go to **Object->Unlock** to unlock the background border. Press Command-A (Macintosh) or Control-A (Windows) to **Select all** of the objects.

17. From the **Window** menu, choose **Show Align**. Click the Vertical Centering icon under Align Objects to center both the type and the border.

There are times when the info palette is invaluable in determining very accurate effects. At other times, it just takes up space. If you don't use a particular palette, put it away by clicking in the small close box in the upper left hand corner of the window.

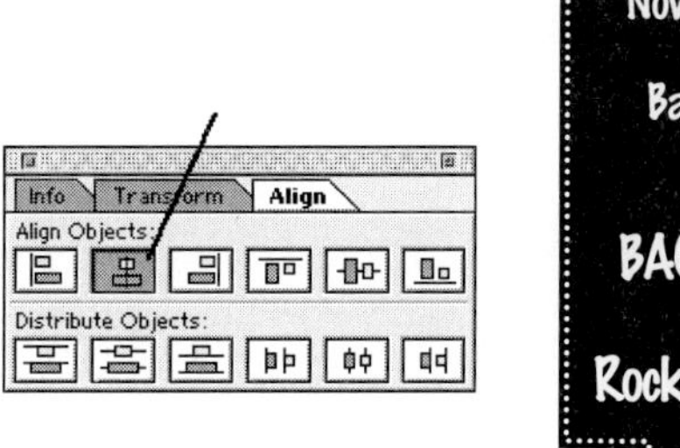

18. **Save As** the document in **Illustrator** format, naming the file "Baggy Announcement.AI." **Close** the document.

The Info Palette

Knowing distances, X/Y positions, angles, width, height and scaling is important in certain situations.

The **Info** palette gives these figures in its window. There are two ways to access the palette. You can go to **Window->Show Info**, or one click on the Measure tool in the Toolbox, then click the crosshair on the page.

Scale Info   **Shear Info**   **Rotate Info**

The information it shows is:

- X and Y position of the object or the cursor on the page. The object's X/Y location is determined by the upper left corner of the object.

- Width and height dimensions of the object.

- Distance between clicks when the Measure tool is selected and the crosshair cursor is clicked on two points.

- Angle of rotation as an object is being rotated, or when the Measure tool is clicked on two positions.

- Scaling percentage.

- Shearing angle.

1. Create a **File->New** document. With the Rectangle tool, draw a 2" square.

2. Select the Measure tool, then click the cursor on the page. The **Info** palette will appear.

3. Move the square around the page with the Selection tool. While moving, observe how the X/Y position changes in the palette. The "D:" shows the distance of the move, and, to its right, the angle the square was moved.

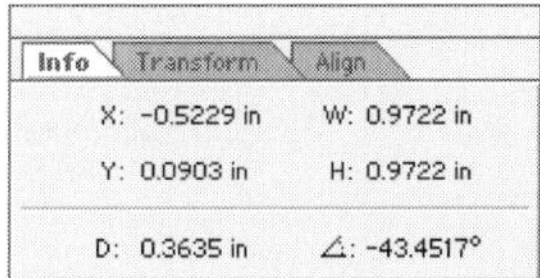

4. With the square selected, access the Rotate tool. Click on the square's upper right point and manually rotate the square. Observe how the rotation angle changes in the palette as you rotate.

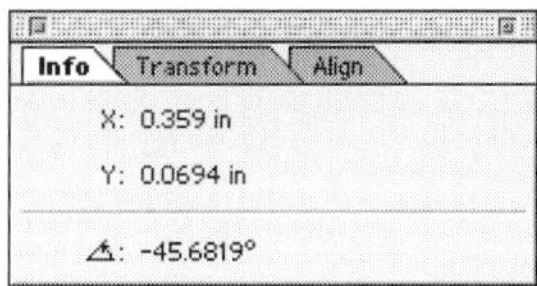

5. With the square selected, double-click on the Scale tool. In the dialog box, select **Non-Uniform** with **Horizontal** = 105, **Vertical** = 75. Click OK. Observe how these figures appear in the **Info** palette.

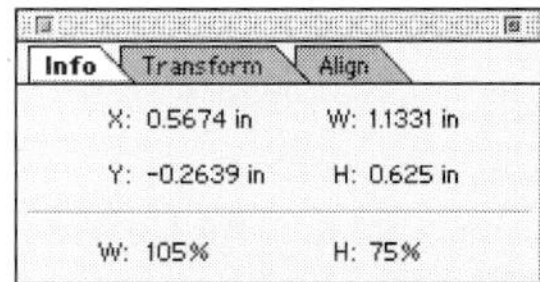

6. Select the Measure tool in the Toolbox. Click on the square's lower left corner point, then the upper right corner point. Observe the **Info** palette after clicking. It will show the distance between clicks, and the angle the tool was moved for the second click.

7. **Close** the document without saving.

The Transform Palette

The **Transform** palette, found in the **Window** menu, is very similar to the **Info** palette, but allows you to perform transformations on selected objects. It shows necessary information about size, location, and orientation of the object(s).

Keep in mind that all the values in the palette concern the imaginary bounding box that surrounds an object or group of objects. If you select an object and type figures into these boxes, the object will react to these changes as if you did them with the appropriate tools. Remember to press Return (Macintosh) or Enter (Windows) to apply the changes.

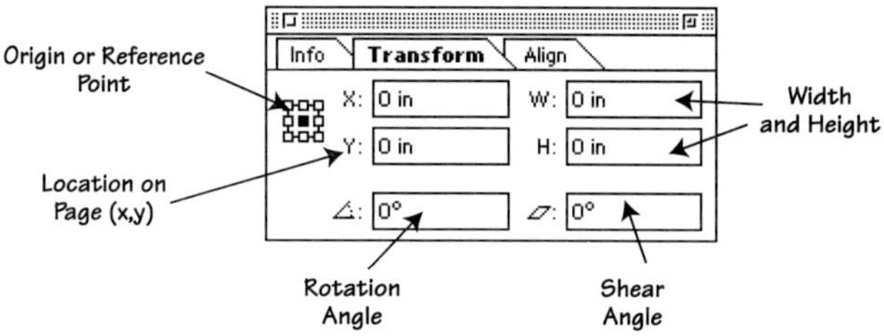

- Reference point is the axis which the object uses as an Origin point for rotation, scaling, shearing, and X/Y point.

  If you click on the upper left reference point, then type 0 for both X and Y axis, the selected object will move so that its upper left point will be on the zero point of the rulers.

  If you type "45" in the Rotation angle box, the rotation will occur around the upper left point of the selected object.

- X/Y location is the location on the page that the selected object will move to, matching its reference point to the figures typed in the X and Y boxes.

  The figures in the X/Y boxes are referenced to the rulers. If you move the zero point of the rulers, these locations move with it.

- Rotation/Shear Angles are the boxes to type in the increments you want applied to the selected object.

- Width/Height are the dimensions of the bounding box. If you type figures into these boxes, the object(s) will respond appropriately.

  This is a quick way to refine dimensions of an object to be more exact.

1. Use **File->New** to create a new document.

2. With the Rectangle tool, draw a 1" square. Keep it selected.

3. Go to **Window->Show Transform**.

4. Click on the upper left reference point in the palette. Type "45" in the Rotation box. Press Return (Macintosh) or Enter (Windows) to apply.

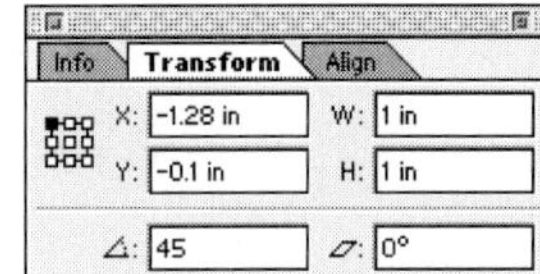

5. The square will rotate 45 °, pivoting on its upper left corner point. Go to **Edit->Undo**.

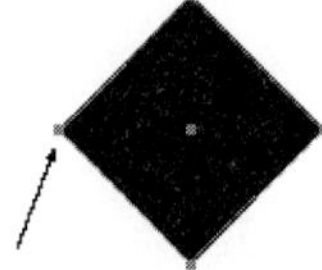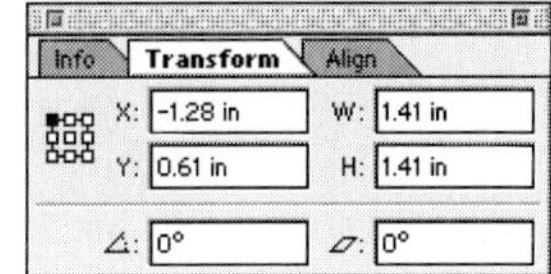

6. Click on the Zero Point and drag the crosshair to be near the square. This will reset where the ruler's zeros meet.

   Select the square. In the **Transform** palette, click on the bottom right reference point. Type 0 for both the X and the Y. Press Return (Macintosh) or Enter (Windows) to apply.

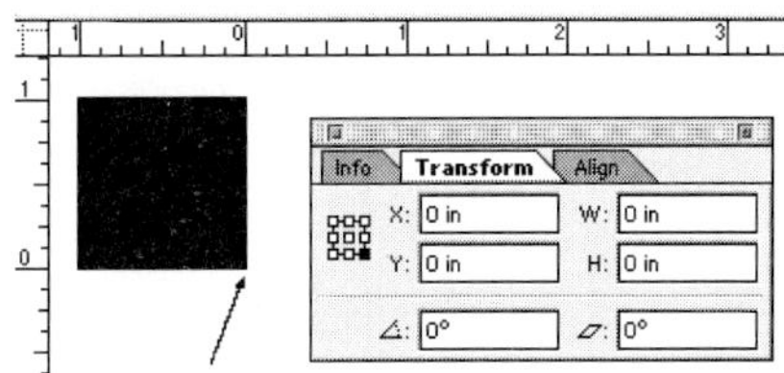

7. You will now enlarge the selected square. Click on the center reference point. Type in the boxes, Width = 2", Height = 3". Press Return (Macintosh) or Enter (Windows) to apply.

Remember, continue to practice the techniques you've learned in the book. Copy existing artwork, trace scanned images, and try to recreate entire display ads using nothing but Illustrator. Congratulations! You've just completed the course. Following this section are the individual projects that you've been asked to complete throughout the various sections of the course.

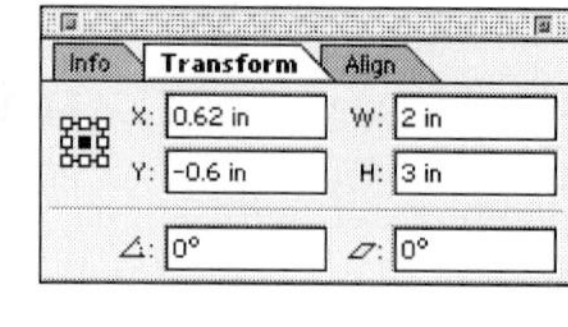

8. Click on the bottom left reference point in the Transform palette. Type "12" for the Rotation angle. Now click the cursor into the Shear box. Notice how the 12° rotation was applied when you did this. This is another way to apply settings, rather than pressing Return (Macintosh) or Enter (Windows).

    In the Shear box, type "22". Click the cursor back into the Rotation box to apply this.

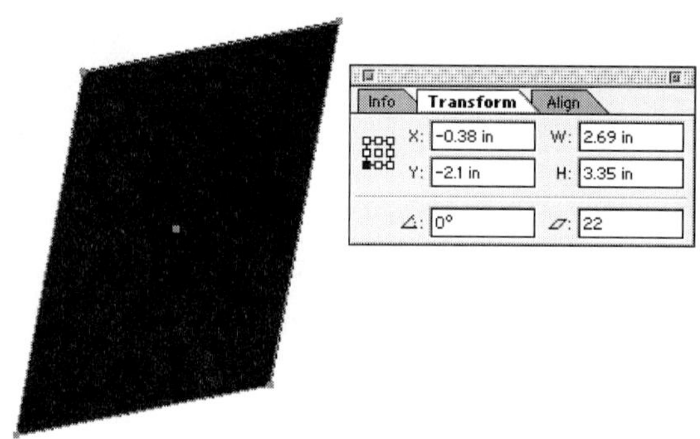

9. **Close** the document without saving.

Project I: Tropical Treasure Mailer

Project J: Last Mango Business Card

CHAPTERS *10* THROUGH *17*:

In Chapters 10 through 17 of the course we provided you with both hands-on activities and a range of self-paced projects. In addition to having a solid knowledge of how to create basic shapes and objects using the Pens, Pencils, Brushes, and primitive tools, you should, by this point, also be comfortable with:

✓ Modifying and editing the two components of a path: anchor points and segments. You should be familiar with averaging and joining paths, as well as how to cut objects apart into separate, distinct objects. You should have begun experimentation with some of the filters that can be used to modify or distort objects within a drawing.

✓ Putting type elements onto the page. By now you should be fully familiar with changing fonts, applying various styles (such as bold and italic) to type characters. You should be able to put type on a single line, into linked boxes, and into irregular "containers." You should also know how to wrap type around an object, and how to convert type into outlines, where it can be treated as a regular art object.

✓ Most aspects of coloring and shading objects, including understanding the difference between a stroke and a fill. You should understand how to use the Swatch palette to color objects or strokes, and you should know how to create new colors and add them to the palette. Using industry-standard color libraries such as the Pantone™ library is another color-related skill that you've practiced with. You should be familiar with the basic difference between four-color process and "spot" colors.

✓ How to create blends, or gradients, containing two or more colors. You should know the difference between linear and radial blends, and how to control their location and direction within a specific object. You should know how to add, modify, and delete blends within the Swatches palette.

✓ The four basic transformation functions: Rotating, Scaling, Reflecting, and Skewing. You should possess a basic knowledge of how to use these functions — either alone or in combinations — to develop many common design treatments. You should have an understanding of the "origin point," and how to apply transformations visually and also mathematically, through the use of the transformation dialog boxes.

✓ Importing scanned and other photographic images into a drawing, and how to manage them once they've been placed.

✓ Controlling objects and shapes accurately and quickly within your drawing, through the use of such features as Locking, Hiding, Showing, Grouping, and Ungrouping elements. You should also know how to use the various alignment and distribution tools provided by Adobe Illustrator.

Project A: Steaming Coffee

Drawing Curved Lines

1. Create a new document using **File->New**.

2. You will need to create a template to use as a guide for your layout.

3. Go to **Window->Show Layers** to access the **Layers** palette. Click on the small page icon at the bottom of the palette. This will create a new layer, called Layer 2. Move it to the bottom of the layer levels.

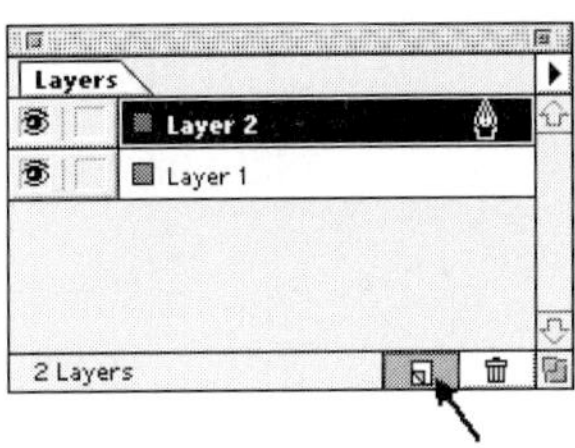

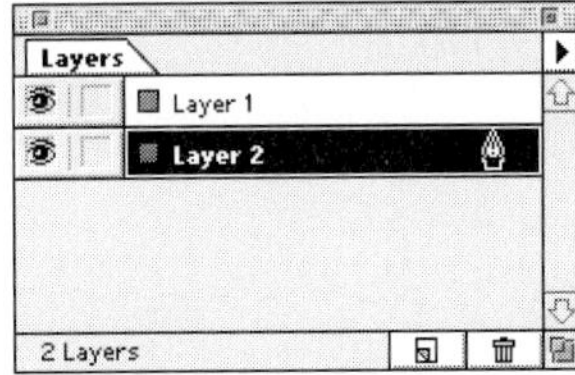

4. Double-click on Layer 2.

5. In the appearing **Layer Options** dialog box, rename the layer "Template."

   Click on **Dim Images**. Click on **Print**, to turn it off.

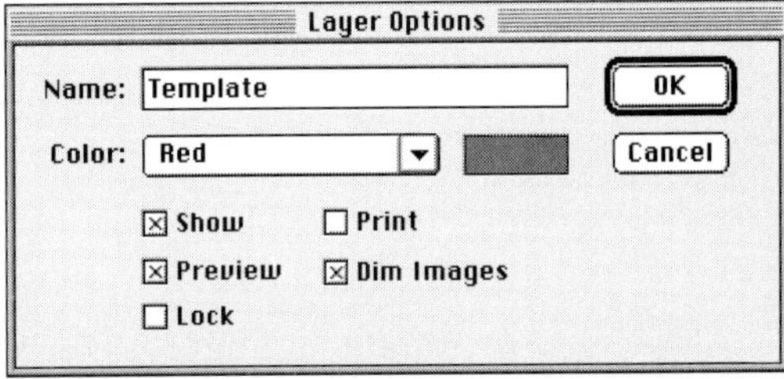

Use Command-N
(Macintosh) or Control-N
(Windows) to create a New
document.

Press **OK**. Leave the Template layer selected in the palette, so it will be the active layer.

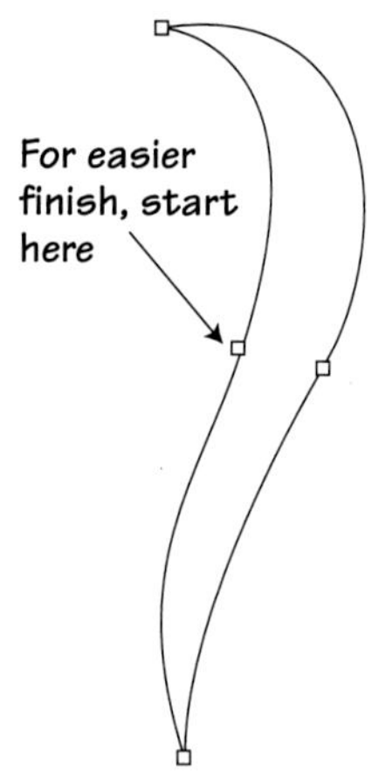

6. Use **File->Place** to go to the **SF-Intro Illustrator** folder and **Place** the **Steaming Coffee.TIF** image. The Placed image will be dimmed gray. Position this image at the top-center of the page.

7. Go to **Window->Show Layers**. Click on the **Lock** button to lock the Template layer. Click on Layer 1 to continue.

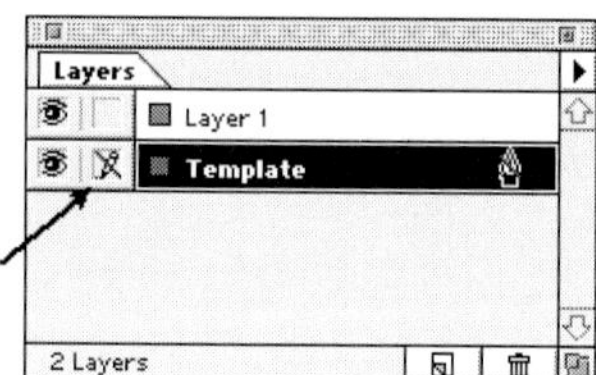

8. Use the Pen tool to draw the illustration.

   The coffee steams are closed paths which should be Filled only.

   The cup and saucer are open paths needing to be Stroked only. To the Strokes, add the rounded caps to give a hand-drawn look.

9. Paint the three coffee steams: **Fill** = 30% Black, **Stroke** = None.

10. Paint the cup and saucer strokes: **Fill** = None, **Stroke** = 3.5 pt. 100% Black, rounded caps.

11. The illustration is finished. **Save As** the file in **Illustrator** format, naming it "Steaming Coffee.AI." **Close** the document.

Project B: Java Jungle

Modifying Elliptical Objects

1. Create a new document using **File->New.**

2. You will need to create a template to use as a guide for your layout.

3. Go to **Window->Show Layers** to access the **Layers** palette. Click on the small page icon at the bottom of the palette. This will create a new layer, called Layer 2. Move it to the bottom of the layer levels.

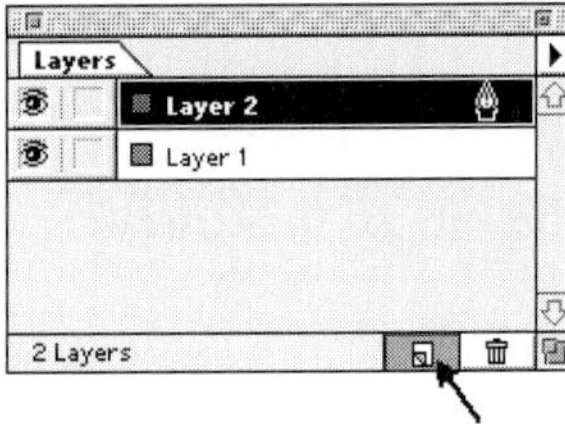
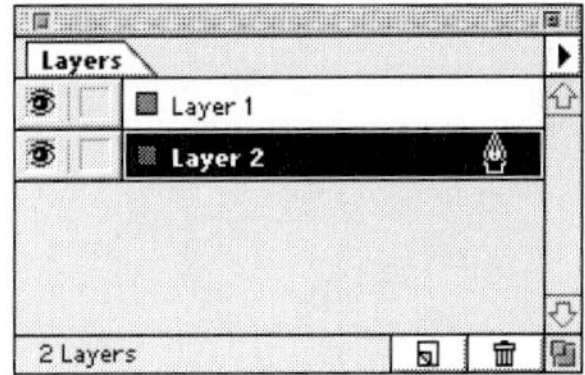

4. Double-click on Layer 2.

5. In the appearing **Layer Options** dialog box, rename the layer "Template."

   Click on **Dim Images.** Click on **Print,** to turn it off.

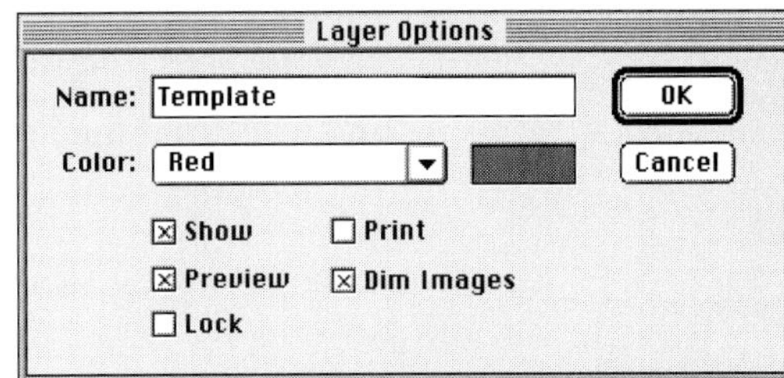

   Press **OK.** Leave the Template layer selected in the palette, so it will be the active layer.

6. Use **File->Place** to go to the **SF-Intro Illustrator** folder and **Place** the **Java Jungle Cup.tif** image. The Placed image will be dimmed gray. Position this image at the top-center of the page.

To create a New document use Command-N (Macintosh) or Control-N (Windows).

To change to the Ellipse tool press "N". Pressing "N" will toggle through all of the Ellipse tools, including the Star and Spiral.

The Scissors and Knife tools can be accessed by utilizing their keyboard toggle "C" key.

Change to the Selection tool by pressing the "V" key.

The "A" key can be used to toggle between the Direct Selection and Group tools.

7. Go to **Window->Show Layers**. Click on the **Lock** button to lock the Template layer. Click on Layer 1 to continue.

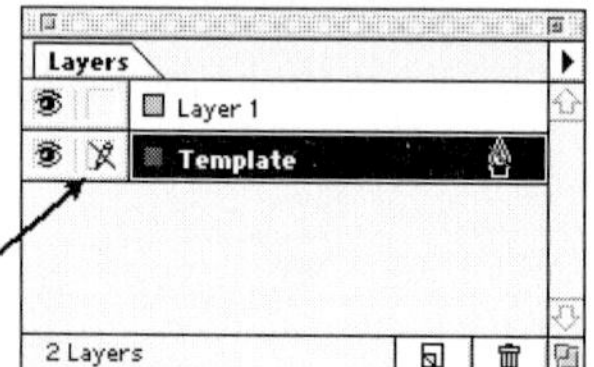

8. With the Ellipse tool, draw an oval to match the size and shape of the template.

9. Use the Scissors tool to cut the side anchor points. Deselect.

10. With the Selection tool, pull the bottom curve downward. After starting the move, hold the Shift key to keep it aligned with top curve. Deselect.

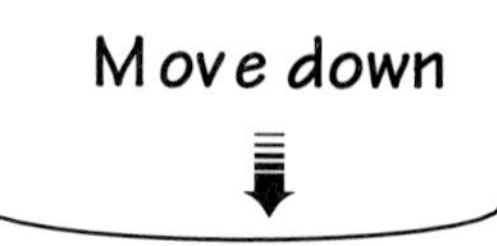

11. With the Direct Selection tool, select the left anchor points of the two objects, then select **Object->Path->Join**.

Now, with the Direct Selection tool, select *right* anchor points of the same objects and select **Object->Path->Join**.

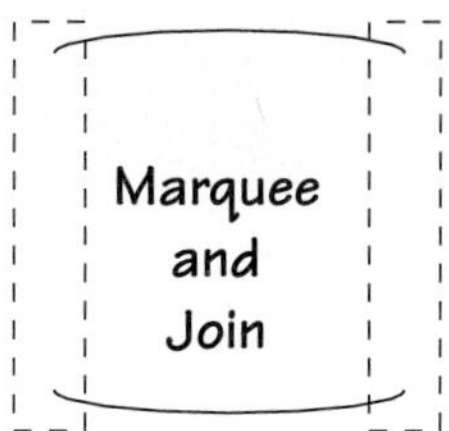

12. Click on the bottom center anchor point with the Direct Selection tool and press the keyboard Down Arrow 8 times.

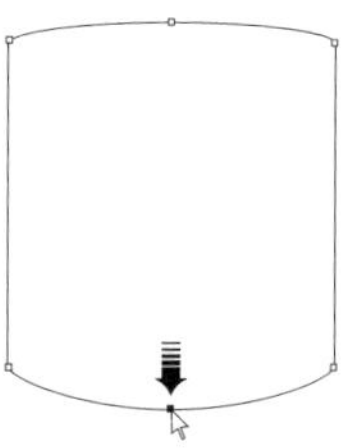

13. Paint the cup: **Fill** = White, **Stroke** = Black 1 pt. rule.

14. Draw an oval, starting out from the center, so that it will fit the cup exactly.

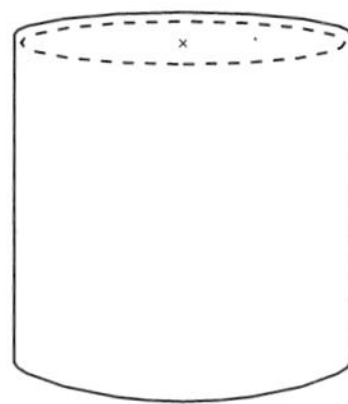

15. Paint this oval: **Fill** = Black, **Stroke** = None.

Changing the arrangement of objects within a document aids the illustrator. With an object selected, you can alter its position, not only horizontally and vertically on a page, but its stacked order. You can use Shift-Command-] to Bring an object to Front, Shift-Command-[to Send to Back, and Command-] or Command-[to send an object Forward or Backward respectively. Windows users should use the Control key in place of the Command key.

Save As a file by using Shift-Command-S (Macintosh) or Shift-Control-S (Windows).

16. Draw another oval to make the cup handle.

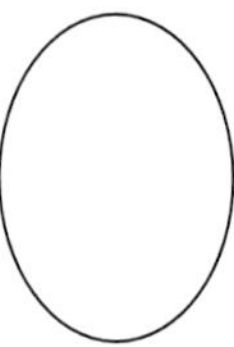

17. Draw a smaller oval that will fit on top of the larger oval. **Fill/Stroke** them the same as the cup.

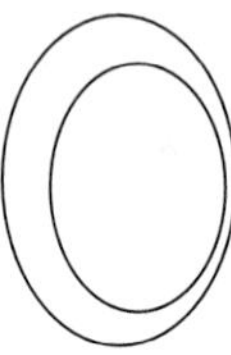

18. Position the smaller oval on top of the larger.

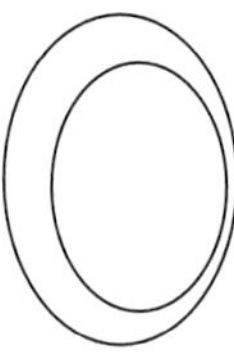

19. Move the two ovals to create the look of the coffee cup handle. With the ovals selected, **Object->Arrange->Send to Back.**

20. **Save As** the document in **Illustrator** format, naming it "Java Jungle Logo.AI." Keep the document open.

Lock and Unlock objects to manipulate your document easier. To Lock selected objects, press Command-L (Macintosh) or Control-L (Windows). To Unlock all objects (yes, you have to unlock all of them), press Shift-Command-L (Macintosh) or Shift-Control-L (Windows).

Change to the Selection tool by pressing the "V" key.

With type selected you can convert to Outlines. With the Selection tool, click on any type and press Shift-Command-O (Macintosh) or Shift-Control-O (Windows) to convert the type to Outlines.

21. Click on the cup to select it and press Command-L (Macintosh) or Control-L (Windows) to Lock it. This will eliminate accidental moving or deleting of the cup.

22. Access the Type tool and click the cursor near the Java Jungle template.

23. Type the words:

Java

Jungle

Highlight the words with the Type cursor.

24. Press Command-T (Macintosh) or Control-T (Windows) to see the **Character** window. Set these attributes to the type: **Font** = ATC Nassau, **Size** = 80 pt., **Leading** = 65 pt., **Tracking** = -30, **Horizontal scale** = 75%.

In the **Paragraph** palette, set the alignment to Center.

25. Click on the Selection tool in the Toolbox.

26. In the **Type** menu, select **Create Outlines**. Press Command-G (Macintosh) or Control-G (Windows) to Group the outlines.

27. Move the outlines to fit the cup.

28. Go to **Object->Unlock All** to unlock the cup. Fine-tune the position of the type on the cup so that it is centered and pleasing to the eye.

Save a document at any time by pressing Command-S (Macintosh) or Control-S (Windows).

Close a window (the current document) with Command-W (Macintosh) or Control-W (Windows).

29. **File->Save** the document. **Close** the document.

When you see any objects or designs that are symmetrical, you need only draw half of the design and Reflect the rest.

Helpful Hints:
Set up guides to show the distance between paths, as well as the flat level the umbrella sits on.

Project C: Last Mango Cafe

Drawing Curved Lines

1. Create a new document using **File->New**.

2. You will need to create a template to use as a guide for your layout.

3. Go to **Window->Show Layers** to access the **Layers** palette. Click on the small page icon at the bottom of the palette. This will create a new layer, called Layer 2. Move it to the bottom of the layer levels.

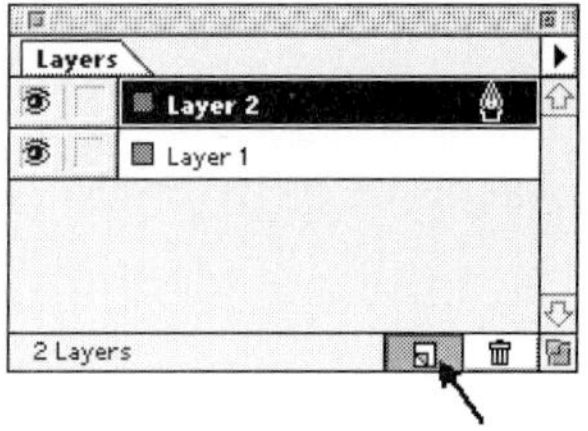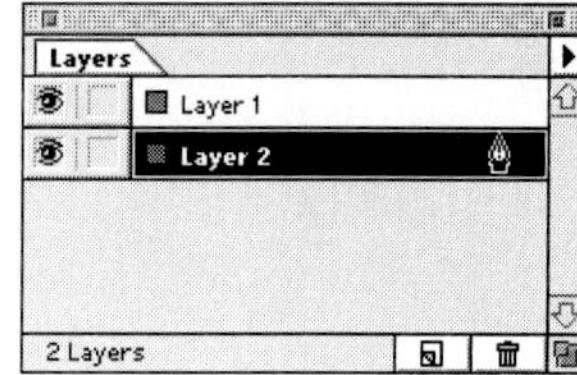

4. Double-click on Layer 2.

5. In the appearing **Layer Options** dialog box, rename the layer "Template."

   Click on **Dim Images**. Click on **Print**, to turn it off.

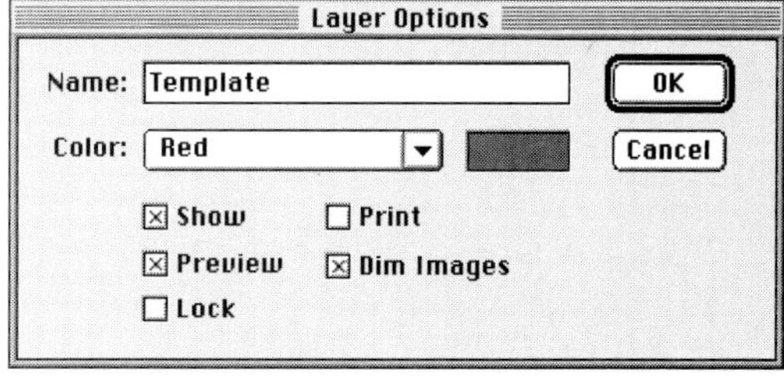

Press **OK**. Leave the Template layer selected in the palette, so it will be the active layer.

6. Use **File->Place** to go to the **SF-Intro Illustrator** folder and **Place** the **Last Mango Logo.TIF** image. The Placed image will be dimmed gray. Position this image at the top-center of the page.

7. Go to the **Layers** palette. Click on the **Lock** button to lock the Template layer. Click on Layer 1 to continue.

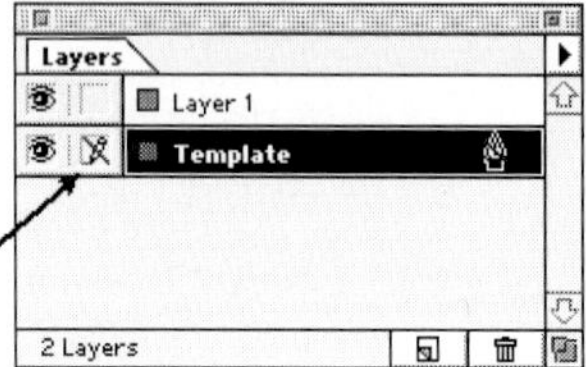

8. Turn on your rulers, if they are not on, with **View->Show Rulers**. Drag a vertical guide to match the template, where the handle of the umbrella pops out of the top of the hood.

    Use the Pen tool to draw the paths of the umbrella's hood. These paths are made up of two curving segments and one straight.

    Here is a shortcut to save time drawing all five paths and adjusting their curves. Look at the umbrella hood and you will see that it is symmetrical. One half is exactly the same as the other. Draw only the paths on the left side of the template. Draw half of the path that crosses the centerline(a.).

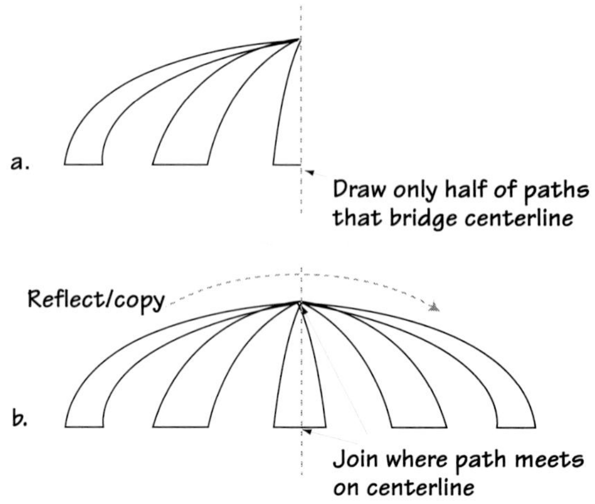

9. Select the three paths. Single-click on the Reflect tool in the Toolbox. Holding the Option key (Macintosh) or Alt key (Windows), click the crosshair cursor on the imaginary centerline down the middle of the umbrella.

10. In the **Reflect** window that appears, choose **Vertical axis**, then click **Copy**.

11. Use the Direct Selection tool to select and **Join** where the two paths meet on the centerline. If any of the other paths interfere, use **Lock** or **Hide** to get them out of the way.

   You have now made a symmetrical design, and you have cut your drawing time almost in half.

12. You will need to import some custom colors from another document. Go to **Window->Swatch Libraries->Other Library**. In the next window, go to the **SF-Intro Illustrator** folder and select **ATC Custom Colors.AI**.

13. Select the five paths drawn. Press Command-G (Macintosh) or Control-G (Windows) to **Group** them. This will avoid accidentally moving or separating the paths that belong together.

14. Paint the paths: **Fill** = ATC Red, **Stroke** = None.

15. **Save As** the document in **Illustrator** format, naming it "Last Mango Logo.AI." Keep the file open.

Modifying Objects

16. With the Ellipse tool, draw a circle to match the curvature of the handle at the bottom.

Change to the Direct Selection Tool by pressing "A" until it is active.

17. With the Direct Selection tool, highlight the top anchor point only and delete it. With the Pen tool, click on the anchor point on the right side of the half circle.

18. Follow the template as a guide to click the Pen tool again at the top of the umbrella, holding down the Shift key as you click, to maintain alignment.

19. With the handle selected, **Send to Back.** Go to the **Swatches** palette.

20. Paint the handle with: **Fill** = None, **Stroke** = 7 pt. Black, rounded caps.

Setting Type to Fit the Layout

21. Access the Type tool and click the cursor on the page.

22. Type "Last Mango Cafe."

23. Click the I-beam inside the text block. Press Command-A (Macintosh) or Control-A (Windows)to **Select All** the letters. Press Command-T (Macintosh) or Control-T (Windows) to access the **Type Character** window. Apply these settings to the type: **Font** = ATC Mango, **Size** = 76 pt., **Leading** = 65 pt., **Tracking** = -30, **Horizontal scale** = 100%.

24. Select the text block with the Selection tool. Go to **Type->Create Outlines.**

25. Select the outlines of the word "Last" and **Group** them. Select the outlines of the word "Mango" and **Group** them.

26. Select the outlines of the word "Cafe." Press Command-G (Macintosh) or Control-G (Windows) to **Group.** Double-click on the Scale tool in the Toolbox. Type 80 in **Uniform** box. Move all the objects to fit the template.

Use Shift-Command-] to Bring an object to Front, Shift-Command-[to Send to Back, and Command-] or Command-[to send an object Forward or Backward respectively. Windows users should use the Control key in place of the Command key.

27. The Last Mango Cafe logo is finished. **Save** and **Close** the document.

Project D: Tropical Fish

Creating a Polygon

1. Create a new document using **File->New**.

2. You will need to create a template to use as a guide for your layout.

3. Go to **Window->Show Layers** to access the **Layers** palette. Click on the small page icon at the bottom of the palette. This will create a new layer, called Layer 2. Move it to the bottom of the layer levels.

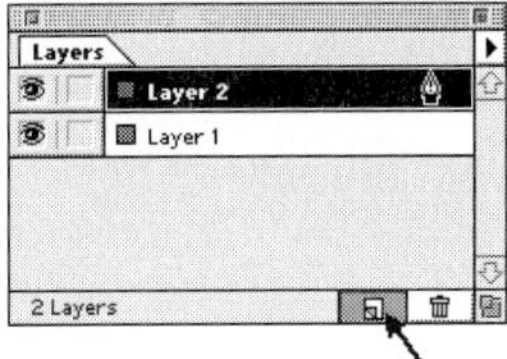

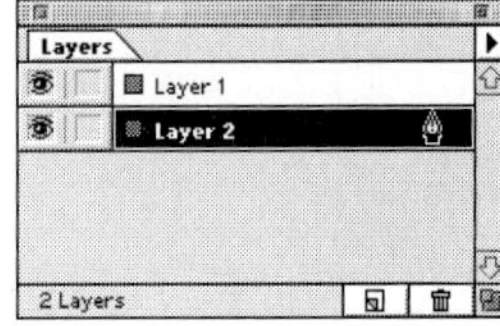

4. Double-click on Layer 2.

5. In the appearing **Layer Options** dialog box, rename the layer "Template." Click on **Dim Images**. Click on **Print**, to turn it off. Press **OK**. Leave the Template layer selected in the palette, so it will be the active layer.

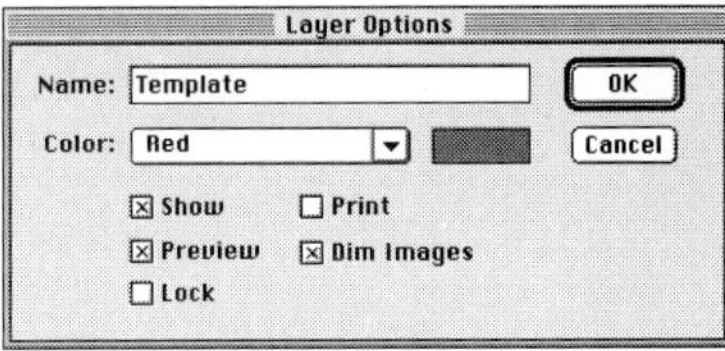

6. Use **File->Place** to go to the **SF-Intro Illustrator** folder and **Place** the **Tropical Fish.TIF** image. The Placed image will be dimmed gray. Position this image at the top-center of the page.

This Project is an exercise that is geared to demonstrate the use of Layers.

Layers are very important for the artist to use, even in the simplest of designs. The arrangement and management of elements in the piece becomes much easier.

Save As a file by using Shift-Command-S (Macintosh) or Shift-Control-S (Windows).

To change to the Ellipse tool press "N". Pressing "N" will toggle through all of the Ellipse tools.

7. Go to the **Layers** palette. Click on the **Lock** button to lock the Template layer. Double-click on Layer 1 to bring up the **Layers Options** window.

8. Rename the layer "Background." Click on the Background layer to make it the active layer, and continue.

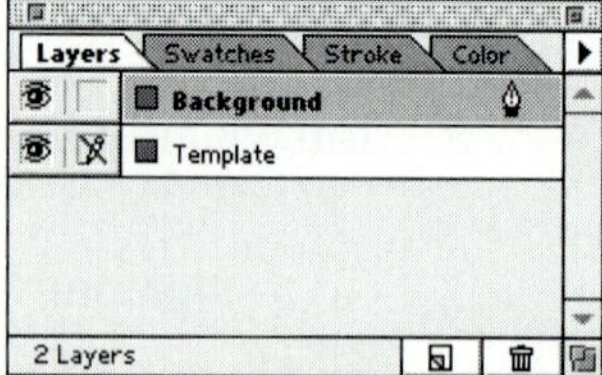

9. You will need to import some custom colors from another document. Go to **Window->Swatch Libraries->Other Library.**

10. In the next window, go to the **SF-Intro Illustrator** folder and select **ATC Custom Colors.AI.** This will give you the custom colors needed in this exercise.

11. **Save As** the file in **Illustrator** format, naming it "Tropical Fish Illustration.AI."

Creating Elliptical Shapes

12. Go to the Layers palette and click on the New Item icon at the bottom of the palette. A new layer, Layer 3, will appear at the top of the list.

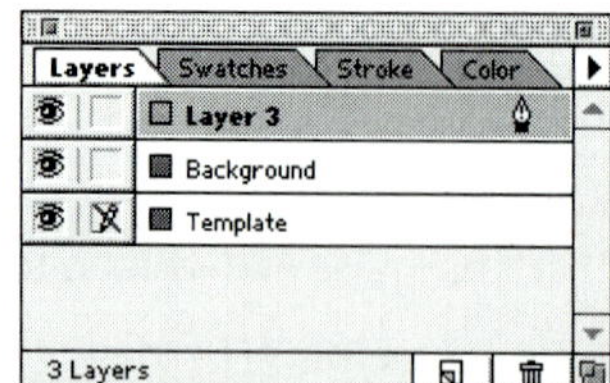

13. Double-click on this new layer to bring up **Layers Options**. Rename the layer "Fish."

14. In the **Layers** palette, Hide the Background layer. Click on the Fish layer to make it the working layer.

15. With the **Ellipse** tool, draw an oval that matches the fish body, also the small fin on its side. Hold the Shift key to draw the circle for the eye.

INTRODUCTION TO ADOBE ILLUSTRATOR/TROPICAL FISH

To change to the Pencil or Paintbrush tool, use the "Y" key.

16. Go to the **ATC Custom Colors** palette. View the named Spot (Custom) colors. Paint the paths this way:

    Body — **Fill** = ATC Coral, **Stroke** = None.
    Side fin — **Fill** = ATC Aqua, **Stroke** = None.
    Eye — **Fill** = ATC Yellow, **Stroke** = None.

17. Go to the **Layers** palette, create a new layer and name it "Fins." Move the Fins layer to be the next layer under the Fish layer.

    Click on the Eye icon of the Fish layer to Hide it. Click on the Fins layers to make it the working layer.

18. Access the Pencil tool in the Toolbox, and use it to draw the top fin, and the tail fin, of the fish, matching the template.

19 Go to the **ATC Custom Colors** palette. Paint the paths:
    Top fin — **Fill** = ATC Yellow, **Stroke** = ATC Blue 1.5 pt.
    Tail fin — **Fill** = ATC Blue, **Stroke** = None.

20. Double-click on the Paintbrush tool in the Toolbox. Set the Width for 2 pt. Make the Caps rounded.

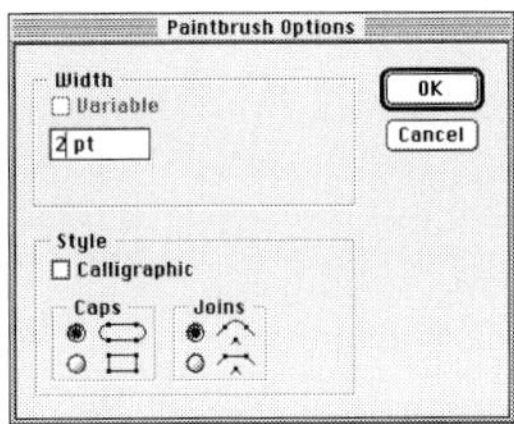

21. Draw the mouth of the fish.

22. For the eye pupil, click the Paintbrush tool on the eye.

23. Go to the **ATC Custom Colors** palette.

24. Paint the mouth: **Fill** = ATC Aqua, **Stroke** = None.
    Paint the pupil: **Fill** = ATC Blue, **Stroke** = None.

25. In the **Layers** palette, click on the Eye icon of the Fish and Fins layers to Hide them.

26. Go to the **Layers** palette and create a new layer, naming it "Coral."

27. Click on the Coral layer to make it the working layer.

28. Double-click on the Paintbrush tool icon in the Toolbox. In the dialog box, set the **Width** for 20 pt.

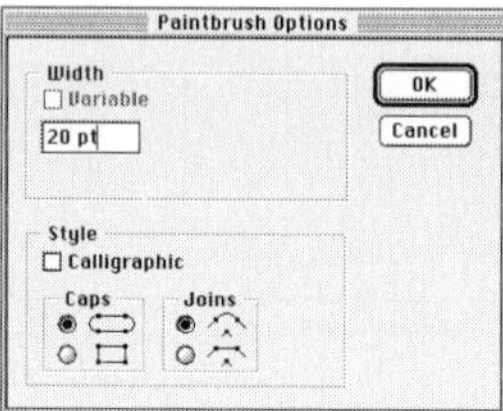

Utilize the View mode toggle. Press Command-Y (Macintosh) or Control-Y (Windows) to change between Preview and Artwork Mode.

29. Draw the coral piece in the template. This will take four strokes of the Paintbrush tool to do all the stems.

30. Go to **Artwork** mode to see the actual outlines of the Paintbrush path. Select all four of the paths with the Selection tool.

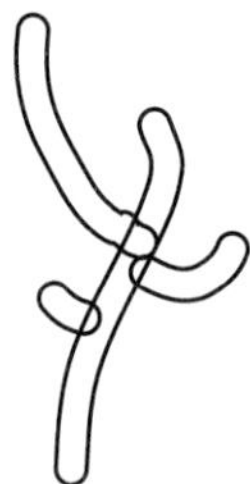

31. Go to **Object->Pathfinder->Unite** to combine them into one path.

32. Go back to **Preview** mode. Go to the **ATC Custom Colors** palette.

33. Paint the coral path: **Fill** = ATC Coral, **Stroke** = None. Deselect the coral.

34. Double-click on the Paintbrush tool in the Toolbox. In the dialog box, set the **Width** for 3 pt. Click **OK**.

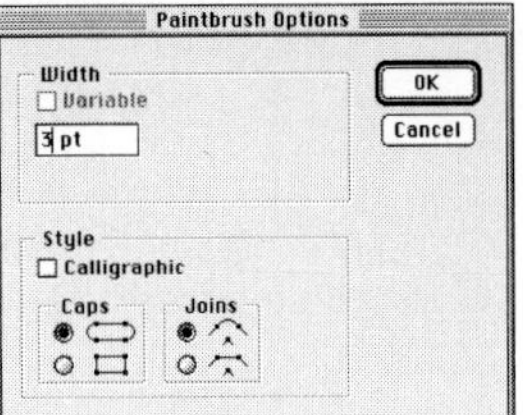

35. With the Paintbrush tool still selected, go to the Fill and Stroke boxes of the toolbox and set them for **Fill** = White, **Stroke** = None. This will set the next painting attributes of the Paintbrush tool.

    Click several times on the coral piece in the template to give it some texture with dotting brushstrokes.

36. When through, select all the dots (holding the Shift key). From the **Object** menu, choose **Group**. From the same menu, choose **Arrange->Bring to Front** so they are in front of the coral piece.

37. Go to the **Layers** palette and click on the Eye icon of the Coral layer to Hide it.

    Click on the Background layer to make it the working layer.

38. With the Pen tool, click on the four corners of the 4-sided shape in the template. Use your artistic imagination to pinpoint the corner that is not seen, but is hidden behind the fish.

39. After you have clicked the fourth anchor point, click a fifth time on the first anchor point you drew to complete a closed path. Go to the **ATC Custom Colors** palette. Paint the object: **Fill**= ATC Blue, **Stroke** = None. Deselect this object.

40. Double-click on the Paintbrush tool in the Toolbox. Set the **Width** for 9 pt. Click **OK**.

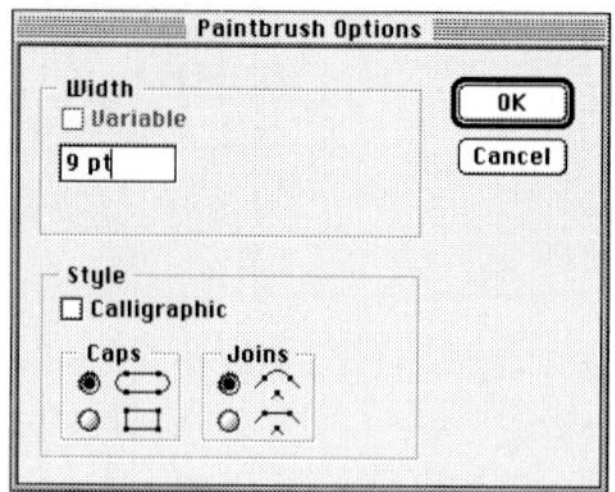

To change to the Pencil or Paintbrush tool use the "Y" key.

To change to the Star tool press "N" until it is active.

41. Draw the thick, curving line that is behind the coral and above the random dots and the starfish in the template.

42. Go to the **ATC Custom Colors** palette. Paint the curving object: **Fill**= ATC Aqua, **Stroke** = None.

43. Double-click on the Paintbrush tool in the Toolbox. Set the **Width** for 2 pt.

44. Go to the Fill and Stroke boxes of the toolbox and set them for **Fill** = ATC Coral, **Stroke** = None. Click the Paintbrush tool to make the random dots under the curving line in the template.

45. With the Paintbrush tool, draw the wavy lines to match the template.

Using the Punk & Bloat Filter

46. Use the Star tool (found in the Ellipse tool section) to draw a star fitting the size and angle of the starfish in the template. Keep the star selected.

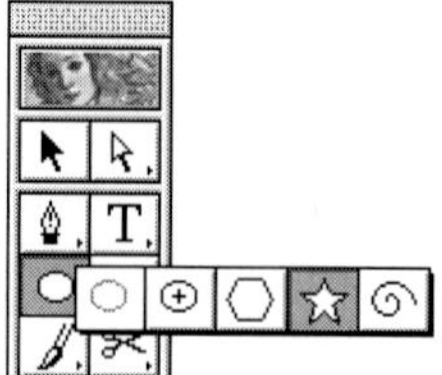

47. Go to the **Filter->Distort->Punk/Bloat**. Make sure the Preview button in the dialog box is clicked. Experiment with the Bloating by moving the slider towards the Bloat side. Finally, type in 20% for more precision of the bloating effects. Click **OK**.

Use Command-C to Copy, Command-X to Cut, and Command-V to Paste. Windows operators use the Control key in place of Command.

48. **Edit->Copy** the starfish to the clipboard.

49. Paint the starfish: **Fill** = ATC Coral, **Stroke** = ATC Coral 6 pt.

50. With the star selected, press Command-B (Macintosh) or Control-B (Windows) to **Paste in Back** the copy.

51. Press the keyboard Left Arrow key 5 times and Down Arrow 5 times.

52. Paint the duplicate: **Fill** = 100% Black, **Stroke** = 6 pt. Black.

53. The design components are all finished. You have drawn the various elements separately, and placed them on separate layers. Many of the layers you have Hidden, to get them out of view for better drawing ease. It is now time to bring the layers back to view, and organize them.

54. Go to the **Layers** palette and click on the Eye icon box, where the Eye was previously shown, to bring all the Hidden layers back to view.

    Now, drag each layer to its appropriate layer level, so that the correct layers will be in front of, or behind other layers.

    The layer at the top of the list should be the Fish layer. Then, in succession, the next layers should be: Fins, Coral, Background, Template.

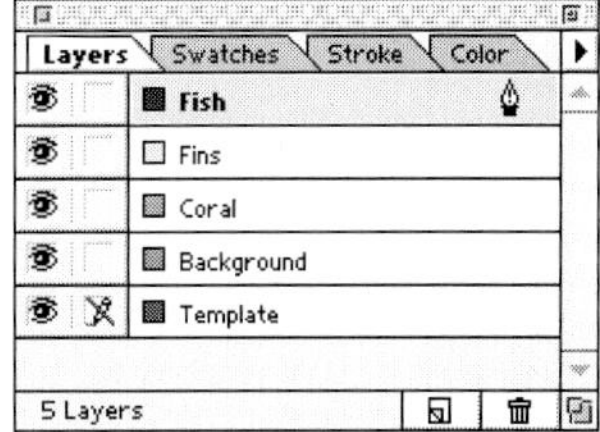

55. The final design, with layers organized, should look similar to this:

56. The illustration is finished. Press Command-S (Macintosh) or Control-S (Windows) to Save the file. **Close** the document.

Use Command-N
(Macintosh) or Control-N
(Windows) to create a New
document.

Project E: Tropical Treasure

Drawing Lines with the Pen Tool

1. Create a new document using **File->New**.

2. You will need to create a template to use as a guide for your layout.

3. Go to **Window->Show Layers** to access the **Layers** palette. Click on the small page icon at the bottom of the palette. This will create a new layer, called Layer 2. Move it to the bottom of the layer levels.

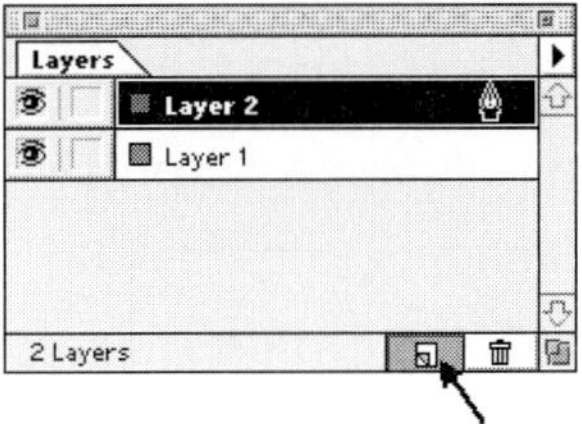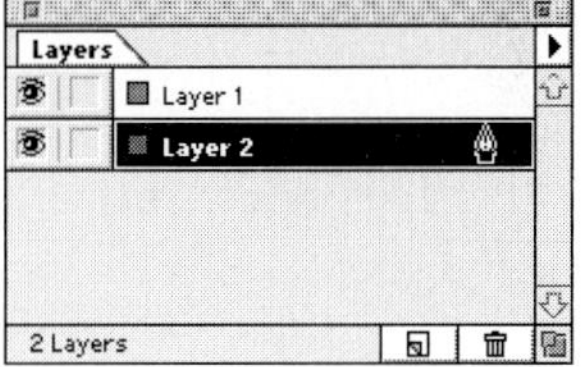

4. Double-click on Layer 2.

5. In the appearing **Layer Options** dialog box, rename the layer "Template."

   Click on **Dim Images**. Click on **Print**, to turn it off.

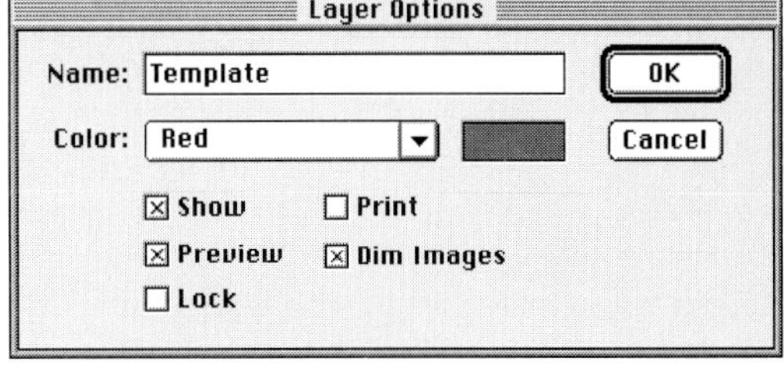

   Press **OK**. Leave the Template layer selected in the palette, so it will be the active layer.

6. Use **File->Place** to go to the **SF-Intro Illustrator** folder and **Place** the **Tropical Treasure.TIF** image. The Placed image will be dimmed gray. Position this image at the top-center of the page.

Click-hold on the Pen tool and you will see further choices for editing a path. These are the Add Anchor Point and Delete Anchor Point tools.

 **Add**

 **Delete**

Cycle through the multipe pen tools by pressing "P".

7. Go to **Window->Show Layers**. Click on the **Lock** button to lock the Template layer. Click on Layer 1 to continue.

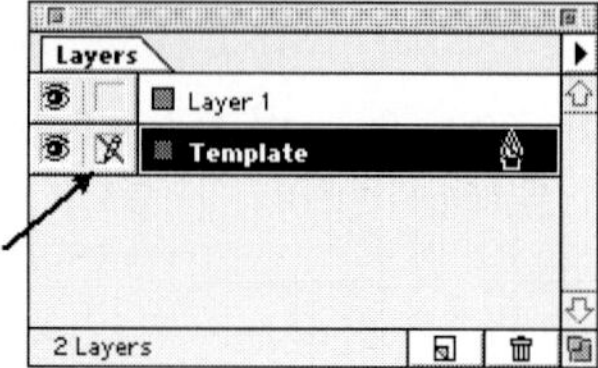

You will need to import some custom colors from another document. Go to **Window->Swatch Libraries->Other Library**. In the next window, go to the **SF-Intro Illustrator** folder and select **ATC Custom Colors.AI**. This will give you the custom colors needed for all logos created in this course.

8. Start with the rules at the top of the logo. With the Pen tool click on the left end of the thick rule. Holding the Shift key, click again on the right side of the rule with the Pen tool.

9. Select the rule with the Selection tool. Press the Option key (Macintosh) or Alt key (Windows) and drag this rule downward to duplicate it. Match the position of the thin rule underneath the thick.

10. Select the first rule drawn. Go to the **Swatches** palette. Paint the rule: **Fill** = None, **Stroke** = ATC Aqua, 4 pt.

11. Select the duplicate rule. Paint it: **Fill** = None, **Stroke** = ATC Aqua 1 pt.

12. Add the second rule to the selection while holding the Shift key. Click on the Reflect tool in the Toolbox. Then, holding the Option key (Macintosh) or Alt key (Windows), click below the rules you just drew. In the dialog box, click **Horizontal** and **Copy** to Reflect duplicates of these rules. Position them to fit the bottom rules on the template.

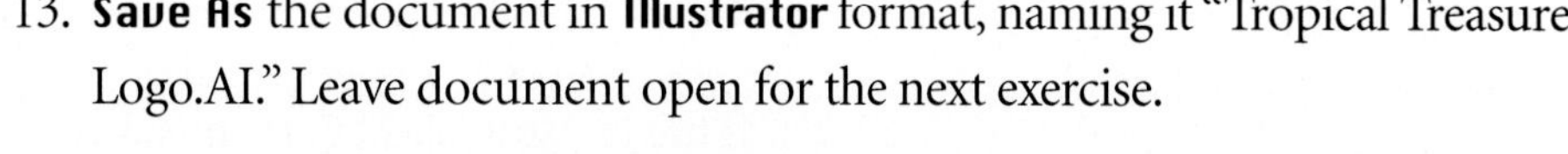

13. **Save As** the document in **Illustrator** format, naming it "Tropical Treasure Logo.AI." Leave document open for the next exercise.

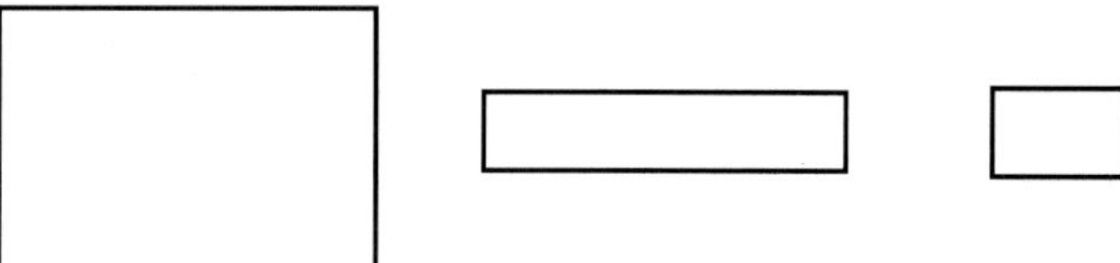

Drawing Objects with Rectangle and Oval Tools

14. Use the Rectangle tool to draw directly on the treasure chest in the template. Create the rectangles that make up the treasure chest, such as the large box, the lid, the lock face, and the small keyhole. Move these rectangles to match the template treasure chest. Make sure the chest lid touches the chest so there is no separation or space between them.

15. The triangles found at the corners of the box are created by drawing a square and using the Delete Anchor Point tool to delete a single point.

    Take this shortcut for the triangles: Draw one square that will fit any corner. Then, holding the Option key (Macintosh) or Alt key (Windows) (press Shift key after the drag is started), duplicate the square to each of the other corners. When all the squares are in place, use the Delete Anchor Point tool (found when you hold down the Pen tool icon) to delete the one anchor point that will make a triangle fit the corner.

16. The coins that get smaller when descending into the perspective are simply ovals drawn with the Ellipse tool to fit the coins in the template.

17. Use the Ellipse tool to match the various-sized oval coins of the template.

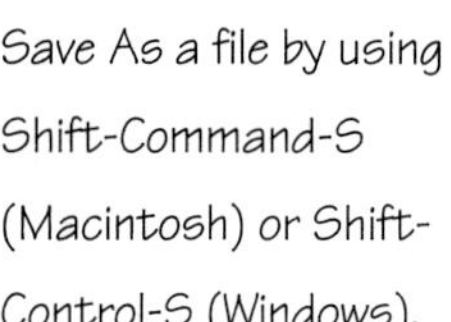

Save As a file by using Shift-Command-S (Macintosh) or Shift-Control-S (Windows).

Change to any of the Rectangle tools by pressing the "M" key.

To change to the Ellipse tool press "N". Pressing "N" will toggle through all of the Ellipse tools, including the Star and Spiral.

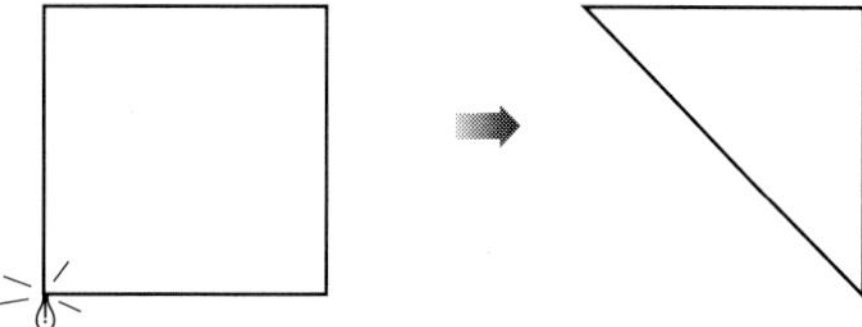

Change to the Direct Selection tool by pressing "A" until it is active.

To Group all selected objects press Command-G (Macintosh) or Control-G (Windows).

18. Go to the **ATC Custom Colors** palette.

19. Paint the treasure chest parts this way:

    Corners and lock face — **Fill** = ATC Gold, **Stroke** = None.

    Chest body and lid — **Fill** = ATC Brown, **Stroke** = None.

    Keyhole on lock face — **Fill** = Black, **Stroke** = None.

    Coins — **Fill** = ATC Gold, **Stroke** = 1 pt. ATC Aqua.

20. Leave the document open.

Creating Gradients

21. Continue in the open document. You will now build a gradient.

22. Go to the **Window** menu and select **Show Gradient**.

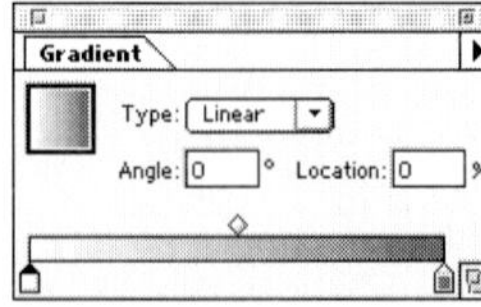

23. Make **Linear** the gradient style.

24. From the **ATC Custom Colors** palette of Spot (Custom) color, drag the color ATC Orange to the left gradient slider to apply color.

To Copy a selected object to the clipboard press Command-C (Macintosh) or Control-C (Windows).

In addition to Paste, you can Paste in Front by pressing Command-F (Macintosh) or Control-F (Windows), or Paste In Back with Command-B (Macintosh) or Control-B (Windows).

Toggle through the Type tools by pressing the "T" key.

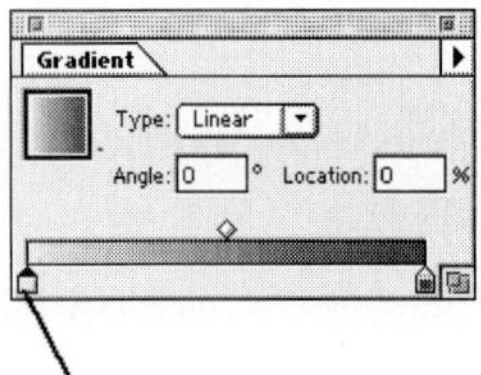

25. From the **ATC Custom Colors** palette, drag ATC Brown to the right gradient slider to apply color.

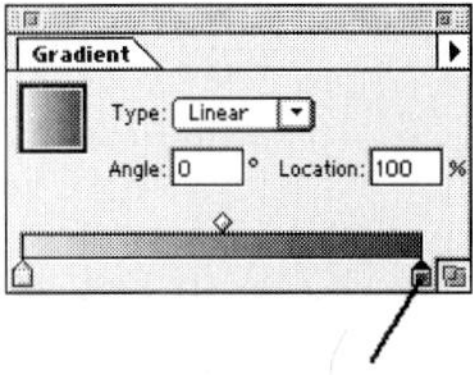

26. With the Direct Selection tool, select both the chest lid and body.

27. Go to the **Gradient** palette where you are building the gradient.

28. From the **Gradient** palette, drag the swatch to the Fill box in the Toolbox. Set the Stroke box in the Toolbox for None. This paints the selected chest objects.

29. With the Selection tool, select all the coins, then **Object->Group** them. Go to **Edit->Copy**. Press Command-B (Macintosh) or Control-B (Windows) to **Paste in Back** of the selected coins.

30. Press the keyboard Right Arrow 2 times and the Down Arrow 2 times to move the duplicate coins.

31. Go to the regular **Swatch** palette. Paint the duplicate coins: **Fill** = 100% Black, **Stroke** = None.

Setting Type to Fit a Layout

32. Access the Type tool. Click the I-beam once and begin typing the words "TROPICAL TREASURE."

33. Highlight the text with the I-beam and press Command-T (Macintosh) or Control-T (Windows) to access the **Character** window.

With the Selection tool click on any type and press Shift-Command-O (Macintosh) or Shift-Control-O (Windows) to convert the type to Outlines.

Use Command-C to Copy, Command-X to Cut, and Command-V to Paste. Windows operators use Control in place of Command.

Paste In Back with Command-B (Macintosh) or Control-B (Windows).

Utilize the View mode toggle. Press Command-Y (Macintosh) or Control-Y (Windows) to change between Preview and Artwork Mode.

34. Apply these settings: **Font** = ATC Tequila, **Size** = 78 pt., **Leading** = 65 pt., **Tracking** = -60, **Horizontal scale** = 110%. Kern between the words so that they match the template.

35. Click on the baseline with the Selection tool. In the **Type** menu, choose **Create Outlines**. Press Command-G (Macintosh) or Control-G (Windows) to **Group** all the letter outlines.

36. From the **ATC Custom Colors** palette, paint the group: **Fill** = ATC Blue, **Stroke** = None.

37. Select this group and **Copy**. From the **Edit** menu, choose **Paste in Back**.

38. With this duplicate selected, press the keyboard Right Arrow 2 times and the Down Arrow 2 times. View in **Artwork** and **Preview** modes.

39. Paint the duplicate: **Fill** = White, **Stroke** = White 1 pt.

40. Select this duplicate and **Copy**. From the **Edit** menu, choose **Paste in Back**. Go to **Artwork** mode.

41. With this second duplicate selected, press the keyboard Right Arrow 2 times and the Down Arrow 2 times.

42. Paint this second duplicate: **Fill** = ATC Coral, **Stroke** = 1 pt. ATC Coral.

43. In **Preview** mode, the outlines should look like this.

Press Command-Y (Macintosh) or Control-Y (Windows) to change between Preview and Artwork Mode.

Save a document at any time by pressing Command-S (Macintosh) or Control-S (Windows).

Close a window with Command-W (Macintosh) or Control-W (Windows).

Modifying Type with the Character Palette

44. Access the Type tool, then click on the page to type:

Gifts From Under The Sea

45. Highlight the text with the Type I-beam and apply these settings in the **Type Character** palette: **Font** = ATC Daquiri, **Size** = 36 pt., **Leading** = 65 pt., **Tracking** = -60, **Horizontal scale** = 120%.

46. Click the baseline with the Selection tool. In the **Type** menu, choose **Create Outlines**. Press Command-G (Macintosh) or Control-G (Windows) to **Group** all the letter outlines.

47. Paint the group: **Fill** = ATC Aqua, **Stroke** = ATC Aqua 0.5 pt.

48. The outlines should look like this in **Preview** mode.

Gifts From Under The Sea

49. Move "Gifts From Under The Sea" in position on the template.

50. The completed Tropical Treasure type objects should look like this in **Preview** mode.

TROPICAL   TREASURE

Gifts From Under The Sea

51. Move all the objects into position on the template and fine-tune them.

52. The logo is now complete. **Save** the file. **Close** the document.

Notes:

Project F: Ball & Mirror

1. Create a new document using **File->New**.

2. You will need to create a template to use as a guide for your layout.

3. Go to **Window->Show Layers** to access the **Layers** palette. Click on the small page icon at the bottom of the palette. This will create a new layer, called Layer 2. Move it to the bottom of the layer levels.

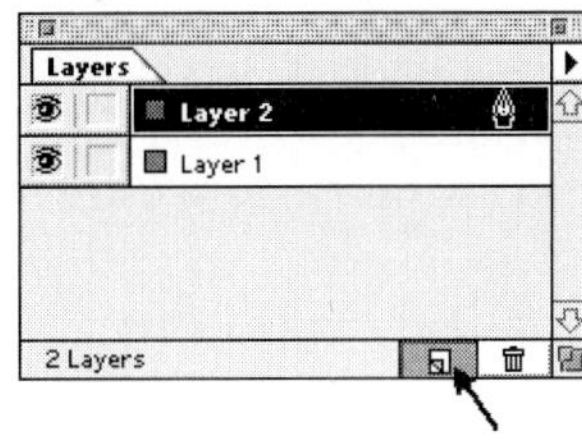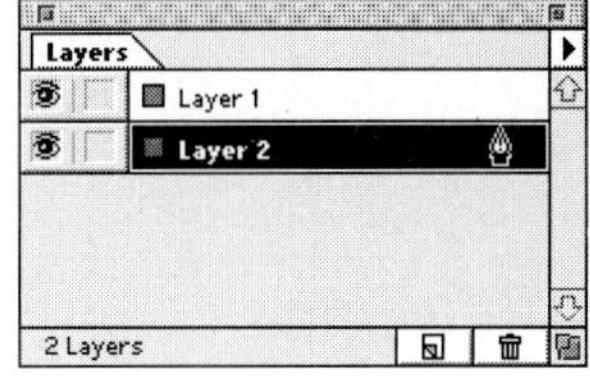

4. Double-click on Layer 2.

5. In the appearing **Layer Options** dialog box, rename the layer "Template."

    Click on **Dim Images**. Click on **Print**, to turn it off.

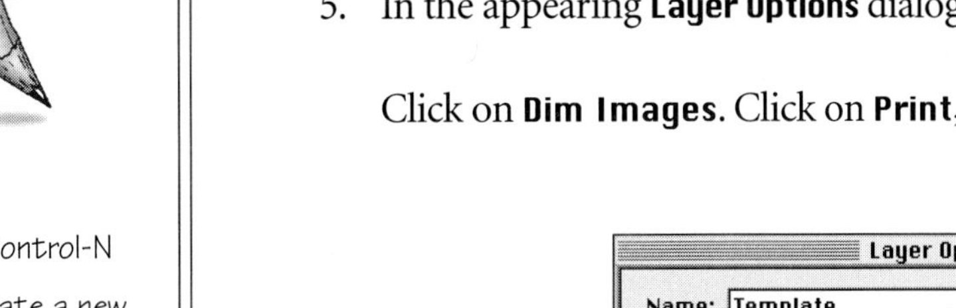

    Press **OK**. Leave the Template layer selected in the palette, so it will be the active layer.

6. Use **File->Place** to go to the **SF-Intro Illustrator** folder and **Place** the **Ball & Mirror.TIF** image. The Placed image will be dimmed gray. Position this image at the top-center of the page.

Use Command-N (Macintosh) or Control-N (Windows) to create a new document.

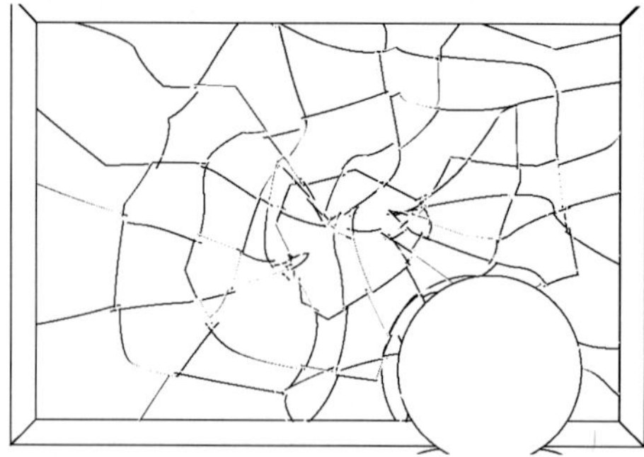

7. Go to **Window->Show Layers**. Click on the **Lock** button to lock the Template layer. Click on Layer 1 to continue.

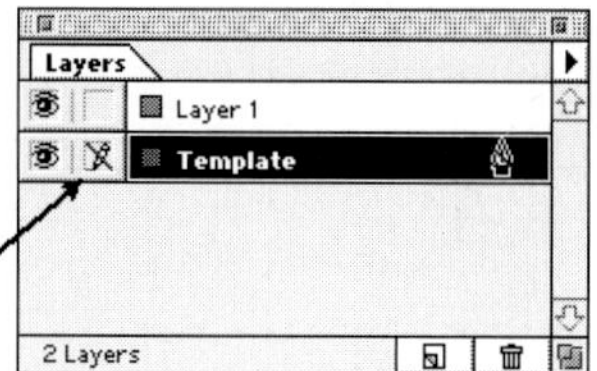

8. In **Artwork** mode, select the Rectangle tool and click the crosshair on the page, holding Option (Macintosh) or Alt (Windows) to bring up the dialog box. Set the rectangle dimensions for 5.5" x 3.75".

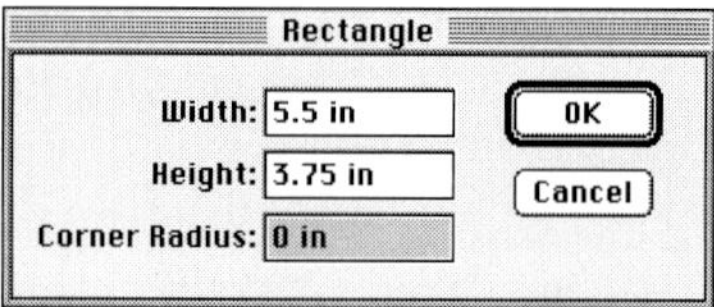

Inside this rectangle, draw another rectangle 5.1" x 3.35". Paint this rectangle: **Fill** = White, **Stroke** = None.

Select the two rectangles and go to **Window->Show Align**. Click on both the **Center Vertical** and then the **Center Horizontal** options under **Align Objects**. This will center the two rectangles.

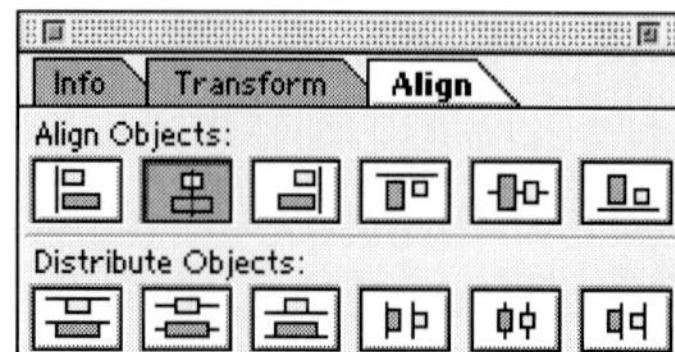

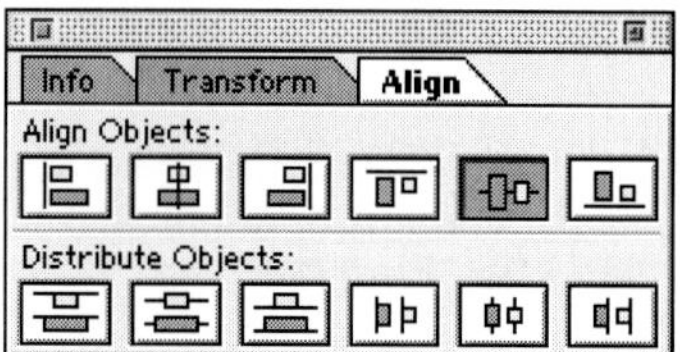

9. Select the Pen tool. Holding the Shift key to constrain the angle, draw 45°
diagonal lines across each corner of the rectangles, as shown. Make sure
the diagonal lines cross the anchor points of the two rectangles.

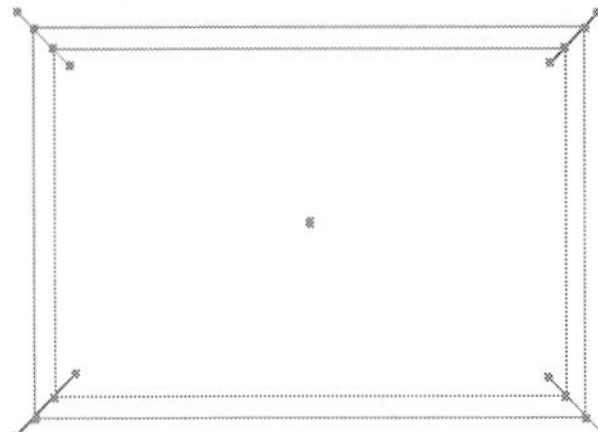

Paint these lines with: **Fill** = None, **Stroke** = None.

Select the inner rectangle. **Edit->Copy**, then **Edit->Paste in Front**. Press
Command-U (Macintosh) or Control-U (Windows) to **Hide** this dupli-
cate. Now, press Command-A (Macintosh) or Control-A (Windows) to
Select All of the paths. Go to **Object->Pathfinder->Divide**.

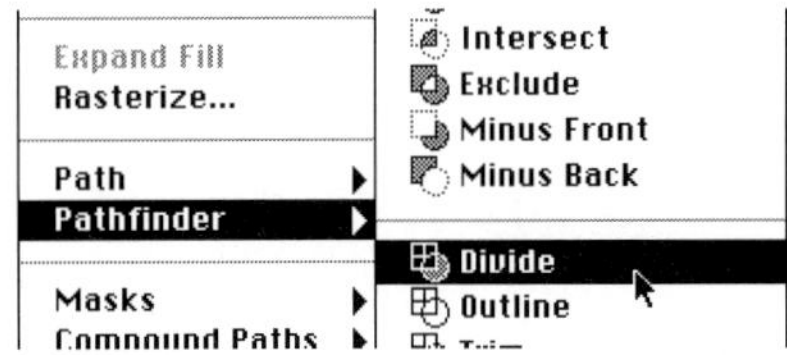

This will divide the rectangles into four separate objects: top, bottom, left
side, and right side. Click on the remaining inside rectangle with the
Direct Selection tool and Delete it.

Touching at the corners, the four sides appear to make up a single frame,
but each is independent, capable of being painted different from the other
sides (shown separated here).

To Group a selection press Command-G (Macintosh) or Control-G (Windows).

Press Command-Y (Macintosh) or Control-Y (Windows) to change between Preview and Artwork Mode.

Change to the Gradient tool by pressing "G".

Select the four frame pieces and **Group** them.

Go to the **Layers** palette. Create a new layer, and name it "Frame." Move the frame group to this layer by moving its colored dot from Layer 1 to the Frame layer. Move Layer 1 up to the top of the layer list.

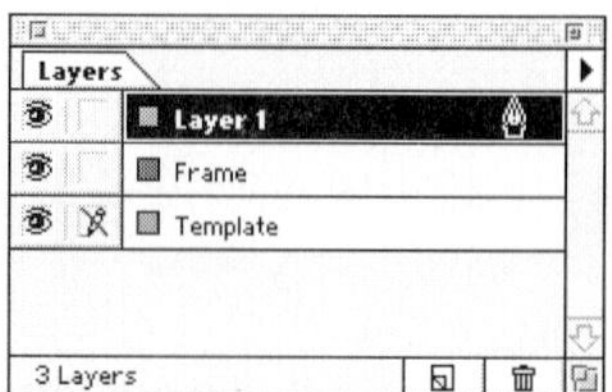

10. Go to **Preview** mode. With the Selection tool, click on the grouped frame. **Fill** the frame (**Stroke** of None) with a gradient created this way:

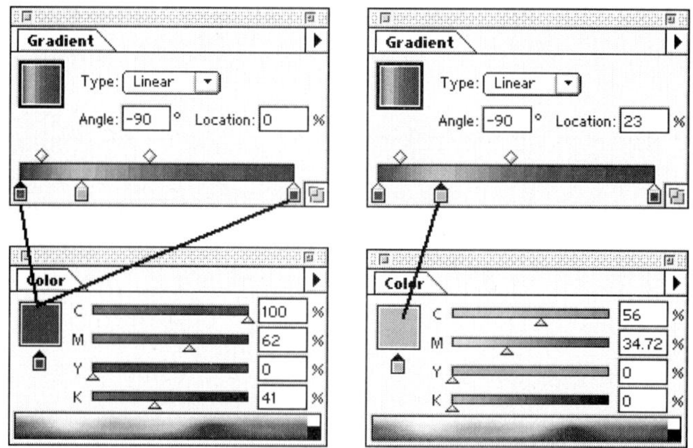

Use the Gradient tool to set the direction of each frame side. To do this, use the Direct Selection tool to click on an individual side to select it.

Click on the Gradient tool in the Toolbox. Make the first click-hold on the extreme outside of the side. Drag the crosshair (while holding the Shift key to keep constrained) to the other side of this section, then release the mouse. The direction of the gradient will be changed.

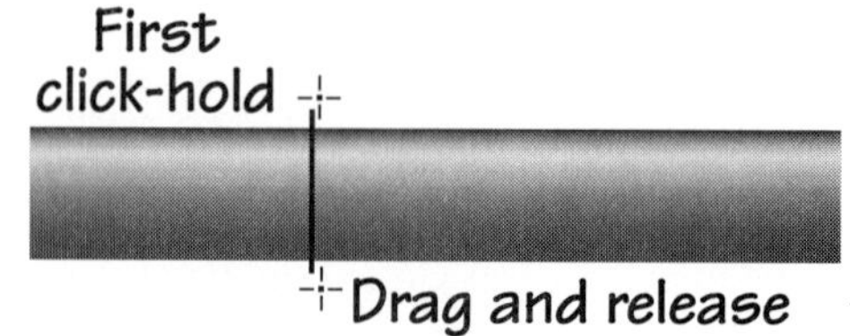

INTRODUCTION TO ADOBE ILLUSTRATOR/BALL & MIRROR

11. Press Command-Shift-U (Macintosh) or Control-Shift-U (Windows) to show the duplicate rectangle. Assign it to the Frame layer, then **Object->Arrange->Send to Back. Fill** it with the following gradient:

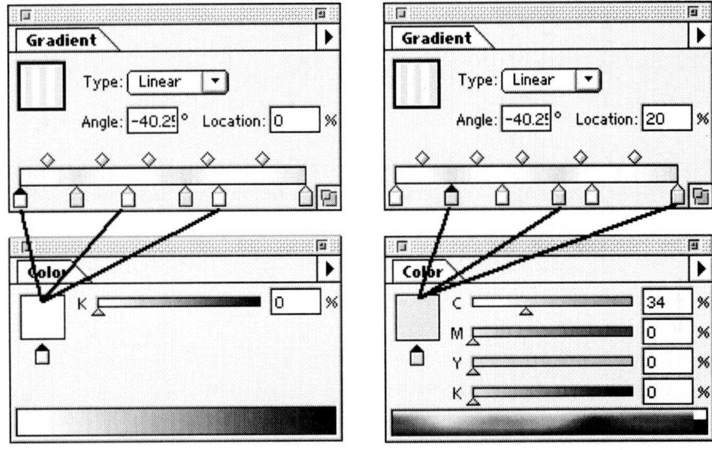

12. Double-click on the Layer 1 layer to bring up **Layer Options**. Rename it "Cracked Layer." Move the Template up to the top of the layer list so it will be visible. Next should be the Cracked Layer, then the Frame layer. **Lock** the Frame layer.

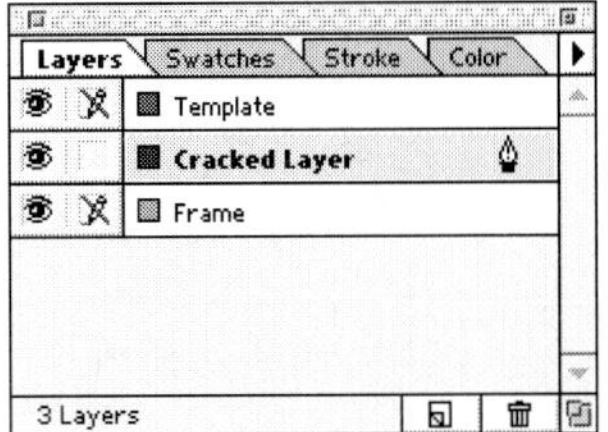

To Copy a selected object to the clipboard press Command-C (Macintosh) or Control-C (Windows).

Paste in Front by pressing Command-F (Macintosh) or Control-F (Windows).

Use Shift-Command-] (Macintosh) or Shift-Control-] (Windows) to Bring an object to Front.

To change to the Ellipse tool press "N". Pressing "N" will toggle through all of the Ellipse tools, including the Star and Spiral.

Click on the Cracked Layer in the **Layers** palette to begin drawing on that layer. Select the Pencil tool, and draw the cracks in the mirror.

Do not let the cracks extend past the exterior of the frame.

Press Command-A (Macintosh) or Control-A (Windows) to **Select All**, which will select all the cracks drawn. Press Command-G (Macintosh) or Control-G (Windows) to **Group** them.

Paint this cracked group with: **Fill** = None, **Stroke** = 1 pt. 100% cyan, 60% magenta.

Edit->Copy this cracked group and **Paste in Front** the cracks. Press the Right Arrow key of your keyboard three times to offset them slightly. Paint the duplicate cracks with: **Fill** = None, **Stroke** = 1 pt. white.

With the white group selected, select **Object->Arrange->Bring to Front**.

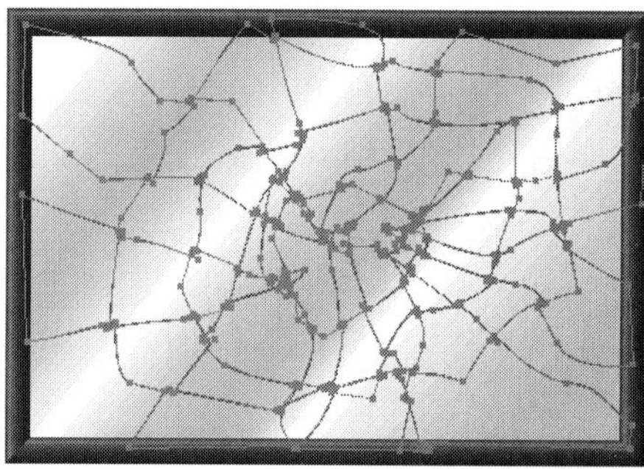

13. Create a new layer in the **Layers** palette, naming it "Ball." Keep the Ball layer selected to be the active layer.

14. With the Ellipse tool, draw a circle 1.6 " in diameter. Paint the circle with **Stroke** = None, and **Fill** with the following radial gradient:

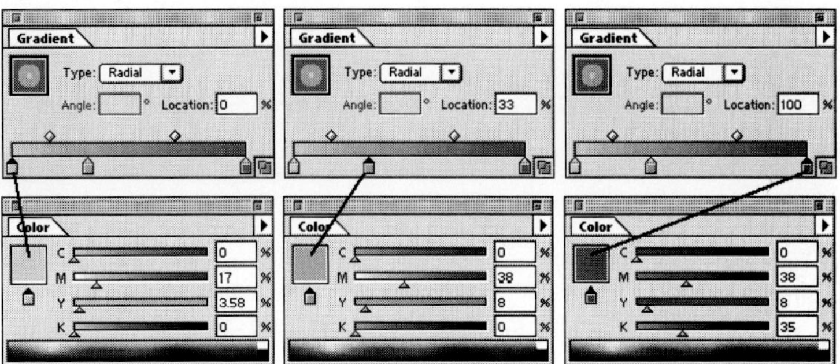

Change to the Gradient tool by pressing "G".

With the Gradient tool, position the center of the gradient so that it looks like a highlight of the ball.

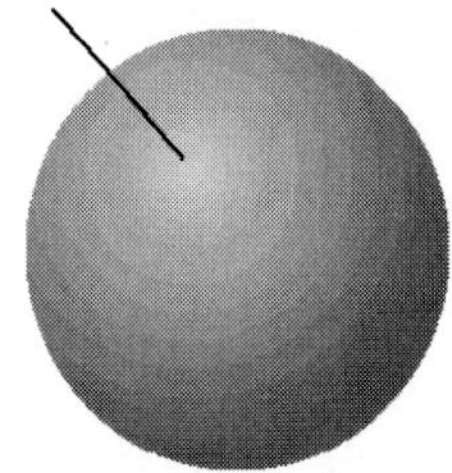

To change to the Ellipse tool press "N" until the Ellipse is active.

15. Select the Ellipse tool, and draw an oval 1.6" wide x 0.25" tall. Using the Scissors tool, cut the circle at the side anchor points. Delete the top half.

Paint the path with: **Fill** = None, **Stroke** =1 pt., 40% magenta, 10% yellow and 30% black.

Rotate the path 15°, then position it on top of the rubber ball to give the impression of a protruding ridge on the surface of the ball.

Macintosh opperators use Shift-Command-] to Bring an object to Front, Shift-Command-[to Send to Back, and Command-] or Command-[to send an object Forward or Back-ward respectively. Windows users should use the Control key in place of the Command key.

Change to the Knife or Scissor Tools by pressing the "C" key.

In addition to Paste, you can Paste in Front by pressing Command-F (Macintosh) or Control-F (Windows), or Paste In Back with Command-B (Macintosh) or Control-B (Windows).

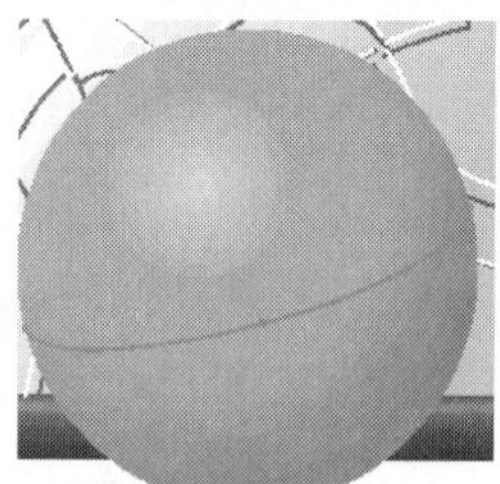

16. To create the reflection in the mirror, click on the ball. **Edit->Copy** the circle, then press Command-B (Macintosh) or Control-B (Windows) to **Paste in Back** of the ball. Press the Left Arrow key on the keyboard 10 times to act as a shadow. **Fill** it = 45% Magenta, 10% Yellow and 40% Black, **Stroke** = None.

Assign this shadow circle to the Cracked Layer. Then **Object->Arrange ->Send to Back**, to be behind the cracks on that layer. **Lock** the Ball layer.

Use the Knife tool (holding the Shift key to constrain it) to cut the lower portion of the circle. Delete the lower half so that it won't show below the frame.

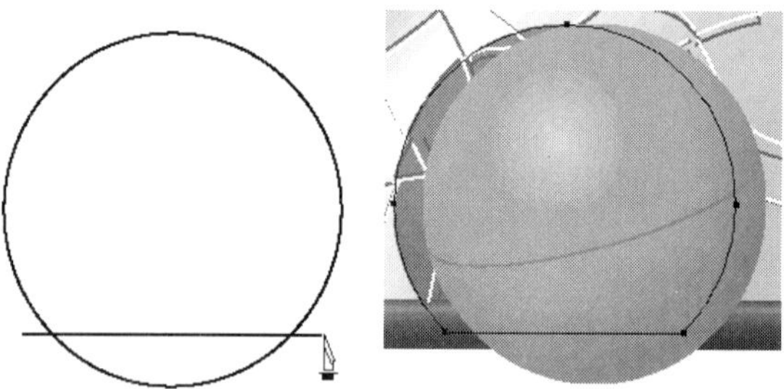

Unlock the Ball layer.

17. Finally, to make the shadow under the rubber ball, draw another oval 1.6 " x 0.25". Paint it: **Fill** = White, **Stroke** = None.

18. **Copy** this oval, then **Edit->Paste in Front**. Scale the duplicate 50%. **Fill** the duplicate with 40% Black, **Stroke** = None.

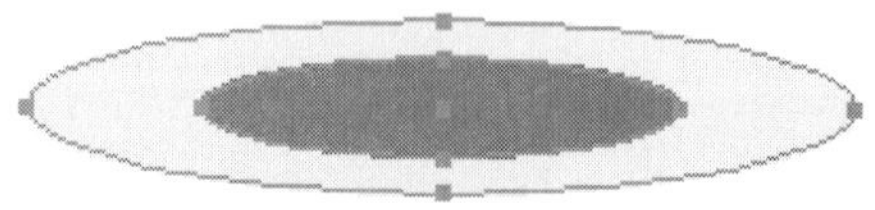

19. Select both ovals, and choose the Blend tool in the Toolbox. With the tool's cross-hair cursor, click on the far left anchor point of the larger oval. Now, click on the far left anchor point of the duplicate oval.

20. The **Blend** dialog box will now appear. Enter these numbers:

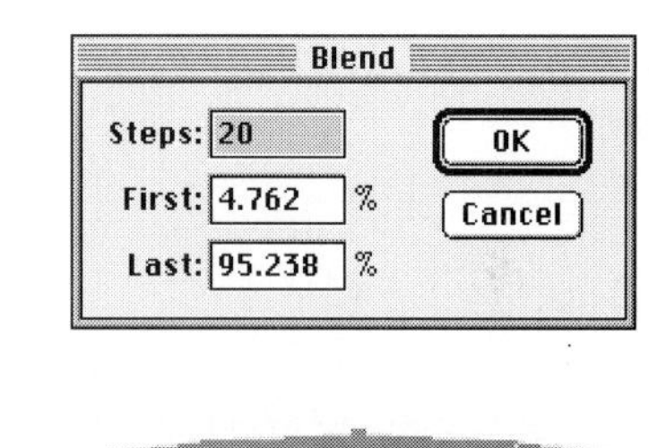

21. **Unlock** the Frame layer. Select all the paths of this blend. Go to **Object->Group**. Position the grouped shadow under the rubber ball, and assign it to the Frame layer, then **Object->Arrange->Send to Back**.

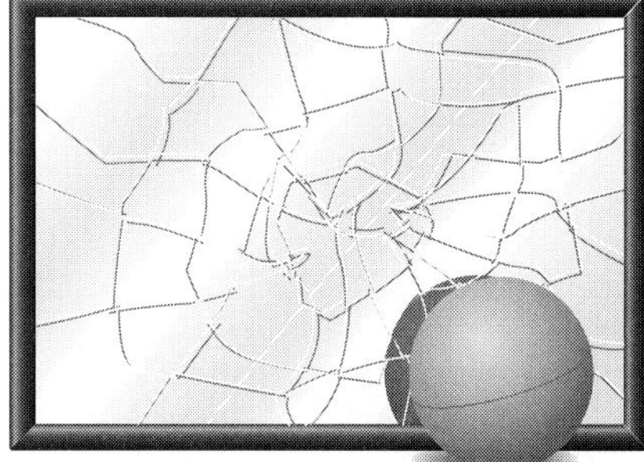

22. The design is finished. Hide the Template layer.

23. **Save As** the file in **Illustrator** format, naming it "Ball & Cracked Mirror.AI." **Close** the document.

To Group a selection press Command-G (Macintosh) or Control-G (Windows).

Use Shift-Command-[(Macintosh) or Shift-Control-[(Windows) to Send to Back.

Notes:

Project G: Jokers Wild

Joker's Wild

1. Create a new document using **File->New**.

2. You will need to create a template to use as a guide for your layout.

3. Go to **Window->Show Layers** to access the **Layers** palette. Click on the small page icon at the bottom of the palette. This will create a new layer, called Layer 2. Move it to the bottom of the layer levels.

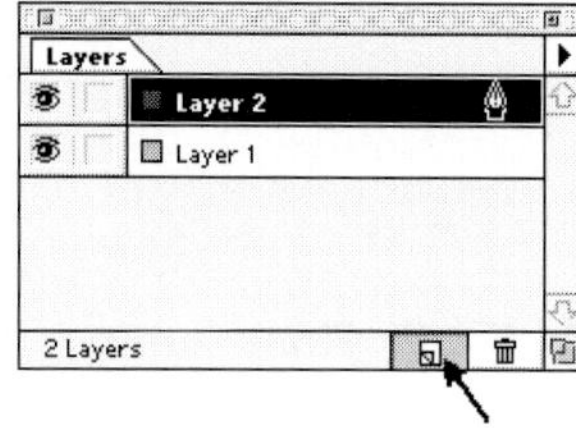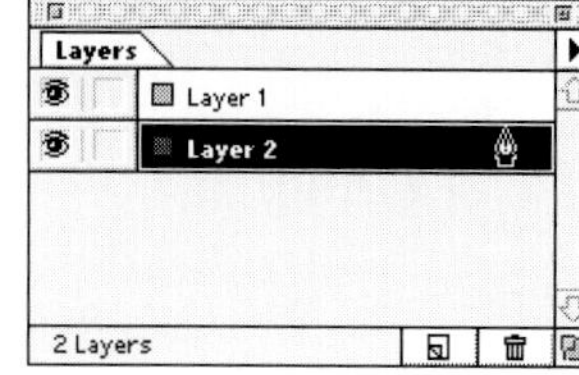

4. Double-click on Layer 2.

5. In the appearing **Layer Options** dialog box, rename the layer "Template."

   Click on **Dim Images**. Click on **Print**, to turn it off.

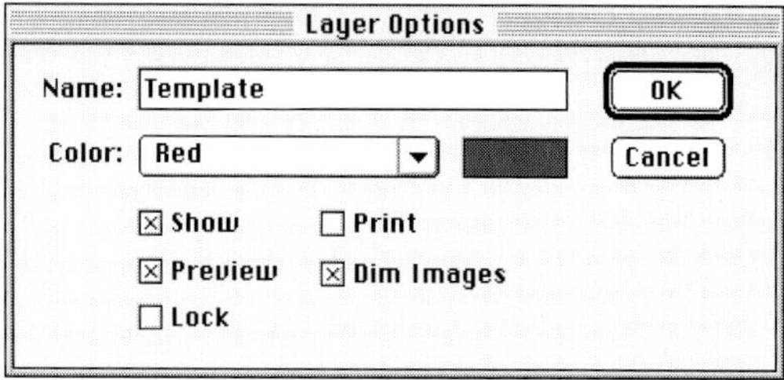

Use Command-N (Macintosh) or Control-N (Windows) to create a New document.

Press **OK**. Leave the Template layer selected in the palette, so it will be the active layer.

6. Use **File->Place** to go to the **SF-Intro Illustrator** folder and **Place** the **Joker.TIF** image. The Placed image will be dimmed gray. Position this image at the top center of the page.

7. Go to **File->Preferences->Units & Undo** and set the **General** units to **Inches**. Click **OK** to return to the Joker template.

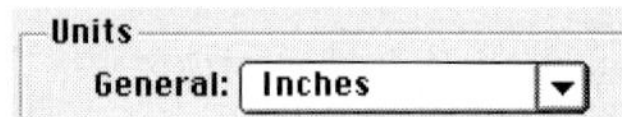

8. Go to **View->Show Rulers**. Make a center guide by dragging a guide from the vertical ruler to the 4.25" mark on the horizontal ruler at the top of the document. This is to mark a center guide of the page to work from.

9. Move the Joker template so the center of his crown is on the center guide you created.

10. When the Joker template is in place, go to the **Layers** palette. Click on the **Lock** button to lock the Template layer.

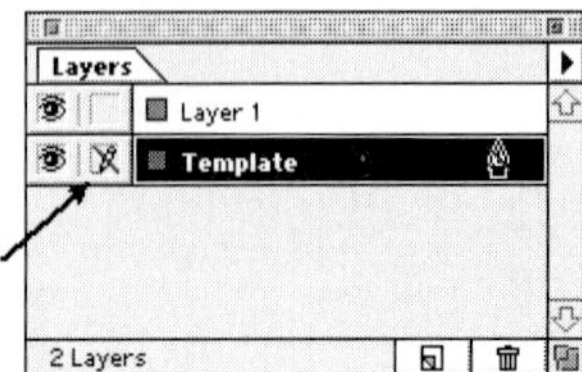

Click on Layer 1 to continue.

11. Zoom in on the crown. Select the Pen tool. Working on the left side of the center guide, start drawing the half-crown shape shown below. End the last point of the path on the center guide.

    Select the Reflect tool. Hold the Option key (Macintosh) or Alt key (Windows) and click on the guide. In the dialog box that appears, select **Vertical** and **Copy**.

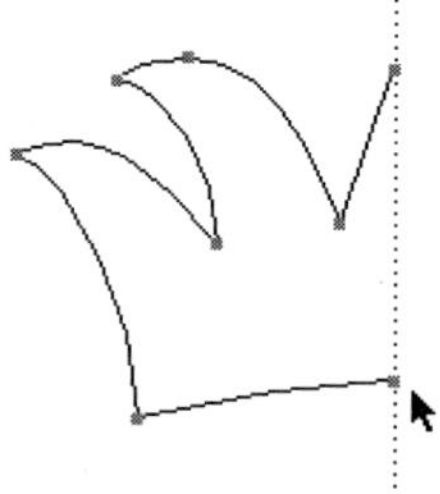

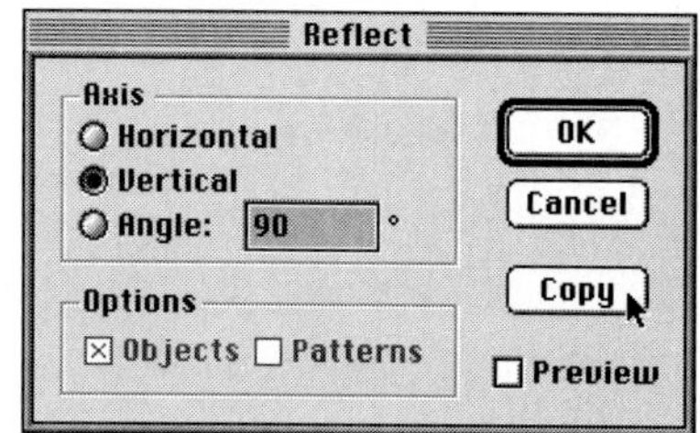

12. With the Direct Selection tool, select the top two points of the crown and choose **Object->Join** for the top two points to join as a Corner Point. Repeat this procedure with the two bottom points. However, use a Smooth Point instead of a Corner Point. Paint the object: **Fill** =100% Cyan, 100% Magenta, **Stroke** = 0.5 pt. Black.

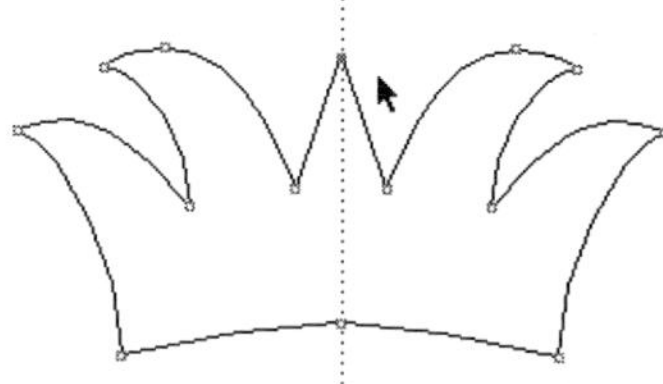

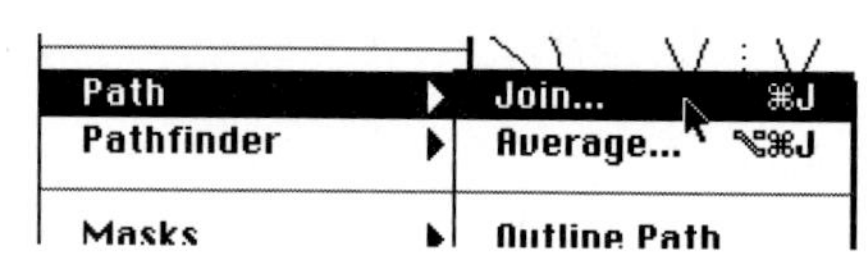

13. With the Pen tool, draw the left half of the cheek and jaw shapes below the crown shape as two separate shapes.

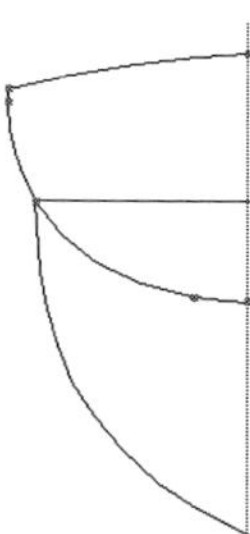

    Select the jaw shape and go to **Object->Arrange->Send to Back**.

The "A" key is the Direct Selection tool and Selection tool toggle.

When Anchor points are selected, you can Join them by pressing Command-J (Macintosh) or Control-J (Windows).

Use Shift-Command-] to Bring an object to Front, Shift-Command-[to Send to Back, and Command-] or Command-[to send an object Forward or Backward respectively. Windows users should use the Control key in place of the Command key.

14 Select and paint both face objects a flesh tone: **Fill** = 5% Cyan, 25% Magenta, 25% Yellow, **Stroke** = 0.5 pt. Black.

15. With both objects selected, click on the Reflect tool in the Toolbox. Hold the Option (Macintosh) or Alt (Windows) key and click the crosshair on the center guide to set an Origin point. In the dialog box, choose **Vertical** and **Copy**.

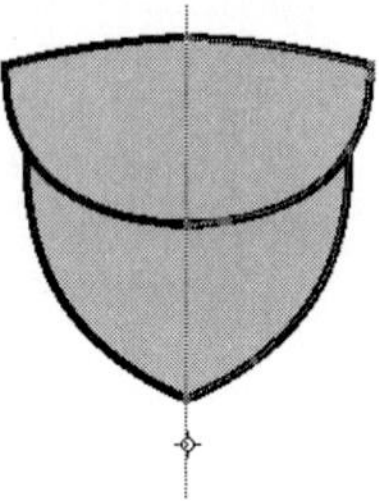

16. Go to **Artwork** mode so you can see the paths and their anchor points more separately. Marquee-select the endpoints of the left and right side paths with the Direct Selection tool. With the two endpoints selected, go to **Object->Join**. Do this so that the cheek and jaw are separate, closed paths.

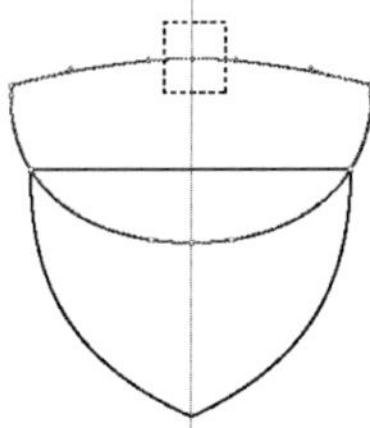
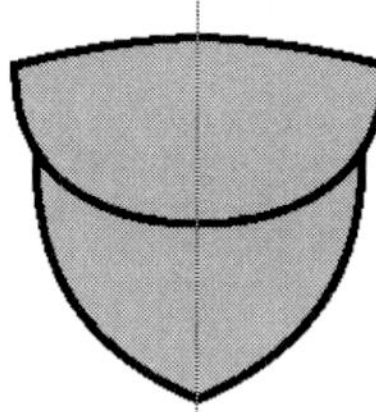

Go to **Preview** mode. Position all of the paths in the jaw and cheek shapes behind the crown shape, using **Object->Arrange->Send to Back**.

17. You will now work on the crown ornaments. Use the Ellipse tool to draw circles to match the crown on the template.

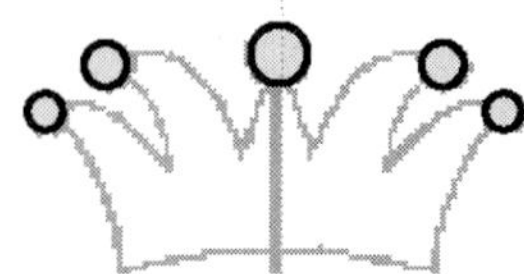

Paint the circles: **Fill** = 100% Yellow, **Stroke** = 0.5 pt. Black.

To change to the Ellipse tool press the "N" key.

18. Do you remember what the eyes, nose, and mouth of the Joker look like? Hide Layer 1 by clicking on the furthest left icon next to the layer name in the **Layers** palette. Take a look at the template, then click on the eye again to view Layer 1.

19. With the Ellipse tool, draw a circle for the Joker's nose. Paint the nose: **Fill** = 100% magenta, 100% yellow, **Stroke** = 0.5 pt. Black.

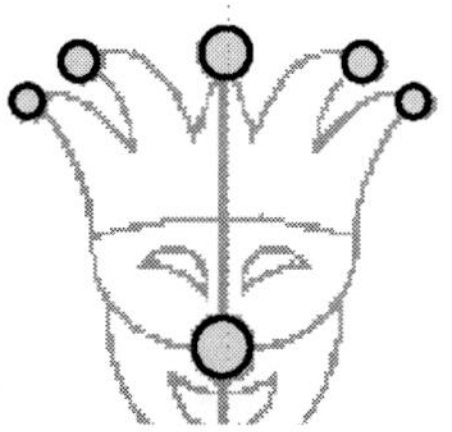

20. The Joker's eyes and mouth are created with overlapping circles, modified with the Pathfinder feature. With the Ellipse tool, draw a circle for the eye. Hold the Option (Macintosh) or Alt (Windows) key and drag a duplicate just below and to the left of the original. Select both objects. Go to **Object->Pathfinder->Minus Front.**

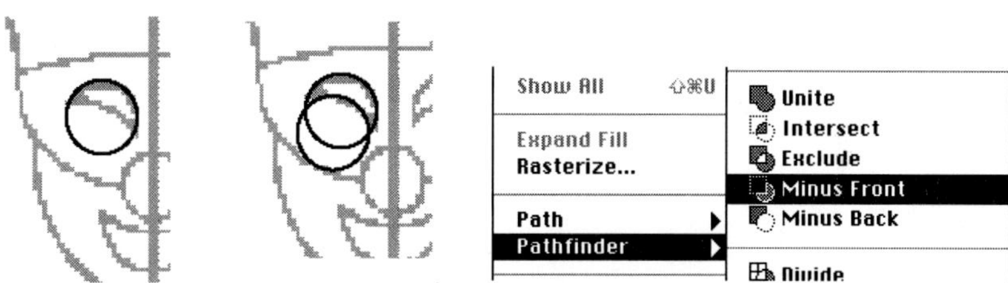

Minus Front means that the object in front is subtracted from the circle that is behind it, leaving this:

Paint the eye: **Fill** = 50% Cyan, 100% Magenta, **Stroke** = 0.5 pt. Black.

Select the eye, access the Reflect Tool in the Toolbox, then click the cross-hair on the center guide while holding the Option (Macintosh) or Alt (Windows) key. In the dialog box that appears, click **Vertical** and **Copy**, to create the second eye.

21. The mouth is created the same way. Draw the first circle for the mouth. Option-drag (Macintosh) or Alt-drag (Windows) the circle to duplicate it.

22. Select both objects. Use **Object->Pathfinder->Minus Front** to modify the circles into one object. Paint the mouth: **Fill** = White, **Stroke** = 0.5 pt. Black.

23. The angled circles on the chest are created a different way. Off to the left of the template, use the Ellipse tool to draw a small 0.05" circle. Paint the circle: **Fill** = 100% Yellow, **Stroke** = 0.5 pt. Black.

Select it and go to **Object->Transform->Move**. Type in these settings, then press **Copy** to make a duplicate underneath.

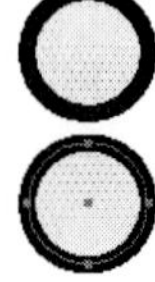
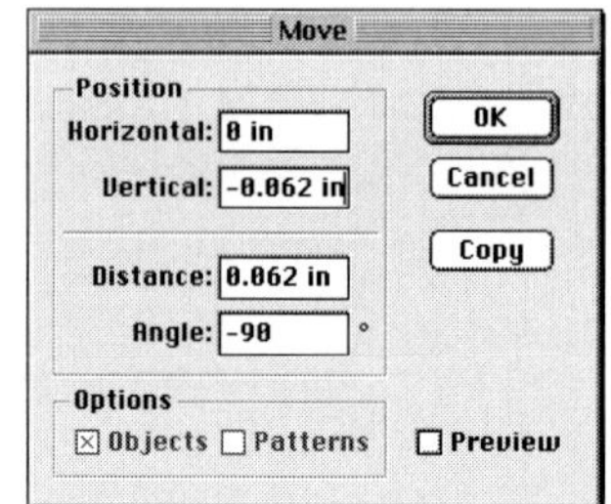

Press Command-D (Macintosh) or Control-D (Windows) to Transform
Again 9 times.

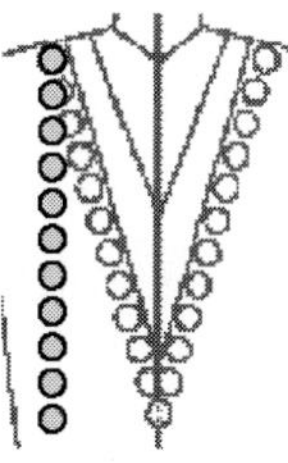

24. Select the circles, press Command-G (Macintosh) or Control-G
    (Windows)to **Group** them. Move the group over so that the top circle
    matches the top circle of the template.

25. Keep the circle group selected. Select the Rotate tool. Hold the Option
    (Macintosh) or Alt (Windows) key and click the crosshair on the center of
    the top circle. In the next dialog box, type "17" for the **Angle**, and click **OK**.

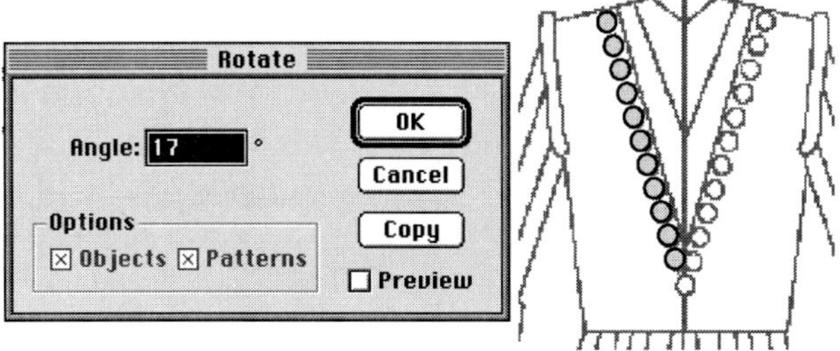

The "A" key is the Direct Selection Tool/Group Selection Tool toggle.

To Hide a selected object press Command-U (Macintosh) or Control-U (Windows). To show all hidden objects, press Shift -Command-U (Macintosh) or Shift-Control-U (Windows).

26. With this angled group selected, access the Reflect tool in the Toolbox. Click the crosshair on the center guide. In the next dialog box, set the **Angle** for 90°, and click **Copy**.

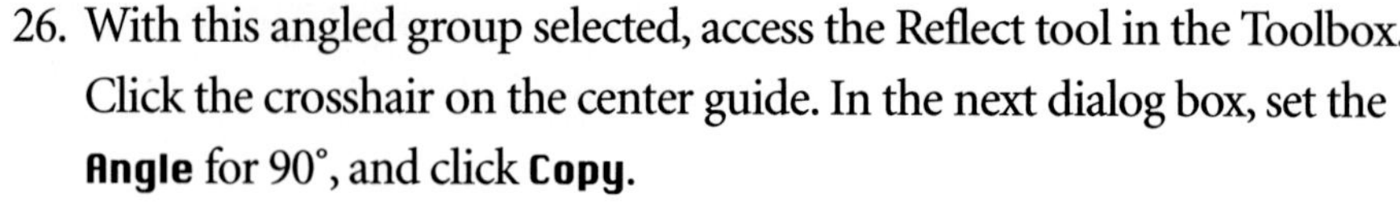

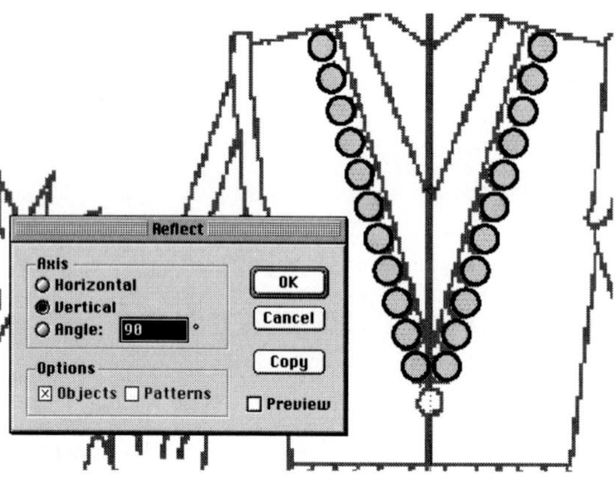

Click on one of the bottom circles with the Direct Selection tool to select just that one circle. **Edit->Copy** and **Edit->Paste** the circle.

Move the duplicate into position where the two groups meet at the bottom. Select all the circles and press Command-U (Macintosh) or Control-U (Windows) to **Hide** them.

27. The upper chest area is merely drawing straight lines with the Pen tool. Draw the three pieces on the left side of the center guide.

After you draw each half, select it and Reflect vertically, then **Join** to make a closed path.

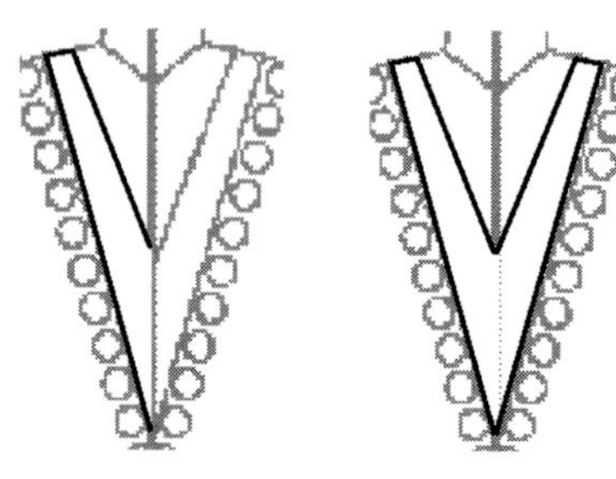

Paint the shape you just drew with: **Fill** = 100% Yellow, **Stroke** = 0.5 pt. Black. Press Command-U (Macintosh) or Control-U (Windows) to **Hide**.

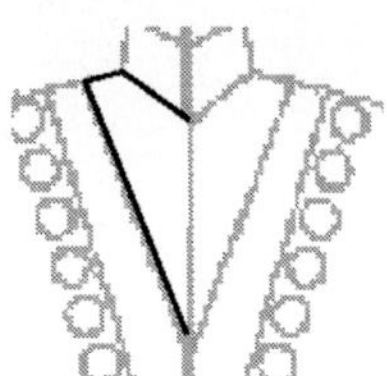 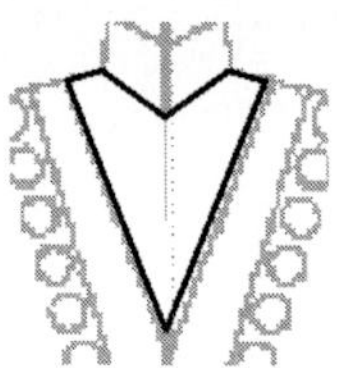

Repeat the process of drawing with the pen tool, reflecting vertically, then joining. Paint the above shape with: **Fill** = 100% Magenta, 100% Yellow, **Stroke** = 0.5 pt. Black. Press Command-U (Macintosh) or Control-U (Windows) to **Hide**.

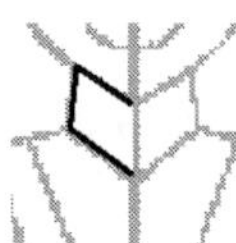 

Repeat the process of drawing with the pen tool, reflecting vertically, then joining. Paint the above shape with: **Fill** = 5% Cyan, 25% Magenta, 25% Yellow, **Stroke** = 0.5 pt. Black. Press Command-U (Macintosh) or Control-U (Windows) to **Hide**.

28. The next object to create is the full chest piece. Drawing on the left side of the center guide, use the Pen tool to click the three segments. Reflect, then **Join** them. Then paint this chest piece with: **Fill** = 50% Cyan, 100% Magenta, 25% Yellow, **Stroke** = 0.5 pt. Black. Select this piece, then go to **Object->Arrange->Send to Back**.

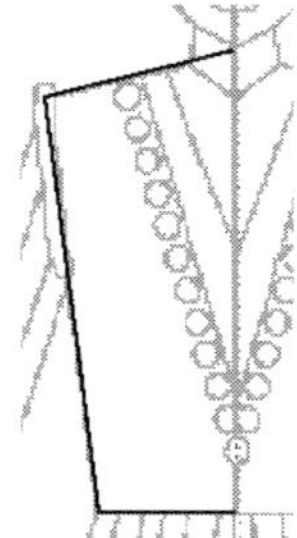 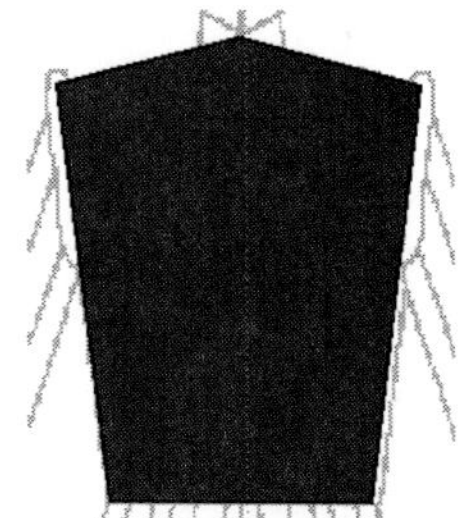

29. After creating the angled circles and the chest pieces, press Command-Shift-U (Macintosh) or Shift- Control-U (Windows) to **Show All** hidden objects. You should see this:

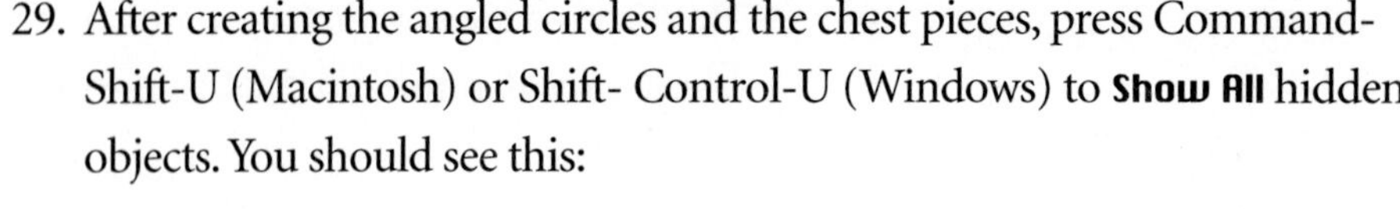

30. The Joker's hands and feet are created using the Pencil tool. Draw the hand/foot to the left side of the center guide. Make sure each is a closed path because you do not need to **Join**. When the left side hand/foot are done, use **Reflect/Copy** to make duplicates on the right side.

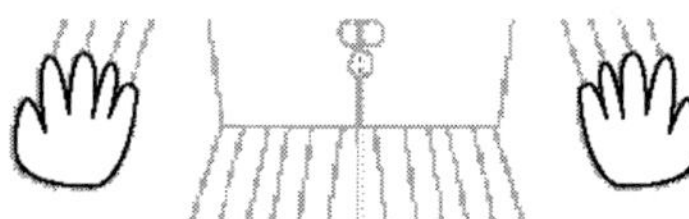

Paint the hands: **Fill** = 5% Cyan, 30% Magenta, 30% Yellow, **Stroke** = 0.5 pt. Black.

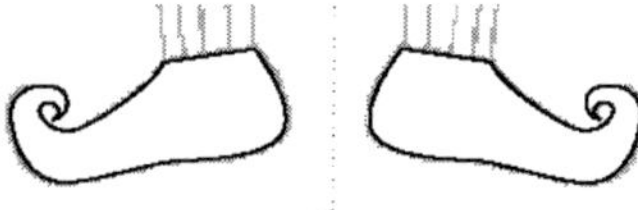

Paint the feet: **Fill** = 100% Yellow, **Stroke** = 0.5 pt. Black.

31. To create the arm, draw the sleeve. Then, draw two separate line segments that go up and down the sleeve.

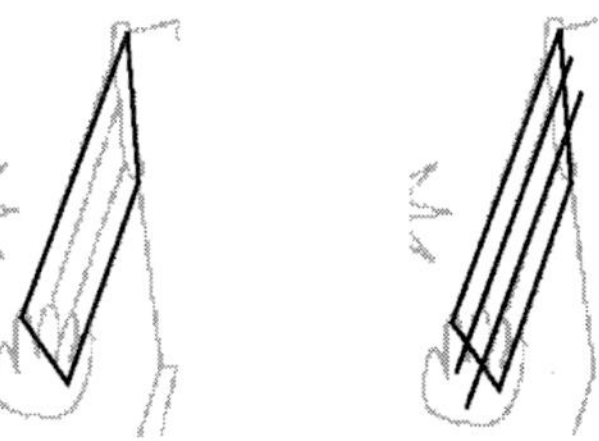

Paint these two segments with **Fill** = None, **Stroke** = None. Select the sleeve and the segments. Go to **Object->Pathfinder->Divide**. This is also shown separated, to show you how the Dividing function created three individual closed paths.

To change to the Pencil or Paintbrush tool use the "Y" key.

When Anchor points are selected you can Join them by pressing Command-J (Macintosh) or Control-J (Windows).

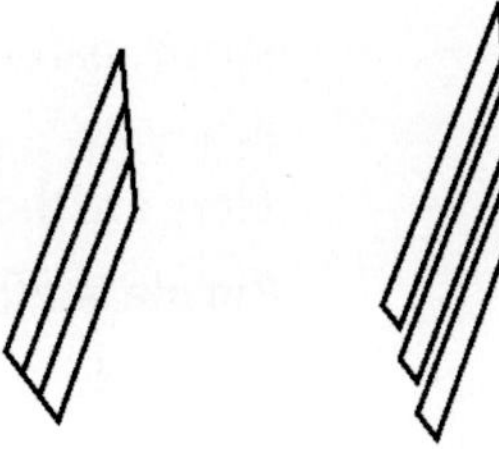

Select each stripe with the Direct Selection tool.
Paint the top path: **Fill** = 100% Magenta, 100% Yellow, **Stroke** = 0.5 pt. Black. Paint the middle path: **Fill** = 50% Cyan, 100% Magenta, **Stroke** = 0.5 pt. Black. Paint the bottom path: **Fill** = 100% Yellow, **Stroke** = 0.5 pt. Black.

Select the stripes and **Object->Group** them. Select the group, then **Object-Arrange->Send to Back**. Then, use **Reflect/Copy** across the center guide to make a duplicate for the right side.

32. The shoulder pads are drawn with the Pen tool, as closed paths. Draw the left side first, then use **Reflect/Copy** to make the right side duplicate. Paint the shoulder pads: **Fill** = 100% Yellow, **Stroke** = 0.5 pt. Black.

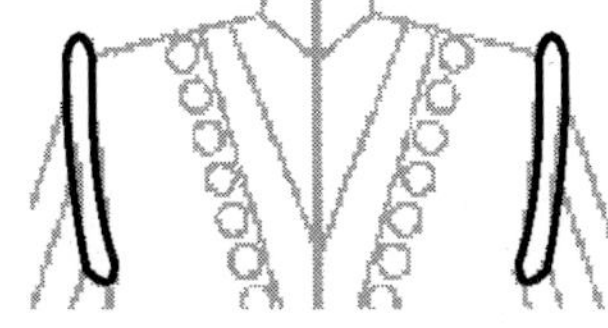

33. Use the same procedure as the sleeve to make the pants. With the Pen tool, draw the outline of the pants. Then draw several segments that act as the stripes. Paint the segments with **Fill** = None, **Stroke** = None.

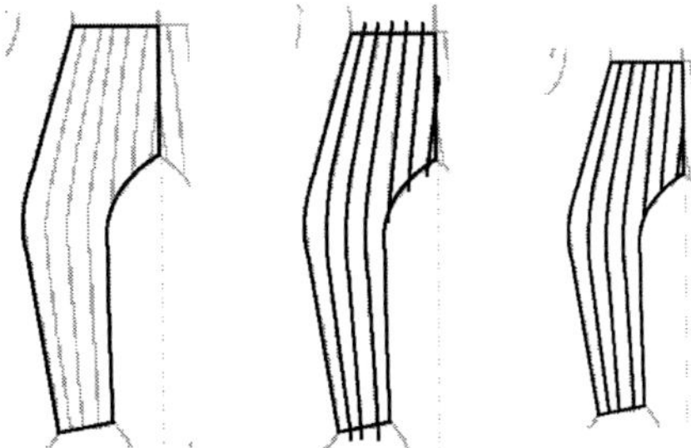

Select each stripe with the Direct Selection tool. Starting from the far left stripe, paint them by alternating the Fills red, then purple, red, purple, etc.

Here are the color breakdowns. **Red** = 100% Magenta, 100% Yellow. **Purple** = 50% Cyan, 100% Magenta. Make the **Strokes** for all stripes 0.5 pt. Black.

34. Press Command-Shift-U (Macintosh) or Control-Shift-U (Windows) to **Show All** objects and paths. Use **Bring to Front** and **Send to Back** from the **Object->Arrange** menu if any of the objects are obscuring another.

    The Joker should be complete, up to this point. From crown to shoes, the various elements should be painted and in place.

35. To make sudden color changes, use the Divide feature. Draw a vertical line along the center guide; color it with no **Fill** or **Stroke**. Press Command-A (Macintosh) or Control-A (Windows) to **Select All** body paths and the vertical line. Go to **Object->Pathfinder->Divide** to split the Joker.

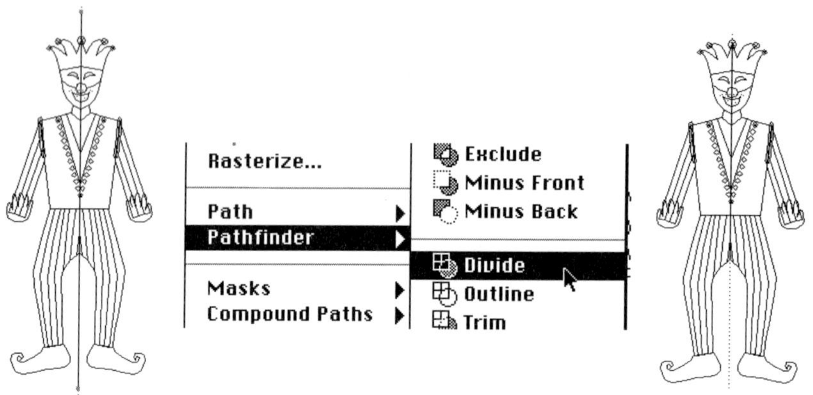

36. With the Direct Selection tool, select the right half of the Joker and go to **Filter->Colors->Invert Colors**.

To change to the Star tool press the "N" key until it is active.

Change to the Rotate or Twirl tool by pressing the "R" key.

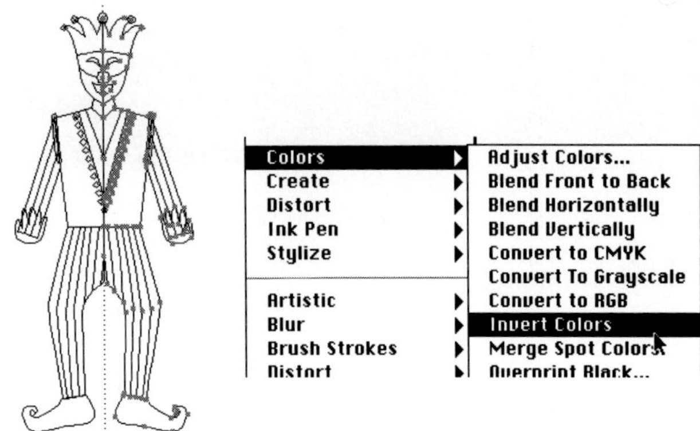

37. Next you will make the starbursts the Joker juggles. Select the Star tool and Option-click (Macintosh) or Alt-click (Windows) above the Joker's head. In the dialog box that appears, enter these numbers:

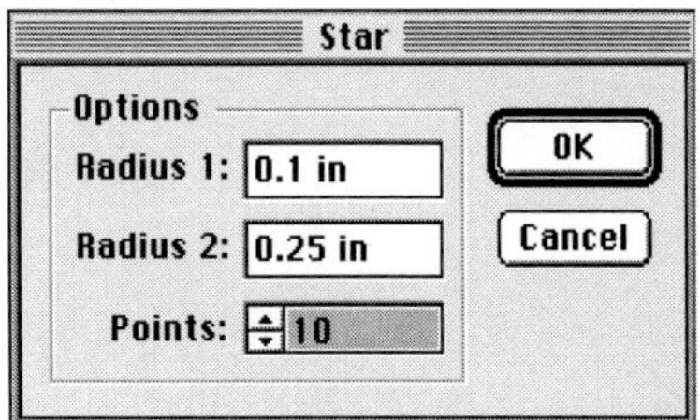

38. With the star selected, paint it: **Fill** = White, **Stroke** = 0.5 pt. Black. Click on the Rotate tool in the Toolbox. Holding the Option key (Macintosh) or Alt key (Windows), click the crosshair on the center of the Joker's nose to set the Point of Origin. In the **Rotate** dialog box that appears, set the Angle for -45 and press **Copy**.

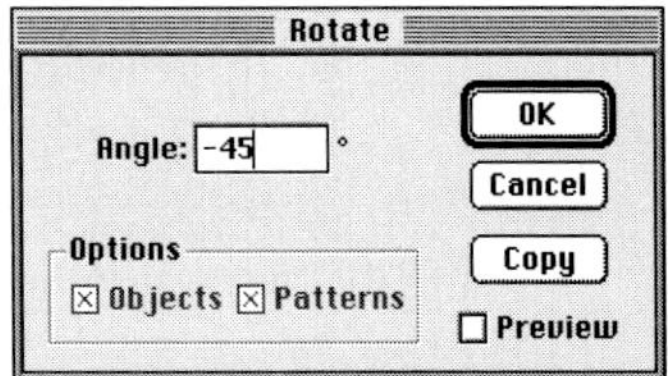

Press Command-D (Transform Again) six times to put the stars in a circle. Delete the star that covers the Joker's stomach.

Fine-tune the stars to better fit the template.

Change to any of the
Rectangle tools by pressing
the "M" key.

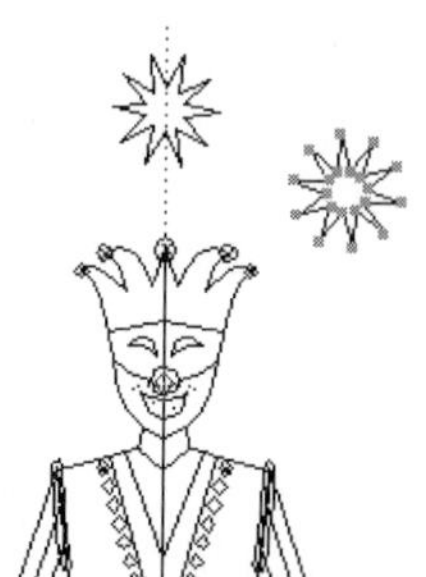

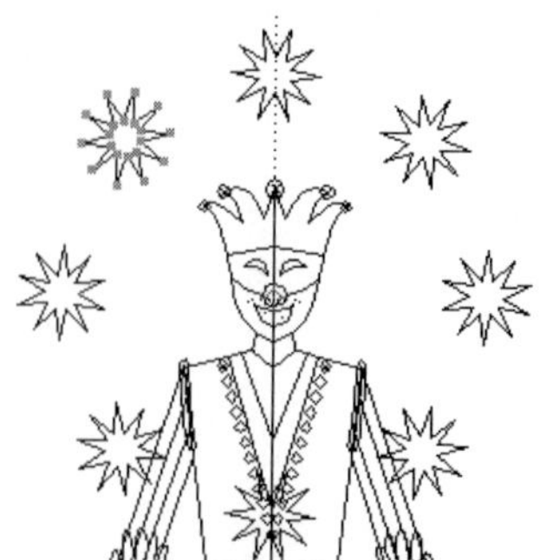

39. Color the middle-left star. Paint it: **Fill** = 100% Yellow, **Stroke** = 0.5 pt. Black. Paint the middle-right star: 100% magenta and 100% yellow, **Stroke** = 0.5 pt. Black.

   Select all stars, and access **Filter->Colors->Blend Horizontal.**

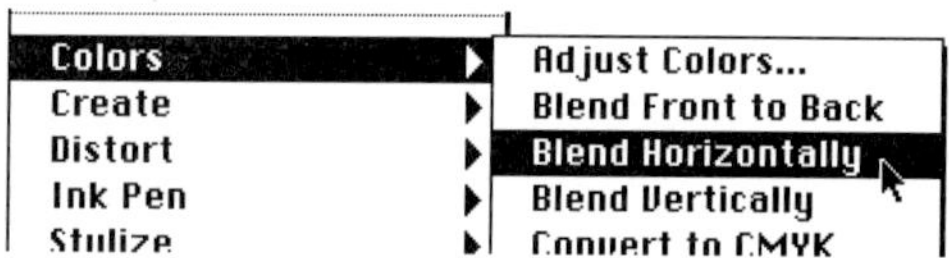

40. To create the card shape and shadow, select the Rectangle tool. Hold the Option key (Macintosh) or Alt key (Windows) and click in the middle waistline of the Joker. In the dialog box that appears, enter these settings:

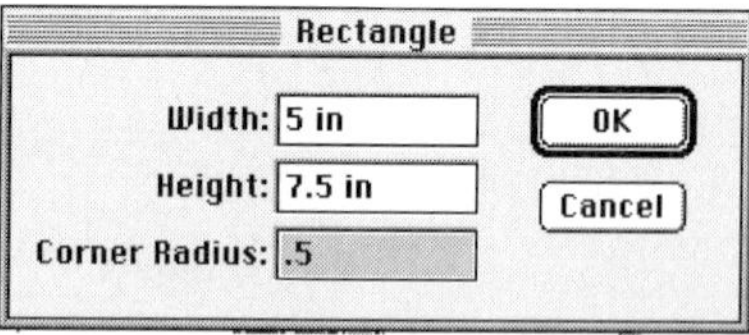

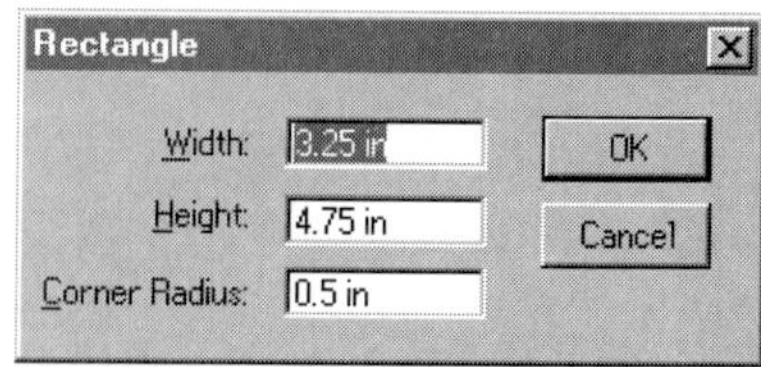

Macintosh   Windows

Color the rectangle with **Fill** = White, **Stroke** = 0.5 pt. Black.

Select the rectangle, then **Copy.** Press Command-B (Macintosh) or Control-B (Windows) to **Paste in Back** the shadow rectangle. Press the Right Arrow key 10 times, and the Down Arrow key 10 times. Paint the shadow: **Fill** = 30% Black, **Stroke** = None.

In addition to Paste, you can Paste in Front by pressing Command-F (Macintosh) or Control-F (Windows), or Paste In Back with Command-B (Macintosh) or Control-B (Windows).

Toggle through the Type tools by pressing the "T" key.

With type selected you can convert to Outlines. With the Selection tool click on any type and press Shift-Command-O (Macintosh) or Shift-Control-O (Windows) to convert the type to Outlines.

Select the rectangle and shadow, position them so that the Joker and stars are centered.

41. Finally, for the letter "J," click the Type tool in the Toolbox, then click the cursor in the upper left corner of the card. Type the capital letter "J."

Click on the Selection tool in the Toolbox. Press Command-T (Macintosh) or Control-T (Windows) to access the **Type Character** palette.

Use this palette to make these settings: **Font** = ATC Tequila, **Size** = 66 pt., **Leading** = Auto, **Tracking** = 0, **Horizontal scale** = 100%.

Position the "J" to fit the template. Go to **Type->Create Outlines**, which will turn the text letter into a path outline.

Click on the rectangle card border. A center point will appear. Mark this point with vertical and horizontal guides you can drag from the rulers.

Click on the letter outline to select it. Click on the Rotate tool in the Toolbox. Holding the Option key (Macintosh) or Alt key (Windows), click the crosshair on the center point you marked with the guides. In the dialog box, type "180" for **Angle**, then click **Copy**. Leave the letter outlines painted Black.

Save As a file by using Shift-Command-S (Macintosh) or Shift-Control-S (Windows).

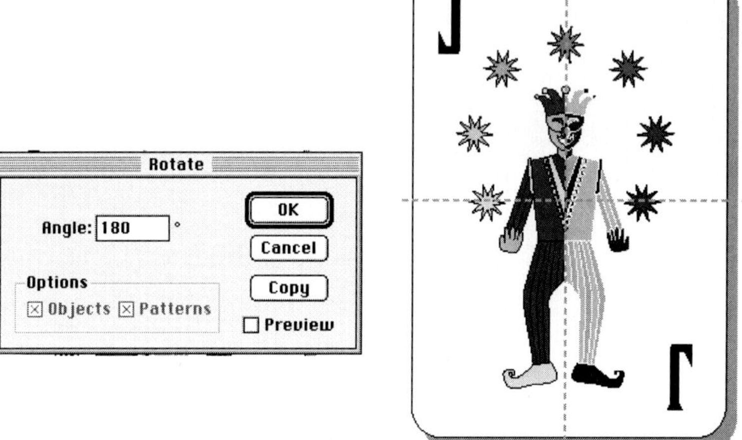

The finished art should like this.

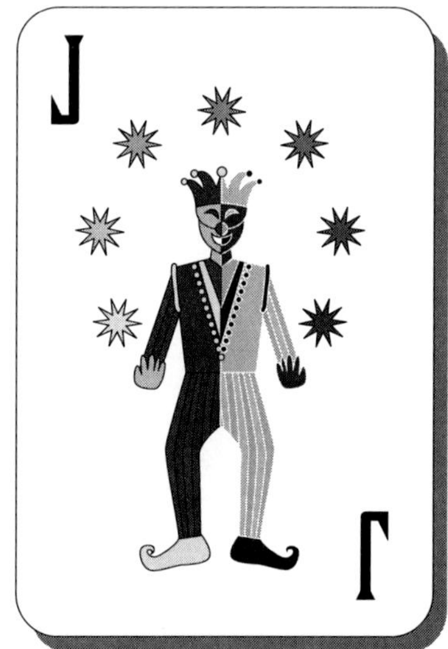

42. **Save As** the file in Illustrator format, naming it "Joker's Wild.AI". **Close** the document.

Project H: Coffee Du Jour Ad

Coffee Du Jour Will Make Your Day

1. Create a new document using **File->New**.

2. You will need to create a template to use as a guide for your layout.

3. Go to **Window->Show Layers** to access the **Layers** palette. Click on the small page icon at the bottom of the palette. This will create a new layer, called Layer 2. Move it to the bottom of the layer levels.

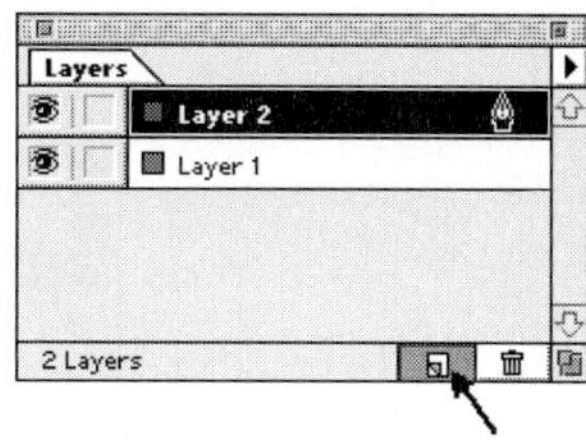
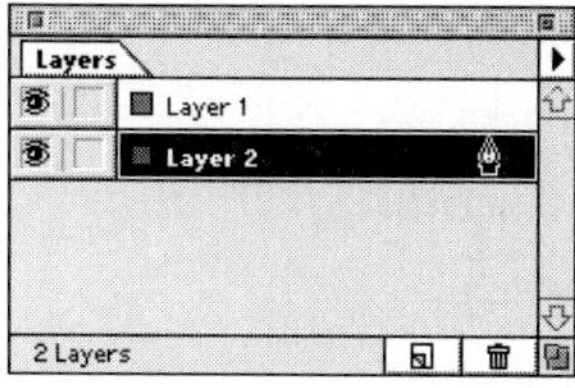

4. Double-click on Layer 2.

5. In the appearing **Layer Options** dialog box, rename the layer "Template."

   Click on **Dim Images**. Click on **Print**, to turn it off.

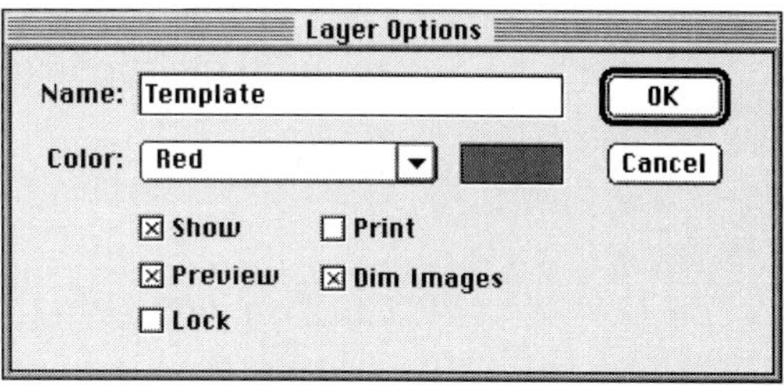

Press **OK**. Leave the Template layer selected in the palette, so it will be the active layer.

6. Use **File->Place** to go to the **SF-Intro Illustrator** folder and **Place** the **Coffee Du Jour Ad.TIF** image. The Placed image will be dimmed gray. Position this image at the top-center of the page.

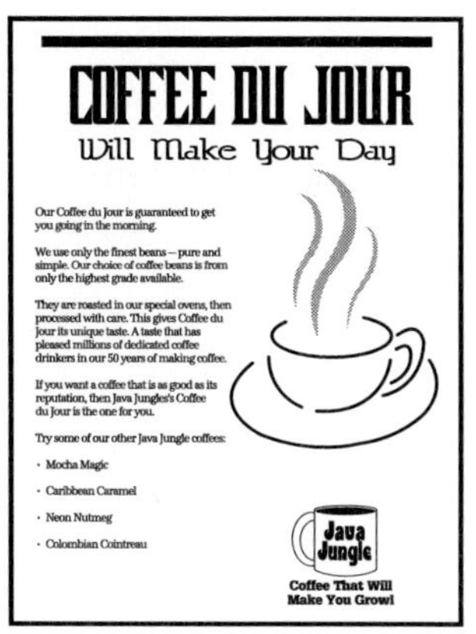

Use Command-N (Macintosh) or Control-N (Windows) to create a new document.

The Crop Marks found in the Object menu will set up crop marks that can be used only by the Illustrator and Photoshop programs. If this were saved as an EPS and Placed into a publishing program, the crop marks will not appear. Using the **Trim Marks** from the **Filter->Create** menu ensures that the crop marks will work in Illustrator as well as in other programs.

When an Illustrator image is opened in Photoshop, the crop marks define the edges of the document.

To Group all selected objects press Command-G (Macintosh) or Control-G (Windows). To Ungroup a selection press Shift-Command-G (Macintosh) or Control (Windows) -G.

7. Go to **Window->Show Layers**. Click on the **Lock** button to lock the Template layer. Click on Layer 1 to continue.

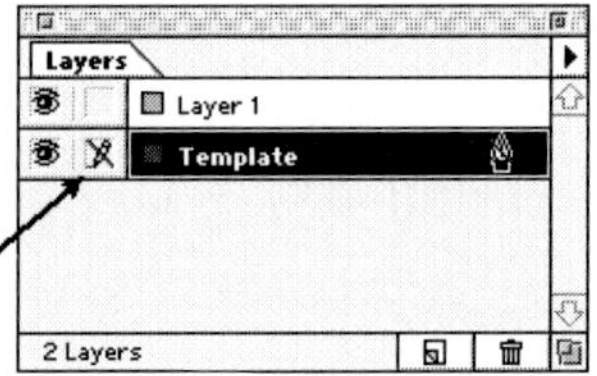

8. **Open** the Illustrator document **Steaming Coffee.AI**. Press Command-A (Macintosh) or Control-A (Windows) to **Select All** paths. Press Command-G (Macintosh) or Control-G (Windows) to **Group** them.

9. Press Command-C (Macintosh) or Control-C (Windows) to **Copy** the group to the clipboard.

10. Close the **Steaming Coffee.AI** document without saving.

11. Click on Layer 1 in the Layers palette. **Paste** the copied group into the working document. Position it to match the template layout, and **Scale** to fit, if necessary. Press Command-L (Macintosh) or Control-L (Windows) to **Lock** the pasted image.

12. **Open** the **Java Jungle Logo.AI** file.

13. Press Command-A (Macintosh) or Control-A (Windows)to **Select All** paths. Press Command-G (Macintosh) or Control-G (Windows) to **Group** them. **Copy** the group to the clipboard.

14. **Close** the **Java Jungle Logo.AI** document without saving. **Paste** the contents of the clipboard into the working document. Position it to match the template layout. Scale if necessary.

15. Click on the Type tool in the Toolbox. Click it once near the headline at the top of the ad. Type the words:

COFFEE DU JOUR

Highlight this phrase with the I-beam cursor. Press Command-T (Macintosh) or Control-T (Windows) to get the **Type Character** window.

16. Set the type as shown in this window. **Font** = ATC Tequila, **Size** = 78 pt., **Leading** = 93.5 pt., **Tracking** = -80, **Horizontal scale** = 120%. Set type alignment to Center. Position this headline with the Selection tool, matching the template layout.

17. Click the I-beam once near the headline at the top of the ad. Type the words:

Will Make Your Day

Highlight this phrase with the I-beam. Press Shift-Command-C (Macintosh) or Shift-Control-C (Windows) to center the alignment. Highlight the type and apply these settings. **Font** = ATC Daquiri, **Size** = 30 pt., **Leading** = 36 pt., **Tracking** = -80, **Horizontal scale** = 140%. Position the type to match the layout in the template.

18. For the body text, you will be importing a text file from the **SF-Intro Illustrator** folder. Access the Type tool and draw a text block where you want the text to be positioned.

19. Place **Coffee Du Jour Ad.TXT** found in the **SF-Intro Illustrator** folder.

20. The text block you drew will fill up with the imported text. Press Command-A (Macintosh) or Control-A (Windows) to **Select All** the text.

21. In the **Type->Character** window, apply these settings to the imported text: **Font** = ATC Colada, **Size** = 12 pt., **Leading** = 13 pt., **Tracking** = -60, **Horizontal scale** = 90%. Press Return to apply the settings. Deselect the text block.

Toggle through the Type tools by pressing "T".

Activate the Character window by pressing Command-T (Macintosh) or Control-T (Windows).

Change to the Zoom tool by pressing the "Z" key.

Change to any of the Rectangle tools by pressing the "M" key.

Save As a file by using Shift-Command-S (Macintosh) or Shift-Control-S (Windows).

22. Use the Zoom tool to zoom in on the bottom of the ad where the Java Jungle logo is located.

23. With the Type tool cursor, click one time and type the phrase:

Coffee That Will

Make You Growl

Highlight the phrase with the I-beam. Make these settings: **Font** = ATC Coconuts, **Size** = 14 pt., **Leading** = 14 pt., **Tracking** = -20, **Horizontal Scale** = 100%. Press Return (Macintosh) or Enter (Windows) to apply.

24. Set the alignment of the type to Center. Position the type to match the type in the template.

25. For the black rule across the top of the ad, use the Rectangle tool to draw a bar that matches the template.

26. Paint the bar: **Fill**= Black, **Stroke** = None.

27. Use the Rectangle tool to draw a 7" x 9" border around the ad. Select this border. Go to **Filter->Create->Trim Marks** to set Trim Marks. Delete the border you drew. The completed ad should look similar to this:

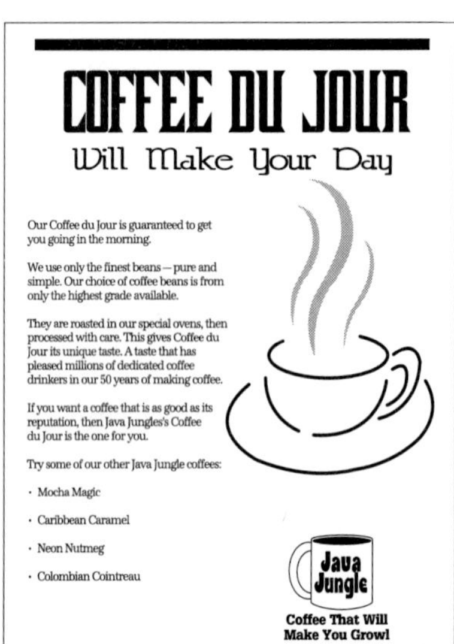

28. **Save As** the file in **Illustrator** format, naming it "Coffee Du Jour ad.AI." **Close** the document.

Project I: Tropical Treasure Mailer

Creating the Layout

1. Create a new document using **File->New**.

2. You will need to create a template to use as a guide for your layout.

3. Go to **Window->Show Layers** to access the **Layers** palette. Click on the small page icon at the bottom of the palette. This will create a new layer, called Layer 2. Move it to the bottom of the layer levels.

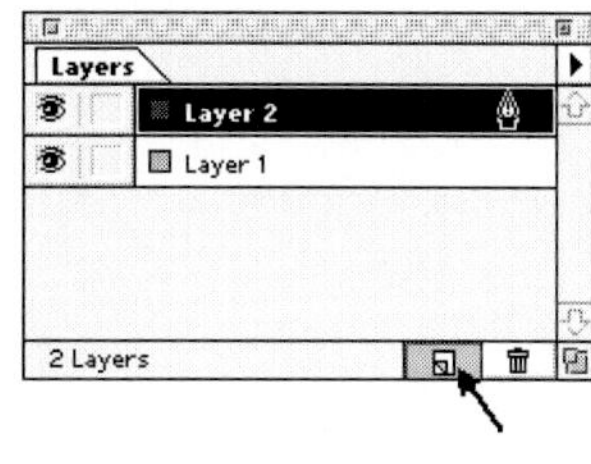
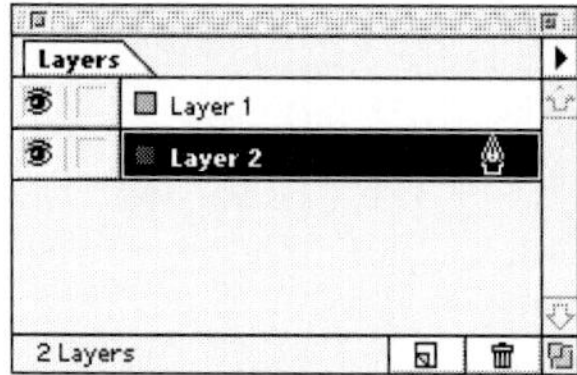

4. Double-click on Layer 2.

5. In the appearing **Layer Options** dialog box, rename the layer "Template."

   Click on **Dim Images**. Click on **Print**, to turn it off.

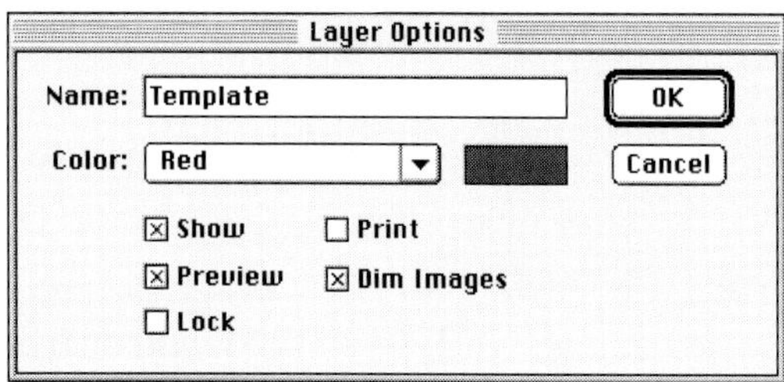

Press **OK**. Leave the Template layer selected in the palette, so it will be the active layer.

6. Use **File->Place** to go to the **SF-Intro Illustrator** folder and **Place** the **Tropical Mailer.TIF** image. The Placed image will be dimmed gray. Position this image at the top center of the page.

If any objects are unable to be selected with the Selection tool, they could be **Locked**. To **Unlock** them, press Shift-Command-L (Macintosh) or Shift-Ctrl-L (Windows). **Unlock All** will unlock every locked object. It cannot single out specific objects.

Press Command-O (Macintosh) or Control-O (Windows) to Open a document.

To Copy a selected object to the clipboard, press Command-C (Macintosh) or Control-C (Windows).

To Paste, press Command-V (Macintosh) or Control-V (Windows).

7. Go to **Window->Show Layers**. Click on the **Lock** button to lock the Template layer. Click on Layer 1 to continue.

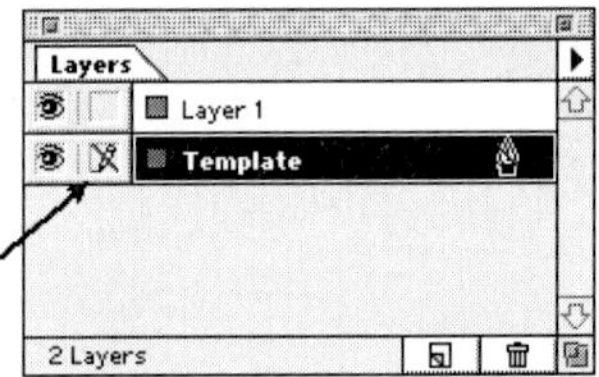

8. **Open** the document, **Tropical Fish Illustration.AI.**

9. Press Command-A (Macintosh) or Control-A (Windows) to **Select All** paths. Press Command-G (Macintosh) or Control-G (Windows) to **Group** them. **Copy** the group to the clipboard.

10. **Close** the **Tropical Fish Illustration.AI** document without saving.

11. **Paste** the group into the working document. Position it to match the template.

12. **Open** the **Tropical Treasure Logo.AI** file.

13. Press Command-A (Macintosh) or Control-A (Windows) to **Select All** paths.
    Press Command-G (Macintosh) or Control-G (Windows) to **Group** them. **Copy** the group to the clipboard.

14. **Close** the **Tropical Treasure Logo.AI** document. **Paste** the group into the working document. Position it to match the template.

15. Click on the Tropical Treasure Logo group to select it.

16. Double-click on the Scale tool in the Toolbox. In the **Uniform** box type "42". Make sure the **Scale Line Weight** box is clicked. Press **OK**. This will reduce the logo to fit the layout. Position it to match the template.

17. Select the Type tool, then click the cursor on the page to type these words:

Don't Make Waves!

18. Highlight this phrase with the Type tool. Press Command-T (Macintosh) or Control-T (Windows) to get the **Type->Character** window. Set the type to be: **Font** = ATC Sea Breeze, **Size** = 36 pt., **Leading** 43 pt., **Tracking** = 0, **Horizontal scale** = 50%.

19. In the **Paragraph** palette, set the alignment to Center. Position this headline into place, matching the template layout.

20. Use **Window->Swatch Libraries->Other Library** to access colors from **ATC Custom Colors.AI.** Paint the headline: **Fill** = ATC Coral, **Stroke** = None.

21. Select this headline. **Copy** it. Choose **Edit->Paste in Back** .

22. With the Pasted duplicate still selected, press the keyboard Right Arrow 2 times, and the Down Arrow 2 times.

23. Paint the duplicate headline: **Fill** = ATC Blue, **Stroke** = None. Deselect the duplicate.

24. In the **Type->Character** window, make: **Font** = ATC Colada, **Size** =10 pt., **Leading** = 14 pt., **Tracking** = -40, **Horizontal scale** = 90%.

25. Click on the Type tool in the Toolbox. Draw a text block for the body copy to fit the template. Type this text:

> Dive down to Tropical Treasures. Find exquisite gifts and goodies made from purely natural materials from the sea. See our coral, sea shells, sand dollars, and more!

Change to any of the Rectangle tools by pressing the "M" key.

Utilize the View mode toggle. Press Command-Y (Macintosh) or Control-Y (Windows) to change between Preview and Artwork Mode.

Save As a file by using Shift-Command-S (Macintosh) or Shift-Control-S (Windows).

26. With the Selection tool, position the text block to match the body copy in the template.

27. Use the Rectangle tool to draw the color bar across the top of the mailer. Use the image below for reference.
Paint the bar: **Fill** = ATC Blue, **Stroke** = None.

28. In **Preview** mode, use the Rectangle tool to draw a 3" x 6.5" border around the mailer. **Fill** = None, **Stroke** = 1pt. Black.

Fit your border to the border of the template. In the **Filter** menu, select **Create->Trim Marks** to set. Delete the border you just drew. The completed art should look like this.

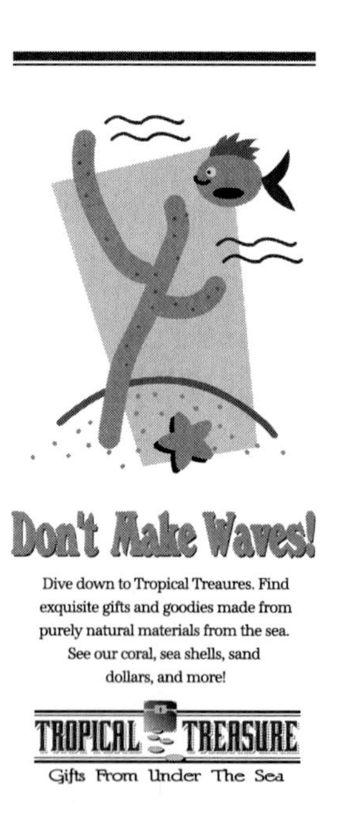

29. **Save As** the file in the **Illustrator** format, and name it "Tropical Treasure Mailer.AI." **Close** the document.

Project J: Last Mango Business Card

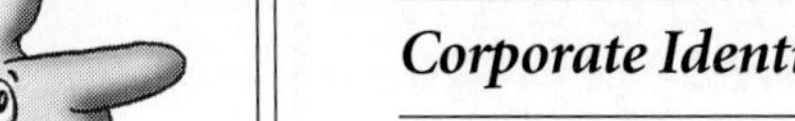

Corporate Identity

1. Create a new document using **File->New**.

2. You will need to create a template to use as a guide for your layout.

3. Go to **Window->Show Layers** to access the **Layers** palette. Click on the small page icon at the bottom of the palette. This will create a new layer, called Layer 2. Move it to the bottom of the layer levels.

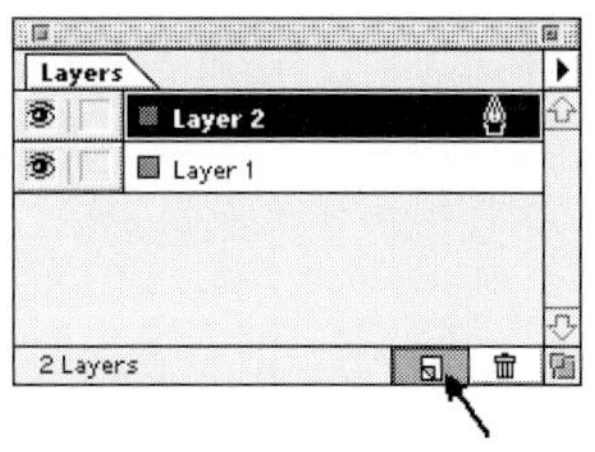
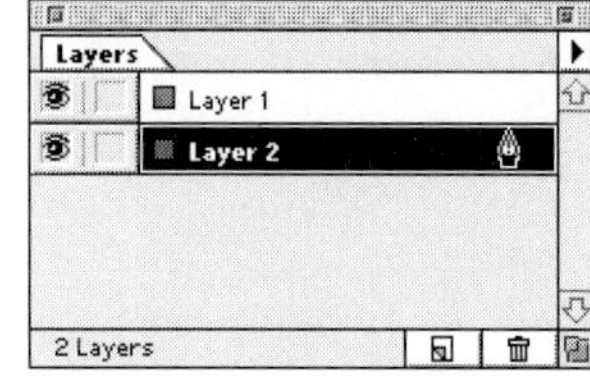

4. Double-click on Layer 2.

5. In the appearing **Layer Options** dialog box, rename the layer "Template."

   Click on **Dim Images**. Click on **Print**, to turn it off.

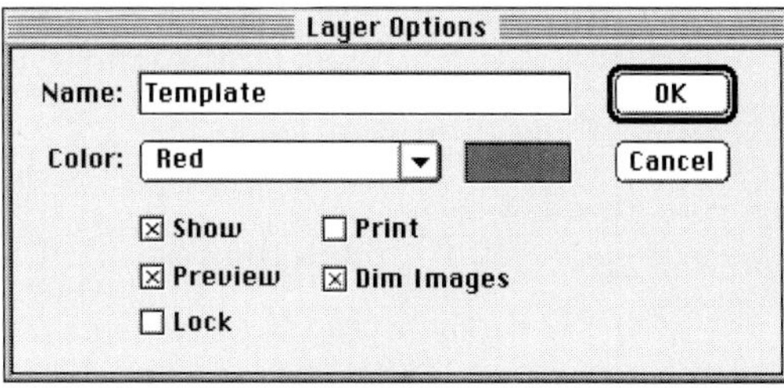

   Press **OK**. Leave the Template layer selected in the palette, so it will be the active layer.

6. Use **File->Place** to go to the **SF-Intro Illustrator** folder and **Place** the **Last Mango Card.TIF** image. The Placed image will be dimmed gray. Position this image at the top-center of the page.

Use Command-N
(Macintosh) or Control-N
(Windows) to create a new
document.

Change to any of the
Rectangle tools by pressing
the "M" key.

Press Command-O
(Macintosh) or Control-O
(Windows) to Open a
document.

7. Go to **Window->Show Layers.** Click on the **Lock** button to lock the
Template layer. Click on Layer 1 to continue.

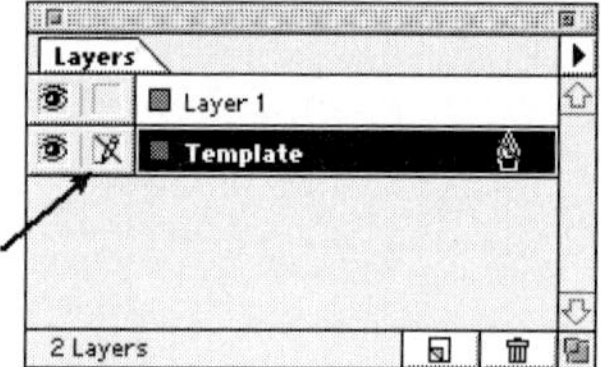

8. Select the Rectangle tool in the Toolbox. Click the crosshair on the page.
In the dialog box that appears, set the **Width** for 3.5 inches, and the
Height for 2 inches. Paint the rectangle: **Fill** = None, **Stroke** = 1 pt. Black.
This will be the working border of the card. Click **OK**.

9. Press Command-L (Macintosh) or Control-L (Windows) to **Lock** the
border.

10. **Open** the document **Last Mango Logo.AI.**

11. Press Command-A (Macintosh) or Control-A (Windows) to **Select All**
paths. Press Command-G (Macintosh) or Control-G (Windows) to
Group them. **Copy** the group to the clipboard.

12. **Close** the **Last Mango Logo.AI** document without saving.

13. **Paste** the group into the working document.

To use the Reshape or Scale tool press the "S" key.

To activate the Paragraph window press Command-M (Macintosh) or Control-M (Windows).

Lock and Unlock objects to manipulate your document easier. To Lock selected objects press Command-L (Macintosh) or Control-L (Windows). To Unlock all objects, yes you have to unlock all of them, press Shift-Command-L (Macintosh) or Shift-Control-L (Windows).

14. Double-click on the Scale tool in the Toolbox. In the **Uniform** box, type "50". Make sure the **Scale Line Weight** box is clicked. Press **OK**. This will reduce the logo to fit the layout. Position it to match the template.

15. Select the Type tool in the Toolbox. Click its cursor on the page. Type the address:

> 1334 Bayshore Circle
> Freeport, Bahamas

16. Click the Type tool in the Toolbox to deselect this text block.

17. Click the Type tool cursor on the page to create a new text block. Type the following words.

> Beer
> Wine
> Food
> Fun

18. With the Selection tool, hold the Shift key and select the two text blocks. This is another way of selecting text in order to apply Type attributes.

    Press Command-T (Macintosh) or Control-T (Windows) to access the **Type->Character** window.

19. Set the type as: **Font** = ATC Daquiri, **Size** = 10 pt., **Leading** = 11 pt., **Tracking** = -40, **Kerning** = Auto, **Baseline shift** = 0.

20. In the **Type->Paragraph** palette, set the alignment to Align Left.

21. Position the address into place, matching the address in the template. Position the body copy items into place, matching those in the template.

22. Press Command-Shift-L (Macintosh) or Control-Shift-L (Windows) to **Unlock** the border.

23. With the border selected, go to **Filter->Create->Trim Marks** to create Trim Marks for the dimensions of the business card. Delete the border.

Press Command-A
(Macintosh) or Control-A
(Windows) to Select All.

Document Setup is
accessible by pressing
Shift-Command-P
(Macintosh) or Shift-
Control-P (Windows).

The completed business card with Trim Marks should look similar to this:

Creating a Four-up Layout

Some commercial printers use the "4-up" ganging technique, in which the art is duplicated and set up so four cards can be printed at once, then cut according to the Trim Marks.

24. **Edit->Select All** to select the entire art pieces. Go to **Object->Group** to group them as one.

25. Go to **File->Document Set**, click on **Use Page Setup**, then click on **Page Setup**. In the next dialog box, select Landscape (wide) orientation. Click OK.

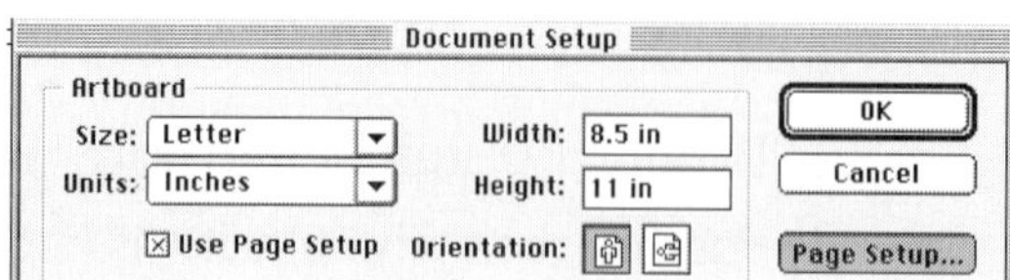

26. Go to **File->Preferences->General** and make sure that **Snap to Point** is clicked on. Click **OK**.

27. Set the ruler Zero Point to the upper left corner of the page. Drag a vertical guide over to the 5.5" mark of the ruler to show a center line.

28. Select the art group with the Selection tool, and position it so the upper right Trim Mark is aligned with the center line guide.

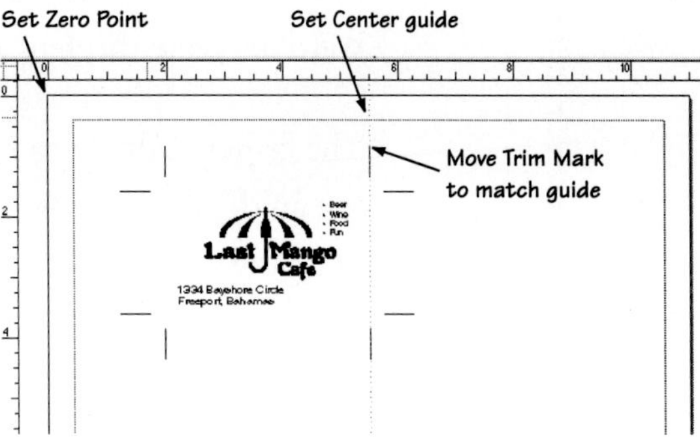

When moving objects, the cursor turns into a solid chevron arrow.

When points become aligned, the chevron turns hollow.

If the Option key is pressed, as the object is moved, the cursor becomes a double cursor.

When points become aligned, the double cursor turns hollow.

29. With the Selection tool, click-hold on the top-left Trim Mark's anchor point. The entire group will be selected for you to move to the right for duplication. When you move the group, the cursor will become a solid chevron arrow (▶).

As you move the art group, hold the Shift key to constrain its alignment. The purpose of this move is to duplicate the group, and keep the Trim Marks perfectly aligned.

30. As the duplicate image's Trim Mark is matching the original's Trim Mark on the center guide, the cursor will become hollow (▷). When this happens, press the Option (Macintosh) or Alt (Windows) key for the duplication to take place. When you press this key, the cursor will become a double-arrow (⇗). Don't be alarmed. This is to show the extra key is pressed.

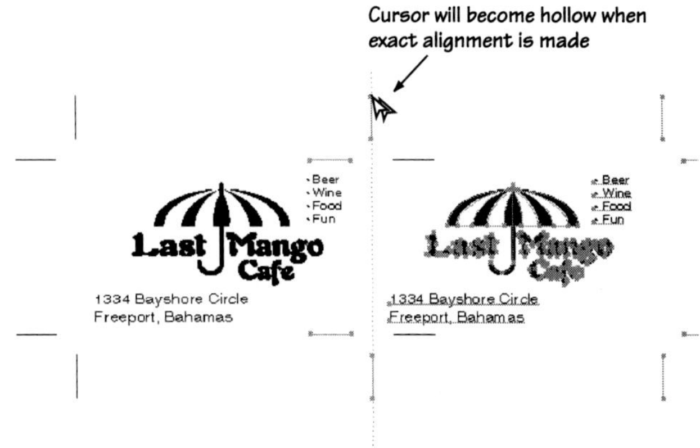

When the hollow arrows appear, the alignment is exact. Let go of the mouse button.

31. Shift-Select both the art groups. You are now going to drag them down-
    ward to create the 4-up layout.

    The center-right Trim Mark will be selected on its anchor point closest to
    the guide, shown here. Click-hold on this point with the Selection tool.
    Drag the groups down so the Trim Mark aligns with the Trim Mark under
    the word "Freeport."

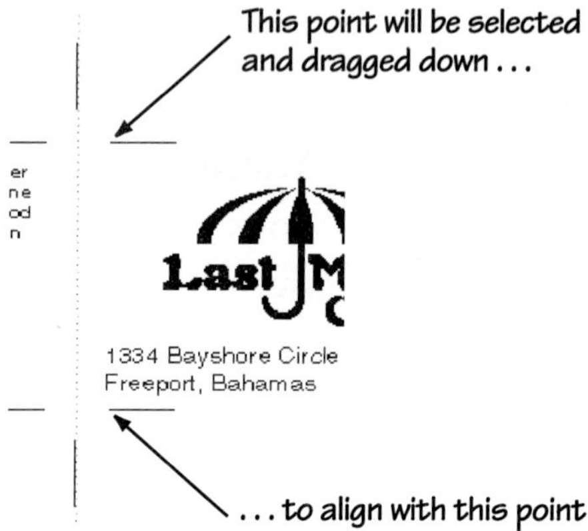

32. After the moving has begun, hold the Shift key to constrain alignment.
    When the two Trim Marks align, and the cursor becomes hollow, press the
    Option (Macintosh) or Alt (Windows) key, so the groups will duplicate.

33. Once the cursor turns hollow, let go of the mouse button. You will now
    have to delete some of the extra Trim Marks.

34. Use this example as a guide for the Trim Marks that are needed. Use the Direct Selection tool to select and delete all the others.

35. The 4-up business card layout is finished, and should look like this.

36. **Save As** the file in **Illustrator** format, naming it "Last Mango Bus Card.AI." **Close** the document.

Notes:

4/1

A job printed using four colors of ink on one side of the sheet, and one color of ink on the other.

4/4

A job printed with four colors of ink on both sides of the sheet. A full four-color project. See *process colors, subtractive color.*

Acetate

A plastic material used to block or expose specific portions of a layout through "windows" cut from the material by a stripper. The resultant "masks" are used to generate film separations for generating printing plates.

Achromatic

By definition, having no color; therefore, completely black or white or some shade of gray.

Acrobat

This program by Adobe Systems, Inc. converts any document from any Macintosh or Windows application to PDF format, which retains the page layout, graphics, color, and typography of the original document. It is widely used for distributing documents online because it is independent of computer hardware. The only software needed is a copy of Acrobat Reader, which can be downloaded free.

Adaptive Palette

A sampling of colors taken directly from an image, and used in a special compression process usually used to prepare images for the world wide web.

Additive Color Process

The additive color process is the process of mixing red, green, and blue light to achieve a wide range of colors, as on a color television screen. See *Subtractive Color.*

Adjacent Color

The eye will respond to a strong adjacent color in such a way as to affect the perception of the particular color in question. That is, a color having different adjacent colors may look different than it does in isolation. Also referred to as metamarism.

Adobe Systems Incorporated

A major software developer responsible for the creation of the PostScript page description language (see *PostScript*), used in almost all graphic arts environments. PostScript resides in a printer or Raster Image Processor (see *Raster Image Processor*) and is used to convert graphics from the screen to high-resolution output. Adobe also develops the highly popular Photoshop, Illustrator, PageMaker, and Premiere graphics and video applications, in addition to a range of others.

Airbrush

A tool driven by compressed air that applies a very fine spray of color to artwork to produce various effects. Its effects are simulated in digital illustration and imaging programs.

Algorithm

A specific sequence of mathematical steps to process data. A portion of a computer program that calculates a specific result.

Alley

The white space, or margin, between columns on a page.

Alpha Channel

An 8-bit channel of data that provides additional graphic information, such as colors or masking. Alpha channels are found in some illustration or graphics programs, and are used in video production.

ANSI

The American National Standards Institute. ANSI establishes and publishes industry standards in many fields including data transmission and graphics.

Anti-aliasing

A graphics software feature that eliminates or softens the jaggedness of low-resolution curved edges.

Apple Computer, Inc.

A computer manufacturer based in Cupertino, California. Apple was responsible for the development of the Macintosh computer and the first Postscript-equipped laser printer, which ushered in the "desktop publishing" revolution.

Archival storage

The process of storing data in a totally secure and safe manner. Archiving differs from backup in that it's meant to be used to restore entire systems or networks, rather than providing quick and easy access to specific files or folders.

Art

Illustrations and photographs in general; that is, all matter other than text that appears in a mechanical.

Artifact

By definition, something that is artificial, or not meant to be there. An artifact can be a blemish or dust spot on a piece of film, or unsightly pixels in a digital image.

Ascender

Parts of a lower-case letter that exceed the height of the letter "x". The letters b, d, f, h, k, l, and t have ascenders.

ASCII

The American Standard Code for Information Interchange, which defines each character, symbol, or special code as a number from 0 to 255 (8 bits in binary). An ASCII text file can be read by any computer, and is the basic mode of data transmission on the Internet.

ATM (Adobe Type Manager)

A utility program which causes fonts to appear smooth on screen at any point size. It's also used to manage font libraries.

Author's Alterations (A/As)

Changes made to the copy by the author after typesetting, and thus chargeable to the author.

Backing Up

The process of making copies of current work or work-in-progress as a safety measure against file corruption, drive or system failure, or accidental deletion. Backing up work-in-progress differs from creating an archive (see *Archiving*) for long-term storage or system restoration.

Backslant

A name for characters that slant the opposite way from italic characters.

Banding

A visible stair-stepping of shades in a gradient.

Banner

A large headline or title extending across the full page width, or across a double-page spread.

Baseline

The implied reference line on which the bases of capital letters sit.

Bézier Curves

Curves that are defined mathematically (vectors), in contrast to those drawn as a collection of dots or pixels (raster). The advantage of these curves is that they can be scaled without the "jaggies" inherent in enlarging bitmapped fonts or graphics.

Binding

In general, the various methods used to secure signatures or leaves in a book. Examples include saddle-stitching (the use of staples in a folded spine), and perfect-bound (multiple sets of folded pages sewn or glued into a flat spine).

Bit (Binary Digit)

The smallest unit of information in a computer, representing one of two conditions, ON or OFF; HIGH or LOW, etc. Eight bits comprise one byte. One byte can represent any text character.

Bitmap

A rectangular array of dots that, taken together, form an image. Bitmap file formats include: .BMP, .DIB, .GIF, .PCX and .TIFF (see *Raster Graphics*).

Bitmapped

An image formed by a grid of dots or pixels whose curved edges have discrete steps because of the approximation of the curve by a finite number of pixels.

Black

The absence of color; an ink that absorbs all wavelengths of light.

Blanket

The blanket, a fabric coated with natural or synthetic rubber wrapped around the cylinder of an offset press, transfers the inked image from the plate to the paper.

Bleed

Page data that extends beyond the trim marks on a page. Illustrations that spread to the edge of the paper without margins are referred to as "bled off."

Blind Emboss

A raised impression in paper made by a die, but without being inked. It is visible only by its relief characteristic.

Blow up

An enlargement, usually of a graphic element such as a photograph.

Body Copy

The text portion of the copy on a page, as distinguished from headlines.

Boldface

A heavier, blacker version of a typeface.

Bond

A sized (coated) writing paper used for business or personal stationery that normally has significant rag (cotton) content.

Border

A continuous line that extends around text; or a rectangular, oval, or irregularly-shaped visual in an ad.

Bounding Box

The imaginary rectangle that encloses all sides of a graphic, necessary for a page layout specification.

Brightness

1. A measure of the amount of light reflected from a surface. 2. A paper property, defined as the percentage reflection of 457-nanometer (nm) radiation. 3. The intensity of a light source. 4. The overall percentage of lightness in an image.

Bug

See *Logo*

Bullet

A marker preceding text, usually a solid dot, used to add emphasis; generally indicates that the text is part of a list.

Burn

1. To expose an image onto a plate. 2. To make copies of ROM chips or CD-ROMs. 3. To darken a specific portion of an image through photographic exposure.

Byte

A unit of measure equal to eight bits (decimal 256) of digital information, sufficient to represent one text character. It is the standard unit measure of file size. (See also *Megabyte, Kilobyte,* and *Gigabyte*).

Calibration Bars

A strip of reference blocks of color or tonal values used to check the registration, quality, density, and ink coverage during a print run.

Calibration

Making adjustments to a color monitor and other hardware and software to make the monitor represent as closely as possible the colors of the final printed piece.

Callout

A descriptive label referenced to a visual element, such as several words connected to the element by an arrow.

Camera Ready

A completely finished mechanical, ready to be photographed to produce a negative from which a printing plate will be made.

Cap Line

The theoretical line to which the tops of capital letters are aligned.

Caps and Small Caps

A style of typesetting in which capital letters are used in the normal way, while the type that would normally be in lower case has been changed to capital letters of a smaller point size. A true small-caps typeface does not contain any lower-case letters.

Caps

An abbreviation for capital letters.

Caption

The line or lines of text that identify a picture or illustration, usually placed beneath it or otherwise in close proximity.

CD-ROM

A device used to store approximately 600MB of data. Files are permanently stored on the device and can be copied to a disk but not altered directly. ROM stands for Read-Only Memory. Equipment is now available on the consumer market for copying computer files to blank CD-ROMs.

Character Count

The number of characters (letters, figures, signs or spaces) in a selected block of copy. Once used to calculate the amount of text that would fit on a given line or region when physically setting type.

Choke

See *Trapping*

Chooser

A part of the Macintosh operating system that permits selection of a printer or other peripheral device. Chooser is also used to access resources on a network.

Chroma

The degree of saturation of a surface color in the Munsell color space model.

Chromaticity Diagram

A graphical representation of two of the three dimensions of color. Intended for plotting light sources rather than surface colors. Often called the CIE diagram.

Cicero/Didot Point

The cicero is a unit of horizontal distance slightly larger than the pica, used widely in continental Europe. A cicero equals 0.178 inches, or 12 Didot points.

CIE (Commission Internationale de l'Eclairage)

An international group that developed a universal set of color definition standards in 1931.

CIE Diagram

See *Chromaticity Diagram*

Clip Art

Collections of predrawn and digitized images stored on disk that can be pasted into word processing and DTP documents.

Clipboard

The portion of computer memory that holds data that has been cut or copied. The next item cut or copied replaces the data already in the clipboard.

Cloning

Duplication of pixels from one part of an image to another.

Color Look-up Table

See *Look-up Table*.

CMS

See *Color Management System*

CMYK (Cyan, Magenta, Yellow, Black)

The process colors (subtractive primaries) used in color printing. The letter K stands for "Key," although it is commonly used to refer to the Black ink that is added to the three colors when necessary. When printing black text as part of a four-color process, only the black ink is used. A normal four-color separation will have a plate for each of the four colors. When combined on the printed piece, the half-tone dots of each color give the impression of the desired color to the eye.

Coated

Printing papers having a surface coating (of clay or other material) to provide a smoother, more even finish with greater opacity.

Cold type

Type produced by photographic or digital methods, as opposed to the use of molten metal as in the old Linotype machine.

Collate

To gather separate sections or leaves of a publication together in the correct order for binding.

Color Balance

The combination of yellow, magenta, and cyan needed to produce a neutral gray. Determined through a gray balance analysis.

Color Bars

See *Color Control Strip*

Color Cast

The modification of a hue by the addition of a trace of another hue, such as yellowish green, pinkish blue, etc. Normally, an unwanted effect that can be corrected.

Color Chart

A printed chart of various combinations of CMYK colors used as an aid for the selection of "legal" colors during the design phase of a project.

Color Control Strip

A printed strip of various reference colors used to control printing quality. This strip is normally placed outside the "trim" area of a project, as a guide and visual aid for the pressman.

Color Conversion

Changing the color "mode" of an image. Converting an image from RGB to CMYK for purposes of preparing the image for conventional printing.

Color Correction

The process of removing casts or unwanted tints in a scanned image, in an effort to improve the appearance of the scan or to correct obvious deficiencies, such as green skies or yellowish skin tones.

Color Gamut

The range of colors that can be formed by all possible combinations of the colorants of a given reproduction system (printing press) on a given type of paper.

Color Key

An overlay color proof of acetate sheets, one for each of the four primary printing inks. The method was developed by 3M Corporation and remains a copyrighted term.

Color Management System

A process or utility that attempts to manage color of input and output devices in such a way that the monitor will match the output of any CMS-managed printer.

Color Model

A system for describing color, such as RGB, HLS, CIELAB, or CMYK.

Color Picker

A function within a graphics application that assists in selecting a color.

Color Proof

A printed or simulated printed image of the color separations intended to produce a close visual simulation of the final reproduction for approval purposes.

Color Scanner

See *Scanner*

Color Separation

The process of splitting an image or PostScript into cyan, magenta, yellow, and black components for offset printing.

Color Sequence

The color order of printing the cyan, magenta, yellow, and black inks on a printing press. Sometimes called rotation or color rotation.

Color Space

Because a color must be represented by three basic characteristics depending on the color model, the color space is a three-dimensional coordinate system in which any color can be represented as a point.

Color Temperature

The temperature, in degrees Kelvin, to which a blackbody would have to be heated to produce a certain color radiation. (A "blackbody" is an ideal body or surface that completely absorbs or radiates energy.) The graphic arts viewing standard is 5,000 K. The degree symbol is not used in the Kelvin scale. The higher the color temperature, the bluer the light.

Color Transparency

A positive color photographic image on a clear film base that must be viewed by transmitted light. It is preferred for original photographic art because it has higher resolution than a color print. Transparency sizes range from 35mm color slides up to 8x10in. (203x254mm).

Colorimeter

An optical measuring instrument designed to measure and quantify color. They are often used to match digital image values to those of cloth and other physical samples.

Column rule

A thin vertical rule used to separate columns of type.

Comp

Comprehensive artwork used to present the general color and layout of a page.

Compose

To set copy into type, or lay out a page.

Compression

A digital technique used to reduce the size of a file by analyzing occurrences of similar data. Compressed files occupy less physical space, and their use improves digital transmission speeds. Compression can sometimes result in a loss of image quality and/or resolution.

Condensed Type

A typeface in which the width of the letters has been reduced. Condensed type can be a specific font, or the result of applying a percentage of normal width by a formatting command.

Continuous Tone

An image such as an original photograph in which the subject has continuous shades of color or gray tones through the use of an emulsion process. Continuous tone images must be screened to create halftone images in order to be printed.

Contrast

The relationship between the dark and light areas of an image.

Copy

Any material furnished for reproduction such as text or illustrations. As a verb, the computer command to copy data to the clipboard in preparation for pasting it to another location.

Copyfitting

Fitting a certain body of text to a given area by changing the font size, leading, justification, or some other parameter.

Copyright

Ownership of a work by the originator, such as an author, publisher, artist, or photographer. The right of copyright permits the originator of material to prevent its use without express permission or acknowledgement of the originator. Copyright may be sold, transferred, or given up contractually.

CorelDraw

A popular drawing program originally designed for the Windows environment, but now available as a Macintosh program. Corel is known to create files that can cause printing and/or output problems in many environments.

Creep

An unwanted movement of the blanket of an offset printing press that causes registration problems.

Cromalin

A single-sheet color proofing system introduced by DuPont in 1971 and still quite popular in the industry. It uses a series of overlaid colorants and varnish to simulate the results of a press run.

Crop Marks

Printed lines used for final trimming of a printed page.

Cropping

The elimination of parts of a photograph or other original that are not required to be printed.

Dash

A short horizontal rule of varying lengths used to indicate a pause or clause in a sentence; see *En-dash* and *Em-dash*.

DCS (Desktop Color Separation)

An EPS file format that creates one file for each of the four primary printing inks, and a fifth file that contains a thumbnail of the image. DCS files are used for building pages with layout programs; when the file is output, the small placement image is discarded, and the four high-resolution files are automatically substituted. This reduces the need to move large, high-resolution files around a network.

Default

A specification for a mode of computer operation that operates if no other is selected. For example, the default font size might be 12 point, or a default color for an object might be white with a black border.

Densitometer

An electronic instrument used to measure optical density. Reflective (for paper) and transmissive (for film) versions are available.

Density

The ability of a material to absorb light. In film, it refers to the opacity of a specific area of the image. A maximum density of 4.0 refers to solid black. Improper density in film images can result in washed-out or overly-dark reproduction.

Descender

The part of a lower-case letter that extends below the baseline (lower edge of the x-height) of the letter. The letters y, p, g, and j contain descenders.

Desktop

1. The area on a monitor screen on which the icons appear, before an application is launched. 2. A reference to the size of computer equipment (system unit, monitor, printer) that can fit on a normal desk; thus, desktop publishing.

Desktop Publishing (DTP)

Use of a personal computer, software applications, and a high-quality printer to produce fully composed printed documents. DTP is, in reality, an incorrect term these days. In the early days of Macintosh and PostScript technology, the term Desktop Publishing inferred that the materials produced from these systems was somehow inferior (as opposed to *professional* publishing). Now, the overwhelming majority of all printed materials – regardless of the quality – are produced on these systems, up to and including nationally famous magazines, catalogs, posters, and newspapers.

Dialog Box

A window in a computer application that – in most cases – presents an opportunity for the user to enter information relative to the process that they're executing. A dialog box might ask, for example, how many copies of a document you want to print, or what size a circle should be, or what color. Dialog boxes are an integral part of today's graphic user interfaces – both on the Macintosh and on Windows-based systems.

Digital Camera

A camera which produces images directly into an electronic file format for transfer to a computer.

Digital

The use of a series of discrete electronic pulses to represent data. In digital imaging systems, 256 steps (8 bits, or 1 byte) are normally used to characterize the gray scale or the properties of one color. For text, see *ASCII*.

Digital Proofs

Digital proofs are representations of what a specific mechanical will look like when output and reproduced on a specific type of printing press. The difference with a digital proof is that it is created without the use of conventional film processes and output directly from computer files.

Dingbat

A font character that displays a picture instead of a letter, number or punctuation mark. There are entire font families of pictographic dingbats; the most commonly used dingbat font is *Zapf Dingbats*. There are dingbats for everything from the little airplanes used to represent airports on a map, to telephones, swashes, fish, stars, balloons – just about anything.

Direct-to-plate

Producing printing plates directly from computer output without going through the film process.

Disk

A computer data storage device, either "floppy," "hard," or a high-capacity removable disk, that stores data magnetically.

Disk Operating System (DOS)

Software for computer systems that supervises and controls the running of programs. The operating system is loaded into memory from disk by a small program which permanently resides in the firmware within the computer. The major operating systems in use today are Windows95 and WindowsNT from Microsoft, the Macintosh OS from Apple Computer, and a wide range of UNIX systems, such as those from Silicon Graphics, SUN Microsystems, and other vendors.

Dithering

A technique used in images wherein a color is represented using dots of two different colors displayed or printed very close together. Dithering is often used to compress digital images, in special screening algorithms (see *Stochastic Screening*) and to produce higher quality output on low-end color printers.

Document

The general term for a computer file containing text and/or graphics.

Dongle

A security device that usually plugs into your keyboard or printer port, that allows copy-protected software to run on your system. Such protected software will only run on systems with the dongle present. This prevents a single copy of software from running on any but one machine at a time.

Dot Gain

The growth of a halftone dot that occurs whenever ink soaks into paper. This growth can vary from being very small (on a high-speed press with fast-drying ink and very non-porous paper) to quite dramatic, as is the case in newspaper printing, where a dot can expand 30% from its size on the film to the size at which it dries. Failure to compensate for this gain in the generation of digital images can result in very poor results on press. Generally speaking, the finer the screen (and therefore, the smaller the dot) the more noticeable dot gain will be.

Double-page Spread

A design that spans the two pages visible to the reader at any open spot in a magazine, periodical, or book.

Double-Click

Two clicks of a mouse button in rapid succession that are interpreted as the command to open an application, file, or folder.

Downloadable Fonts

Typefaces that can be stored on disk and then downloaded to the printer when required for printing.

DPI (Dots Per Inch)

The measurement of resolution for page printers, phototype-setting machines and graphics screens. Currently graphics screens use resolutions of 60 to 100 dpi, standard desktop laser printers work at 600 dpi, and imagesetters operate at more than 1,500 dpi.

Dragging

The process of moving an object on the screen by clicking on it with the mouse, moving the cursor to another location, then releasing the button.

Drop Cap

A large initial cap, usually set down into the block or body of normal text. Excellent examples of ornate drop caps (called illuminated initials) can often be seen in manuscripts illustrated by hand in the Middle Ages.

Drop Shadow

A duplicate of a graphic element or type placed behind and slightly offset from it, giving the effect of a shadow.

Drum Scanner

A color scanner on which the original is wrapped around a rotary scanning drum. See *Scanner.*

DTP

See *Desktop Publishing*

Duotone

The separation of a black-and-white photograph into black and a second color having different tonal values and screen angles. Duotones are used to enhance photographic reproduction in two-three-or sometimes four-color work. Often the second, third, and fourth colors are not standard CMYK inks.

Dye

A soluble coloring material, normally used as the colorant in color photographs.

Dye Transfer

A photographic color print using special coated papers to produce a full color image. Can serve as an inexpensive proof.

Electrostatic

The method by which dry toner is transferred to paper in a copier or laser printer, and liquid toners are bonded to paper on some large-format color plotters.

Element

The smallest unit of a graphic, or a component of a page layout or design. Any object, text block, or graphic might be referred to as an element of the design.

Elliptical Dot Screen

A halftone screen having an elliptical dot structure.

Em Dash

A dash – often used in place of parentheses or commas to break a sentence – that is usually equal to the point size. For example, in 10 point type, an em dash would be 10 points wide. Formerly the width of a capital M in a particular font; this definition is still used by some type foundries.

Em Space

A space usually equal to the current point size; in 10 point type, an em space should be 10 points wide. Formerly the width of a capital M in a given font; this definition is still used by some type foundries. Hot lead typesetters often used this space as the standard distance for a paragraph indent.

Embedding

1. Placing control codes in the body of a document. 2. Including a complete copy of a text file or image within a desktop publishing document, with or without a *link* (see *Linking*).

Emulsion

The coating of light-sensitive material (silver halide) on a piece of film.

En Dash

A dash – often used in hyphenated word pairs – that is usually half the width of an em dash.

En Space

A space that is usually equal to half the width of an em space.

EPS (Encapsulated PostScript)

A file format used to transfer PostScript data within compatible applications. An EPS file normally contains a small thumbnail that's used to display the image when it's placed into position within a mechanical or used by another program. EPS files can contain text, vector artwork, and images.

Ethernet

A set of software protocols widely used in network communications.

Excel

A spreadsheet application produced by Microsoft; available separately or as part of Microsoft Office.

Exception dictionary

A file, used within a spell-checking or hyphenation process, that provides exceptions to standard spelling or justification rules.

Expanded Type

Also called extended, a widened version of a typeface design. Type may be extended artificially within a DTP application, or designed as such by the typeface designer. See also *Condensed Type*.

Export

To save a file generated in one application in a format that is readable in another application.

Extension

A modular software program that extends or expands the functions of a larger program. A folder of Extensions is found in the Macintosh System Folder.

Fill

To add a tone or color to the area inside a closed object in a graphic illustration program.

Film

Non-paper output of an imagesetter or phototypesetter.

Filter

In image editing applications, a small program that creates a special effect or performs some other function within an image.

Flat

A group of individual camera-ready pages mounted in the proper order and ready for photographing to produce a signature plate.

Flat Color

Color that lacks contrast or tonal variation.

Flatbed Scanner

A scanner on which the original is mounted on a flat scanning glass. See *Scanner*.

Flexography

A rotary letterpress process printing from rubber or flexible plates and using fast drying inks. Mainly used for packaging.

Floating Accent

A separate accent mark that can be placed under or over another character. Complex accented characters such as in foreign languages are usually available in a font as a single character.

Flop

To make a mirror image of visuals such as photographs or clip art.

Flush Left

Copy aligned along the left margin.

Flush Right

Copy aligned along the right margin.

Folder

1. The digital equivalent of a paper file folder, used to organize files in the Macintosh and Windows operating systems. The icon of a folder looks like a paper file folder. Double-clicking it opens it to reveal the files stored inside. 2. A mechanical device which folds preprinted pages into various formats, such as a tri-fold brochure.

Font

A font is the complete collection of all the characters (numbers, uppercase and lowercase letters and, in some cases, small caps and symbols) of a given typeface in a specific style; for example, Helvetica Bold.

Force Justify

A type alignment command which causes the space between letters and words in a line of type to expand to fit within a line. Often used in headlines, and sometimes used to force the last line of a justified paragraph, which is normally set flush left, to justify.

Four-color Process

See *Process Colors*

FPO

"For Position Only": a low-resolution graphic or simple box to designate the location of a graphic in the final file.

Frame

In desktop publishing, an area or block into which text or graphics can be placed.

FreeHand

A popular vector-based illustration program available from Macromedia.

Full Measure

A line set to the entire line length.

Galley Proof

Proofs, usually of type, taken before the type is made up into pages. Before desktop publishing, galley proofs were hand-assembled into pages.

Gamma Correction

1. Adjusting the contrast of the midtones in an image. 2. Calibrating a monitor so that midtones are correctly displayed on screen.

Gamma

A measure of the contrast, or range of tonal variation, of the midtones in a photographic image

Gamut -

See *Color Gamut*

GASP

Acronym for Graphic Arts Service Provider, a firm that provides a range of services somewhere on the continuum from design to fulfillment.

GCR (Gray component replacement)

A technique for adding detail by reducing the amount of cyan, magenta, and yellow in chromatic or colored areas, replacing them with black.

GIF - Graphics Interface File

A CompuServe graphics file format that is used widely for graphic elements in Web pages.

G (Gigabyte)

One billion (1,073,741,824) bytes (2^{30}) or 1,048,576 kilobytes.

Global Preferences

Preference settings which affect all newly created files within an application.

Gradation

A smooth transition between black and white, one color and another, or color and no-color.

Gradient

A fill pattern that goes from dark to light or light to dark, or from one color or shape to another.

Grain

Silver salts clumped together in differing amounts in different types of photographic emulsions. Generally speaking, faster emulsions have larger grain sizes.

Graininess

Visual impression of the irregularly distributed silver grain clumps in a photographic image, or the ink film in a printed image.

Gray Balance

The values for the yellow, magenta, and cyan inks that are needed to produce a neutral gray when printed at a normal density.

Gray Component Replacement

See *GCR*

Gray Scale

An image containing a series of tones stepped from white to black that is used for monitoring tone reproduction.

Grayscale

An image composed in grays ranging from black to white, usually using 256 different shades of gray.

Greeking

1. A software technique by which areas of gray are used to simulate lines of text below a certain point size. 2. Nonsense text use to define a layout before copy is available.

Grid

A division of a page by horizontal and vertical guides into areas into which text or graphics may be placed accurately.

Group

To collect graphic elements together so that an operation may be applied to all of them simultaneously.

GUI

Acronym for Graphical User Interface, the basis of the Macintosh and Windows operating systems.

Guides

Lines created in layout application programs to assist in aligning various design elements.

Gutter

The white space between two facing pages. Sometimes used interchangeably with Alley to describe the space between columns on a page.

Hairline Rule

The thinnest rule that can be printed on a given device. A hairline rule on a 1200 dpi imagesetter is 1/1200 of an inch; on a 300 dpi laser printer, the same rule would print at 1/300 of an inch.

Halftone

An image generated for use in printing in which a range of continuous tones is simulated by an array of dots that create the illusion of continuous tone when seen at a distance.

Halftone Tint

An area covered with a uniform halftone dot size to produce an even tone or color. Also called tint or screen tint.

Hanging Indent

Formatting text so that the first line is not indented, and all subsequent lines within the paragraph are indented. Often used with bullets.

Hanging punctuation

Punctuation marks such as quotation marks that are set outside the text block; similar to a hanging indent.

Hard Copy

A tangible permanent image such as an original, a proof, or a printed sheet.

Hard Drive

A rigid disk sealed inside an airtight transport mechanism that is the basic storage mechanism in a computer. Information stored may be accessed more rapidly than on floppy disks and far greater amounts of data may be stored.

Hard Return

A manual line ending (created by pressing the Return or Enter key) that denotes the end of a paragraph.

Header

A fixed body of copy that appears at the top of each page of a section of a book. It may contain variable quantities such as page number, time, date, or file name.

Hide

A command in DTP applications that will render certain elements on the screen invisible, but will not remove them from the file.

High Key

A photographic or printed image in which the main interest area lies in the highlight end of the scale.

High Resolution File

An image file that typically contains four pixels for every dot in the printed reproduction. High-resolution files are often linked to a page layout file, but not actually embedded in it, due to their large size.

Highlights

The lightest areas in a photograph or illustration.

HLS

Color model based on three coordinates: hue, lightness (or luminance), and saturation.

HSV

A color model based on three coordinates: hue, saturation and value (or luminance).

HTML (HyperText Markup Language)

The language, written in plain (ASCII) text using simple tags, that is used to create Web pages, and which Web browsers are designed to read and display. HTML focuses more on the logical structure of a page than its appearance.

Hue

The wavelength of light of a color in its purest state (without adding white or black).

Hyperlink

An HTML tag that directs the computer to a different Anchor or URL (Uniform Resource Locator). The linked data may be on the same page, or on a computer anywhere in the world.

Hyphenation Zone

The space at the end of a line of text in which the hyphenation function will examine the word to determine whether or not it should be hyphenated and wrapped to the next line.

Icon

A small graphic symbol used on the screen to indicate files or folders, activated by clicking with the mouse or pointing device.

Illustrator

A vector editing application owned by Adobe Systems, Inc.

Imagesetter

A raster-based laser device used to output a computer page-layout file or composition at high resolution onto photographic paper or film, from which to make printing plates.

Import

To bring a file generated within one application into another application.

Imposition

The arrangement of pages on a printed sheet, which, when the sheet is finally printed, folded and trimmed, will place the pages in their correct order.

Indent

A typographical technique that lines up the beginnings or ends of lines at a position other than the preset margin.

Indexing

In DTP, marking certain words within a document with hidden codes so that an index may be automatically generated.

Indexed Color Image

An image which uses a limited, predetermined number of colors; often used in Web images. See also *GIF*.

Initial Caps

Text in which the first letter of each word (except articles, etc.) is capitalized.

Inline Graphic

A graphic that is inserted within a body of text, and may be formatted using normal text commands for justification and leading; inline graphics will move with the body of text in which they are placed.

Intensity

Synonym for degree of color saturation.

International Paper Sizes

The International Standards Organization (ISO) system of paper sizes is based on a series of three sizes A, B and C. Series A is used for general printing and stationery, Series B for posters, and Series C for envelopes. Each size has the same proportion of length to width as the others. The nearest ISO paper size to conventional 8-1/2 x 11 paper is A4.

ISO

The International Standards Organization.

Italics

A version of a typeface designed with letters slanted to the right.

Jaggies

Visible steps in the curved edge of a graphic or text character that results from enlarging a bitmapped image.

JPG or JPEG

A compression algorithm that reduces the file size of bitmapped images, named for the Joint Photographic Experts Group, an industry organization that created the standard; JPEG is a "lossy" compression method, and image quality will be reduced in direct proportion to the amount of compression.

Justification

The alignment of text along a margin or both margins..

Kelvin (K)

Unit of temperature measurement based on Celsius degrees, starting from absolute zero, which is equivalent to -273 Celsius (centigrade); used to indicate the color temperature of a light source.

Kerning

Moving a pair of letters closer together or farther apart, to achieve a better fit or appearance.

Key (Black Plate)

In early four-color printing, the black plate was printed first and the other three colors were aligned (or registered) to it. Thus, the black plate was the "key" to the result.

Kilobyte (K, KB)

1,024 (2^{10}) bytes, the nearest binary equivalent to decimal 1,000 bytes. Abbreviated and referred to as K.

Knockout

A shape or object printed by eliminating (knocking out) all background colors. See *Overprinting*.

L*a*b

The lightness, red-green attribute, and yellow-blue attribute in the CIE Color Space, a three-dimensional color mapping system.

Landscape

Printing from the left to right across the wider side of the page. A landscape orientation treats a page as 11 inches wide and 8.5 inches long.

Laser printer

A high quality image printing system using a laser beam to produce an image on a photosensitive drum. The image is transferred to paper by a conventional xerographic printing process. Current laser printers used for desktop publishing have a resolution of 600 dpi. Imagesetters are also laser printers, but with higher resolution and tight mechanical controls to produce final film separations for commercial printing.

Layer

A function of graphics applications in which elements may be isolated from each other, so that a group of elements may be hidden from view, locked, reordered or otherwise manipulated as a unit, without affecting other elements on the page.

Layout

The arrangement of text and graphics on a page, usually produced in the preliminary design stage.

Leading ("ledding")

Space added between lines of type. Usually measured in points or fractions of points. Named after the strips of lead which used to be inserted between lines of metal type. In specifying type, lines of 12-pt. type separated by a 14-pt. space is abbreviated "12/14," or "twelve over fourteen."

Leaders

A line of periods or other symbols connecting the end of a group of words with another element separated by some space. For example, a table of contents may consist of a series of phrases on separate lines, each associated with a page number. Promotes readability in long lists of tabular text.

Letterspacing

The insertion or addition of white space between the letters of words.

Library

In the computer world, a collection of files having a similar purpose or function.

Ligature

Letters that are joined together as a single unit of type such as oe and fi.

Lightness

The property that distinguishes white from gray or black, and light from dark color tones on a surface.

Line Art

A drawing or piece of black and white artwork, with no screens. Line art can be represented by a graphic file having only one-bit resolution.

Line Screen

The number of lines per inch used when converting a photograph to a halftone. Typical values range from 85 for newspaper work to 150 or higher for high-quality reproduction on smooth or coated paper.

Linen Tester

A magnifying glass designed for checking the dot image of a halftone. See *Loupe*.

Linking

An association through software of a graphic or text file on disk with its location in a document. That location may be represented by a "placeholder" rectangle, or a low-resolution copy of the graphic.

Linotype

A typecasting machine (now obsolete) that injected hot metal into a line of molds to produce lines of type. After printing, the type was melted and used again.

Linotype-Hell

The manufacturer of imagesetters such as the Linotronic that process PostScript data through an external Raster Image Processor (RIP) to produce high resolution film for printing.

Lithography

A mechanical printing process used for centuries based on the principle of the natural aversion of water (in this case, ink) to grease. In modern offset lithography, the image on a photo-sensitive plate is first transferred to the blanket of a rotating drum, and then to the paper.

Logo

A graphic element normally used as a design to represent a company or product.

Lossy

A data compression method characterized by the loss of some data.

Loupe

A small free-standing magnifier used to see fine detail on a page. See *Linen Tester*.

Lowercase

The uncapitalized letters of the alphabet; so named when type was composed by hand, and the small letters were in the lower part of the type case.

LPI

Lines per inch. See *Line Screen*.

Luminosity

The amount of light, or brightness, in an image. Part of the HLS color model.

LZW

The acronym for the Lempel-Ziv-Welch lossless data- and image-compression algorithm.

M, MB (Megabyte)

One million (1,048,576) bytes (2^{20}) or 1,024 Kilobytes.

Macro

A set of keystrokes that is saved as a named computer file. When accessed, the keystrokes will be performed. Macros are used to perform repetitive tasks.

Manuscript (MS or Mss)

The original written or typewritten work of an author submitted for publication.

Margins

The non-printing areas of page, or the line at which text starts or stops.

Mark up

To prepare copy for a compositor, setting out in detail all the typesetting instructions, or to denote corrections on a printed proof.

Mask

To conform the shape of a photograph or illustration to another shape such as a circle or polygon.

Masking

A digital technique that blocks an area of an image from reproduction by superimposing an opaque object of any shape.

Master Page

A page that holds repeating elements of a layout, such as guides or graphics.

Match Print

A color proofing system used for the final quality check.

Mechanical

A pasted-up page of camera-ready art that is to be photographed to produce a plate for the press.

Mechanical Dot Gain –

See *Dot Gain*

Medium

A physical carrier of data such as a CD-ROM, video cassette, or floppy disk, or a carrier of electronic data such as fiber optic cable or electric wires.

Megabyte (MB)

A unit of measure of stored data equaling 1,024 kilobytes, or 1,048,576 bytes (10^{20}).

Megahertz

An analog signal frequency of one million cycles per second, or a data rate of one million bits per second. Used in specifying computer CPU speed.

Menu

A list of choices of functions, or of items such as fonts. In contemporary software design, there is often a fixed menu of basic functions at the top of the page that have pull-down menus associated with each of the fixed choices.

Menu-driven

Programs which allow the user to request functions by choosing from a list of options.

Metafile

A class of graphics that combines the characteristics of raster and vector graphics formats; not recommended for high-quality output.

Metallic Ink

Printing inks which produce an effect of gold, silver, bronze, or metallic colors.

Midtones or Middletones

The tonal range between highlights and shadows.

Mock-up

The rough concept or layout of a publication or design.

Modem

An electronic device for converting digital data into analog audio signals and back again (MOdulator-DEModulator.) Primarily used for transmitting data between computers over analog (audio frequency) telephone lines.

Moiré

An interference pattern caused by the out-of-register overlap of two or more regular patterns such as dots or lines. In process-color printing, screen angles are selected to minimize this pattern.

Monochrome

An image or computer monitor in which all information is represented in black and white, or with a range of grays.

Monospace

A font in which all characters occupy the same amount of horizontal width regardless of the character. See also *Proportional Spacing*.

Montage

A single image formed by assembling or compositing several images.

Mottle

Uneven color or tone.

Mss

See *Manuscript*

Multimedia

The combination of sound, video images, and text to create a "moving" presentation.

Network

Two or more computers that are linked to exchange data or share resources. The Internet is a network of networks.

Neutral

Any color that has no hue, such as white, gray, or black.

Neutral Density

A term that describes images or filters that are gray with no apparent hue.

Noise

Unwanted signals or data that may reduce the quality of the output.

Non-breaking Space

A typographic command that connects two words with a space, but prevents the words from being broken apart if the space occurs within the hypenation zone. See *Hyphenation Zone*.

Nonreproducible Colors

Colors in an original scene or photograph that are impossible to reproduce using process inks. Also called out-of-gamut colors.

Normal Key

A description of an image in which the main interest area is in the middle range of the tone scale or distributed throughout the entire tonal range.

Norton Utilities

A software product that provides programs for maintaining a computer's hardware or software; for example, locating and restoring a file that was accidentally "erased."

Nudge

To move a graphic or text element in small, preset increments, usually with the arrow keys.

Oblique

A slanted character (sometimes backwards, or to the left), often used when referring to italic versions of sans-serif typefaces.

OCR (Optical Character Recognition)

A special kind of scanner software that provides a means of reading printed characters on documents and converting them into digital codes that can be read into a computer as actual editable text rather than pure images.

Offset

In graphics manipulation, to move a copy or clone of an image slightly to the side and/or back; used for a drop-shadow effect.

Offset Lithography

A printing method whereby the image is transferred from a plate onto a rubber covered cylinder from which the printing takes place (see *Lithography*).

OLE

Object Linking and Embedding, a software technique that permits linking an object in a document to its original file and enabling automatic updating. OLE applications may be OLE containers (able to accept OLE documents) or OLE servers (able to create OLE documents), or both.

Opacity

1. The degree to which paper will show print through it. 2. Settings in certain graphics applications that allow images or text below the object whose opacity has been adjusted, to show through.

OPI

Open Prepress Interface, a software device that is an extension to PostScript that replaces low-resolution placeholder images in a document with their high-resolution sources for printing.

Optical Disks

Video disks that store large amounts of data used primarily for reference works such as dictionaries and encyclopedias.

Orphan

The last line of a paragraph that appears alone at the top of a column or page.

Outline

A typeface in which the letters have outlines only and no fill.

Overlay

A transparent sheet used in the preparation of multicolor mechanical artwork showing the color breakdown.

Overprint Color

A color made by overprinting any two or more of the primary yellow, magenta, and cyan process colors.

Overprinting

Allowing an element to print over the top of underlying elements, rather than knocking them out (see *Knockout*). Often used with black type.

Page Description Language (PDL)

A special form of programming language that describes both text and graphics (object or bit-image) in mathematical form. The main benefit of a PDL is that makes the application software independent of the physical printing device. PostScript is a PDL, for example.

Page Layout Software

Desktop publishing software such as PageMaker or QuarkXpress used to combine various source documents and images into a high quality publication.

Page Proofs

Proofs of the actual pages of a document, usually produced just before printing, for a final quality check.

PageMaker

A popular page-layout application produced by Adobe Systems.

Palette

1. As derived from the term in the traditional art world, a collection of selectable colors. 2. Another name for a dialog box or menu of choices.

Panose

A typeface matching system for font substitution based on a numeric classification of fonts according to visual characteristics.

Pantone Matching System

A system for specifying colors by number for both coated and uncoated paper; used by print services and in color desktop publishing to assure uniform color matching.

Pasteboard

In a page layout program, the desktop area outside of the printing page area, on which elements can be placed for later positioning on any page.

PCX

Bitmap image format produced by paint programs.

PDF (Portable Document Format)

Developed by Adobe Systems, Inc. (and read by Adobe Acrobat Reader), this format has become a de facto standard for document transfer across platforms.

PDL

See *Page Description Language*

Perfect binding

A common method of binding paperback books in which the pages are glued directly to the binding.

Perspective

The effect of distance in an image achieved by aligning the edges of elements with imaginary lines directed toward one to three "vanishing points" on the horizon.

Photoshop

The Adobe Systems image editing program commonly used for color correction and special effects on both the Macintosh and PC platforms.

Pi Fonts

A collection of special characters such as timetable symbols and mathematical signs. Examples are Zapf Dingbats and Symbol. See also *Dingbats*.

Pica

A traditional typographic measurement of 12 points, or approximately 1/6 of an inch. Most DTP applications specify a pica as exactly 1/6 of an inch.

PICT/PICT2

A common format for defining bitmapped images on the Macintosh. The more recent PICT2 format supports 24-bit color.

Pixel

A picture element – the smallest dot or unit on a computer monitor or in a bitmapped image.

Plate

Paper, polyester, or metal sheet used in a printing press to transfer an image onto paper.

PMS –

See *Pantone Matching System*

PMT

Photo Mechanical Transfer – positive prints of text or images used for paste-up to mechanicals.

Point

A unit of measurement used to specify type size and rule weight, equal to (approximately, in traditional typesetting) 1/72 inch.

Polygon

A geometric figure consisting of three or more straight lines enclosing an area. The triangle, square, rectangle, and star are all polygons.

Portrait

Printing from left to right across the narrow side of the page. Portrait orientation on a letter-size page uses a standard 8.5-inch width and 11-inch length.

Positive

A true photographic image of the original made on paper or film.

Posterize, Posterization

The deliberate constraint of a gradient or image into visible steps as a special effect; or the unintentional creation of steps in an image due to a high LPI value used with a low printer DPI.

Postprocessing Applications

Applications, such as trapping programs or imposition software, that perform their functions after the image has been printed to a file, rather than in the originating application.

PostScript

A page description language developed by Adobe Systems, Inc. that describes type and/or images and their positional relationships upon the page; the resulting file is processed by a RIP (see *Raster Image Processor*) into a format a laser printer or imagesetter can understand.

PPD

Acronym for PostScript Printer Definition file, the information that ensures that output remains within the capabilities of the selected output device.

PPI

Pixels per inch; used to denote the resolution of an image.

Prepress

All work done between writing and printing, such as typesetting, scanning, layout, and imposition.

Preferences

A set of defaults for an application program that may be modified.

Prepress Proof

A color proof made directly from electronic data or film images.

Primary Colors

Colors that can be used to generate secondary colors. For the additive system (i.e., a computer monitor), these colors are red, green, and blue. For the subtractive system (i.e., the printing process), these colors are yellow, magenta, and cyan.

Printer Command Language

PCL — a language, that has graphics capability, developed by Hewlett Packard for use with its own range of printers.

Printer fonts

The image outlines for type in PostScript that are sent to the printer.

Printer's Spreads

Pages arranged so that, when printed as spreads and assembled, the pages appear in the proper order. For example, the front and back covers are printed on a spread, the inside front and inside back covers are printed on another spread, etc.

Process Colors

The four colors (cyan, magenta, yellow, and black) that are combined to print a wide range of colors. When blended, they can reproduce many, but not all of the colors found in nature. See also *CMYK*.

Profile

A file containing data representing the color reproduction characteristics of a device determined by a calibration of some sort.

Proof

A representation of the printed job that is made from plates (press proof), film, or electronic data (prepress proofs). It is generally used for customer inspection and approval before mass production begins.

Proportional Spacing

A method of spacing whereby each character is spaced to accommodate the varying widths of letters or figures, thus increasing readability. Books and magazines are set proportionally spaced, and most fonts in desktop publishing are proportional. With proportionally spaced fonts, each character is given a horizontal space proportional to its size. For example, a proportionally spaced "m" is wider than an "i."

Pt.

Abbreviation for point.

Pull Quote

A phrase extracted from the copy and used as a graphic to break up a quantity of text visually, and to call attention to an important point.

QuarkXPress

A popular page-layout application.

Queue

A set of files input to the printer, printed in the order received unless otherwise instructed.

QuickDraw

Graphic routines in the Macintosh used for outputting text and images to printers not compatible with PostScript.

Ragged Left

See *Flush Right*

Ragged Right

See *Flush Left*

RAM

Random Access Memory, the "working" memory of a computer that holds files in process. Files in RAM are lost when the computer is turned off, whereas files stored on the hard drive or floppy disks remain available.

Raster

A bitmapped representation of graphic data.

Raster Graphics

A class of graphics created and organized in a rectangular array using bitmaps. Often created by paint software, fax machines, or scanners.

Raster Image Processor (RIP)

That part of an imagesetter that converts the page information from the Page Description Language into the bitmap pattern that is applied to the film or paper output.

Rasterize

Converting mathematical and digital information into a series of dots by an imagesetter for the production of negative or positive film or paper output

Ray Tracing

A software technique for rendering the surface of a reflecting object realistically by tracing the light rays from the source of illumination to the eye of the viewer.

Reader's Spreads

A two-page spread as seen by the reader after printing and collation; thus, the two pages may have been printed in separate locations on the signature.

Reference Marks

Symbols such as the asterisk (*), dagger, double dagger, section mark (§), and paragraph mark (¶) used in text to direct the reader to a footnote.

Reflective Art

Artwork that is opaque, as opposed to transparent, that can be scanned for input to a computer.

Registration

Aligning plates on a multicolor printing press so that the images will superimpose properly to produce the required composite output.

Registration Color

A default color selection that can be applied to design elements so that they will print on every separation from a PostScript printer. "Registration" is often used to print identification text that will appear outside the page area on a set of separations.

Registration Marks

Small crosshairs on film used to align the individual layers of film separations.

Resolution

The number of dots or pixels per inch of a monitor or output device.

Retouching

Making selective manual or electronic corrections to images.

Reverse Out

To reproduce an object as white, or paper, within a solid background, such as white letters in a black rectangle.

RGB

Red, Green, Blue, the additive primary colors used to create images on a computer monitor or television screen.

Rich Black

A process color consisting of sold black with one or more layers of cyan, magenta, or yellow.

Right Reading

A positive or negative image that is readable from top to bottom and from left to right.

Right-Click

Clicking the right mouse button on a Windows system, usually to reveal a pop-up menu. A Macintosh mouse has only one button.

RIP

See Raster Image Processor

River

An accidental and undesirable pattern of white space between words in text that appears to flow from one corner to another.

ROM

Read Only Memory, a semiconductor chip in the computer that retains startup information for use the next time the computer is turned on.

Roman Type

The primary serif typeface of a family.

Rosette

The pattern created when color halftone screens are printed at traditional screen angles.

Rotation

Turning an object at some angle to its original axis.

RTF

Rich Text Format, a text format that retains formatting information lost in pure ASCII text.

Rubylith

A two-layer acetate film having a red or amber emulsion on a clear base used in non-computer stripping and separation operations.

Ruler

Rulers displayed at two sides of the working space on a monitor that show measurements in units that can be selected in the set-up process.

Running Head

A line of type at the top of a page that repeats the same information. Also called header.

S/S (Same Size)

An instruction to the printer to reproduce at the same size as the original.

Sans Serif

Sans Serif fonts are fonts that do not have the tiny lines that appear at the top of and bottom of letters.

Saturation

The intensity or purity of a particular color; a color with no saturation is gray.

Scaling

The means within a program to reduce or enlarge the amount of space an image will occupy by multiplying the data by a scale factor. Scaling can be proportional, or in one dimension only.

Scanner

A device that electronically digitizes images point by point through circuits that can correct color, manipulate tones, and enhance detail. Color scanners will usually produce a minimum of 24 bits for each pixel, with 8 bits each for red, green, and blue.

Screen

To create a halftone of a continuous tone image (See *Halftone*).

Screen Angle

The angle at which the rulings of a halftone screen are set when making screened images for halftone process-color printing. The equivalent effect can be obtained electronically through selection of the desired angle from a menu.

Screen Frequency

The number of lines per inch in a halftone screen, which may vary from 85 to 300.

Screen Printing

A technique for printing on practically any surface using a fine mesh (originally of silk) on which the image has been placed photographically. Preparation of art for screen printing requires consideration of the resolution of the screen printing process.

Screen Shot

A printed output or saved file that represents data from a computer monitor.

Screen Tint

A halftone screen pattern of all the same dot size that creates an even tone at some percentage of solid color.

Script

A typeface designed to imitate handwriting.

SCSI

Small Computer Systems Interface, a standard software protocol for connecting peripheral devices to a computer for fast data transfer.

Selection

The act of placing the cursor on an object and clicking the mouse button to make the object active.

Self-Cover

A cover for a document in which the cover is of the same paper stock as the rest of the piece.

Serif

A line or curve projecting from the end of a letter form. Typefaces designed with such projections are called serif faces.

Service Bureau

A business that specializes in producing film for printing on a high-resolution imagesetter.

Set Solid

Type set with no extra spacing between the lines; for example, 12-pt. type with 12-pt. leading, or 12/12.

SGML

Standard Generalized Markup Language, a set of semantics and syntax that describes the structure of a document (the nature, content, or function of the data) as opposed to visual appearance. HTML is a subset of SGML (see *HTML*).

Sharpness

The subjective impression of the density difference between two tones at their boundary, interpreted as fineness of detail.

Sheet Fed

A printing press that prints single sheets of paper rather than from a continuous roll.

Shortcut

1. A quick method for accessing a menu item or command, usually through a series of keystrokes. 2. The icon that can be created in Windows95 to open an application without having to penetrate layers of various folders. The equivalent in the Macintosh is the "alias."

Show

The opposite of "Hide," a toggle command. For example, the tabs and paragraph marks in a text document can either be shown or hidden by clicking on an icon in the toolbar.

Sidebar

Supplementary text positioned at the side of a page.

Signature

A group of pages ganged together on a large, single sheet for printing, usually comprising an individual section of a publication.

Silhouette

To remove part of the background of a photograph or illustration, leaving only the desired portion.

Skew

A transformation command that slants an object at an angle to the side from its initial fixed base.

Small caps

A type style in which lowercase letters are replaced by uppercase letters set in a smaller point size.

Smart Quotes

The curly quotation marks used by typographers, as opposed to the straight marks on the typewriter. Use of smart quotes is usually a setup option in a word processing program or page layout application

Snap-to (guides or rulers)

An optional feature in page layout programs that drives objects to line up with guides or margins if they are within a pixel range that can be set. This eliminates the need for very precise, manual placement of an object with the mouse.

Soft Font

See *Downloadable Font*

Soft or Discretionary Hyphen

A hyphen that is coded for display and printing only when formatting of the text puts the hyphenated word at the end of a line.

Soft Return

A return command that ends a line but does not apply a paragraph mark that would end the continuity of the style for that paragraph.

Spectrophotometer

An instrument for measuring the relative intensity of radiation reflected or transmitted by a sample over the spectrum.

Specular Highlight

The lightest highlight area that does not carry any detail, such as reflections from glass or polished metal. Normally, these areas are reproduced as unprinted white paper.

Spine

The binding edge at the back of a book that contains title information and joins the front and back covers.

Spot Color

A color not created by CMYK separations, usually specified by a Pantone swatch number. A spot color is printed by mixing given proportions of various inks in accordance with the percentages given by the Pantone number.

Spread

Two facing pages that can be worked on as a unit, and will be viewed side by side in the final publication.

Stacking Order

The order of the elements on a page, wherein the topmost item will obscure the items beneath it.

Standard Viewing Conditions

A prescribed set of conditions under which the viewing of originals and reproductions are to take place, defining both the geometry of the illumination and the spectral power distribution of the light source.

Standing Cap

A large capital letter sharing baseline with the adjoining text but rising above it. See *Drop Cap*.

Standoff

The distance between a graphic and the text that wraps around it. See *Wrap*.

Stat

Photostat copy.

Stet

Used in proof correction work to cancel a previous correction. From the Latin; "let it stand."

Stipple

Black and white line art where shading is accomplished by the placement of pinpoint dots.

Stochastic Screening

A method of creating halftones in which the size of the dots remains constant but their density is varied; also known as frequency-modulated (or FM) screening.

Stripping

The preparation and assembling of film prior to platemaking.

Stroke, Stroking

Manipulating the width or color of a line.

Stuffit

A file compression utility used in the Macintosh environment.

Style

A set of formatting instructions for font, paragraphing, tabs, and other properties of text.

Style Sheet

A file containing all of the tags and instructions for formatting all parts of a document; style sheets create consistency between similar documents.

Subhead

A second-level heading used to organize body text by topic.

Subscript

Small-size characters set below the normal letters or figures, usually to convey technical information.

Substitution

Using an existing font to simulate one that is not available to the printer.

Substrate

The paper or any other generally flat material upon which an image is printed.

Subtractive Color

Color which is observed when light strikes pigments or dyes, which absorb certain wavelengths of light; the light that is reflected back is perceived as a color. See *CMYK* and *Process Color*.

Superscript

Small characters set above the normal letters or figures, such as numbers referring to footnotes.

Swash Letters

Letters with extra flourishes usually used in logos, headlines, or as initial caps.

Swatch

A sample of a set of papers, inks, etc. that may be provided in physical form, or appear as a menu in a word processing or illustration application program.

Syntax

The rules that govern the structure of statements in a computer language, or in a language in general.

System Folder

The location of the operating system files on a Macintosh.

Tabloid

A paper size 11 inches wide and 17 inches long.

Tabular

Text set in columns or tables.

Tagged Image File Format (TIFF)

A common format used for scanned or computer-generated bitmapped images.

Tags

The various formats in a style sheet that indicate paragraph settings, margins and columns, page layouts, hyphenation and justification, widow and orphan control and other parameters.

Template

A document file containing layout and styles by which a series of documents can maintain the same look and feel.

Text Attribute

A characteristic applied directly to a letter or letters in text, such as bold, italic, or underline.

Text Block

A set of characters that may be manipulated as a group.

Text File

A file containing text in ASCII format that does not contain style formatting.

Text Type

Typefaces used for the main text of written material. Generally no larger than 14 point in size, and variable with the type of publication.

Text wrap

See *Wrap*

Text

The characters and words that form the main body of a publication.

Texture

1. A property of the surface of the substrate, such as the smoothness of paper. 2. Graphically, variation in tonal values to form image detail. 3. A class of fills in a graphics application that give various appearances, such as bricks, grass, etc.

Thin Space

A fixed space, equal to half an en space or the width of a period in most fonts.

Thumbnails

1. The preliminary sketches of a design. 2. Small images used to indicate the content of a computer file.

Tick Mark

A small mark at right angles to the axis of a graph that indicates the location of a certain measurement; such as tick marks indicating the numbers 1, 2, 3, etc.

TIFF

See *Tagged Image File Format*

Tight

A characteristic of text in which the characters are set very close together.

Tile

1. A type of repeating fill pattern. 2. Reproduce a number of pages of a document on one sheet. 3. Printing a large document overlapping on several smaller sheets of paper.

Tint

1. A halftone area that contains dots of uniform size; that is, no modeling or texture. 2. The mixture of a color with white.

Tip In

The separate insertion of a single page into a book either during or after binding by pasting one edge.

Toggle

A command that switches between either of two states at each application. Switching between Hide and Show is a toggle.

Tone

Any variation in lightness or saturation while hue remains constant.

Toolbox

An on-screen mouse-operated palette that allows the user to choose from a selection of tools available in computer application programs.

Tracking

Adjusting the spacing of letters in a line of text to achieve proper justification or general appearance.

Transfer Curve

A curve depicting the adjustment to be made to a particular printing plate when an image is printed.

Transparency

A full color photographically produced image on transparent film.

Transparent Ink

An ink that allows light to be transmitted through it.

Trapping

Compensating for potential gaps between two adjoining colors because of misregistration.

Trim

After printing, mechanically cutting the publication to the correct final dimensions. The trim size is normally indicated by marks on the printing plate outside the page area.

TrueType

An outline font format used in both Macintosh and Windows systems that can be used both on the screen and on a printer.

Type 1 Fonts

PostScript fonts based on Bézier curves encrypted for compactness that are compatible with Adobe Type Manager.

Type Family

A set of typefaces created from the same basic design but in different weights, such as bold, light, italic, book, and heavy.

Typesetting

The arrangement of individual characters of text into words, sentences, and paragraphs.

Typo

An abbreviation for typographical error. A keystroke error in the typeset copy.

Typographer

A specialist in the design of printed matter and generally an expert in type and letterforms.

Typography

The design and planning of printed matter using type.

U&lc

An abbreviation for UPPER and lower case. Also the name of a popular design publication.

UCR (undercolor removal)

A technique for reducing the amount of magenta, cyan, and yellow inks in neutral or shadow areas and replacing them with black.

Undertone

Color of ink printed in a thin film.

Unsharp Masking

A digital technique (based on a traditional photographic technique) performed after scanning that locates the edge between sections of differing lightness and alters the values of the adjoining pixels to exaggerate the difference across the edge, thereby increasing edge contrast.

Uppercase

The capital letters of a typeface as opposed to the lowercase, or small, letters. So called because when type was hand composited, the capital letters resided in the upper part of the type case.

Utility

Software that performs ancillary tasks such as counting words, defragmenting a hard drive, or restoring a deleted file.

Varnish Plate

The plate on a printing press that applies varnish after the other colors have been applied.

Varnishing

A finishing process whereby a transparent varnish is applied over the printed sheet to produce a glossy or protective coating, either on the entire sheet or on selected areas.

Vector Graphics

Graphics defined using coordinate points, and mathematically drawn lines and curves, which may be freely scaled and rotated without image degradation. Two commonly used vector drawing programs are Illustrator and FreeHand.

A class of graphics created using mathematically described geometric shapes that overcomes the limitations of bitmapped graphics.

Velox

Strictly, a Kodak chloride printing paper, but used to describe a high-quality black & white print of a halftone or line drawing.

Vertical Justification

The ability to automatically adjust the interline spacing (leading) to make columns and pages end at the same point on a page.

Vignette

An illustration in which the background gradually fades into the paper; that is, without a definite edge or border.

Visible Spectrum

The wavelengths of light between about 380 nm (violet) and 700 nm (red) that are visible to the human eye.

Watermark

An impression incorporated in paper during manufacturing showing the name of the paper and/or the company logo. A "watermark" can be applied digitally to printed output as a very light screened image.

Web Press

An offset printing press that prints from a roll of paper rather than single sheets.

Weight

1. The thickness of the strokes of a typeface. The weight of a typeface is usually denoted in the name of the font; for example, light, book, or ultra (thin, medium, and thick strokes, respectively). 2. The thickness of a line or rule.

White Space

Areas on the page which contain no images or type. Proper use of white space is critical to a well-balanced design.

White Light

Light containing all wavelengths of the visible spectrum.

Widow

First line of a paragraph that appears alone at the bottom of a column or page.

Window Shade

A type of text block used in certain applications, such as PageMaker. Windowshades have handles at the top and bottom which, when dragged with the mouse, will reveal or conceal text.

Wizard

A utility attached to an application or operating system that aids you in setting up a piece of hardware, software, or document.

Word Break

The division of a word at the end of a line in accordance with hyphenation principles.

Word Processor

A desktop publishing application program designed for creating and formatting text, but not for page layout.

Word Space

The space inserted between words in a desktop publishing application. The optimal value is built into the typeface, and may usually be modified within an application.

Word Wrap

In word processing, the automatic adjustment of the number of words on a line of text to match the margin and hyphenation settings, resulting in shifting a word to the next line as required.

Wrap

Type set on the page so that it wraps around the shape of another element.

WYSIWYG (pronounced "wizzywig")

An acronym for "What You See Is What You Get," meaning that what you see on your computer screen bears a strong resemblance to what the job will look like when it is printed.

X-height

The height of the letter "x" in a given typeface, which represents the basic size of the bodies of all of the lowercase letters (excluding ascenders and descenders).

Xerography

A photocopying/printing process in which the image is formed using the electrostatic charge principle. The toner replaces ink and can be dry or liquid. Once formed, the image is sealed by heat. Most page printers currently use this method of printing.

Zero Point

The mathematical "origin" of the coordinates of the two-dimensional page. The zero point may be moved to any location on the page, and the ruler dimensions change accordingly.

Zip

1. To compress a file on a Windows-based system using a popular compression utility. 2. A removable disk made by Iomega (a Zip disk) or the device that reads and writes such disks (a Zip drive).

Zooming

The process of electronically enlarging an image on a monitor to facilitate detailed design or editing.